THE
HORNET'S
STING

THE HORNET'S STING

The amazing untold story
of Second World War spy
Thomas Sneum

MARK RYAN

PIATKUS

PIATKUS

First published in Great Britain in 2008 by Piatkus Books

Copyright © 2008 Mark Ryan

A CIP catalogue record for this book
is available from the British Library

ISBN 978-0-7499-0990-1

Edited by Philip Parr
Text design by Paul Saunders
Maps by Rodney Paull
Typeset in Sabon by M Rules
Printed and bound in Great Britain by
MPG Books, Bodmin, Cornwall

Papers used by Piatkus Books are natural, renewable and recyclable
products made from wood grown in sustainable forests and certified
in accordance with the rules of the Forest Stewardship Council

Mixed Sources
Product group from well-managed
forests and other controlled sources
www.fsc.org Cert no. SGS-COC-004081
© 1996 Forest Stewardship Council

FSC

Piatkus Books
An imprint of
Little, Brown Book Group
100 Victoria Embankment
London EC4Y ODY

An Hachette Livre UK Company
www.hachettelivre.co.uk

www.piatkus.co.uk

This story is dedicated to the memory of Thomas Sneum, Kjeld Pedersen, Kaj Oxlund, Arne Helvard, Sigfred and Thorbjoern Christophersen, Lorens Arne Duus Hansen, Christian Michael Rottboell, Paul Johannesen, Hasager Christiansen, John Christmas Moeller, Roland Olsen, Niels Richard Bertelsen, Hans Henrik Larsen and the many others who risked, suffered and sacrificed so much in the Second World War. We are all human, with our fears and faults, and we possess varying degrees of courage and competence in the challenges we face in this life. All those who set out to undermine Adolf Hitler's Nazis in occupied Europe, however successful, whatever their eventual fate, deserve the respect of future generations. Let the power of their story put to shame those politicians and teachers who already seem to be forgetting the creators of our freedom.

CONTENTS

Acknowledgements   x

Maps   xii

Introduction   1

1 The Tightrope to Radar   7

2 Trapped   18

3 Himmler and the Longbow   25

4 A Taste of Freedom   31

5 On Location   38

6 Flight Plan   45

7 The Jigsaw Puzzle   52

8 A Close Shave   61

9 Take-Off   68

10 Up Close and Personal   74

11 Wing-Walker   81

12 The Welcome   88

13 Disbelief   93

14 Sending for the Doctor 99

15 The Spymaster 108

16 SIS, SOE and a Strained Marriage 115

17 Spy School 126

18 A Recipe for Disaster 134

19 Into Action 140

20 A Fragile Foothold 146

21 Bed Manners 153

22 The Threat 160

23 Meet the Wife 167

24 Brothers in Arms 173

25 History-Makers 178

26 Infighting 186

27 Christmas Horrors 193

28 Hunted 199

29 Bohr's Bombshell 205

30 London Beckons 213

31 Trek to the Unknown 218

32 Closing In 226

33 Surrounded 233

34 Defiance and Loyalty 239

35 Living on the Edge 247

36 Walking with Ghosts 252

37 Spilling the Beans 261

38 The Gamble 267

39 The Consequences 272

40 The Ordeal   277

41 A Diplomatic Incident   287

42 Smear Campaign   293

43 Powerless   297

44 A New Betrayal   304

45 All's Fair in Love and War   310

46 When Life is Too Short   314

47 The Accident   321

48 Rewards and Memories   328

49 Coming Home   336

    Epilogue: The Hornet's Sting   343

    Index   358

Acknowledgements

This book would not have been possible without the help of two people – Thomas Sneum and Alan Brooke.

Tommy, the hero of the story, was patient, helpful and amusing, especially once he had overcome an early impulse to shoot me. He was, quite simply, the most fascinating man I have ever met. I will always cherish our many hours of taped conversations, Sneum's cigar smoke thick in the air, the table littered with history books and the occasional bottle of schnapps, red wine or beer. His gift to me was the material for this book, mine to him the preservation of his story, though I will always be sorry that I didn't earn him more recognition while he was still alive. It took many years to piece together the full story, perhaps too many, though I hope it has been worth it, both for you, the reader, and for Tommy's family.

In sharp contrast it took Alan Brooke, Editor-at-Large for Piatkus, no time at all to see the potential of the story once I sent it to him. Like all great 'bosses,' having made his key observations, Alan then left the writer to come up with the right blend. If I have succeeded, and only others can be the judge of that, much of the credit should go to Alan for his firm but wonderfully economical guidance.

In the Sneum family, I want to give particular thanks to Tommy's son Christian, whose knowledge of English and Danish (among many other languages) helped so much with the translation of important documents, such as Danish police reports, history books and newspaper articles. It is one of the enduring joys of having worked on this book that I can now count Christian among my friends. And although some of the tales of Tommy's womanising may not be entirely comfortable for 'Chris,' his sister Sandra or half-sister

Marianne, neither will they come as any great surprise. I can only hope that everyone will recognise that, since a love for women was so central to Tommy's life, it would have been a less-than-accurate portrayal of his character had some of these romantic adventures not been included here.

In my own family, my wife Victoria has given me invaluable assistance on the technical front, since the computer remains a mysterious beast to some of us. My little son Luca put up with seeing less of his father while the book was prepared, and I hope to make amends.

The late Ronnie Turnbull, who worked for Britain's Special Operations Executive, also deserves special acknowledgement here. While his impact on Sneum's war, however indirect, meant that he doesn't always emerge favourably in the narrative, I always enjoyed our telephone conversations in the years before he died, and I have since been told that he did too. Ronnie was more than capable of arguing his corner, and when we didn't feel like talking about the war any more we would talk about football instead. I developed an affection for Ronnie and tried without success to persuade Tommy to meet him, so that Sneum could overcome the bitterness he still felt towards SOE. The fact that I had to remain objective in the telling of this story should in no way devalue the personal rapport I developed with Turnbull, whether I agree with some of his wartime decisions or not.

There are so many people to thank: Denise Dwyer and Andy Hine in the Little, Brown London office for their cool professionalism and enthusiasm, and my excellent copy editor, Philip Parr, whose immediate grasp of the story's various elements and eagle eye for consistency were truly amazing.

Undoubtedly there are many more helpful individuals in England and Denmark who have been overlooked here, so let this page be for you too, and for all those at the National Archives in Kew, London, and the Frihedmuseet in Copenhagen, who put up with my bad temper as I tried to uncover the truth.

Here is the product of all our hard work.

Every effort has been made to identify and acknowledge the copyright holders. Any errors or omissions will be rectified in future editions provided that written notification is made to the publishers.

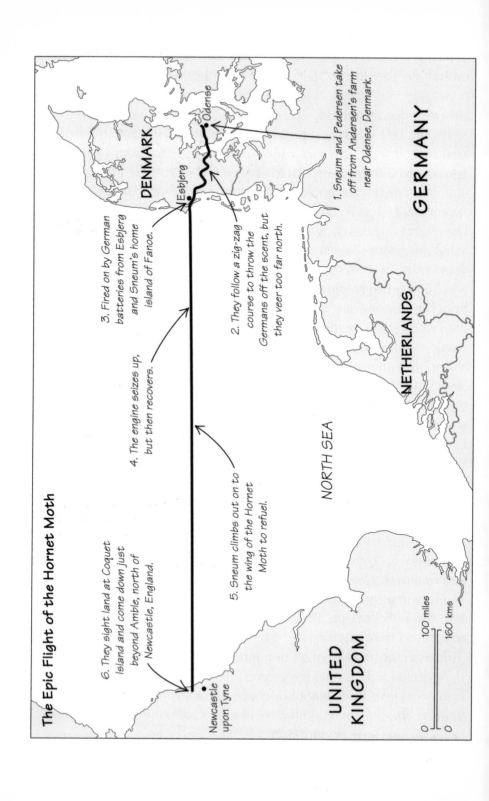

The Epic Flight of the Hornet Moth

DENMARK

Odense

Esbjerg

GERMANY

NETHERLANDS

NORTH SEA

UNITED KINGDOM

Newcastle upon Tyne

1. Sneum and Pedersen take off from Andersen's farm near Odense, Denmark.

2. They follow a zig-zag course to throw the Germans off the scent, but they veer too far north.

3. Fired on by German batteries from Esbjerg and Sneum's home island of Fanoe.

4. The engine seizes up, but then recovers.

5. Sneum climbs out on to the wing of the Hornet Moth to refuel.

6. They sight land at Coquet Island and come down just beyond Amble, north of Newcastle, England.

100 miles

160 kms

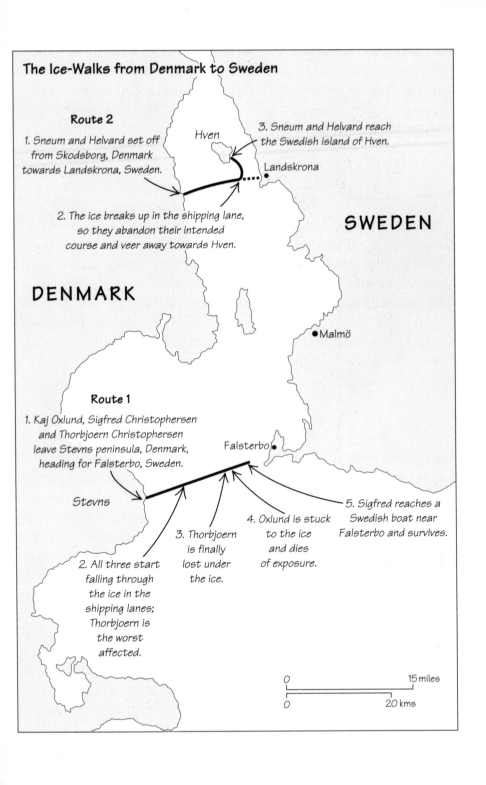

The Ice-Walks from Denmark to Sweden

Route 2

1. Sneum and Helvard set off from Skodsborg, Denmark towards Landskrona, Sweden.

Hven

3. Sneum and Helvard reach the Swedish island of Hven.

Landskrona

2. The ice breaks up in the shipping lane, so they abandon their intended course and veer away towards Hven.

SWEDEN

DENMARK

●Malmö

Route 1

1. Kaj Oxlund, Sigfred Christophersen and Thorbjoern Christophersen leave Stevns peninsula, Denmark, heading for Falsterbo, Sweden.

Falsterbo●

Stevns

5. Sigfred reaches a Swedish boat near Falsterbo and survives.

4. Oxlund is stuck to the ice and dies of exposure.

3. Thorbjoern is finally lost under the ice.

2. All three start falling through the ice in the shipping lanes; Thorbjoern is the worst affected.

0   15 miles

0   20 kms

INTRODUCTION: ZURICH, FEBRUARY 1998

WHEN A FORMER MI6 SPY is pointing a Browning 9mm pistol straight at your chest, there isn't much time to think about why you wanted to meet him in the first place. You are consumed by more immediate concerns, such as whether his wild-eyed stare means that he might just be crazy enough to pull the trigger. You search frantically for the right words to persuade him to calm down and point the pistol somewhere else. But all the time there is the fear that the wrong words might push him over the edge.

This living nightmare's origins lay in Denmark, where a British national newspaper had sent me on an assignment. Some money had gone missing during the transfer of a Danish footballer to an English club. While investigating, I was driven along a busy Copenhagen highway which ran parallel with the Oeresund, the treacherous sea channel between Denmark and Sweden.

'Did you know,' said the taxi driver, 'that some people tried to walk across that stretch of water to escape the Nazi occupation during the Second World War?' He must have noticed the disbelieving expression on his passenger's face. 'It was frozen over at the time,' the driver added, 'but the ice wasn't very solid. Some people made it; others didn't.'

His story started me thinking: who were these people, so

desperate to get away from the Nazis that they braved the fragile
ice to try to reach a neutral country? I picked up history books and
attempted some research. The years passed. Then I discovered that
one of the men to whom the Copenhagen taxi driver had alluded
was still alive. His was a particularly intriguing case, because he
had spied for Britain during the war and remained a controversial
figure, even as the twentieth century drew to a close. He was now
said to be living in Switzerland. His name was Thomas Sneum.
This sounded like a man worth meeting, even if it meant tracking
him down in my spare time.

In February 1998 I flew to Switzerland in the hope of hearing
Sneum's story first hand. I called him as soon as the plane landed,
the phone conversation was cordial, and he agreed to meet me the
following day . . . or so I thought. Waiting on his doorstep in
peaceful, suburban Zurich on a cold, clear morning, I had no
inkling of the reception he had prepared. Suddenly the door flew
open and there he was, brandishing the pistol menacingly. Did
Sneum think his visitor was merely pretending to be a reporter and
was really someone far more threatening, recruited to exact revenge
for some past misdemeanour? Maybe he held such a dim view of
journalists that he felt this was the best way to greet them.

It was hard to see the funny side as this short, shrivelled man
continued to aim his Browning directly at my heart. I kept my
hands where he could see them and pleaded my case, trying to
point out that there must have been a dreadful misunderstanding.
Later he told me: 'I can read people within the first few seconds of
meeting them.' In my case it wouldn't have been difficult: the look
of panic probably confirmed that I didn't constitute any major
threat. Gradually his anger seemed to give way to a more
controlled suspicion. He refused to put the gun away, but he did
eventually invite me in.

For such a notorious ladies' man even to consider spending time
in the company of someone who wasn't a woman represented quite
exceptional behaviour, I would later discover. The fact that Tommy
adored women – and they adored him – emerged quickly as one of
the more obvious aspects of his story. As we became friends over
the years, other vital components took much longer to establish.

Sneum's pistol was just the first of many barriers to the truth over the next decade: for example, MI5 were still being obstructive in 2007. But from early on I was determined to get to the bottom of the story, which contained hidden depths almost as challenging as the Oeresund itself. It is fair to say that James Bond films have been made with more likely storylines. But Tommy Sneum's story really happened. Ian Fleming's hero wasn't based on Sneum, but it is no exaggeration to say that he could have been.

'James Bond was just a film character, and I would never have gone around shooting people under ridiculous conditions like he did,' Sneum once pointed out. 'Anyway, there were times during the war when James Bond would have gone back. I carried on.'

Tommy's humour, his women and above all his spectacular stunts meant that he passed into wartime legend as either a lovable maverick or a deadly loose cannon, depending on your point of view.

'People talk so much of what they will do,' he told me. 'I prefer to do it.'

The author Ken Follett readily admits that his novel *Hornet Flight* was inspired by just one extraordinary episode in Sneum's eventful war. However, Follett's understandable distortions in the name of fiction mean that the true story has, until now, never been told. Similarly, no film has ever been made to celebrate Tommy's sheer audacity, or to examine his ruthless willingness to fight dirty when cornered.

In a letter dated 11 July 2006, MI5 did at least confirm two facts about Thomas Sneum: he had been investigated by the organisation during the Second World War for possible treachery; and he had ultimately been cleared. But if they were prepared to admit that much, why wouldn't MI5 release more information from their files about this agent?

Perhaps the answer lies in the shabby way Britain's Secret Intelligence Service (SIS) treated Sneum during the war. That he was investigated at all probably says more about the political infighting between the established SIS and its upstart rival, the wartime Special Operations Executive (SOE), than it does about Sneum's capacity to double-cross those who stood in his way. At the same time, Tommy's conduct wasn't always exemplary either, largely because he considered himself too important, as a source of intelligence, to be compromised. That selfish streak was understandable, perhaps even excusable, in a brave man who risked his life for the Allied cause time and again. But the reader can be the judge of Tommy's contribution to that cause, and the controversial conduct that often accompanied it.

R.V. Jones was so convinced of Sneum's value to the Allies that he partly dedicated his book, *Most Secret War*, to the dashing young pilot. During the war, in addition to being a key scientific adviser to Winston Churchill, Jones was the assistant director of British Scientific Intelligence, one of the component sections of SIS. So he was better placed than most to determine whether Sneum's name belonged in a list of celebrated super-spies. The dedication read:

> To all those in Nazi-occupied Europe who in lone obscurity and of their own will risked torture and death for scientific intelligence, like 'Amniarix' (Jeannie Rousseau, Vicomtesse de Clarens), Leif Tronstad, Thomas Sneum, Hasager Christiansen, A.A. Michels, Jean Closquet, Henry Roth, Yves Rocard, Jerzy Chemielewski, and the author of the Oslo Report: To reconnaissance pilots like Eric Ackermann and Harold Jordan: and to the men of the Bruneval Raid.

> 'For courage is the quality that guarantees all others.'

Sneum had a paperback edition of the book in his Zurich apartment. It contained a more personal, handwritten dedication from the author: 'To Thomas Sneum, one of the heroes of this book and the war.'

However, Foreign Office documents recently revealed a very different view of Sneum's wartime activities in the field, particularly when he was working with a wireless operator called Sigfred Christophersen. When the following extract was written, Major Geoffrey Wethered, who hunted double-agents on behalf of MI5 during the war, had just met with Commander Hollingworth of SOE's Danish Section. Wethered reported: 'During their adventures they [Sneum and Christophersen] appear to have given a great deal of information to the Germans about our activities in

Denmark, to such an extent SOE sent a message to ARTHUR [the codename of leading SOE agent Mogens Hammer] . . . informing him that Sneum had spilt the beans. None of this was told to us until today.'

Was Hollingworth's accusation motivated by genuine concern about the loyalty of Sneum, an SIS agent, or by his own desire for political gain at a time when his position as an SOE spymaster was under threat? To what extent was Sneum simply caught in the crossfire of London's interdepartmental rivalry between SIS and SOE? There was no love lost between the two British covert organisations, who rarely told each other what they were doing in the field, and often seemed at least as anxious to outwit their domestic rival as they were to undermine Adolf Hitler's Third Reich.

After years of investigation into Sneum's action-packed story, the true course of events can finally be told here. Was Sneum a hero or a traitor; a scapegoat or a villain? When it comes to the dark world of spooks, where does perception end and reality begin?

Chapter 1

THE TIGHTROPE TO RADAR

THOMAS SNEUM DIDN'T have time to think of a subtle way out of his first big crisis as a spy. It was unfortunate because no one on the British side knew about the extraordinary risks he was taking. The spy world in London was not even aware of his existence, and British Scientific Intelligence had no knowledge of the new Nazi installation which had drawn Sneum into such immediate danger. Mysterious towers had suddenly been erected where pine trees met sand dunes on his native island of Fanoe. And their strategic position, just off the west coast of Denmark, suggested that Adolf Hitler was preparing an unpleasant welcome for any British planes eyeing a route to mainland Europe across the North Sea.

The installation was visible in the distance, almost taunting Sneum; but his attempt to uncover its secrets, as he pretended to hunt rabbits on the surrounding heathland, had just been foiled by a rogue Alsatian's ability to pick up his scent on the sea breeze. 'That bloody dog came out of nowhere,' he explained many years later, as if still struggling to make sense of what had happened.

Tommy knew he was in deep trouble. He could reason with people; he could play mind games and win. That was why he had struck up what he thought would become a useful rapport with the Germans who had occupied his country for the last few months. He even liked some of them. As a youngster, Sneum had played with

German children on the tourist beaches of Fanoe just as often as he had played with their British counterparts. The rugged holiday island, just three kilometres wide and sixteen kilometres long, had been a paradise. Tommy still called it home, but now the game had changed. The Germans had turned from tourists to invaders, and the British were nowhere to be seen. Despite these dramatic changes to his world, Tommy's childhood experiences had helped him to adapt and turn the new balance of power to his advantage – until now.

No amount of carefully chosen words was going to stop this dog. It seemed to have made up its mind about how to deal with any suspicious-looking locals and was now eating up the last stretch of ground between them at such a frightening speed that Sneum could already see its razor-sharp teeth. He knew he had only a few seconds to come up with a solution, but he was still struggling to understand how the Alsatian had appeared so suddenly. The German guards kept their dogs on leads at all times, so this one had either broken free or been released deliberately by its handler. The guard was nowhere to be seen and the Alsatian was ready to leap. Instinctively, Tommy raised his shotgun and fired. 'I blew a hole in that animal just in time,' he recalled. 'But I also knew straight away that I was still in trouble.'

His desperate act of self-defence left an ominous silence, broken only by the sound of a German soldier scrambling up the slope towards him. As the guard drew closer and raised his rifle, Tommy saw that 'He was literally shaking with anger and looked as though he might be ready to do anything.'

At that moment he knew his charm offensive among the invaders, launched in the hope of unearthing intelligence for the British, was going to count for nothing. The dream of an escape to England and a new life as a fighter pilot in the RAF looked no more than a hollow fantasy. Right there, at home, was where the war seemed about to end for Thomas Sneum.

* * *

Tommy had been a twenty-two-year-old flight lieutenant in Denmark's Fleet Air Arm when the Nazis had rolled across the border on 9 April 1940. He had wanted to fight them there and then, and bitterly resented being denied the opportunity to take off in his Hawker Nimrod biplane to meet the Luftwaffe in the skies above Copenhagen. He hadn't been allowed to fire a single round in defence of his country and now, when he had finally pulled the trigger against the occupying forces, all he had done was blast a gaping hole in a dog. Worse still, it appeared that he might now be about to pay for that killing with his own life.

For a proud patriot, the situation was so absurd that it rivalled the farce of 9 April itself. Tommy had rebuilt his self-esteem by showing a distinct lack of respect for his own country's conduct on that momentous day, and in particular for the decisions of his military superiors. Since then, word had spread among the occupying forces that a feisty individual had stood out during the meek capitulation, and might yet require careful handling. Hauptmann Meinicke, Hitler's plump, middle-aged commander on the island of Fanoe, expressed some sympathy when he heard how the young Danish pilot had been grounded on the morning the German forces had swept in. The commander, a professional soldier without a Nazi bone in his body, seemed genuinely impressed by the local man's defiant spirit, and had the opportunity to tell him so when the pair were introduced by an administrative official in nearby Esbjerg, Denmark's most westerly port.

Although Sneum wasn't particularly tall, there was something of a fighter in his rugged features. He hadn't been given the chance to test himself, and that had obviously hurt, even though he would surely have been killed if his plane had been allowed to engage the enemy. Meinicke heard how the fiery Dane had conveyed his disgust to his superiors in Fleet Air Arm. First he had protested at the decision not to defend the country. Then he had asked to leave the service. Finally, when asked to put in writing a valid reason for his discharge, he had scribbled: 'The shit behaviour of the Danish Navy on 9 April.' It was blatant insubordination.

As spring turned to summer on Fanoe, Meinicke clearly enjoyed the rapport that developed between them. The glint in Tommy's eye and the cheeky smile were never more evident than when he refused to accept what Meinicke personally regarded as inevitable – that Germany would win the war by Christmas.

'I don't think you'll win the war this year, next year or the year after that,' insisted Tommy bravely.

Meinicke scoffed and said: 'You can't be serious.'

But Sneum was adamant. 'Look at Napoleon,' he pointed out. 'He had all of Europe and never got to England. You'll lose too, when the English and the Americans get together.'

They bet a bottle of whisky on the war being over by New Year 1941. Since the Americans were officially neutral and looked set to remain so, Meinicke confidently predicted that his new friend would never taste a drop of that Scotch. As a small consolation for Germany's occupation of his country, however, he gave Sneum permission to use a firearm, if only to hunt near his family's home. On this pretext, Tommy had edged towards the sinister-looking installation as it took shape between the dunes and the trees. He wondered what menace this new facility represented to the British across the North Sea. And if his suspicions were correct, he knew he would have to find a way to warn them. But now the only challenge he faced was how to stay alive long enough to get himself out of this mess.

With the Nazis sweeping all before them in 1940, Tommy could have taken a back seat like so many of his fellow countrymen. But he wasn't built that way; he had to be involved somehow. And when, soon after the invasion, Reichsmarschall Hermann Goering invited Flight Lieutenant Thomas Sneum to join his mighty Luftwaffe, some very troubling ideas began to form in Tommy's head. Although he had been outraged by the invasion, Sneum had nothing against the Luftwaffe's commander-in-chief personally. He had met Goering and even acted as a translator for him a couple of years earlier, when Hitler's trusted ally had visited Avnoe, the Danish air base where Sneum was stationed. Later in life, Tommy observed: 'Goering looked like a fat, stupid bastard – flabby. But he had already proved himself to be a man – one of the best fighter pilots in the First World War. He had downed a lot of Allied planes in that war, and I admired him at the time. Personally, I don't think he was ever a Nazi at heart. By the time we finished touring the air base, he was calling me by my name, addressing me as "Flight Lieutenant Sneum".'

It hadn't been easy to resist the temptation to fly again,

particularly after an officer on Goering's staff had taken Tommy on a tour of airfields on both sides of the border between Denmark and Germany. The German's persuasive, probing manner led Tommy to believe he might be an intelligence officer. Nevertheless, he was impressed by the respect he was shown, something entirely absent in the treatment he had recently suffered at the hands of his own military superiors. (Danish Fleet Air Arm had even threatened to arrest him after he had distributed naval food supplies among local households without permission in the confused hours immediately after the invasion. But Sneum hadn't seen any point in leaving those supplies where they were, just waiting for the Germans to seize them, and he didn't see why he should continue to take orders from men he now regarded as cowards.)

As he was courted by the invaders, Tommy reflected bitterly that at least the Germans were true fighters, like himself. To be among fellow warriors in the skies above Europe would be appealing. From another perspective, he also considered that signing up with the Luftwaffe would give him the opportunity to learn a great deal about the German war machine, valuable intelligence that could be passed on to the Allies. Looking back, Tommy reasoned:

> I wanted to know as much as possible about the way the Germans built people up, so I thought seriously about accepting Goering's invitation. But then I got afraid. Even at that point I saw my future in England. Who would have believed that my intentions were genuine? If I had gone to London and said: 'I've just spent six months in the German Air Force and now I want to join you,' who would have welcomed me? No one. They would just have thought I was a bloody spy. So I sent a nice reply to Goering, thanking him for his offer, but explaining that I didn't think I could accept.

However, the fear of being a bystander throughout the war was strong in these emotive times. Still hungry for action of some kind, Sneum fed his natural addiction to danger by edging ever closer to the new Fanoe installation, and in particular the strange rectangular shapes by the sea, with their mesh frames and mysterious rods protruding like antennae. The mystery behind their precise function had begun to consume him, with his curiosity only sharpened by an equal determination among the Germans to protect their secrets. For months, local traffic had been diverted so that no islanders could come close to the new giants on their doorstep.

But Tommy knew this island better than the back of his hand. He was also intelligent – 'My IQ is 164,' he later claimed. And, crucially, he had sufficient imagination to grasp the enormous military potential of scientific innovation. As he edged ever closer to the facility, he could see that each giant structure was constructed around a searchlight. The metal grids were built on huge cubic bases, with the two connected by long levers which offered horizontal and vertical mobility. He suspected he was looking at some kind of early-warning system, and if he was right the consequences would be grave indeed. Any British bombers hoping in the future to attack the Nazis at Esbjerg, or pass unnoticed over this strategic coast on their way to targets in Germany, would be blasted out of the sky.

But before he could contact the British to sound the alarm, Tommy felt that he needed to be sure of his facts. And so, on this particular summer's day, he had climbed Kikkebjerg – 'Lookout Hill' – not far from the German base. He was trying to monitor the installation through a powerful pair of binoculars, and make sure the coast was clear before he moved closer still. But the Alsatian had ruined everything, and the shotgun blast had left one angry German guard looking distinctly trigger-happy.

When he saw the remains of his dog, and the intruder with a shotgun, the guard aimed his rifle as if ready to exact instant revenge. Rather than fire, though, he shouted: 'Put it down. Now!' Sneum thought it wise to comply, and also raised his hands in the air. The guard was still shaking with anger as he walked forward; and there were tears in his eyes. The steel bayonet attached to the barrel of the German's rifle was soon an inch from Tommy's temple.

'Look, there's no need for this,' Sneum suggested as calmly as he could, in fluent German. 'I had no choice but to shoot. Your dog was about to rip my throat out. I don't know why. I was just hunting.'

'Hunting?' The German wasn't buying it. 'No one is allowed here.'

'I have a permit,' Tommy insisted. 'Why wasn't your dog on a leash?'

'I'll ask the questions, not you!' screamed the guard. 'Now move!'

'I'll do as you say,' said Sneum, then added, 'but I'll report you, too.'

He was frog-marched to an office just inside the perimeter of the German base. 'This bastard has just shot my dog,' the soldier told his colleagues. 'What shall we do with him?'

Typically, Sneum suppressed his fear and moved on to the attack. 'Now look, if you carry on like this, I'll make sure Hauptmann Meinicke hears about your behaviour. He's a personal friend of mine. Your dog was out of control and an obvious threat. Under Danish law, I was well within my rights to shoot it.'

The Germans looked at one another for a moment. The mention of their commanding officer's name had clearly given them food for thought.

'Take his name and address then get him out of here.' Having delivered his verdict, the guard in charge turned on the troublemaker. 'We'd better not see you around here again. Believe me, you won't be so lucky if we do, whether you know Hauptmann Meinicke or not.'

* ※ *

When he next met the formerly amiable Meinicke, Sneum noticed immediately that the Hauptmann's jovial manner had disappeared. There was no more banter about how quickly Hitler would win the war. And there was no apology for the dog's sudden attack, or for the threats from his guards. Worse still, as he led the young islander to his office, Meinicke behaved as though he now required proof of Tommy's allegiance.

'Flight Lieutenant Sneum,' said the German officer rather formally, 'some of our bigger vessels have been experiencing some difficulties trying to negotiate the narrow sea-lane around Fanoe as they approach Esbjerg on the mainland.'

'Is that so?' Tommy sensed he was about to be pushed further than he wanted to go.

'Indeed it is. In fact, some of our ships have almost run aground. So I wonder if you could help us.'

Sneum looked for a way out. 'Hauptmann Meinicke, I'm an aircraft pilot, not a ship's pilot.'

'But you're a navy man, you're an islander and you know the waters. We just need confirmation of the best way into Esbjerg. And it so happens that I have a map right here.'

Tommy had to think quickly. He could give Meinicke false information about the sea depths around Fanoe and Esbjerg, but this could easily be checked and he would soon be found out. If he wanted to solve the mystery of the installation, he would have to cooperate. Besides, it wouldn't be much of a betrayal. The so-called secrets of the channel could be found in any copy of *Danish Harbour Pilot*, the bible of the Danish Navy, so Sneum was sceptical that the Germans had encountered any navigational problems: he strongly suspected this was a test; and if it was, he didn't intend to fail. But he still felt uncomfortable as he studied the map and finally opened his mouth.

'The trick is to approach from here,' he said, pointing to a specific coordinate. 'Only start to sail east when you reach this point. The channel is deep enough there to take even the biggest of your vessels.'

'Just draw it for me, would you, Sneum?'

Feeling like salt was being rubbed in his wounds, Tommy duly obliged, trying to think of the intelligence he might one day glean in return for his cooperation.

'Well, now we know, Flight Lieutenant,' said Meinicke with some ambivalence. 'Thank you. I'm sure that will make life much easier.'

Both Sneum's character and the waters around the west coast of Denmark suddenly seemed much easier for Meinicke to fathom. So he suggested that his young Danish friend might want to meet some Abwehr (German Intelligence) officers, who were now firmly established in Copenhagen's Hotel Cosmopolit. Tommy didn't know how to react as Meinicke penned a note of introduction. The German explained that it amounted to a reference and could open doors in the capital, should Tommy so desire.

Most Danes with Allied sympathies would have come up with

an excuse to steer clear of such a snake pit. 'But I always liked to do what was least expected of me,' Sneum explained years later. So, within a week, he travelled to Copenhagen for an informal meeting in the bar of the Hotel Cosmopolit. He quickly persuaded the occupiers that his loyalties were now firmly with them, and that he was keen to be of service. Over a casual drink, he was asked his opinion on a number of issues, including the strategic importance of various airfields in Denmark. Tommy defended his actions later, insisting:

> I only gave them information that I knew they already had, or could easily get hold of. And I took the opportunity to plant information too, or ideas that I thought could hurt them. For example, I might tell them they had no reason to be afraid of one particular thing, and suggest that there was more reason to be afraid of another instead, when in fact the opposite was true. If they appeared confident of something I would say, 'Are you sure?' in a way that might plant a seed of doubt in their minds. They asked me: 'How are the Danes feeling about us?' And of course I replied: 'You're nice people.'

As the evening gathered pace, Tommy took his new acquaintances to an illicit drinking den he knew, hidden away in the cellar of a nearby tobacconist's. Ove Petersen, who owned both businesses, illegal and legal, took Sneum aside and told him in no uncertain terms that he feared the consequences of this impulsive visit. Now that Tommy had shown the Germans his secret bar, right across the road from their Intelligence Headquarters, Petersen was worried that he would either be closed down by the occupiers or branded a traitor by the locals. Sneum assured him that neither would happen, since the Germans were far too fond of their beer to eliminate such an inviting option. He also argued that it would be perfectly patriotic for Petersen to welcome the occupiers, because he intended to mislead them on certain key issues. Tommy told his friend that if the Abwehr officers seemed interested in someone as a potential source of intelligence, he would raise questions about the contact's sympathies. Meanwhile, if a loyal Dane's behaviour had aroused suspicion, he would allay the Germans' fears.

Although Petersen understood the logic, he still looked relieved when they all left in the early hours, with the drunken Nazis barely able to climb the stairs. And he was not too thrilled to see the process repeated several times in the following weeks, until the sudden appearance of Germans in his little den became almost routine.

Later Tommy revealed that throughout this time he was walking a tightrope with his new acquaintances: a single verbal slip could have led to his imprisonment, deportation or worse. He insisted: 'I kept conversation down to small-talk. I was never so inquisitive that they could be suspicious. I just talked and talked. Now and again I came in with a question that could mean nothing but could mean a bit. You had to show the Germans you were pro-German. Once I had done that, some of the Abwehr even told me where they were going and where their troops were.'

After a few weeks of these exchanges, Tommy returned to Fanoe and took a stroll one summer's evening down the Western High Street of Nordby, with Meinicke and his adjutant walking on either side of him. They were spotted by two of Sneum's friends from childhood, Hugo Lee Svarrer and Jens Nielsen. Tommy smiled as they passed. The Danes' greeting was not so warm: 'They spat at me,' Tommy revealed later. 'And one said to the other: "That fucking German-loving swine." When you hear something like that, it hurts.' At the time, Tommy was too shocked to react. Though they probably hadn't understood the Danish words, the Germans were certainly left in no doubt about the sentiment, and they remained silent for some time. Then Meinicke gently began a conversation on more trivial matters, almost as though the incident had never happened. But Sneum would never forget the exchange, and he vowed that one day those former friends would have to apologise for what they had done. He recalled when that moment finally came: 'Soon after the war, I was at a hunting-club dinner and they came up to my table and said: "We feel terrible about what we said that day. We didn't know any better." I forgave them.' At the time, however, there was nothing Tommy could do but play up to his new reputation for treachery. 'Some of the Germans took me around the port of Esbjerg not long after that incident, and I went drinking with Luftwaffe officers. I think many more Danish people despised me when they saw that.'

But eventually, after all the abuse and accusations, Tommy struck gold. 'I got to know an *Unteroffizier* – a sergeant major – who was very fond of his beer; a big, friendly fellow. He used to go to a restaurant near the ferry port in Nordby. I went down there, bought him a drink and we started talking.' After several bottles of beer and some meaningless chat, Tommy saw that his drinking partner was sufficiently relaxed to allow the conversation to be steered in a specific direction. What followed stuck in his mind for the rest of his life.

Sneum asked: 'Are you afraid of the British coming here, bombing us, because of the installation?'

'They'd never reach us,' said the *Unteroffizier* with another swig. 'We'd be able to see them coming from far away if they brought ships.'

'Surely you can't see them any further away than the normal range of binoculars,' replied Sneum, as innocently as he could.

'Yes, we can. We've got special technology,' said the German, with a touch of arrogance.

'Does that mean you can also see aircraft?' asked Tommy, knowing he was taking a bigger risk with every question.

'Naturally,' replied the *Unteroffizier* casually.

Sneum thought he had better express relief at this news, though that was far from what he was feeling. 'My heart was beating very fast after what I had been told,' he said later. 'I knew that the British had to try to put this new technology out of action. Because, if the Germans were to be warned by the installation at Fanoe about British planes coming their way, that same warning would immediately go out to all the stations in southern Denmark and northern Germany. Nothing would be able to come in unobserved.'

Chapter **2**

TRAPPED

By THE END of the summer of 1940, Else Sneum knew she was pregnant. She was only twenty-three, and her striking features were lit by a new excitement. The pretty brunette clearly felt ready for motherhood, though she was much less willing to accept some of her husband's new habits. Hunting by day and boozing by night, Thomas Sneum seemed far less attentive than he had been before they were married. Else told him that his priorities would have to change now that she was expecting their first child.

When the couple had tied the knot on 17 April and walked down the steps of Copenhagen's spectacular Radhus (Town Hall) to cheers from friends, Else had known that their life together would be far from perfect. The blend of Italian Renaissance and medieval Danish architecture had provided a dramatic setting for the ceremony; but with the Nazi occupation barely a week old, there would be no honeymoon. Else accepted that, and she didn't even seem to mind living with Tommy's parents on Fanoe for a while, although the arrangement afforded the newly-weds little privacy. But she wanted Tommy at least to try to act like a loving husband to compensate for the awkwardness of the situation. Thus far, he hadn't done so.

And, as her pregnancy progressed, Else gradually realised that he never would. For Tommy was rarely in the family home in Nordby long enough to make the relationship feel like a true marriage. He didn't want to feel married, and craved the freedom he used to enjoy. The idea of being a parent at such a young age didn't thrill him either. Only the war captured his imagination; and to get involved in that war he needed to be out and about. Back at the house, his father Christian did little to help ease the family tension: 'My father liked Else because she flirted with him. My mother disliked Else intensely for the same reason.'

But it was Else's father, Carl Jensen, who had created many of the problems they now faced, for he had forced Tommy to go through with the wedding in the first place. Jensen, a good-looking salesman of newspaper advertising space, was never going to give Sneum an inch once he realised the young couple were sleeping together. 'He was a fucking shit,' his son-in-law said, still bitter half a century later. Jensen had reacted with horror when a tearful Else had told him, the day after the invasion, that Tommy was already talking about trying to escape to England so that he could fight against the occupiers. Confronting Sneum hours later, Jensen warned him that he wasn't about to allow a flashy flight lieutenant to leave his daughter in the lurch and make a break for the bright lights of London.

Sneum recalled:

Else and I were engaged early in 1940. I had proposed to her partly because she was a very good-looking girl and I made the mistake of treating her like a trophy. Then I had gone off the idea of marrying her, because I could see we wouldn't get on and I had realised she wasn't the woman for me. But when my future father-in-law found out that the engagement was off, and that I'd said I was going to England, he made a hell of a lot of trouble. He and his wife said they would denounce me to the Germans and reveal my plans if I didn't marry their daughter, because I had taken away her innocence.

'Her virginity?' I asked.

'Oh Christ, yes!' responded Tommy enthusiastically. 'Anyway, Else's father told me this: "I don't like you. I think you've led my daughter astray and I don't want you in my family. But you've compromised her and now you're going to make a respectable woman out of her. If you don't . . . well, the consequences for you don't bear thinking about." So I married his daughter,' concluded Tommy simply.

There were some advantages to this arrangement, though. At least the marriage would briefly take Tommy's mind off the humiliation of having been a member of an armed service that had refused to fight. It also gave him some cover because the Germans would be less likely to suspect a newly married man of planning to escape to England.

Jensen probably thought he had won the battle of wills with his son-in-law through basic blackmail. Sneum knew differently: 'The wedding didn't make any difference. I had made up my mind to go to England and I didn't think I would ever be back, so it was all the same to me. Otherwise, I would never have married Else, because we were getting tired of each other. It was her family who put enormous, stupid pressure on us both.'

Even as Else had made her way down those Radhus steps on 17 April, her new husband had been distracted – although, unusually for him, not by another beautiful woman. He noticed uniformed Germans in the Radhuspladsen, moving confidently among the wedding guests, as though this were their own capital. The cheers for the bride were almost drowned out by Nazi propaganda as Danes sat silently on benches and listened dutifully. Tommy hated what he saw. The Radhus, with its 350-foot tower, was an impressive venue, but there had been more romantic weddings in Copenhagen's history.

Five months later, with his wife now pregnant, Tommy felt that everything was moving too quickly. Though the couple had enjoyed some good times, he knew he didn't want to spend the rest of his life with Else. He loved all women, not just one, and most seemed to love him in return, even though he was too short to be considered classically good-looking. And he had sought the company of women long before his father acknowledged his adolescence by trying to teach him the facts of life. 'I'll never forget his opening line,' remembered Tommy, smiling affectionately at the memory. 'He began: "I suppose you have heard some dirty stories." And I had, so it wasn't too bad a start. He went on to tell me that

I should always please the woman before I pleased myself, and I think that was a good lesson to learn.'

Tommy enjoyed his first major affair as a fifteen-year-old on Fanoe, when a married woman twice his age taught him everything else he needed to know about the opposite sex. 'That created quite a scandal,' he recalled. 'My father found out by reading a note she had left for me at our family home, and he wanted to give me a good thrashing. For the first time I resisted, and told him not to raise his hand to me again.'

The amorous Tommy already considered himself to be a man. As the years went by, he was flattered to be told on more than one occasion that he reminded girls of the tough and charismatic film star Humphrey Bogart. Tommy's military uniform did him no harm either in his pursuit of the opposite sex. Indeed, he remembered: 'Else and I met in a tailor's, and she was originally fascinated by my naval cadet's uniform. She was very complimentary and I suppose I was a bit flattered by the attention.' But what had attracted him to Else? 'She had a lot of nice girlfriends,' he said mischievously. And when asked to describe his wife's personality, Tommy replied rather uncharitably: 'She didn't have one.' That wasn't true, of course, but Tommy could never forgive or forget that he had been forced to marry the wrong woman too young.

❊ ❊ ❊

With so many other women in the world, Else was always going to have a hard time holding on to her man. 'I like all girls, they are lovely and charming,' Tommy explained simply. However, he loved the idea of making a difference in the war even more than he loved women. So when Else found herself alone in bed again one night during the late summer of 1940, it wasn't because of a love rival. Her husband was creeping between sand dunes and pine trees, not in and out of the bedrooms of beautiful women. He had eyes only for the mysterious installation on his native island of Fanoe.

In the darkness, Tommy spotted the rectangular outline of one of the strange devices and heard the faint drone of a plane's engine somewhere overhead. He thought it sounded like a German sea-plane, though he couldn't see it. Suddenly, the entire piece of machinery ahead of him began to swivel, as if it were following the aircraft. Then something even more extraordinary happened: 'They switched on the searchlight and the beam hit the silver-coloured Junker immediately.' The light's aim was so precise that Tommy knew he hadn't witnessed a chance event. There had been no random scanning of the darkness for the origin of the sound: the searchlight had known exactly where to point. For that to have happened, the plane must have been spotted by something far more powerful and sophisticated than the naked eye or binoculars. The precision left Tommy temporarily awestruck. 'It was that demonstration which made me certain we were dealing with some kind of early-warning system. I was convinced that they now had the capability to plot the position of a ship or plane using radio waves.'

Sneum was well aware that this could be disastrous for the Allied war effort. Since a nearby lighthouse offered a reference point for British planes crossing the North Sea to bomb potential targets in Germany, innumerable aircraft could fall into the trap before the Allies realised what was happening. Tommy had to find a way to warn the British of the dangers that awaited their unsuspecting pilots. Fortunately, he had an ally who could help him achieve this.

Kaj Oxlund, who was friends with both Tommy and Else, had already begun to smuggle reports on the basic logistics of the German occupation across to neutral Sweden. At thirty-five years old, he was a thickset individual with neat brown hair and a reassuring smile. Tommy was convinced he could trust him. After all, it had been Kaj, an anti-aircraft battery gunner at the time, who had warned Tommy in a phone call to Avnoe air base on 7 April that the Nazi invasion was imminent. Tommy explained: 'We were already close friends by then, and I had often stayed with him in Copenhagen. He left me a message to call him, and when I did he told me what was going to happen. He was getting the sort of high-quality information from Army Intelligence that we didn't get in the navy. Kaj told me: "I'm sure they're coming. We're prepared."'

In reality, neither man could have done much more than die, since there had been little chance of Danish forces surviving the Nazi onslaught if they had resisted. Now all the enjoyable

weekends they had spent as a foursome with Else and Kaj's wife
Tulle seemed a world away, along with the exhilarating sense of
freedom both men had felt while riding powerful Frederiksborg
stallions around the perimeter of Tommy's airfield. Sneum retained
fond memories of those carefree days before the war: 'Oxlund liked
shooting, riding, the country life, just as I did. He had a classy wife
and we liked each other too. Else and Tulle got on well together
and we spent some lovely weekends that way.'

Between 7 and 9 April 1940, however, Kaj and Tommy became
resigned to the fact that they would probably never see their
women again. Their grim assumption soon proved unfounded,
though: while the trustworthy Oxlund's intelligence had been
accurate, Denmark's King Christian decided to spare his forces
from inevitable slaughter by ordering no resistance to the invasion.
Even so, life would never be the same again for either man. Their
stubborn and increasingly complicated struggle against the
occupation was only just beginning.

In the aftermath of the invasion Oxlund left the army to go into
business, a move which made him the best possible courier for
Sneum's precious intelligence. As a genuine businessman, he had a
perfect excuse to travel; and as a former military man he had the
nerve to carry incriminating evidence without arousing suspicion.
Tommy therefore compiled a preliminary report to go with his
sketches of the Fanoe installation, put them into a dossier and gave
it to Kaj, who took a ferry across the Oeresund to Sweden and
posted a thick envelope to the British Legation in Stockholm. It
contained the first news from Denmark of the early-warning
technology that would soon be known as 'radar'.

In case the British required more detail, Tommy intended to pay
them a visit in person before long. Through autumn and midwinter,
however, increased patrols and thick ice frustrated his efforts to
escape the Nazi occupation of Denmark by boat. His
disappointment was shared by two friends who were equally
desperate to reach Britain, Kjeld Pedersen and Christian Michael
Rottboell. Taller and better looking, Pedersen had been Tommy's
best friend in the Danish Navy's Fleet Air Arm before the
occupation grounded both men. 'We trusted each other completely,'
Sneum would later say. And by late 1940 they shared a new

dream – to fly aerial combat missions for Britain's Royal Air Force. Meanwhile, Rottboell, a confident young aristocrat, was an aircraft mechanic and staunch supporter of the resistance. He was determined to reach England so that he could fight the Nazis, and his family had noticed a change in his demeanour whenever they were together in their magnificent castle at Boerglum Cloisters. Suspecting his intentions and realising there was little he could do to stop him, Rottboell's father confronted Sneum when he visited one day. 'Look, I know what you are getting my son into,' he said. Before Tommy could answer, Mr Rottboell added, 'Just promise to keep an eye on Christian Michael for me as best you can.' Tommy looked the older man in the eye and said that he would. Now, though, it appeared that Rottboell's father had no immediate reason to worry, because they seemed to be going nowhere.

In early 1941, however, Tommy Sneum became obsessed with a novel plan which, if executed successfully, would allow him to write his name in history.

Chapter **3**

HIMMLER AND THE LONGBOW

THE FOCAL POINT for Tommy's new assault on the Nazis was no longer the daunting installation on Fanoe but a swanky hotel in the centre of the Danish capital. And his ambitious – some would say crazy – assassination plot was linked to his enduring love for a woman who fascinated him like no other. Talking about the origins of his plan, he explained:

> I had an ex-girlfriend called Oda Pasborg, a beautiful blonde who had starred in a film called *En Fuldendt Gentleman – The Complete Gentleman*. Her father had given her a penthouse apartment on one of the approaches to the Hotel d'Angleterre, where all the top German officers used to stay. I was still close to Oda and I had keys for the apartment. It started me thinking.
>
> One day in 1940, I had been visiting Oda when I found myself down on the street just a few metres from a German staff car. Inside was an officer and I felt the urge to shoot him, but I wasn't carrying a pistol, because I had been to see Oda and she didn't like anything to do with the war. Afterwards I realised that I could, in theory at least, have killed the German officer from Oda's apartment window, as he went past.

But why aim only for a lowly army officer? Tommy began to dream of assassinating a top Nazi official. If he was in the right place at the right time, and given sufficient warning of such a visit to central Copenhagen, it certainly seemed feasible. He said later:

> I wanted to kill Heinrich Himmler more than any of the others because I knew I was never going to get to Adolf Hitler. Not many people knew who Himmler was at the time, but I did. He was Reichsfuhrer of the SS, and even a lot of German officers didn't like him. But I was prepared to kill any of the top Nazis if I got the chance, even the Luftwaffe chief, Hermann Goering, a man I had met personally and found to be very charming. Now it was different: they had invaded Denmark and I wanted revenge.

The challenge was to think of a way to avoid capture after making the attempt, since such a fate would mean a terrible death for Sneum and any associates who could be linked to the hit. 'The problem was that if you used a pistol or rifle, the Germans would soon see where the shot had come from, and I wasn't prepared to risk getting Oda into such serious trouble. She would have been tortured, and I couldn't have that. Oda was one of the very few girls that I ever really loved. I probably loved her more than she ever realised.'

It seems that Tommy's desperation to impress Oda may have gone hand in hand with his desire to play a more active part in the war, a potentially explosive combination in a man who hated rejection or defeat of any kind. He revealed later:

> We had known each other since long before I married Else, and Oda was much classier. We met on a boat while sailing back from Harwich in England to Esbjerg, a journey which took about thirty hours in those days. It was the mid-1930s; I was seventeen or eighteen and she was a couple of years older. She was beautiful, tall, blonde, charming and intelligent. I saw her and thought, This is the woman I'm going to make my wife one day.
>
> What was so special about her? Just to be near her made you happy. I felt so relaxed on that boat that I could talk about anything with her. We went out on deck and it was cold, and we held each other tight. We kissed and it was the most extraordinary, lovely experience. We didn't do much more than that on the

voyage, but we both knew we were already very much in love. She went on to Copenhagen at the end of the voyage, and I went to Fanoe. A couple of days later I went to Copenhagen to see her again, and took a room at the Grand Hotel. She was shocked and afraid when I called to tell her where I was, because a friend of her father owned that hotel. So I had to move to another hotel before she would come and see me. But when she did it was worth it, because every moment together was a pleasure.

She was snooty in an awfully nice way, from a good but stupid family. Stupid because in her father's eyes I wasn't good enough for her. In those days fathers thought about prospective sons-in-law in terms of career and breeding. Although he couldn't complain about my family, I was still at polytechnic and had a reputation for being a wild child, so he did everything he could to keep us apart. In those days it was difficult for young people to meet away from their parents, and fathers believed that boys should be properly introduced to their daughters through the family or not at all.

We still found ways to see each other and we stayed together for a couple of years, but in the end Oda couldn't stand the strain because of her family's disapproval, and we agreed it was better to part. That was probably in 1936, but we stayed good friends. The situation was painful, and we did no more than kiss each other warmly on the cheek whenever we met. That's how it was when the war came, but secretly I still loved her. And I think my original decision to marry Else was also partly motivated by my desire to send a message to Oda, saying: 'Look what happens if you don't marry me.'

I still wanted Oda, you see, and whatever was left between us lasted for several years without coming to a final end. I didn't try to force things, which would have been the worst possible way, but I used to go up to her penthouse near the Hotel d'Angleterre so that we could talk intimately. She was single, and she trusted me enough to give me my own set of keys to her apartment. From a war perspective, the location was too good to be true, and I was convinced there had to be another way to use this opportunity without damaging Oda.

It didn't take me long to come up with the answer. I bought a steel longbow from a hunting shop in Copenhagen. It was perfect because it came in two pieces, which you could quickly assemble or fold away as you liked. It didn't take up too much room and I had used a longbow as a child to hunt birds and rabbits. But to draw back this bow required a force equivalent to lifting a twelve-stone man; and it weighed about seventy-five pounds. The power it unleashed meant that the arrows, wooden with duck-feather flights, were lethal.

The beauty of the longbow is that it can be a silent killer, and I felt confident that I could escape the scene before the Germans pinpointed the source of the arrow. With luck, I would be able to carry out the perfect assassination. So I went into Copenhagen's Tivoli Gardens, and put targets up on trees. After a while, I could hit playing cards from fifty metres. Then I went back to Fanoe and practised against moving targets. The seagulls gliding along had no chance against my steel longbow. I knew it would be a much harder challenge to hit a moving German while aiming downwards from an apartment window, but I believed that from fifty metres I could not only hit a man but strike whatever part of his body I was aiming for.

As part of my preparations, I even wrote '9 April 1940' – the day of the invasion – on my arrows. Now I only needed a tip-off that a top German was coming to the d'Angleterre. As long as Oda was well away from the apartment on that day, I would have time to do the job.

By now it was early 1941, and Tommy had spent many days at the central Copenhagen home of a resistance sympathiser called Jens Dahl, waiting for the phone call from one of Dahl's contacts that might give his plan the green light. At Kastrup Airport, Arne Helvard, an old colleague from Fleet Air Arm, was monitoring the movements of top Nazis. Another ally was Tommy's brother-in-law, Niels-Richard Bertelsen, who as a Copenhagen detective was sometimes given prior warning when senior Nazi figures were heading into the Danish capital.

In early February Bertelsen called to say that a top Nazi was about to leave Kastrup for Copenhagen, though his identity was unknown. Tommy called Oda's apartment and for once was delighted to hear no reply. Wherever she was, she had unwittingly taken herself out of the firing line. Tommy used his set of keys to let himself in, assembled his longbow and waited for his prey. Then Oda's phone rang. Tommy took a chance and picked up the receiver. 'It was Bertelsen. There had been a change of plan: the leading Nazi had felt unwell and decided to fly directly to Germany. It soon became clear that the man I had been waiting for was Heinrich Himmler. In the end, they had just landed at Kastrup, refuelled and flown away.'

History shows that on 6 February 1941 Himmler did indeed land at Copenhagen's Kastrup Airport on his way back from visiting SS recruits in Norway. He had no idea how close he had come to being the target of an assassination attempt. It is impossible to say whether that attempt would have succeeded, particularly given Sneum's unusual choice of weaponry. However, it is conceivable that the course of history, and especially the fate of millions of Jews, might have been different had Himmler stuck to his schedule. The very Nazi that Tommy had most wanted to kill had nearly flown into his trap, only to escape thanks to a headache.

In 2007 Tommy's son, Christian, asserted:

I am absolutely sure Himmler was the target. We still had that steel longbow in the family house near Zurich when I was a boy. I used to try, without success, to pull back its string. My father always told me that he had almost assassinated Himmler with that longbow. I believed him at the time and I still believe it today. I don't think he wanted to make any more of it later in his life, because he didn't actually get round to killing Himmler. And there was so much that he did manage to do that there wasn't much point in going on about what he might have done.

To some extent, Tommy himself was relieved that he failed to carry out the hit:

There is a desire in every man for revenge at some level or other, and Adolf Hitler, the uneducated little bastard, had invaded my country. I became obsessed with getting revenge for that, because I was so proud to be a Danish officer. If you have a rotten society like Nazi Germany, it is no good killing low-level members of that society. You have to kill the leaders. But I was so enthusiastic about my ideas that I only realised the possible consequences when my sister Margit challenged me around that time. She said: 'What about the family? What about Father and Mother? You can't do it.' They would probably have shot my family if I'd killed a top Nazi, so I'm lucky that it didn't happen in the end. Sometimes I felt ashamed that I didn't consider the consequences for my family while I was laying those plans.

Also, if you killed Himmler, you immediately spoiled the whole intelligence-gathering game for ever, because there would have been so much more security. So there was an advantage attached to not killing him. As for Oda, I never told her what I had been planning to do from the window of her flat. And I still loved her for many years after the war. But we never got back together.

Although he later found positives in the fact that the assassination attempt had to be aborted, at the time it was deeply frustrating for Tommy. In early 1941 he felt he had lost both the girl and the chance to make a telling impact on the course of the war. But soon enough many more opportunities would arise in both spheres, and Thomas Sneum would be ready to seize them.

Chapter **4**

A TASTE OF FREEDOM

A S HIMMLER FLEW AWAY to safety in that first week of February 1941, Tommy was left in Denmark, still feeling trapped. Yet he remained as determined as ever to break through the wall of ice that enveloped the Danish coast. Instead of looking west to Britain for an escape route, he turned his attentions eastwards, to neutral Sweden. Since it was much closer, Tommy knew he would have a more realistic chance of getting there. And perhaps the Swedes could provide the first stepping stone to Britain.

Sneum was beaten to the British Legation in Stockholm by a young man he knew only vaguely, but one whose arrival would have serious repercussions for his war. Ronald Turnbull was a charming young Scot who was busily establishing a field headquarters for the Special Operations Executive's Danish Section in the Swedish capital. The SOE, created with the personal approval of Winston Churchill, was tasked with setting Nazi-occupied Europe ablaze with the fires of resistance. Anyone who had known Turnbull just five years earlier would have been surprised by his appointment. As a Cambridge University student in the 1930s, he had sent fan mail to Hitler, declaring himself to be a keen supporter of all things German. 'I wrote to Hitler and I've got a letter from him somewhere,' he said later. 'In the early days I thought Hitler was a great man, which turned out not to be the case. I was vice-president of the Anglo-German Association at Cambridge. We wanted to get closer to the Germans, particularly their youth.'

Before long the scales fell from Turnbull's eyes and his opinion of what was happening in Germany changed. When he left university he stood as a Liberal candidate for Bethnal Green and then worked as a journalist on the London *Evening Standard*. He was under no illusions about Hitler's intentions by the time Neville Chamberlain returned from a meeting with the Fuhrer in September 1938. The Prime Minister claimed triumphantly that he had secured 'peace in our time' for Britain. Turnbull knew the truth: 'I felt sick when Chamberlain waved that white paper,' he said. 'I knew what was coming.'

But even the perceptive Ronnie, who by 1940 was a press attaché at the British Legation in Copenhagen, was taken aback when the Germans invaded Denmark on 9 April. He was celebrating his engagement to Maria Thereza do Rio Branco, daughter of the Brazilian Ambassador, when the Nazis rolled in. He escaped thanks to his diplomatic immunity, but some of the British journalists with whom he had liaised in the Danish capital were trapped.

Though Ronnie didn't exactly cover himself in glory during those frightening, chaotic days, his affinity with Denmark was remembered in Britain's corridors of power, and he had also broadcast anti-German propaganda to Denmark from the BBC in London. Thereza made her way to England soon after her husband had arrived, and they had been married for two months when SOE came calling in July. Turnbull accepted the organisation's offer enthusiastically, but then realised that just to reach his new office would present a serious challenge.

Due to the extreme dangers of travelling from Britain to Sweden by air in the winter of 1940–1, Turnbull was sent on an extraordinary, roundabout route to Stockholm. Ronnie and Thereza, who was by now pregnant, were accompanied by his secretary, Pamela Tower. They sailed to the Cape of Good Hope in South Africa, then went north, reaching Istanbul before the Turnbulls' son Michael was born. As soon as mother and baby were strong enough to continue, they headed overland to Moscow, via Tiflis, Baku and Rostov. Once in the Russian capital they boarded yet another train, this time to Leningrad, and from there travelled to Finland. Eventually, in February 1941, the exhausted Turnbulls reached Stockholm by ship. They had left Liverpool more than two months earlier.

This epic journey drew only derision from Lord Haw-Haw, Hitler's infamous propagandist William Joyce, who announced on Berlin radio: 'The British must really be in a sad condition if they have to send a fellow from the Foreign Office halfway around the world to get to Stockholm.'

The resistance organisation that the 'fellow from the Foreign Office' had been sent to run – SOE Denmark – would eventually become a thorn in the side of Tommy Sneum. But he couldn't have known that as he started to make his way to the very building in which Turnbull was now based.

※ ※ ※

Smarting from his failure to assassinate a high-ranking Nazi with his longbow, Sneum had finally spotted a weakness in the German ring of steel around his country. He upset his good friend Kjeld Pedersen and their resistance colleague Christian Michael Rottboell by insisting that he must use the route alone. It would be safer that way, he told them firmly, and they had to accept his decision, however reluctantly.

So, on 20 February 1941, Tommy set out for Kastrup Airport. He carried with him an update on the radar installation on Fanoe, where the Germans had been building a third tower for their early-warning system. He also had facts and figures about the Nazi occupation of Denmark and German troop movements. An hour on a civilian plane took him to Roenne Airfield on Bornholm, a Danish island within striking distance of the Swedish mainland. A couple of days later he climbed aboard a huge ferry which, aided by ice-cutters, carved a path to Ystad on the Swedish coast. The first, nervous minutes of 23 February saw him posing as a businessman in front of a yawning customs official on the quayside. Tommy dreaded a search of his belongings or clothes, but the lazy official simply stamped his passport and directed him to the night train for

Stockholm. Sneum couldn't show any signs of the exhilaration he felt. He was free of the Nazi occupation, however temporarily.

Sleep came easily on the train once the adrenalin wore off. Before dawn, making sure that he wasn't followed as he left Stockholm train station, Tommy made his way to the Strandvagen peninsula outside the city. Soon after it opened for official business, he proudly entered the British Legation.

'I'm Flight Lieutenant Thomas Sneum of the Danish Fleet Air Arm and I have a lot of important information,' he announced at reception. He was led to Squadron Leader Donald Fleet, the ageing but enthusiastic Assistant Air Attaché. A smiling Fleet decided to take Sneum straight to the office of Captain Henry Denham, the Naval Attaché, who operated from the kitchen wing of the Legation.

Turnbull, who had attended some of the same Copenhagen functions as Sneum during the winter of 1939–40, was nowhere to be seen. Had Tommy renewed his acquaintance with Ronnie that day, the brave Dane's war could have turned out very differently. Turnbull might well have taken one look at all the excellent information in Sneum's possession and recruited him on the spot for SOE Denmark. Denham worked in close proximity to Turnbull, but answered to a different British chain of command. 'I wasn't employed to help the Admiralty,' Turnbull pointed out. By the same token, Denham wasn't employed to help SOE.

The dynamic between the two men was curious. Both had worked at Britain's Copenhagen Legation, and they had been repatriated by the Nazis on the same sealed train. Turnbull now worked with Denham's former secretary, Pamela Tower, but 'She was still in love with Henry,' Ronnie claimed. Since Turnbull's arrival in Stockholm, Denham had offered him access to any routine naval information at his disposal, but the SOE man later said dismissively, 'We didn't need ordinary intelligence.' It seemed that Denham and Turnbull shared almost everything, but when it came to the precious new secrets that Sneum had brought into the building, there would be no sharing, even though this was precisely the sort of extraordinary intelligence Turnbull craved.

As a regular naval officer, Denham was obliged to pass any significant intelligence through the established Admiralty channels, which led through Naval Intelligence to the Secret Intelligence

Service in London. Turnbull, meanwhile, had to report to his own SOE spymaster back in Britain, Commander Ralph Hollingworth. Denham wasn't about to entrust the 'amateurs' at SOE with vital scientific intelligence, no matter how much he liked Turnbull on a personal level. Had Sneum's discoveries landed on Turnbull's desk rather than Denham's, he too would have wanted to send them exclusively to his own organisation, SOE. And the source of such valuable intelligence was to be treated in a similarly possessive fashion: Tommy was already becoming a trophy, the sort of prize that one covert British organisation would jealously guard against overtures from its rival.

Naturally, Tommy didn't know any of this. As he began his presentation, he viewed 'the British' as one united force lined up against the Germans. He could never have imagined that, behind the scenes, they were squaring up to each other. Starting with something simple and tangible, he told Denham that some German sea-planes had been brought out of the water in the northern Danish port of Thisted and were now arranged on the quayside like sitting ducks. Then he moved swiftly on to the more pressing issue of the installation on Fanoe, and the remarkable capacity of the rectangular devices to pick out planes in the night sky with their searchlights.

Denham and Fleet betrayed no prior knowledge of the installation. If Oxlund's thick envelope had arrived at the British Legation as intended the previous summer, these officers seemed determined to give the impression that they had not seen it. But Denham had been around long enough to know when he was being told something important. He quickly excused himself, giving the impression that he hoped to contact London for further guidance on what action to take in light of what he had just heard. Tommy barely had time to ask him if he could be put on the next available flight to Britain, so that he could join the RAF and fight the Luftwaffe.

'Well done on the sea-planes, Flight Lieutenant Sneum,' said Fleet in his colleague's absence. 'We might be able to do something with those. By the way, there's a Mosquito arriving in Stockholm in the next few days. We should be able to pull a few strings to get you over to Britain on that.'

An elated Sneum felt as though he had almost made it to London already. He chatted for what seemed like hours to Fleet about the situation in Denmark, and what the British might do to undermine the Germans there. Finally they were interrupted by the return of Denham, who was noticeably more intense than before. 'Look, I've got a proposal for you,' he said.

'First I have one for you,' cut in Sneum. 'There are about twenty Danish pilots, skilled in their jobs, just like me, men who want nothing more than to join the Allied forces and fight the Nazis. There is a large expanse of water at Lake Tissoe, near the west coast of Zealand, where they can be ready for you on any given night. All you have to do is send a message through to one of my people in Denmark. I can give you some names. Lake Tissoe is as big and as easy to recognise as any rendezvous point you could think of. One of your Sunderland flying boats will have no trouble finding it, especially if I coordinate everything.'

'How could you do that from England?' asked Fleet.

Tommy didn't hesitate: 'If I receive a guarantee in London that the Sunderland will be sent, I'll volunteer to parachute back into Denmark and prepare my friends for the pick-up.'

Both Englishmen could see that Sneum was deadly serious. 'We could arrange that for you in theory,' said Denham cautiously. 'But maybe you won't have to parachute into Denmark. Not if you're already there for us.'

Tommy sensed he was about to be told something he didn't want to hear. 'I had hoped you could get me to England,' he reiterated with as much insistence as he dared show.

But Denham was equally stubborn. 'This installation of yours on Fanoe may be more important, I'm afraid,' he explained. 'We need to understand exactly how these things work. Get as much technical detail as we can.'

'I don't see what more I could do,' replied Sneum.

'You could take photographs,' suggested Denham.

Tommy almost laughed. He imagined strolling nonchalantly around the restricted areas like a tourist, taking snaps at will.

'You could use a little Leica,' continued Denham calmly. 'Nothing too conspicuous. And if that works out, you could use a Movikon camera. They take moving pictures.'

Sneum couldn't believe his ears. Make a film? But he agreed, and at that moment effectively became a British agent. He was well aware that his first assignment was only one step short of a suicide mission, despite Denham's casual description of what was required. But Thomas Sneum wasn't the sort to back out of a challenge.

Chapter 5

ON LOCATION

BY THE LAST WEEK of March 1941, Tommy Sneum was ready to take Leica and Movikon cameras across to Fanoe on the ferry from Esbjerg. He wore his naval uniform, including a billowing cloak, to make it easier to hide the bulky cameras. As he stood on the ferry deck and took in the crisp spring air, the engines began to rumble in preparation for departure. Then they suddenly stopped, and Tommy stumbled across the most amazing piece of good fortune. Lifted on board at the last moment by crane was what looked like a control cabin for one of the Fanoe radar towers. As it landed with a jolt on the lower deck, its door was flung open to reveal the internal workings in all their glory. So that the ferry could leave without too much delay, the control cabin was secured rather hastily with ropes at an awkward angle. Crucially, the door was left open in the rush. The excitement was still visible in Tommy's eyes decades later when he said with a smile: 'I couldn't believe it. This was too good to be true, and I wasn't about to miss my chance.'

He peered down from the upper deck at this priceless piece of intelligence then looked around him carefully. No one seemed to have noticed the attention he was paying to the cargo. But there was no time to waste as he reached for his Leica, pointed it at the control cabin and prayed that he had focused correctly. With adrenalin racing through his veins, he snapped three pictures. He winced at every click of the shutter, hoping the stiff sea breeze would carry the sound away before it reached the wrong ears. Holding his nerve, he took a few paces to the right and left, taking more shots from a variety of angles before deciding to quit while he was ahead.

With the Leica tucked safely back inside his cloak, Tommy sat down and tried to make himself as inconspicuous as possible. Combat, he imagined, could scarcely be more exhilarating than this. As he disembarked at Fanoe without so much as a second glance from the Germans waiting to unload their control cabin, he felt as though he had achieved a massive victory in his one-man war. 'It was one of the most dangerous moments but also one of the most satisfying,' he observed later.

Encouraged by such a dramatic change in fortune, Sneum was soon ready to take the Leica to the Fanoe installation. Before he set out, he hid the camera under his windcheater jacket, leaving his arms free to carry his shotgun. He thought nothing of risking the wrath of the occupiers by sporting a shotgun again so soon after dispatching the Alsatian. And it was still vital that he had a cover story to explain his presence so close to the installation, so he bagged himself a few rabbits on the open heathland. They made handy props, though Tommy suspected that any guards who remembered him from the previous year might not be easily fooled.

Using the trees and dunes as cover, Sneum observed the routine of the guards as they patrolled the fences that surrounded the installation. The plane-tracking devices were only just inside the perimeter, so in theory they could be photographed without even breaking in. Tommy waited for a window of opportunity. When one guard walked past, there was a gap of a good minute before another came into view, marching from the opposite direction. If that pattern remained consistent, he thought he could get the pictures he wanted; but if there was any unexpected variation in the Germans' routine, he feared he would be caught with the camera. Thumbscrews, pliers and whips were all favoured tools when German interrogators questioned suspected spies. An agent who couldn't cope with the pain, and revealed his mission to the Nazis, could then expect a firing squad at the end of his ordeal.

Tommy watched the first guard disappear out of sight, and raced forward to take pictures of the huge towers through the fence. Then he retreated in the nick of time, and waited for the next gap in the German patrol. With growing faith in his hit-and-run technique, he photographed the giant contraptions from a variety of angles. But he knew this was a high-risk strategy, and decided it was better to escape with what he had than to look for the perfect picture. Hiding his camera for the last time, he began his retreat. Each step towards safety filled him with elation and relief. By the time he had returned to the Sneum family home in Soenderho, on the southern tip of the island, Tommy couldn't wait to contact Kaj Oxlund with news of what he had achieved.

In April 1941, Oxlund arranged a hasty business trip to Sweden and took with him scores of superb still pictures of the Fanoe radar installation. He negotiated the border checks unchallenged, and took a night train to Stockholm. Reaching the Strandvagen peninsula, he presented the precious intelligence to a grateful Denham and Fleet at the British Legation. The triumphant return journey, free of all incriminating evidence, was dampened only by the disappointing fact that he had received no guarantee that the British would send a Sunderland to Lake Tissoe to pick up the Danish officers who wished to serve the Allies.

For Tommy Sneum, meanwhile, the most dangerous part of his mission still lay ahead. He knew that the next time he trekked north to the Fanoe installation, he would face a stiffer challenge. To use the Leica was one thing; to use the Movikon right under the noses of the Germans would be quite another. And he didn't think he would succeed without an accomplice to watch his back. He chose a fellow islander and resistance sympathiser known simply as Peter to act as an extra pair of eyes. For speed and mobility, they would travel to the vicinity of the installation on bicycles. The alternative, a long march with the large Movikon bulging under his jacket, would be asking for trouble.

As they set out with their shotguns to kill some more props before they reached the trees and dunes of the north, Sneum began to wonder whether his objective was entirely realistic. To capture the early-warning devices in action, as they rotated and searched the sky for planes, he would need to stay in one position for a considerable length of time. The fir trees which bordered the installation on one side might provide the cover he required, but would they allow him an adequately clear view of the target for effective filming?

Half an hour later Tommy and Peter were approaching the installation when the vast rectangular sensors started to turn slowly in the distance, probably as they followed a friendly Junker or Messerschmitt in the sky. Though the Danes hadn't yet reached the cover of the trees, this was the moment for which Tommy had waited. On impulse, he decided to abandon his bicycle and begin filming immediately. At least he would have something in the can before he assessed whether it was feasible to film from any nearer. He removed the Movikon from under his windcheater, crept a little closer and turned round to give Peter an encouraging wink before he started up the camera. Crouching low, he then focused the lens. He heard a worrying rattle and then a gentle whirring that signalled the automatic rotation of the reel. Every second seemed to last a lifetime, but he had to hold firm and capture in full the revolving action of the German installation. Suddenly, fifty metres behind him, he heard a frantic scrambling. 'There's somebody coming,' hissed Peter as he dashed for his bike and pedalled away for all he was worth. Sneum stopped filming, turned and tucked the Movikon back inside his jacket. Then he spun round to identify the source of his companion's anxiety. A German guard, pointing a rifle menacingly, was marching directly towards him from less than a hundred metres away.

Tommy recalled what happened next:

I crouched down in the tall grass. In that squatting position, my knees were sticking out. That helped to hide the bulge created by the movie camera under my jacket. At the same time I pulled down my trousers and pants. The German officer came up with his rifle pointed at me. This was one of the most dangerous moments of my entire war. If he made me get up he would see the bulge of the camera and soon know I was a spy. He got close and shouted: '*Was machen sie hier?'* – What are you doing here? So I replied: *'Ich scheisse'* – I'm taking a shit. He looked embarrassed and said: 'Oh, OK.' Then he walked off.

When the German had retreated, Sneum pulled up his trousers and walked briskly back to his bicycle. He pedalled off as nonchalantly as he could, amazed that he was still a free man. The radar installation had been recorded in action, but filming it had almost cost Tommy his life. Had the guard been more experienced and refused to accept his story, there would have been no way out.

Tommy could have quit at this stage, while he was ahead. But he imagined the reaction of Denham and Fleet if he crossed over to Sweden with no more footage. 'It's good work, old chap,' Denham would say. 'But it isn't very clear from that distance. Would you mind going back for us and getting in closer?'

Even before he reached Soenderho that night, and registered a familiar, disapproving look from Else, Tommy knew that he would have to return to the installation. 'I'd chosen this business now and I had to see it through,' he explained later. This time, however, he would face the threat of the German guards and their dogs alone.

＊ ＊ ＊

Three days later, just before dawn, Tommy set off again with his shotgun and Movikon, bagging some ducks and rabbits on his way north. Would he too know what it was like to become prey before the day was out? All his life, he had been taught to suppress his fear. Now, though, as he approached the installation in a wide loop, he was finding it harder than ever to hold his nerve.

About fifty metres from the radar station, on a small, natural mound, stood a water tower, which was often used by the Nazis as a lookout point. However, 'I thought I might still be able to reach it unnoticed, because the trees came right up to the tower on one side,' Tommy said later. The installation was crawling with Germans, but there was one place the guards wouldn't be looking: 'Their blind spot was at the foot of the water tower itself,' Tommy remembered. 'When you are up in the tower, you are not going to be looking directly below you for the enemy, in your own area. You are going to be looking out to sea for ships or aircraft. It wasn't easy for them to look down anyway, because they had fortified the water tower like the wall of an old castle.'

As he crouched behind the trees, Tommy could see the outlines of guards moving in the tower and could even hear them talking and laughing. Although they were only silhouettes, he felt he knew when they turned around because their voices grew fainter. Reckoning they were facing away from him, he sprinted for the base of the tower, grateful that the sandy soil cushioned his approach. But the tone of the German voices above suddenly changed dramatically, as if someone had seen or heard something. Very gingerly, Tommy peered upwards. The guards were looking out in almost all directions – everywhere but directly below. He hardly dared breathe as he carefully reached into his jacket to extract the camera. The sun was still rising, but by now there was enough light in which to work. The radar station was directly in front of him, and it looked even more impressive at close quarters. It was about to demonstrate its intimidating power again.

Tommy heard a faint drone in the sky as a patrolling German Junkers set about its morning business, though he couldn't pinpoint its position. However, the vast rectangular sensors turned immediately in the direction of the plane's engines. They had spotted their potential target long before Sneum could see anything specific. Though the giant, revolving structures seemed to be performing a dance just for him in the perfect morning light, Tommy knew he had to pick the right moment to take advantage.

The guards seemed to have calmed down, perhaps assuming that the noise below had been caused by a frightened rabbit. Impatiently, Sneum waited to hear some German voices again, and he was delighted when the majority began to poke fun at whoever had reacted to the sound of his approach. The increasingly boisterous conversation was the cover Tommy had desired. He clicked on the Movikon. *Action!* Frame by detailed frame, one of Hitler's most precious secrets was being stolen from under German noses. The stakes were unbelievably high. This time, there could be no cover story if he was caught; no reasonable explanation for his presence.

As soon as Tommy knew he had what the British wanted, he

turned off the camera, tucked it back into his jacket and waited for an opportunity to retreat. The guards in the water tower, who were making the mistake of acting as a unit in everything they did, crossed their perch to survey the north-western horizon. Sneum made a dash for safety, back the way he had come, still scarcely daring to breathe. At any time he knew he might hear the order to stand still and raise his hands. 'I had already decided to keep running if that happened, even if it meant I risked being shot in the back,' he recalled. 'To be captured would have meant torture.' He ran like the wind and heard nothing but his own deafening gasps for breath. Finally, the last remnants of fear left him. 'I wanted to shout with joy, but I couldn't,' he said.

It wasn't easy to act normally. No Hollywood film director had ever managed to create anything quite like this. One of the most priceless war movies ever made was safely in the can. The only problem now was how to get Tommy's precious, undeveloped prize to the British.

Chapter **6**

FLIGHT PLAN

TOMMY DECIDED THE REELS of film were too bulky and therefore too dangerous to be taken to Sweden by Kaj Oxlund. Besides, he had risked too much to see the results of his heroics carried away by another man. Kaj was a highly proficient courier, but the security checks were becoming more thorough between Denmark and Sweden by the day. And that gave Tommy the excuse to insist upon taking his precious intelligence to England directly. His reward for bringing the British such valuable cargo, he believed, would be the chance to fly a Spitfire in the RAF. The chance to test his skills against the Luftwaffe was Tommy's ultimate target. But there was only silence from Captain Henry Denham in Stockholm on the Sunderland sea-plane Tommy had requested for Danish pilots with similar ambitions. The proposed airlift from Lake Tissoe seemed as far away as ever.

While Tommy wondered about the best way to escape, he realised he had a more immediate problem. As he attempted to liaise with Oxlund, Kjeld Pedersen and Christian Michael Rottboell, he was forced to abort several arranged meetings because he had the impression he was being followed. At first he thought it might just be his imagination, a symptom of the pressure he had begun to feel, but as he made several unorthodox twists and turns through the streets of Copenhagen, the same faces kept reappearing behind him. Three- or four-man teams seemed to be taking it in turns to trail him. But if that were true, Sneum didn't see why he hadn't already been dragged away for interrogation. Perhaps the enemy were after bigger fish than a young naval pilot. Maybe the Abwehr had suspected him all along, and thought he could lead them to more important resistance figures. Tommy explained later: 'I don't think I was under surveillance every day, and I always managed to shake them off eventually. But just when I had begun to relax for a day or two, they were back.'

At no time was Sneum challenged or arrested, so it occurred to him that the surveillance team, which might report to the Danish police or directly to German Intelligence, were unsure of his role in any subversive activity. If they were still guessing, that was fine with Tommy. Perhaps he had already done enough to confuse them. But he decided that the safest course of action was to get out of Denmark as soon as possible.

As a pilot, he naturally favoured an escape plan that would allow him to bring his flying skills into play. There had to be civilian planes in Denmark, aircraft which hadn't yet been found and disabled by the Nazis. But where? He knew that the British company de Havilland had always employed a representative in Copenhagen. Such a man ought to know the whereabouts of enough civilian-owned planes to be able to form a squadron, and it seemed reasonable to ask him for some practical help. But when Tommy tracked down and called the representative, whose name was Thielst, he was distinctly unhelpful. Perhaps he feared his phone line had been tapped by the Nazis. At the end of an awkward conversation, giving the man the benefit of the doubt, Sneum decided to visit him at the de Havilland offices in the city centre.

Tommy arrived hoping that Thielst would prove more amenable in person. Unfortunately, the rep remained as evasive and suspicious as he had been on the phone. Tommy's only success during another tense conversation was to steal a manual from one of the office desks. But his disappointment evaporated when he opened the manual and found inside a list of all the owners of de Havilland planes in Denmark. Now it was just a question of picking the name and address that were most likely to bear fruit. And for this task he decided that two heads were better than one.

Tommy contacted an army pilot called Holger Petersen, an old friend, and they met up in Copenhagen to go through the manual together. They noticed that a Hornet Moth was registered to a lieutenant in the Army Reserve named Poul Andersen, who owned a dairy farm called Elseminde near Odense on the island of Fyn. Petersen – who was known simply as 'H.P.' – thought he remembered something about the history of this plane. He was convinced that Elseminde had been used as a base by Sylvest Jensen, an aerial photographer who had made a fortune just before the war by snapping people's houses and charging huge amounts for the souvenir pictures. He also believed there might be more than a Moth on the farm: crucially, there could be stockpiles of fuel, since Jensen had run several planes from Elseminde's very basic airfield before the arrival of the Germans had brought an abrupt halt to his lucrative enterprise. Although H.P. wasn't keen to fly to England himself, he seemed to share his friend's excitement as the bare bones of an audacious plan began to form in their heads. And Tommy could hardly wait to follow up this new lead.

First, however, he had to face new responsibilities, however temporarily. His daughter, Marianne Sneum, had arrived on 14 April. With a mixture of excitement and apprehension, Tommy visited his wife and child in hospital that evening. When he held the infant in his arms and saw the sheer pride on the face of his beaming, exhausted wife, he was surprised by a strange elation he hadn't known before. But deep down he knew more than ever that the war would soon take him away from his new family. The spying, the adrenalin, the refusal to be bullied during the occupation, these were all factors which consumed him. And he felt no more ready for fatherhood than he had for marriage.

By now, his relationship with Else was beyond repair. He had never been faithful to her, primarily because he liked other women too much – the excitement they brought and the independence they guaranteed. Trips around the country, picking up intelligence reports here and there, had afforded him many opportunities for casual conquests. The thrill that came with danger meant everything to him, though he was never stupid enough or sufficiently smitten to tell the girls his real name. And he was even able to justify his behaviour by arguing that his infidelities helped his resistance missions: 'Talking to the girls was a good way to get the true picture in an area, and to understand where local loyalties lay. And which was better, to stay in a private bedroom or in a hotel, where the Nazis might have a sympathiser working? I used to say I was on business and never let anyone too close. The women never suspected what I was really doing. I gave them other things to think about.'

He always managed to remain detached from romantic and family complications. The desire to escape to Britain with his recently shot films dominated his feelings and thoughts. If that footage could help prevent British planes from being blown out of the sky, it would surely book his passage into the RAF. He already missed flying more than he would ever miss another human being, including his wife and baby. And at least he knew they would be supported by four loving and healthy grandparents, who could offer comfort while he risked his life overseas.

＊ ＊ ＊

The day after Whitsun 1941, Tommy Sneum took a taxi to Elseminde. He was driven down a track through dusty fields full of turnips and knee-high barley, past a herd of more than a hundred cattle and up to the manicured lawns of an impressive old farmhouse.

The lady who opened the front door seemed surprised at the intrusion.

'Sorry to disturb you,' Tommy said. 'May I speak with Lieutenant Poul Andersen, please?'

'My husband is officiating at the racecourse,' the woman said suspiciously, as though this information were common knowledge.

Sneum thanked her and headed straight for the race meeting in Odense. Battling his way through the crowds, he found a steward and asked him to tell Andersen that Flight Lieutenant Nielsen would like to speak with him.

Before long, a very stern-looking man in his forties approached from the main stand, clearly caught somewhere between curiosity and irritation. With slicked-back hair and cheekbones of granite, Poul Andersen cut an intimidating figure. Tommy was glad he hadn't used his own name, and was suddenly concerned that this might not be the right plane-owner to approach.

Andersen looked even more suspicious of Tommy than his wife had been. 'You'll have to make it quick,' he said impatiently. 'There's another race in fifteen minutes.'

'Then I'll come straight to the point, sir. I hear you have a few planes on your farm. I'm looking for a bargain now, so that I'll have something to fly after the war. If the price is right, I'm interested in buying one.'

Andersen shook his head. 'I have only one left, Nielsen, and I wouldn't want to sell her. As you say, the war has to end some day.'

Sneum wasn't about to give up. 'I could give you cash.'

'Sorry, Nielsen. She's not for sale. Now, if you'll excuse me, I must—'

At that moment, Tommy knew he had to gamble. 'Sir, before you go, what would your answer be if I told you the plane would go west?' Telling the truth, even in such an ambiguous way, was a terrible risk.

Andersen stared at the younger man, instantly realising that 'west' meant Britain. There was a tense silence. 'Then she's yours,' he finally replied.

'How much?' Tommy asked.

'No charge. Meet me when the races have finished.'

＊ ▓ ＊

Andersen drove Sneum back to the farm, down a track adjacent to the main house and through one of the turnip fields to a barn. Made of corrugated tin, it had been converted into a hangar. When Andersen threw open the double doors, Tommy's heart sank as he was confronted by the dirty, dusty old fuselage of a de Havilland Hornet Moth. The registration number – OY-DOK – was scarcely visible through the grime. The rest of the plane was nowhere to be seen. In short, the grubby wreck that lay before them was pathetic.

As he tried to hide his disappointment, Tommy was shown the wings. They had been detached before the plane was wheeled into the hangar and were now stacked neatly at the back of the building, dusty but apparently undamaged. In a big linen bag were some bolts, which might one day be used to reattach the wings and struts to the fuselage. Just as he was feeling slightly more optimistic, though, Tommy's hopes were dashed again.

'The tail fin didn't fare so well in transit from Kastrup,' explained Andersen. 'It got a bit warped and torn, so we sent it to Aalborg for repairs. When it came back, we took it into the farm workshop. It's still in there now, in a crate.'

Tommy tried to muster some enthusiasm. 'I see. That's handy.'

'The best thing about this plane', added Andersen, 'is the engine. It's still very sound. Doesn't need much doing to it at all. That's the beauty of her.'

Sneum processed this information in silence.

'I did have a Klemm,' continued the farmer, almost apologetically. 'But I crashed the thing.'

'What's the maximum range for a Hornet Moth?' asked Tommy, hoping that everything he knew about the little sports planes was wrong.

'About six hundred kilometres, I think.'

The confirmation came like a kick in the teeth. Even if a plane were flown due west from Odense, the north-east coast of England would still be out of reach.

Then Tommy saw two huge fuel drums in the shadows at the back of the hangar. 'Are they full?'

'Oh, yes,' replied Andersen. 'Three or four planes used this field as their base before the Germans came.'

Ideas were flying through Sneum's mind, but for now he simply shook hands with his host and confirmed that he would soon be in touch.

'Don't bother,' said Andersen. 'At least not until you're ready to go. Fake a break-in at my workshop when you want the tail fin, but I don't want to hear from you until you know which night you're leaving. On that particular night, I intend to be seen by as many witnesses as I can find, as far away from here as possible. And one other thing, Nielsen: if you're caught in my hangar in the meantime, I'll say you're a thief and claim I've never met you. I have a family to protect, you understand.'

Tommy returned to Copenhagen to seek out Kjeld Pedersen, his closest friend from Fleet Air Arm. He recalled later:

> We volunteered at the same time and became great friends. He had a wonderful sense of humour and he was an excellent boxer, much better than I was. He could judge distances to the millimetre and that helped with his jab. We went into the ring together many times, and on each occasion he would be beating me easily due to his superior technical ability. Then I would get mad and give him a beating. We remained friends after leaving the navy, and he joined the police in 1940. He won a bravery award for diving into a canal to rescue a drowning girl. But we both wanted to get away, we never gave up and he always stood by me when plans to escape went wrong.

But Pedersen's loyalty must have been stretched to the limit by Sneum's blind faith in his latest scheme, as his dumbfounded reaction seems to suggest.

'We're flying to England,' announced Tommy when he found his friend in a deserted corner of their favourite bar.

'Are they sending a plane?'

'No, I've found us one here and we'll fly it ourselves.'

'What sort of plane is it?' asked Kjeld.

'A Hornet Moth.'

Pedersen burst out laughing. 'What? You want to fly to England in a Moth? It hasn't got the range.' He was right: even on a direct route from Odense they would drop into the North Sea over a hundred kilometres short of their destination.

'I think it can be done,' maintained Sneum. 'We can refuel.'

'Just land in the North Sea and take off again? It isn't a seaplane, you know.'

Sneum looked his friend in the eye. 'We'll do it in mid-air.'

Pedersen's mouth dropped open. 'Now I know you're mad,' he said.

'Trust me,' said Tommy. 'I'll have us both flying for Churchill's RAF by midsummer.'

Chapter 7

THE JIGSAW PUZZLE

IN MAY 1941 Sir Charles Hambro, chief of Britain's Special Operations Executive, took a look at the situation in Denmark and wondered why his organisation had achieved nothing tangible there since Ronald Turnbull had been sent to Stockholm. Infuriated, he sent a series of communications to Turnbull's superiors in SOE's Scandinavian Section. One of them read: 'Turnbull wants jerking up. He thinks he is in the Ministry of Information. What is he doing about SO2 [sabotage] work?'

When the complaint was passed on to Turnbull, two thoughts went through his mind. He revealed later:

> Firstly Hambro probably didn't realise it had taken me so many months to reach Stockholm, and that I had only been there since February. Secondly, Hambro probably didn't understand the situation in Denmark as well as I did. It was all very well blowing up trains and taking risks, but it was much better to forge good links with the professionals in Danish Intelligence and see what we could achieve.

While there was something to be said for gaining valuable intelligence through passive observation, Turnbull was thoroughly outclassed in his favoured art by a fellow Brit who was working out of the very same building. Ironically, it was his good friend Captain Henry Denham, the Naval Attaché with whom Turnbull had escaped from Copenhagen the previous year, who got wind of a vital piece of information for the Allies. And the news was every bit as important as the radar intelligence Denham hoped to gather with the help of Tommy Sneum.

On 19 May, the *Bismarck*, Hitler's greatest warship, had suddenly made a break from the port of Gotenhafen (now Gdynia, in Poland) for the Atlantic, where Allied convoys would be at her mercy. To reach the ocean she had first to sail through Scandinavian waters, and hope that details of her movements didn't reach the Allies in time to cause her any trouble. Denham's extensive contacts in the Swedish Navy meant that he was the officer who gave London the first news of the *Bismarck*'s breakout. The ship was chased, crippled and eventually sunk on 27 May, at enormous human cost on both sides. For every Allied life lost, however, many more were saved by the intelligence Denham had supplied.

Danish Intelligence, an organisation in which Turnbull was soon to place all his faith, had remained strangely silent on the *Bismarck*'s movements. Later, its senior officers tried to excuse their oversight with the fatuous claim that their main lookout, a lighthouse keeper, had been ill on the day the mighty ship had sailed past.

Given this failure, one might have thought that Danish Intelligence, who often seemed as close to the Germans as they were to the Allies, might have come under the microscope. If their balancing act troubled anyone in London, however, it didn't seem to bother Turnbull, as he began to explore ways to strengthen links with the men he felt mattered most in Copenhagen.

* * *

Over in Denmark, Tommy Sneum and Kjeld Pedersen were in more of a hurry than Turnbull on the matter of delivering intelligence. Instinctively, Tommy knew the value of the secrets he had already uncovered, and he convinced his deeply sceptical colleague that a dismantled Hornet Moth was the answer to their prayers. Now they just needed to find a way to reach the hangar unnoticed, so that they could begin to patch up the machine. They took a train to Odense one Saturday afternoon, bought a gigantic parcel of sandwiches and packed them into a suitcase, along with numerous bottles of beer. In a restaurant that evening, they planned the last leg of the journey to Elseminde like a military operation.

In order to avoid detection, they took an Odense tram all the way to its terminus on the city's outskirts and walked the last three kilometres across country towards the farm. Once in the vicinity, they waited for the cover of twilight. At 8.45 p.m., they finally managed to cross the turnip fields unnoticed and slip into the hangar. But the murky half-light that had helped them on the outside was a hindrance inside the converted barn. To use a torch or even strike a match risked unwelcome attention from German patrols, since the light might be spotted through the cracks in the hangar walls. They decided to sleep until sunrise, which would allow a more thorough inspection of the plane. Each man took a wing out of its felt wrapping and used the cover as a sleeping bag. They passed a restless, nervous night, but when dawn broke at 4.00 a.m. they were relieved to be able to begin their assessment of the aircraft.

'The wings are in one piece – can't see any cracks or breaks anywhere,' whispered Sneum. 'They should slot in nicely. The fuselage is OK, too.'

'The wings will only stay in place if we have the right bolts,' pointed out Pedersen, holding up the linen bag.

It soon emerged that Kjeld's fears were well founded. The bolts in the bag obviously weren't for the wings. They looked more likely to fit the tail fin, but that was still in the farm's workshop. Furthermore, a detailed search of the linen bag and the rest of the hangar revealed that even some of the tail fin bolts, made of specially hardened molybdenum steel, were missing.

'Don't worry, we'll get some more tail fin bolts,' whispered Sneum, 'when we order the new bolts for the wings.'

'We can't,' warned Kjeld.

'Why not?'

'Molybdenum isn't available in Denmark any more. And certainly not at short notice.' Kjeld, who had been sceptical even before he had seen the plane and discovered the shortage of bolts, now thought they should abort the whole project before it killed them. 'Come on, Sneum, there's nothing to hold this plane together. I know we're desperate, but this is suicide.'

Tommy refused to throw in the towel. 'We'll find some bolts. They don't have to be molybdenum.'

'They do if you don't want the bloody thing to fall apart halfway across the North Sea,' maintained Kjeld.

Sneum didn't see it that way. 'Compressed carbon steel bolts may be softer but they can do the job. It's only one flight.'

'One bloody long flight,' warned Pedersen. 'She's got to be able to withstand some pretty fearsome pressure up there.'

'We can do it,' insisted Sneum. 'We'll order everything to precise specifications. We've got enough mates from Fleet Air Arm to do that. Are you still in?'

Grudgingly, Pederson replied, 'If the engineers say it can be done.' He seemed pretty sure that they would say the exact opposite.

At 7.30 a.m. farm workers appeared in the fields around the barn, just as Tommy and Kjeld were about to leave. The pilots hid under sacks at the back of the hangar. It was a frustrating morning, but they feared discovery if they dared to move. One man slept while the other kept an eye out for any nosy labourers. Tommy took the first nap and woke mid-morning with a stretch and a carelessly noisy yawn. Kjeld scrambled frantically towards him, with one forefinger pressed to his lips. With the other, he pointed to the far corner of the hangar. At the base of the corrugated-tin wall, where the ground had crumbled away, a crouching man was creating a stench, and the pilots realised that the relative privacy afforded by the hangar walls meant that the area had been designated as the farm workers' unofficial lavatory.

At lunchtime the workers left the fields at last, but locals out for a Sunday stroll had begun to pass regularly on a road just fifty metres to the north of the hangar. Tommy wondered if they would ever be able to get out without being noticed. Luckily a cornfield, with the crop already half a metre high, caressed the western wall of the hangar, and offered just enough cover if they kept low. After much uncomfortable crawling and cursing, the two men reached the road, picked themselves up and brushed themselves down. No sooner had they done so than a party of German officers appeared on horseback, just where the road forked off to nearby Sanderum. The Germans viewed the young men suspiciously, but their commander seemed reluctant to interrupt his ride. After a moment's hesitation, which seemed like an eternity to Tommy and Kjeld, the horsemen continued on their way without demanding papers or a reason for the Danes' presence in the area.

Relieved, Tommy and Kjeld slipped away down a country lane, only to be confronted with the sight of a newly built drill-ground for German soldiers. It was less than a kilometre from Elseminde. Privately, Tommy wondered whether this escape plan was cursed, but he assured himself that the occupiers couldn't hold parades around the clock, no matter how disciplined they were, and therefore he and Kjeld would still have the opportunity to fly away if they chose their moment carefully.

They made it back to the capital using the skeleton Sunday transport services, and launched a search for petrol cans or drums. These containers needed to be small enough to carry without attracting suspicion, and practical enough to be used in Sneum's outlandish plan to refuel in mid-air. No such cans seemed to exist, however, so Tommy asked a trusted workshop to make some to order, along with a hose and filters. He also specified the size and number of bolts they needed to attach the wings and the tail fin to the fuselage. While these orders were being met, Tommy and Kjeld tracked down two former Fleet Air Arm mechanics called Lindballe and Wichmann. They wanted their old colleagues to run an expert eye over the plane, check the carburettor and the magneto, and generally reassure them that the entire scheme wasn't lunacy.

⁂

The following Saturday, all four men travelled to Odense, carrying a rather conspicuous amount of sackcloth, and slipped into the hangar as darkness fell. They used the sackcloth to seal the cracks in the walls, and when they were sure no tell-tale light could escape, they switched on their torches to begin work in earnest.

By dawn, they had cleaned the carburettor, given the magneto the all-clear, examined the wiring and changed the oil. However, they still couldn't start the engine – the only sure way to discover if all was well – because the sound would be heard far and wide. At least there seemed to be nothing wrong with the compression when they turned the propeller by hand, so Lindballe and Wichmann cheerfully gave the engine a clean bill of health. Whether they would have been so confident if they were destined to fly across the North Sea in the Moth is open to question.

* * *

When the carbon steel bolts were finally ready, Tommy and Kjeld began the painstaking process of reassembling the plane. Tommy admitted to his friend that a large amount of guesswork would be involved in this process. They attached the wings to the fuselage in the folding position, but as they completed this delicate task it was impossible to be sure that they had stayed faithful to the original angles and elevations. Any miscalculation, even by a few degrees, and the Moth would nosedive or flip in the slightest turbulence.

Every night for a month Tommy and Kjeld made the best of their limited materials to cobble together their fragile dream. They relied upon lashings of copper wire to fasten the ill-fitting bolts, and hoped the pressures of flight would not tear apart these makeshift bindings. The pilots regularly turned the propeller in a bid to ensure that the oil would flow freely when it mattered.

The last piece of the jigsaw was the tail fin, which still lay in a box in Poul Andersen's workshop. Sneum followed the farmer's instructions to the letter. 'To keep Andersen out of it I had to break the padlock so that the Danish police and the Germans could see there was evidence of a break-in,' he remembered. Tommy took the vital component and crept back to the barn before anyone noticed.

With the tail finally attached, the plane at least looked as though it might be capable of flight. By now, the petrol cans were ready at the Copenhagen workshops too, so the pilots began to transfer them across the country to Odense in small paper parcels. There were four zinc cans, each with a capacity of two gallons, and twelve smaller tins that could hold about one and a half gallons apiece. Once they were all safely stockpiled in the hangar, the fuel was transferred from the huge drums into the more manageable containers. Tommy and Kjeld then ensured that the fuel tank in the plane itself was full to the brim, and prepared to put the finishing touches to their plan.

But the long midsummer days had already brought fresh complications. The turnip-pickers seemed to use every last minute of light for their toil now; and one man in particular tested the pilots' patience. Perhaps he was keen to impress the boss, or maybe he just had extra mouths to feed, but he seemed obsessed with picking as many turnips as was humanly possible. And his chosen field was the one nearest to the hangar. Often he would work a seventeen-hour day, from 5.00 a.m. to 10.00 p.m. The harder he worked, the less time the pilots had to prepare their plane. Nevertheless, they seized every opportunity to finish their job. And halfway through June they knew they were ready.

Out of courtesy to their former associate, Tommy and Kjeld revealed their intentions to Christian Michael Rottboell. After such a frustrating winter of aborted escapes by sea, Rottboell had declared himself anxious to be kept informed of any plans. When told of the plane, he insisted upon coming to Odense so he could gauge their chance of success. (Although he had never been a pilot, he had some basic mechanical knowledge of planes.) Though Tommy and Kjeld didn't particularly want to hear his opinion, they thought it best to keep him happy.

When Rottboell was brought into the hangar in the dead of night his eyes lit up, especially when he saw the size of the cockpit. 'There's room for a third man at the back,' he declared. 'I'll show you.'

Pedersen looked stunned. 'No, Rottboell, it's out of the question.'

But the younger man was determined to illustrate his point. He clambered inside the cockpit and curled up in a little ball behind the two seats. 'See?' he said triumphantly. 'It can be done.'

'And where,' asked Tommy, 'do you suppose we'll put the fuel?'

'On top of me. Or around me. It doesn't matter. There's room.'

Sneum was losing patience. 'Rottboell, you don't seem to understand. The tank isn't much more than half the size it should be for this journey. The extra fuel is going to fill every inch of the cockpit not already taken up by Pedersen and me.'

Rottboell wouldn't give up. 'But we're a trio. That's how we planned the escape by boat.' The silence with which his comments were greeted only made him more desperate. 'I thought we were going to stick together. Don't leave me behind, for Christ's sake.'

Tommy could see the hurt in Christian Michael's eyes. 'Listen,' he explained, 'I made your father a promise that I would do my best to look after you. Believe me, if we try this with three people, we'll crash. Or never even get off the ground.'

Rottboell turned away, hardly able to hide his anger and frustration. Tommy recalled later: 'Rottboell was furious that he couldn't go with us in the plane but he was too well bred to cause a scene. He thought there was room in the back, but he didn't understand the weight problem. I told him to stay put until I could find a way to pick him up, along with the others who wanted to come to England.'

* * *

Determined to arrive in England with fully updated intelligence in addition to the precious radar installation film, Sneum and Pedersen decided to make a final sweep of their contacts around Denmark. Kjeld toured Jutland, while Tommy covered Zealand and Copenhagen. What they discovered was encouraging. The batteries and garrisons at Holbaek, Roskilde and Naestved had all been left intact, despite the Nazi occupation. Hundreds of men deemed harmless by the Nazis had secretly hidden thousands of rounds of ammunition in readiness to support the Allies if and when a liberating invasion came. After the capitulation of April 1940, the British had doubted the will of the Danish armed forces to fight the Nazis, but Sneum and Pedersen now felt they had evidence that the reality might be rather different. Danish servicemen were just waiting for the signal from London to mount a massive diversion in support of an Allied landing force.

Although Tommy and Kjeld were taking a risk in compiling this report, there were pleasures to be had too. Tommy, in particular, enjoyed the sexual freedom such assignments afforded him, and continued to tell himself that his behaviour was in the interests of good security. 'I thought that the more fun I had, the less suspicious

I would appear to the locals,' he later claimed with a smile. Whatever the validity of this argument, he certainly had plenty of fun on the tour. And he wasn't caught.

The take-off area near Odense, however, had recently become more dangerous. To keep his troops on their toes, the local German commander had ordered that manoeuvres should take place in the fields near the hangar on the night of 20 June. On 18 June, blissfully ignorant of this development after their tour of the country, Pedersen and Sneum agreed a precise moment for their dramatic escape by air – midnight in two days' time.

Tommy and Kjeld were on a collision course with the Third Reich.

Chapter **8**

A CLOSE SHAVE

As SOON AS HE'D AGREED the take-off time with Kjeld, Tommy visited his wife and child, who were now living with Else's parents in Copenhagen. He knew there was a fair chance that he would never see them again. But he was also aware that if he told Else about his escape plan, she would protest and try to stop him. She would probably also tell her father, who might even alert the authorities. So Tommy concocted a cover story: 'I'm leaving for Aalborg,' he announced. 'I've been given work to do at the airfield there.'

'What kind of work? And when do we join you?' Else was one of the few people who could tell when Tommy was lying.

'Maybe not for a while,' said her husband. 'Things have to be properly assessed there first, before the precise nature of my work becomes clear.'

'Well, don't be too long,' warned Else, clearly unconvinced. She gave Tommy his baby daughter, and he held her for a while in his arms. Lovely as she was, he knew he wasn't cut out to watch the war from a cosy domestic setting. All over Europe, he told himself, other husbands were making the same sacrifice for their country by turning their backs on their families. The difference, perhaps, was that he doubted he would ever be able to fulfil the role of doting husband and father. It had all come too soon. The war – along with Mr Jensen – had been responsible for that.

Tommy kissed his wife and baby one last time, and left Else fighting back her tears. Much later, Tommy said: 'I loved the baby and still had some feelings for Else, but the cause was more important to me at that time than family.'

Focusing on the steps he had to take before returning to his beloved plane, Sneum went to see his old friend Kaj Oxlund in the northern suburb of Soeborg. The happy, carefree days the two men had enjoyed with their girlfriends before the war were now just memories, and Tommy was in serious mood. 'Don't ask me anything about the reasons for this,' he begged. 'The less you know, the better. But if I'm absent for a while, just continue the good work we started together. And do me one last favour. This is a letter for Else. I want you to see she gets it.'

'If we hear you're dead?' Oxlund was trying to be helpful.

'On the contrary,' replied Tommy with a grim smile. 'Don't bother giving it to her if you hear I'm dead. She won't need to read it then. But if you've heard nothing in the next two or three weeks, post it to her. Make sure you're in Denmark when you send it.'

Trying to fathom his friend's intentions, Oxlund dutifully took the letter and assured Tommy he would comply with the request. They embraced briefly, with Sneum wishing he could say more.

Then it was time to move the precious Leica and Movikon films of the Fanoe radar installation to the hangar in Odense. They just fitted into two suitcases, which would look less suspicious, Tommy decided, if carried by two men. Posing as brothers visiting relatives in the countryside, Tommy and Kjeld set out on this vital journey on the night of Thursday 19 June. They reached the plane without incident. In addition to the films, the cans of petrol were loaded into the back of the cockpit, along with a length of hose, an axe and a broomstick, to which they had attached a huge white towel. Life jackets were tucked away in the hangar for now, and everything was as it should be.

After working all night, Sneum and Pedersen left the barn and, with the sun already quite high, crept up the track that led through Andersen's fields to the main road. Suddenly, six German officers galloped up on horseback and surrounded them. By now, Tommy was adept at suppressing his fear, but this crisis almost got the better of him: 'This was one of the few moments I was really scared because the plane was ready in the hangar,' he revealed later. Just metres away, the Hornet Moth was loaded with secrets which, if discovered, would provide enough evidence to have both men shot.

'Good morning!' said Tommy cheerfully, hoping his inner terror wasn't showing.

'What are you doing here?' This German officer in particular didn't look happy.

'We're going home.'

'Where's home?'

'Odense,' explained Tommy, smiling.

The occupiers only had to demand to see their papers and Tommy and Kjeld would be finished. There was a tense silence as the Germans assessed the pair in front of them. Then, putting their pleasures before their duty, they decided to continue their morning ride. The Danish pilots were left to breathe in the dust kicked up by the horses' hooves.

'Keep walking,' said Sneum. 'Don't even look relieved.'

Pedersen was too traumatised even to feel relieved, let alone look it.

* * *

After a long daytime sleep at separate hideouts, Tommy and Kjeld met at Valby railway station and returned to the hangar. First they warned Andersen of their intentions, so that the farmer could leave for the evening and make sure he was seen by lots of witnesses far away from his plane. Then they set about cutting a hole in the fuselage near the fuel tank, through which they hoped their hose would be able to fit when it mattered. They imagined this would be a simple process. But after each man had chipped away with a knife for a while Pedersen's blade broke. Gently cursing his friend, Tommy continued more forcefully – and promptly broke his own knife. Now they had to claw and poke at the hole with their bare fingers. By the time they had created a large enough gap for the hose to pass through, twice the allocated time had elapsed and their hands were red raw.

It was already past midnight, and it might still take another three-quarters of an hour to pull the plane out of the hangar and make it ready for take-off. They wondered whether to continue that night. Once airborne, they would take a further hour and a half to cross Denmark to Jutland's coast, where the greatest danger would come from German fighter aircraft. By then, the longest day of the summer would already have begun, making them sitting ducks in perfect visibility. Reluctantly, they decided it would be suicidal to go on. The escape attempt was postponed for twenty-four hours.

After their close shave with the occupying forces the previous morning, they decided that it would be wiser to leave the hangar under cover of darkness. As they crossed the fields and headed back towards Odense, however, they passed the drill-ground, where they were astonished to see an entire German company preparing for night exercises. The two Danish pilots crouched down in bushes and tried not to make a sound as the Germans trundled past noisily. With an expert eye, Sneum noticed in the gloom that the artillery men were pulling 37mm and 20mm anti-aircraft guns, either of which could bring down a plane before it reached an altitude of three thousand metres. He glanced at Pedersen and saw the same realisation etched on his friend's face. Had they tried to fly away in the Hornet Moth that night, they would almost certainly have been blasted to pieces. As it was, though, they were still in grave danger. If discovered breaking the curfew, they could expect to be arrested and questioned. So the pair sat motionless until the last of the heavy artillery cannons had rumbled away in the darkness. Once again, it appeared that they had survived a major crisis by the skin of their teeth.

'We're still leaving,' insisted Sneum. 'Tomorrow night.'

Pedersen wasn't convinced. 'What if the Germans are still here?'

'They were here tonight. They won't be doing manoeuvres in the same fields tomorrow.'

'How do you know?'

'I don't, for sure,' said Sneum, fixing his friend with a stare. 'But I do know we have to get out of here.'

At 2.00 a.m. Sneum and Pedersen disturbed the night porter at the Grand Hotel in Odense. He took one look at their filthy polo-neck sweaters and turned his nose up at them. 'I'm sorry,' he said, not sounding sorry at all. 'There are no rooms available tonight. We're completely full.'

'But I know for a fact there are rooms,' said Tommy, bluffing.

'You'll have to leave,' the porter said. 'I'm afraid we can't take people in your condition.'

'Very well. I'll have you out of your job by midday,' said Sneum with all the authority he could muster.

The porter looked alarmed. 'No, wait a minute, sir. Perhaps I was hasty. Please accept my apology.'

Sneum suppressed a smile. 'Very well, since it's late, let's have an end to this. We'll take one room between us to save you any further trouble.'

'That'll be forty kroner,' said the porter.

Pedersen had just enough money to pay for the twin-bedded room, so while German troops launched exercises all around Elseminde, the two Danes took baths and then sank into a deep sleep until late morning.

When they woke, they devoured bacon and eggs in bed. Tommy phoned his brother Harald for a final weather report, which turned out to be favourable. The escape attempt was on for that night.

Sneum and Pedersen left the hotel with enough money to buy a packet of biscuits for the flight, some Tuborg squash, Carlsberg grape tonic, and two tickets for the Odense open-air swimming pool. They spent the afternoon splashing about in the sunshine in an attempt to wash away their fear. Somewhere in the back of their minds, however, they both entertained the thought that these might be the last hours of their short lives. The pilots treated themselves to some good coffee and Danish *wienerbroed* in the poolside cafeteria before heading back to Elseminde with only a five-krone coin left between them. Now they had to succeed: they were too broke to stay in Denmark.

Later that afternoon, having arrived at the farm, Sneum slipped out of the barn to post a message through Poul Andersen's letterbox. He returned without confirmation that his note had been received. Finally, at 7.00 p.m., the farmer cycled over to the hangar. He greeted Tommy and Kjeld more warmly than before, as though he too suspected that he might be the last person they were ever likely to see. The three men sat outside in the evening sunshine and enjoyed a cigarette together, having safely distanced themselves from all the fuel in the hangar. They were alarmed to notice the large number of people out for a weekend walk in the countryside; but there was nothing they could do to change the longstanding customs of the locals.

As if the cumulative cost was already causing him pain, Andersen explained that he was about to take his entire family to an Odense restaurant called Skoven for the second evening in succession. He would have to come up with another reason for celebration, though he remained confident his alibi would put him beyond suspicion the next time the Germans came calling. Andersen would again ensure that his family were unusually noisy in Skoven to guarantee that their presence registered clearly with the staff. He would also insist that they all stay until very late. They all agreed that a second evening like this would infuriate the waiters enough for them to remember the entire family vividly.

As he shook hands with Tommy and Kjeld, something in Andersen's eyes seemed to acknowledge the pilots' bravery. 'Be careful,' he said. 'It would be such a waste.'

'I agree,' said Sneum. 'But we don't intend to die.'

'I'm not talking about you,' said Andersen with a smile. 'I'm talking about the plane. I'd quite like to have her back when this is all over.' With that, the farmer waved one last farewell and cycled away.

Sneum and Pedersen loaded the last of their equipment into the plane and went over everything one last time. For two hours they turned the propeller to make sure no oil had been left in the cylinders. Then they prayed, but also put on their life jackets in case those prayers weren't answered while they were over the North Sea.

At 11.00 p.m. they opened the hangar doors and pushed the plane to the entrance. But even in their folded position flush with the body of the plane, the wings would not fit through the narrow hangar doors.

Tommy explained later: 'The barn had originally been adapted to house a German Klemm, Andersen's first plane, which was even smaller than a Hornet Moth. Andersen had pranged his Klemm and replaced it with the Hornet Moth, which went in dismantled.

He had never mentioned any possible problem with the door: he thought the plane would just go through like the Klemm had. It wouldn't. We couldn't get it out. The plane jammed in the doorway.'

It's easy to imagine the horror the men must have felt, after all their hard work, to discover that the plane was trapped inside its makeshift hangar. Tommy and Kjeld couldn't remove the wings from the fuselage again; there simply wasn't enough time. A rising sense of panic threatened to overwhelm them. Sneum recalled:

> We worked with axes on the sides of the hangar door, and soon had to take off our life jackets because we were sweating so much. Each barn door was composed of two halves, one designed to fold upwards and the other to fold downwards. Fortunately the framework was made of wood. Little by little, we managed to cut the plane free; and by pulling and pushing, after about fifteen minutes, we finally got it outside, though we heard a tearing sound at the last moment.
>
> We had taken all the cloth off the front of one of the folded wings, exposing the plywood underneath, and bent it. Together we forced the wings back into position and unfolded them, slipping the bolts into place. But we discovered that we had bent the carbon-steel bolts while forcing the plane through the barn door. We just hammered at them until they were almost at one with the parts they were meant to secure, and we hoped they would hold. We had nothing with which to measure the correct inclination of the wings.

The entire scene belonged in some kind of slapstick comedy. But this was deadly serious, and the pilots' lives were in danger like never before.

Chapter **9**

TAKE-OFF

I T WAS NOW 11.30 p.m. and the situation was critical. Both men tried to stay positive. The plywood hadn't cracked and they didn't think the lost canvas at the front of one wing would be enough in itself to bring down the plane. Tommy and Kjeld looked up at the heavens; there was no moon, which at least offered hope that they wouldn't be spotted immediately and blasted out of the sky by a German artillery unit. Overall, however, the weather wasn't going to offer them the protection they desired. Sneum worried about the lack of low cloud cover. The ceiling came between fifteen hundred and seventeen hundred metres, so there would be no hiding place in the first vital minutes after take-off. It would take some time to reach the ceiling, and they didn't know what they might face before they did.

'Sneum, tell me straight.' Pedersen was just three months older than Tommy, and just a little more concerned about their predicament. 'Can we make it?'

'Fuck off,' replied Tommy. 'Of course we'll make it.'

'Seriously,' persisted Kjeld, looking his friend directly in the eye. 'What are our chances?'

'Fifty–fifty,' answered Tommy, and watched Pedersen's face drain a little. 'No, sixty–forty we'll make it,' he added for encouragement. But his attempt at optimism was no longer convincing or infectious.

Neither pilot had flown for more than a year, not since the Nazis had invaded and grounded all Danish planes on 9 April 1940. Tommy hadn't forgotten the roar of the German bombers over Avnoe early that morning, the surge of adrenalin as his adjutant opened sealed orders from King Christian and confirmed that Denmark's sovereign territory was to be defended at all costs. He remembered the frantic sprint to his Hawker Nimrod fighter biplane, and the confusion when mechanics tried to block his path. He recalled the sheer frustration of being told that both the King and the Prime Minister had just announced their change of heart in a radio broadcast, and that Naval HQ in Copenhagen had confirmed the new order to offer no resistance. He had still tried to clamber into his Nimrod, and only gave up when a mechanic told him they had already put all the planes out of action. The shame of that night had never left him. Everything he had done since had been geared towards this moment, when he would beat the ban and fly again.

Pedersen must have known how his friend was feeling, because he too had been a pilot in Fleet Air Arm. But that didn't mean he was so desperate to remember how it felt to fly that he was ready to sacrifice his life for the privilege. This feeble-looking Hornet Moth was a far cry from a Hawker Nimrod. Besides, no one had ever attempted to fly a single-engine aircraft from Denmark to Britain. Pedersen, at least, knew his limitations. 'I'm not going to fly her,' he insisted. 'You must do it.'

'That pleases me,' replied Sneum with a smile. 'You're not a very good pilot.'

They had intended to wait for a night train to run along a nearby embankment and drown out the noise of the plane's engine. But with all the upheaval of getting the plane out of the hangar they had missed their intended locomotive. They expected another train at midnight, so all was not lost; and anyway, Sneum was determined to press ahead even if that one didn't come. He climbed into the cockpit through the port door and checked their luggage one last time. Behind him were several five-litre and ten-litre cans of petrol and the long tube with a funnel attached to one end. Folded neatly were spare shirts and smart naval uniforms for each man. The biscuits and the grape soda sat next to an axe. The broom handle with the two-metre-long white towel nailed to the end had been carefully placed to one side. And nestling innocently among these items were the two cases containing priceless undeveloped cine and still film of the German radar installation on Fanoe. Tucked away equally safely was the detailed report they had just compiled on the military bases where Danish troops were prepared to rise up against the German invaders on a signal from Churchill. To whet the appetites of the British further, Tommy and Kjeld had carefully documented key ports and ship movements around the Danish coast, to guide the bombing of German targets in their country.

By Sneum's own admission, he hadn't been quite so thorough in obtaining a detailed map of their destination: 'Our only map of England was one we had torn from an atlas.'

Britain seemed a far-away place; and it felt like an eternity before they heard the midnight train – just a faint, regular rattle in the distance at first. Gradually it grew louder as the locomotive ate up more track and spewed out more steam. Here at last was the cover they craved. No one would hear a little sports plane above the thunderous roar of the train.

'Contact!' yelled Sneum.

Kjeld gave one mighty downward heave on the propeller and ducked clear as the engine burst noisily to life, with the blades soon scything at the air under their own power. The buzz was beautiful, like a promise of freedom, and adrenalin surged through the pilots' bodies.

As the Hornet Moth began to roll through the turnip fields for the first time in years, clouds of dust flew up in all directions and effectively blinded Tommy in the cockpit. They had a few hundred metres of rough terrain to negotiate before they reached the smoother designated take-off field. During these risky moments, Pedersen ran alongside to act as guide: Sneum could still see his friend, even if he couldn't see what was directly in front of him. Later Tommy recalled: 'He had a crazy look on his face, his revolver was cocked and he was ready to shoot anyone who dared to interfere. He had told me that he would kill as many Germans as he could with his pistol and the rest with his bare hands.' Pedersen pointed and waved so that Sneum could steer the machine through tiny breaks in the ditches between fields. Steadily they headed towards the grassy field that sloped down in a northerly direction and would act as their natural runway.

As Tommy swung the plane into position, Pedersen jumped aboard and tried to take his seat, positioned to the right and fractionally behind his partner's. But the makeshift flagpole had complicated matters by rolling across Kjeld's allocated place, where it now lay jammed. Pedersen had no time to release it gently, so he wrenched it upwards with all his strength. The broomstick and towel shot straight through the cockpit's plexiglas roof, ripping a sizeable hole above their heads. Sneum admitted later: 'I swore at him when he did that. On top of everything else, it meant we would have a cold draught whistling down our necks for as long as we were in the plane.'

Guiltily, Kjeld pulled in the flag of peace and laid it to one side. Knowing there was no time for further recriminations, Sneum coaxed more life out of the engine and sent the flimsy plane hurtling forward. Both men knew this was the point of no return. Happily, the field seemed surprisingly smooth. Tommy feared that one bump might diminish precious speed, but he was able to use the incline of the hill to achieve a furious pace before pulling the joystick towards himself.

There was just one problem – the plane wouldn't take off. Even with the help of the slope, the amount of fuel she was carrying made her just too heavy. The Moth flirted with the air for no more than a few seconds before thumping stubbornly back down to earth. They should have been climbing steeply by now, because pylons and high-voltage cables lay straight ahead; and a hundred metres further on was the ten-metre-high embankment that carried the railway track through the next field. The situation was critical. Even if the temperamental Moth belatedly decided to fly, it no longer seemed possible to make it over the cables. However, it was also too late to abort the take-off. And as if all that were not enough to deal with, Tommy noticed a disturbing development to the left, where another train was snaking its way over the embankment. Even if they could somehow negotiate the cables that stretched like tripwires between the pylons, the formidable wall beyond them had effectively just grown even higher.

Suddenly there was a fresh sensation of weightlessness. The Hornet hovered a foot or two above the grass for five seconds before dropping again, as if exhausted by her effort. By this stage, they were already over halfway down the hill. Time and space were running out fast, and humiliation beckoned: to be shot down over the North Sea was one thing; to crash after fifty metres was quite another.

Then, finally, the Moth took to the air and stayed there. But the prospect of death by electrocution instantly tempered the pilots' elation. With clearing the power cables no longer an option, both men realised their lives now depended upon staying low enough to duck under them instead. Sneum remembered: 'I had to go down, keep the engine running full speed and try not to climb.' He had to perform the stunt at about 100 kilometres per hour, or 55 knots. For Sneum to attempt to achieve that speed without gaining altitude seemed like mission impossible. He was a good pilot, but this sort of aerobatics might demand more skill than even he possessed. The cables were perilously close now, hanging little more than twenty metres above the field. Sneum held his nerve and braced himself, while Pedersen hardly dared look. Just above them, the wires flashed past like cheese-cutters. The anxious pilots waited for what seemed like the inevitable collision. To their amazement, none came.

Now, though, the embankment and train rose before them. And going under them was not an option. As Tommy hauled back on the joystick, Pedersen gestured frantically, his palms turned to the sky, his arms flapping. 'Up! Up!' he screamed. Something stung the Hornet Moth into action. Up she reared, banking steeply to port, until the embankment was almost scaled. But while Tommy tried to work his magic, he saw that the train was about to crush the plane's left wing. The wing tip was level with the top of the engine, which was hurtling towards them. The next few seconds would decide their fate. Sneum caught sight of the train driver and his fireman, seemingly both hypnotised as the Hornet Moth flew towards them. 'They were looking as though we had just fallen down from the moon,' Tommy said later. Those on the train ducked as if to avoid decapitation, but in an instant they were left again to their own world, with their heads and bodies still happily connected. Tommy had cleared them with no more than five or six metres to spare. The plane was still in one piece and so were the pilots. Now there was just the small matter of what the Third Reich might throw at them before they reached the North Sea.

Chapter **10**

UP CLOSE AND PERSONAL

TOMMY CHECKED THE accuracy of the plane's compass against the railway track, which he knew ran directly from east to west. Something was wrong; the instrument was a full thirty degrees wide of the mark. Sneum checked again but the compass was still thirty degrees out. At least there was no variation in its lack of accuracy. Therefore, if he compensated by thirty degrees each time, Tommy was confident he could still plot their course effectively. Unfortunately, however, their problems weren't confined to the compass.

'How is she flying, Sneum?' Pedersen had to shout to make himself heard above the racket of the engine. The answer he received wasn't encouraging.

'The left wing feels twice as heavy as the right, everything is out of alignment, the nose pulls down and she seems to have a life of her own.'

Kjeld looked even more afraid than before. 'Christ, can we make it?'

'Of course we'll make it.'

They flew across the island of Fyn and came out over the Lille Belt Channel near the town of Assens. There, Pedersen looked down on the starboard side and spotted the interrupted flash of a light. The Germans were sending up a message in Morse code. 'Identify yourselves,' it read.

The Danish duo looked at each other and decided to ignore it. Seconds later, over Bogoe, a tiny island between Fyn and Jutland, they looked down again and saw a light moving on a straight course across the water. It was a worrying sight for the pilots. With their request ignored, it seemed the Germans had sent up one of their naval aircraft to investigate.

Sneum and Pedersen thrust their white flag back up through the pierced cockpit roof, but otherwise they felt helpless. The Hornet Moth lacked the power to outrun the enemy. All they could do was train their eyes on the ominous light below, and await their fate. Gradually, however, the light grew fainter, until finally it disappeared. For a while, Tommy and Kjeld were ecstatic.

They had reached an altitude of 1750 metres by the time they began to cross Jutland. Above the town of Haderslev they ran into thick cloud. Now Sneum relied on his Reid and Sigriet blind-flying instruments – compass, altimeter, speed dial and fuel gauge – as he maintained 1900–2000 rotations per minute and checked the oil pressure. It was time now to try to confuse Hitler's forces with a new tactic. A plane heading due west across Denmark in the direction of the North Sea and England would automatically arouse suspicion. The Germans would have it firmly tracked on radar at the Fanoe installation, and no one knew better than Sneum how devastating that new technology could be. But perhaps there was a way to throw them off the scent.

Tommy explained: 'We started to zigzag to prevent the radar from knowing which direction we were going. That's why they thought it was a German aircraft. How the hell could it be anything but a friendly aircraft, flying like that?' By feigning this aimlessness, Tommy hoped to look like a German pilot on a drunken jaunt, or a raw trainee being given his first taste of night instruction. It would still look suspicious, but even if the Nazis thought some defiant Dane was breaking the flight ban, they would read no specific intent into his seemingly random course, and might assume they were witnessing nothing more than a foolhardy protest against the occupation. As Tommy weaved one way then the other, their overall westbound course might have appeared to be no more than a casual coincidence. There was nothing casual about the atmosphere inside the cockpit, though. Cloud condensation and the freezing night air seeped through the hole in the cockpit roof. Then Pedersen became nauseous, his sickness probably aggravated by all the twisting and turning. Soon he vomited. 'I didn't manage to avoid all of it,' Sneum confessed as he remembered the moment with a grimace.

Tommy still thought his tactics worthwhile, though, especially if they had confused Meinicke's staff on Fanoe long enough to delay the scrambling of a night-fighter. Meinicke had often said that spending the war in Denmark, with no real enemy to fight, suited him just fine. Sneum hoped that the German's colleagues, who shared responsibility for monitoring the Danish skies, would have the same non-confrontational approach to the mystery aircraft.

Almost two kilometres up in the sky, plotting a course that ran safely south of Fanoe and its gun batteries, Sneum continued to rely upon a combination of experience and guesswork as he turned time and again in ever-thickening cloud. Both men's lives depended upon Tommy's instinctive skill; and for that reason he preferred not to worry Kjeld unduly as a nagging suspicion began to take hold inside him. For while they may have fooled the Germans, they might also have begun to fool themselves. In short, they might be lost.

'We were in clouds with no visibility and we didn't know where the bloody hell we were,' Sneum admitted. 'In fact, we were fifteen or twenty kilometres too far north.'

Tommy prayed for a tiny window in the wall of swirling cloud, not big enough to be noticed from the ground but sufficient to spot a reassuring landmark. He didn't get one. He still had the compass, and was still taking into account the thirty-degree discrepancy in every calculation he made. However, he had changed direction every two minutes for so long that by now the compass provided little comfort. Mentally it was becoming a struggle to keep up with the new information that his technology was throwing at him.

Having checked with the Luftwaffe, Meinicke's staff on Fanoe would have concluded that none of their planes was supposed to be airborne. So now Sneum's old friend might well have been faced with a tricky dilemma. He had only one plane at his disposal, a Messerschmitt 109 fighter. The rest had been sent east a few days earlier, in preparation for Operation Barbarossa, the invasion of

Russia. The single remaining Messerschmitt and her pilot were being held in reserve for an emergency. The rogue plane heading slowly in their general direction would hardly have constituted a life-or-death crisis, but some sort of action would have to be taken sooner or later. It must have felt like a no-win situation for Meinicke, because if he ordered his pilot to shoot down a foolhardy Dane displaying no malicious intent, it would be a public relations disaster in what had been a relatively peaceful occupation. After all, the Germans were supposed to be keeping the local population on their side, not stirring them to resistance by shooting them in cold blood. On the other hand, if the plane kept coming, Meinicke would have to be uncharacteristically ruthless in order to safeguard the radar installation.

Meanwhile, Sneum felt no need to convey his private concerns about their confused course to Pedersen, because he calculated that the west coast of Jutland was now only minutes away. More often than not, the coast would herald a break in the cloud. If that happened, distinctive landmarks would probably be visible below to tell them precisely where they were.

The plan was to fly out into the North Sea between the islands of Romoe and Mandoe. That was almost as far south as you could go without flying into German air space, and there were no gun batteries in the area. Sneum's brother, Harald, had told them the previous afternoon that they could expect a mild south-easterly breeze – hardly a problem. He had been confident of his calculation, having been supplied with up-to-date information by friends in the Meteorological Office. Although Tommy suspected he had drifted from his intended flight path, he presumed they would still be able to spot either Romoe or Mandoe from wherever they hit the coast. But as the Hornet Moth broke clear of the cloud, the pilots were confronted with a very different sight: 'Puffs of black smoke were exploding all around us from shellfire,' remembered Tommy. 'And tracer bullets seemed to be coming directly at us from below.'

As they looked down and saw orange flashes from battery guns, in an instant the awful truth dawned. This wasn't Romoe or Mandoe. The landmass below was frighteningly familiar. They had left Jutland over Esbjerg, with all its battery defences, and crossed the narrow channel to Fanoe, Sneum's home island. Now they were over Nordby, at the island's northern tip, almost directly above the radar installation that Sneum had filmed so courageously. The same installation was about to exact its revenge by guiding 105mm and 88mm cannon-fire on to their little sports plane. As the flak exploded with increasing venom and accuracy, Tommy and Kjeld braced themselves for a direct hit.

No one was to blame. Harald had made the most accurate forecast he could given the data that was available to him. By midnight, however, conditions had started to change. As Tommy and Kjeld had been taking off, the wind was already coming from due south; then it had continued to shift until now it was a strong sou'westerly. Simply by veering through ninety degrees, the wind had become potentially disastrous. Sneum had been blown further north than he had foreseen, and now it looked as though he and Pedersen would pay for it with their lives.

Kjeld motioned frantically. 'Up, up!' he urged again.

Tommy didn't need telling, and he sent the plane into a steep climb towards what cloud cover was available at 2400 metres. While making this desperate dash for safety, he realised they could be shot down right over his family's mansion, in full view of his parents, who had doubtless been woken by the commotion in the skies.

A direct hit would bring an appropriately explosive end to Sneum's stormy relationship with his father. At least they had recently come to accept their differences, and had even discovered some common ground. Christian Sneum was a complex man. A headmaster at the local school, he was a firm disciplinarian and yet remained a pacifist. He hadn't approved of his son's career in the military. Even so, when the Germans had invaded, Christian knew that his eldest son wouldn't be able to take the occupation lying down. And strangely, given the views he had held for a lifetime, he didn't seem to want Tommy to sit around and do nothing as the Nazis took control of their country.

'Shouldn't you be in England?' he had asked his son pointedly earlier in the year.

Tommy was shocked yet inspired by the message behind the question. It was clearly a time for honesty. 'You know, Father, I probably won't survive the war,' he said.

Christian knew his boy to be a natural risk-taker. 'No, Thomas, I don't suppose you will,' he replied in an equally matter-of-fact way.

Tommy's mother, Karen, overheard the exchange and burst into tears. Soon there were no dry eyes left in the Sneum household, not even among the men, whose emotions were normally well hidden. Despite the war that had changed their lives, Tommy's family found peace among themselves that day.

But a sense of peace or resignation wouldn't keep Tommy alive now. All that could save him and Pedersen were lightning-quick reactions. The gunners on the ground had originally fired too high, fooled perhaps by the seemingly distant noise of the sports plane's tiny engine. Now they were getting closer with every shell, guided by the very radar system Sneum had sought to expose to the British. Somewhere in all the chaos Tommy realised that it might be his old friend Meinicke who was seeking his destruction. Given the strategic importance of the installation, situated just west of the major port of Esbjerg, Sneum couldn't blame him. The highly sensitive nature of the technology there had left him with little choice. But it still seemed like a strange way for their friendship to end.

In spite of the gunners' best efforts, the little plane remained in one piece and flew ever closer to the haven of the clouds. As a result, the German commander was left with no option but to play his last and deadliest card. It was time for the solitary Messerschmitt 109 to be scrambled.

Even when he reached the comforting oblivion of the cloud cover, Sneum sensed that the danger wasn't over. He knew the Germans would send up any fighters they had if the flak failed to find its mark. From what he could see through occasional breaks in the clouds, the night sky was no longer pock-marked by small explosions. The guns below had fallen ominously silent and there had to be a reason why. Twice he doubled back, anticipating the threat of unwelcome visitors. He flew in wide circles, always using the natural cover.

At first the Messerschmitt would have waited in clearer skies, working on the theory that sooner or later the mystery aircraft must head out to sea. When the Moth didn't reappear, however,

Meinicke's man probably followed the rogue plane up through the clouds, to seek out his target from above. The two planes might well have been flying blind in opposite directions on several occasions. At any rate, gambling the Messerschmitt was hunting to the east, Sneum suddenly made a break for the west, out over the North Sea in the direction of England.

If the Messerschmitt pilot ever saw his intended target, perhaps he was fooled by the similarity between the Danish cross that had been painted on the Hornet Moth and the Luftwaffe cross found on all German aircraft. At any rate, to their amazement, Sneum and Pedersen continued to fly out over open sea unchallenged. Meinicke could and perhaps should have ordered his pilot to follow, but there was no pursuit. It's possible he felt that the threat to the radar installation had receded, so there was no need for such ruthlessness. Nevertheless, it seems a miracle that the Hornet wasn't intercepted. Quite how Sneum and Pedersen survived in the skies over Fanoe, no one would ever know.

Chapter 11

WING-WALKER

'LOOK, THERE!' YELLED PEDERSEN when they had put plenty of North Sea between themselves and Denmark.

What greeted Tommy's eyes as he followed Kjeld's gaze filled him with such relief that only now did he fully realise the immense pressure he had been under. He remembered that moment with joy: 'There was an opening in the clouds and we saw the North Star right on the starboard side. I was so happy. It meant we were on the right course, flying due west, and we both knew it immediately.'

They had distrusted the compass right from the start, but it hadn't let them down badly after all. And if the Moth continued to fly like this, then the north-east coast of England lay only a few hours away. They were cold, but pretty soon they realised they had been flying over the North Sea for an hour without incident. They almost relaxed, and freedom felt well within their grasp. Then the Hornet's engine stopped.

At least, that's what it sounded like, for a fraction of a second, before it spluttered back to life. 'No words will ever convey the sheer terror we felt during the following minutes,' admitted Sneum decades later, 'but we didn't panic.' The pilots shot each other a horrified glance and listened in silence for a possible repeat. There it was again, a clanking sound and a strangled groan as the engine threatened to cut out completely. 'We just about went through the roof with fear,' Tommy said. 'But I was also thinking about how the hell I could get out of this situation.'

The first thing he needed was help from his instruments to diagnose the problem. 'Light, for God's sake,' screamed Tommy.

Every half an hour, Kjeld had fed the luminescence of the radium-painted control dials with his torch. Now he hardly dared read what he saw there. 'The oil pressure's flickering between point-five and zero,' he shouted. 'What's it supposed to be again?'

'Three-point-five,' replied Sneum.

'I thought we'd had it,' admitted Tommy later. 'Apparently the oil gauge was working, since the needle was oscillating, and that led to the disastrous conclusion that the whole oil system had broken down. That, in turn, would cause the engine to burn to pieces in a few minutes. Without hesitation I cut the gas and started gliding towards the water.'

He had to control a mounting sense of terror if he was going to control the plane without power. It didn't help that they couldn't even see the sea, because thick cloud was obscuring their view of what lay below them. Imagination ran riot as they braced themselves; family and friends flashed through their minds in snapshots. And all the time there lurked the grim realisation that they had lost everything for the sake of a foolhardy flight they hadn't needed to make.

The only faint hope now was to survive a crash-landing. But the North Sea was a deadly adversary; many others would try to cross this stretch of water during the war and fail. The currents and storms usually finished off anyone unlucky enough to fall into the sea unnoticed. Tommy also knew that once they hit the waves hypothermia would very soon take hold. Even so, he was determined to give them the best chance he could, however slim.

'Find the life jackets,' he screamed.

If they did manage to survive the crash-landing, they could maybe use the axe to hack off a wing and stay afloat on it long enough for a ship or another aircraft to see them.

Kjeld searched the cockpit behind him for the life jackets. 'I can't find them,' he yelled.

Then they looked at each other and remembered. The life jackets were still in the turnip field, thrown off as they sweated and chopped at the frame of the barn door.

'That wasn't a nice moment, when we realised,' recalled Tommy later. 'We were both positive it spelled the end. We said goodbye and thanked each other for our friendship, which had stood the test of time, especially since the German invasion. The flight had been the toughest test of that friendship, because it is one thing to live together as pals, and another to die together.'

Although it was unlikely they would survive, Tommy tried to judge how close they were to the waves. The altimeter, the instrument that should have done that for him, simply couldn't be trusted. At the moment, it read precisely one hundred metres. Tommy described the dilemma he faced:

I had to put on some power in order to avoid tipping over when it came to landing on the water. I thought, How can I fly blind in cloud at stalling speed so the plane hits the sea in a way that we can get out? I was frightened, but never so frightened that I didn't know what we had to do. So I pushed the throttle right forward to try to gain a few more revolutions before stalling. Then the most wonderful thing happened. The engine started up again. But it had another couple of failures straight after that.

Hovering between life and death, Tommy knew he had to act quickly to seize this chance:

It puffed and blew a little to start with, but soon got back to its old, regular hum. There was no oil pressure, or at least the instruments showed zero. But I got the plane to climb a little, and the engine was still purring away, so I climbed a little more. The plane suddenly seemed light as a feather and rose like an angel to five hundred metres. From what I was told afterwards, ice had formed and then melted in the carburettor.

That ice had melted as the plane had dropped into warmer temperatures. 'I could hear solid lumps of things the size of eggs coming loose and clanking against the exhaust,' Tommy recalled. 'That must have been chunks of ice.'

Though Tommy hadn't realised precisely what was going on at the time, he did know that the Moth hadn't liked the higher altitudes, so he wasn't going to take her back up there again.

There wasn't much time for relief, because by now the fuel was running out. Sooner rather than later, the cans in the back of the cockpit, along with the funnel and hose, were going to have to come into play. Which meant Sneum would need to perform the craziest stunt of all in order to keep them airborne. Stepping out onto a wing at a speed of one hundred and twenty knots wasn't in any pilot's manual. But someone was going to have to go out there, unscrew the fuel cap and get the hose into it. Tommy had already promised Kjeld that he would do it.

They had made the task a little easier by punching that hole in the fuselage behind the cockpit and just above the fuel tank. But once they had shoved the hose through the hole, Sneum was going to have to face his fears, step out and make things right.

Pedersen's role would scarcely be pressure-free, though. He would have to fly the plane faultlessly to keep her steady, and Tommy had often poked fun at his friend's lack of prowess as a pilot. He explained later: 'Kjeld wasn't the best of pilots at that time, although he became an excellent pilot later. In Fleet Air Arm he had taken things too seriously, and he didn't like to take risks. We made fun of him for being very, very careful all the time.' However, that perceived lack of spontaneity could now become a life-saving strength. If Pedersen lived up to his billing and demonstrated a plodding lack of ambition in the cockpit, then both men might survive. But he hadn't flown for over a year and this wasn't a plane he knew well. Tommy revealed: 'There were pedals for both seats because the plane had originally been equipped with dual controls. But we had only one fork-shaped stick, and that was in the middle. The stick and the rudder bar could be worked properly only from the pilot's seat. So Kjeld had limited ability to fly the plane from his side.' Pedersen knew that the smallest error could cost his friend his life, which put him under intense pressure. And his well-meaning advice was less than helpful: 'For Christ's sake, don't fall down,' he said.

'Thanks, Pedersen,' Tommy replied. 'That was just what I needed to hear.'

As Sneum pushed the heavy hose further through the hole in the fuselage, he remained composed. 'I wasn't afraid at that point,' he claimed later. 'I wasn't too happy about doing it, but it was necessary. The alternative was certain death. If I failed and fell off before refuelling, maybe Kjeld could survive with a forced landing. But if I got the fuel tube into the tank and then fell off, he could just continue by changing seats.'

When Tommy tried to fling open the port-side door, however, it slammed in his face, shut fast due to the extreme air pressure. The refuelling process had sounded achievable when they had planned it on the ground. Now the reality was proving very different. In order just to get the door open, Tommy decided that Kjeld would have to decelerate. Sure enough, once Kjeld did this, the door could be opened. But as he poked his head out, Sneum was momentarily unnerved: 'The wind was howling and it was pretty dark, because you couldn't see much in the thick fog. It was very cold and in those seconds the full reality and the great danger involved in going out there became clear. I was afraid of getting out.' Nevertheless, 'I stepped out onto the wing with my right foot and held on to the inside of the door frame with my left hand. Then I leaned over and pulled the tube further out of the hole in the fuselage, from the outside this time.'

The plane rocked a little with the shifting weight and Pedersen tilted fractionally to compensate. Sneum was thankful that his left arm and foot were still inside the plane, and he hadn't transferred all his weight outside. But then he brought his left foot out onto the wing too, and only his left hand clung to the inside of the cockpit. At that point he knew that if the plane banked again, he would be gone. 'I think we were about a hundred to a hundred and fifty metres above the sea,' he recalled. 'But it didn't matter if we were a kilometre up in the sky or twenty metres. If I fell off, I'd had it.'

Tommy tried to concentrate on the task in hand, rather than on what could so easily go wrong. He was struggling for breath and fighting to maintain stability, but he knew that to turn back now would be even more suicidal than continuing. With the hose twisted firmly around his right arm, he flexed the freezing fingers of his right hand and attempted to unscrew the fuel cap. 'At first I couldn't do it because my fingers were so numb, and I almost lost my balance,' he explained. But he summoned the courage to try again, and this time he succeeded.

Tommy grabbed the end of the hose and instantly faced a new, tougher battle. 'I struggled to bend the hose down into the fuel tank. It felt so heavy all of a sudden, and I was dizzy and tired.' With one final effort, he pushed it towards the hole and scored a bull's-eye. Plunging the hose deep into the tank, he ensured it would hold firm. Even if he fell now, at least Pedersen would have a chance of survival. Shivering, Tommy slowly edged back towards the cockpit door. He tried to wrap his left knee around the inside of the cockpit wall but faltered slightly, and for a terrible moment only the increasingly desperate grip of his left hand kept him from disaster. Pedersen watched helplessly, knowing that if he abandoned the controls to try to help his friend, the Hornet Moth might shudder enough to throw Sneum into oblivion. Terrified, Tommy launched himself at the cockpit. A split second later he landed in a heap on top of Kjeld. As Pedersen wrestled with the stick, Sneum slammed the door shut behind him. He took over the controls and saw reflected in the face of his friend the relief that he too was feeling. For a while they sat in silence, eating biscuits and drinking grape soda, waiting for their composure to return so that they could begin the next phase of their daring plan.

While Sneum held the end of the hose with one hand and the joystick with the other, Kjeld inserted the funnel. But when he tried to pour the first five-litre can of petrol down the tube, the air currents whistling through the various holes and cracks in the cockpit wreaked havoc. Tommy remembered: 'Kjeld was spilling as much petrol down my back as was going into the tank. As it evaporated I felt colder still. I was covered in petrol. And the stench was overpowering.' Only a fraction of the fuel from that first can found its way into the hose and ultimately into the tank. Not for the first time on the flight, Tommy thanked his partner loudly in his own colourful way. But as the fumes grew unbearable Pedersen was barely conscious to hear him. There was another worry too: any spark in the cockpit would see them going up in flames. If they ever reached Newcastle and were forced to crash-land, the Moth might be an inferno before anyone reached them.

As it was, though, that possibility seemed less likely than

freezing to death or ditching in the sea. Pedersen was drifting in and out of consciousness, seemingly lost in an ever-deepening nausea. However, when he vomited again the effort seemed to bring him momentarily to his senses.

'Come on, Kjeld, I need you now,' Sneum yelled with a hint of desperation in his voice.

Bravely, Pedersen willed himself to continue with his task. He emptied one can after another into the funnel, retching as the petrol splashed all over him. Although the wastage was still considerable, it seemed to both men that a little more liquid reached the fuel tank each time. Tommy later explained: 'We used all the five-litre cans and one of the ten-litre cans. We had plenty of spare fuel, which was just as well.'

Finally, after almost forty-five minutes, they decided they had done all they could. It was time to let the stomach-churning smell dissipate, so that they could breathe enough clean air to recover. If this was freedom, they decided, up to now it was overrated.

Chapter 12

THE WELCOME

SOON A CREEPING, cold monotony became the new enemy. There seemed to be no end to their ordeal, and their strength was fading fast. Their eyelids grew heavy and the gloom invited sleep. It would have been so easy to close their eyes and forget all their troubles. Tommy felt his body shutting down.

Then something wonderful happened to give their fading senses new energy: they felt the warmth of the first rays of morning sunlight breaking over the horizon behind them. And with it came a break in the clouds, as the path to England opened up ahead of them.

'Look!' Pedersen suddenly shouted. 'Land!'

Sneum was confused. It was only 4.30 a.m.; he hadn't expected to see the English coast for another hour. Yet there it was, what seemed to be a wall of land stretching across the horizon.

'We've done it,' yelled Pedersen. 'We've done it!'

'Hang on,' said Tommy. 'That's not land. It's fog.'

Sure enough, the elements had thrown up an optical illusion, as if trying to shatter the spirits of the tiring pilots. The bank of fog had looked exactly like cliffs in the distance. Nevertheless, Tommy and Kjeld knew if they kept flying west, real land would come soon enough.

By 5.15 a.m. (British time) on Sunday 22 June, they had been in the air for almost six hours. Then they spotted a small island ahead of them. 'We were sure we could see breakers crashing against rocks and we looked at each other with joy,' said Tommy. They dropped down to a height of just fifty metres to take a closer look. Although they suspected it was another mirage, soon there seemed no doubt: green vegetation and black rocks beckoned them closer. Then a big white lighthouse came into view. It certainly was an island, and the mainland was now visible beyond it too. A small town. It couldn't be Newcastle, which they knew to be much bigger. So where were they? On one side, there was a sweeping curve in the coastline.

Pedersen suddenly looked worried. 'No sign of an island on the map, Sneum. Do you know what that looks like?'

'What?'

'The mouth of the Zuiderzee.'

'I suppose it could be,' said Tommy, playing along.

'For Christ's sake, we're in Holland!' There was fresh panic in Pedersen's face.

'Fuck off or I'll throw you overboard,' Sneum scoffed dismissively, when he thought Kjeld had suffered enough.

'No, wait, I agree with you,' said Pedersen in a climbdown so sudden that it confused his fellow pilot. 'I think this is England.'

'Why the change of heart?' Tommy asked.

'Because of those,' came the reply. Kjeld pointed, his hand shaking. The sky was alive with Spitfires and Hurricanes. Unbeknown to the Danes, their little sports plane had been spotted as it approached tiny Coquet Island just off the Northumberland coast. David Baston of the Royal Observer Corps was stationed at Gloucester Hill Farm near Amble, the little town seen by Sneum and Pedersen. As soon as the bemused Baston had sighted the Hornet Moth, he had called his headquarters in Durham. The message, quickly relayed to nearby RAF Acklington, had led to four planes being scrambled. Now Sneum and Pedersen were at the mercy of those fighters, which circled and swooped like vultures.

This was just the type of crisis for which the broomstick and giant white towel had been designed. It wasn't for nothing that they had suffered the effects of the pierced cockpit roof all the way across the North Sea. Sneum looked up to check that their symbol of goodwill was still fluttering above them. To his consternation, though, the huge towel had been reduced to the size of a handkerchief – and a ragged, dirty one at that. To British eyes, there would be nothing to distinguish them from the enemy. 'That wasn't a good moment,' Tommy remembered later with considerable understatement.

As they wondered what they could do to avoid being blasted out of the sky, they flew over a small harbour and found themselves just above the rooftops of the town. But something wasn't right about the scene below them. 'Strange, I can't see a soul down there,' observed Kjeld.

Then Sneum realised what was happening. 'They take cover in an air-raid.' Pedersen still looked confused. 'It's because of us.'

The Spitfires came down for a closer look, presumably trying to decide whether to blow the Hornet Moth to pieces. If they hadn't been crossing the town, that might have happened already. Tommy recalled: 'We waved to them and they signalled to us, but we knew we were still in trouble.' One Spitfire pilot responded by pointing downwards. 'Land or we'll open fire' appeared to be the message. As Sneum headed for gently rising fields behind the town, the Spitfires and Hurricanes climbed high above the mystery intruder, though they remained in a perfect position to strike. Then a commotion on the ground caused the Danes to look down again. The Hornet couldn't have been more than thirty metres in the air as the latest threat showed itself below them. Sneum explained: 'I saw some soldiers running into huts and running out again with rifles. I got scared. Some trigger-happy idiot was going to try to shoot us down just for the honour of being able to boast for the rest of his life: "I shot down a plane during the war with nothing more than a rifle." At such close range, any good shot could not only have hit the plane and ignited all the loose fuel; they could have hit our bodies, too.' Fortunately for Tommy and Kjeld, however, this makeshift British firing squad didn't seem able to shoot straight. And Tommy wasn't going to give them any time to practise: 'I dived down so they couldn't see me any more and hopped over hedges.'

By the time he climbed again, he was already out of range, though the Spitfires and Hurricanes responded to the manoeuvre with fresh menace. All Sneum wanted to do was land the plane without starting a fire, and then explain himself to the British personally. In the morning haze, he spotted a suitable field and told Kjeld to brace himself. As he eased down the nose, however, there was panic below: 'The field came alive and I realised the smooth-looking surface I had identified was covered in sheep.' Then, looking ahead, the Danes saw that their epic flight was about to end just as it had begun, with Sneum struggling to avoid potentially lethal wires (this time strung from telephone poles). Pedersen could hardly bear to watch, but once again his friend's reflexes saved them with only metres to spare. One more road, one more hedgerow and then they were over a field of ankle-high corn. If Sneum could just drop the Moth gently down it would all be over.

The first brush with land was a magical moment, though they should have known better than to think it had guaranteed their safety. The Hornet rumbled on noisily, the whole plane vibrating as if she were about to disintegrate in protest at what she had been forced to endure. Pedersen expressed his fear that the speed alone might do them both serious damage if Sneum couldn't bring the machine under control. A country road lay ahead, at a right angle to their approach. Fighting a final battle with a plane that had performed miracles, Tommy slowed her just in time. The Hornet Moth came to a stop just metres from the hedge that marked the edge of the field.

They had done it, and they sat for a moment in silence. Sneum glanced at his watch. It was 5.30 a.m. on 22 June 1941. The crossing had been six hours and five minutes of continuous flight in a single-engine aircraft; nearly eight hundred kilometres, almost entirely over water. They had achieved the impossible. Had they known it, they could have celebrated an unofficial aviation world record. 'We didn't know anything about that at the time. We were just happy to be alive,' admitted Sneum.

With rubbery legs and stiff backs, the Danish pilots climbed down and collapsed briefly into each other's arms. Then they remembered that there were appearances to be maintained. Tommy revealed: 'We had fresh white shirts and uniform jackets folded behind our seats, and in our jacket pocket we each had a tie, which we proceeded to put on. We wanted to be presentable, so that we would be treated like gentlemen.'

Once they considered themselves sufficiently smart, they locked the aircraft and took a short stroll to help their circulation. For a few surreal minutes, it was as if nothing extraordinary had happened. Then they spotted a farm labourer walking down the road, apparently on his way to work. He didn't look very different from the men at Elseminde. When they called him over, however, he seemed startled.

Sneum spoke first. 'Can you please tell us where we are?'

'No,' came the reply. It was a simple word, but the worker pronounced it in a way that didn't sound English to Tommy. And the context seemed even more bizarre.

'No?'

'No.'

'Don't you know where we are?' asked Pedersen.

'Of course I do. I'm not stupid, man.'

'Then why won't you tell us?' asked Sneum.

'I'm not prepared to give that kind of information to strangers,' said the farm worker. 'Don't you know? There's a war on.'

Chapter **13**

DISBELIEF

'YES, WE KNOW there's a war on,' Tommy said patiently. 'But we'd still like to know where we are.'

'I can't tell you,' replied the farm labourer, eyeing the new arrivals suspiciously.

Partly because the Danish pilots were so happy to be alive after all they had been through, they weren't slow to see the funny side of this exchange.

Pedersen tried his luck. 'Please just tell us if we're in England or Scotland,' he asked gently.

There was a moment's silence, as though the labourer were searching for a path between treason and rudeness. 'England,' came the resentful answer at last. 'That's all I'm saying. You'll make me late for work.'

As the local hurried away, Tommy and Kjeld couldn't help but share a smile. And they were no less amused by the sight of an elderly Home Guard officer, a rifle on his back, racing towards them on a bicycle. He saluted, dismounted, looked more closely at their uniforms – and promptly pointed his rifle at them. 'Where the bloody hell have you two come from?' he demanded.

'Denmark,' said Pedersen.

'Rubbish! Don't give me that,' replied the Home Guard officer, and quickly called for reinforcements on his field telephone.

No one seemed to know quite what to do while they all waited for more men to arrive; so for a few strangely silent minutes, Sneum and Pedersen played along with the idea that they had been captured single-handedly by their grey-haired adversary.

Tommy had landed in a cornfield belonging to Bullock Hall Farm, which wasn't far from RAF Acklington. Two Land Rovers appeared from the air base, an RAF officer and his driver in each one. Sneum thought it better to keep his pistol concealed under his jacket, just in case relations took a sudden turn for the worse.

'Identify yourselves,' demanded the first officer to reach them. It was as though they had landed from another planet.

'Flight Lieutenants Sneum and Pedersen, Danish Fleet Air Arm, at your service,' said Tommy, offering his hand. 'We're here to help you fight Hitler. We've just flown across the North Sea.'

'In that?' The second officer looked incredulous as he studied the flimsy-looking Hornet Moth. 'Not a chance.' He had already drawn his pistol.

Tommy and Kjeld weren't smiling any more, though they managed to remain composed. 'That's exactly what we did,' explained Sneum patiently. 'We've come all the way from Denmark, and we've brought some important film of German installations in our country.' He waited for the British officer's expression to change. It didn't.

'Are you armed?' The first English officer had clearly decided to treat the intruders as enemy spies until they proved otherwise.

Reluctantly, Tommy handed over his weapon. 'Look, if you don't want us, we'll carry on to America and to hell with you,' he said.

Later, Sneum revealed: 'I was bloody angry and disgusted with their attitude. Christ Almighty, we had just risked our lives in so many different ways to get there, and now we were being treated like Nazis.'

Tommy pointed the British officers in the direction of the precious undeveloped film and the intelligence files, which were still tucked away in the cockpit. Everything was loaded into the Land Rovers before the crestfallen pilots were driven away. They didn't know it, but neither man would ever see their precious Hornet Moth again. Within half an hour they were in the mess at RAF

Acklington, facing a full English breakfast and plenty of pointing and staring from groups of intrigued local pilots. Some spoke in an uneasy whisper, and Tommy thought he heard at least one refer to them as 'German bastards'. But he couldn't fully trust his ears after a night of being pounded by the elements and deafened by the Hornet's tiny but noisy engine.

Finally a tall, dashing pilot marched confidently over to their table. He said he was Canadian, and had flown one of the Spitfires which had intercepted them. He had been nominated to ask a question, he explained. 'Some of the guys are wondering . . . you see we've taken a good look at your, err, plane.' The derisive tone annoyed Tommy intensely. 'What we can't work out is this: where, exactly, have you guys come from?'

'Denmark,' repeated Sneum.

The Canadian laughed. 'Impossible.'

The two exhausted Danes watched the Spitfire pilot return to his cronies and relay the details of their brief exchange. Then a voice from the huddle rang across the canteen. 'Well, if you ask me, they're German spies.'

The room fell silent. Sneum was seething. He and Kjeld had been in England barely an hour, yet already they had been shot at and accused of treachery.

Despite the insults, their hosts weren't without compassion: the Danes were shown to beds in the sick bay, and invited to sleep until lunchtime. The fresh linen felt luxurious, though they didn't stay awake long enough to savour it.

≈ ▦ ≈

Back in Denmark, Lieutenant Poul Andersen called the police and reported that his plane had been stolen. The farmer was interrogated later that day by policemen from Odense. Their superiors from Copenhagen, and even the Germans, were informed. The authorities correctly suspected that Andersen had cooperated with the 'thieves', but he was a hard man and a capable actor – he managed to summon passable anger when required to express his feelings for whoever had made off with the Hornet Moth, his pride and joy. Since neither the Danish police nor the

Germans had any concrete proof that Andersen had been involved, they had little choice but to accept his story and let him go about his business.

Andersen's consolation for his interrogation came that evening, when he tuned in to the BBC: 'Two Danes have arrived in England this morning,' the broadcaster announced. He didn't elaborate. For Andersen, though, the brief message confirmed that the risks they had all taken to defy the Nazi occupation had been worthwhile. He was confident he knew precisely who those 'two Danes' were; and that meant his Hornet Moth had made it in one piece, too. Perhaps he allowed himself to believe that he would get the plane back at the end of the war. At that moment in 1941, however, the recovery of his property wasn't important. He had done something to undermine the Germans, and he could allow his granite features to crack into a smile of satisfaction. His stubborn little sports plane had defied the odds, and helped to make the dreams of two brave if slightly crazy young men come true.

* * *

In Acklington, Tommy and Kjeld were allowed to shower. To feel hot water on their backs instead of freezing fuel was glorious. They were treated to more hot food for lunch before being taken to their first interrogation. The inquisitors were Wing Commander Pringley, Flight Lieutenant Lord Tangerville and Flight Officer Forest. They were polite and their questioning remained relatively superficial. They never challenged the answers they received, which they wrote down officiously for some kind of preliminary report. Occasionally they sought simple clarification on an issue they didn't understand. Sneum thought it was all too easy. He had a feeling that the serious business would be conducted elsewhere.

That afternoon Tommy and Kjeld were put in a car, driven to Regional Headquarters near the town of Morpeth, and told to relate their story from the beginning again. This time the questions were more searching, and the Danes' answers were sometimes accepted with a detectable scepticism, although they were still never challenged outright. Sneum and Pedersen remained calm, knowing that patience would be the key to getting through this initial phase, and their composure seemed to have paid off when the British abruptly concluded proceedings and offered their uninvited guests a remarkable piece of hospitality. The 'prisoners' were escorted to a restaurant in Morpeth and treated to a lavish evening meal, free to choose from the menu like any other customers. The only sombre moment came when a radio broadcast from Winston Churchill announced that the Germans had invaded Russia.

Tommy said later, 'When we heard all about Operation Barbarossa, we realised why we had managed to get through the previous night without being intercepted. Nearly all the Luftwaffe planes had already gone east.'

By the time the coffees arrived in the restaurant, however, so had two more officers, slightly older and wearing different, darker uniforms. Suddenly Sneum didn't feel so lucky any more. The new arrivals were police sergeants – and being friendly wasn't at the top of their agenda. The RAF men had no choice but to hand over their guests as arranged, and the mood soon changed. The natural camaraderie and mutual respect shared by airmen of every nation was replaced by the strained civility of their new escorts. In little more than half an hour, a police car had rushed the prisoners to Newcastle's railway station, where they boarded a midnight train, closely followed by their guards.

⋅ ▩ ⋅

The first smears of dawn had already turned to morning as Tommy and Kjeld were marched bleary-eyed out of London's King's Cross Station and ushered towards an unmarked police car.

As far as they could see, it was business as usual in England's capital, with few visual signs of a country at war. They were driven through a sleepy West End and across the River Thames, until finally the car drew to a halt at the Royal Patriotic School for Orphan Daughters in Unity Street, Battersea. The large, neo-Gothic building had previously been home to a charitable institution. Now it was a vetting centre for foreigners who had entered the country through unofficial channels. It had been adapted for this new role just five months before, and the chaos inside suggested that an efficient system had not yet been discovered.

For illegal aliens who failed to present a convincing case to the Allies, however, a swift and ruthless procedure did exist. Anyone deemed a security risk was shipped to an internment camp on the Isle of Man. Many of the so-called impostors who were sent there would not be heard of again until the end of the war. Tommy and Kjeld didn't realise it, but their individual wars, indeed their very freedom, would depend upon how they coped with questioning over the next twenty-four hours. And this time the interrogation would be extreme.

Chapter **14**

SENDING FOR THE DOCTOR

THOUGH IT WAS NO LONGER in his possession, Tommy was confident that the Movikon film of the Fanoe radar installation was already in London too. Therefore, he had every reason to believe that it would be only a matter of time before he and Pedersen were congratulated on their intelligence coup and offered the chance to join the Royal Air Force. He presumed that the film had already been developed and was now probably being watched by several senior British officers.

However, there was no evidence of that as yet. Sneum and Kjeld were taken into a spartan room, where they were directed towards a simple wooden table and invited to sit opposite each other on two hard chairs. To their surprise, they were then left alone, and it soon dawned on them why such unexpected breathing space had been offered. Tommy revealed: 'They had installed microphones in our room, which we very quickly found.'

The British guards didn't return for some time, their superiors perhaps hoping for some slip of the tongue inside the cell. Eventually, though, the pilots were separated and taken to even smaller rooms, where the questioning began in earnest. Tommy found himself being interrogated by a fellow Dane, who gave his name as Seaman Peters. In fact he was a naval officer called Olaf Poulsen, and he seemed impressed by the quality of Sneum's intelligence. He called in some British Royal Navy officers, who wanted to focus on two German ships Tommy had mentioned. It quickly occurred to Sneum that the *Nurnberg* and the *Schleswig-Holstein* might just provide his passage to freedom, so he told the fascinated naval men everything he knew about the vessels and their movements.

With the prospect of a Spitfire waiting for a new pilot on some English airfield, Tommy answered questions on a variety of topics as fully and helpfully as he could. In a later military report, he wrote of this interrogation:

> I talked about my work, my family, my sources for intelligence in Denmark and about the people who had helped me economically. Furthermore, I had brought 60 metres of 16mm film of German positions, batteries and airfields, and I also brought Leica films [stills] of the same kind. Then I had made drawings and sketches of the following airfields: Kastrup, Vaerleose, Avnoe, Esbjerg, Aalborg, Knivholt and Karup.
>
> An army officer came in to interrogate me in connection with the messages they had earlier received in Stockholm. I painted a more-or-less correct picture of the situation in Denmark.
>
> To the Admiralty, I gave all the positions of the coastal batteries I knew existed, the comings and goings in the Danish harbours and the result of the English mine-laying in Danish waters. I had brought with me a copy of the *Danish Harbour Pilot*, so I was able to explain to what extent the Germans had a presence in each place by using the maps.

At this point Tommy was placed in the hands of Squadron Leader Denys Felkin's sharp and sceptical team of interrogators: Lieutenants Gregory and Siddons, accompanied by Flying Officer Sanky. The first two men, in particular, were experienced players, whose skills as inquisitors had been honed during their time with Air Ministry Intelligence. They had often dealt with foreign pilots who turned out to be exactly what they first seemed – brave souls who had escaped from occupied countries and were keen to fly against the Germans. However, the interrogators had also come across more complicated characters, men who seemed credible at first and then, after exhaustive forensic questioning, were exposed as German spies.

It wasn't always easy to tell the difference between hero and traitor. MI5, the branch of British Intelligence that dealt with domestic security, believed that pilots, as a breed, made first-class spies because they invariably had a good eye for technical information. The interrogators from the Air Ministry had therefore been given a checklist to help them detect a secret agent:

1. Could the man be an enemy agent? In Sneum's case the answer, in theory at least, was 'yes'.
2. Does his general background make him a likely recruit or bring him within one of the categories that the enemy are known to favour in their search for recruits? Again, the answer in Tommy's case was a strong 'yes'.
3. Are there any possible points in his story suggesting recruitment, training, dispatch? Another affirmative. Sneum had admitted to friendly contact with the enemy, having thought it more dangerous to make a secret of it. As for the escape itself, the British were finding it hard to believe that the Germans hadn't assisted Tommy in some way. It was regular German practice to suggest to a recruited agent an 'escape route' from Nazi-occupied territory, and then call off their patrols on the given day to make sure their man got through. That way, under interrogation, the agent could draw largely on fact when asked to describe how he had reached Britain.
4. Is his whole story of a pattern indicating a German agent? Sneum's MI5 interrogators must have been tempted to answer 'yes' to this question, too.

One might have expected the sheer volume of intelligence that Tommy had brought with him to have worked in his favour. In his report, he said of Gregory, Siddons and Sanky: 'They got my sketches of the German airfields, and information about Anti-Aircraft Batteries around the country.' But in the same document, he admitted: 'The British had extremely good aerial photographs of all the existing German airfields in Denmark already.'

At least Sneum was able to report a more enthusiastic response from the Air Ministry interrogators: 'Those people were especially interested in my information, films and Leica pictures of the German direction-finders on Fanoe.' And yet even the Air Ministry officials suspected that they were being sucked into an elaborate sting. In theory, the Abwehr might have audaciously allowed this information to reach the British. Had the Germans decided that the British already knew enough about their radar activities to render Sneum's new evidence a price worth paying for infiltration? Was this a brilliant ruse to get their man into direct contact with British Intelligence? The British couldn't discount such a possibility at this stage, especially when it became clear that Sneum had enjoyed regular contact with the forces occupying his country.

He admitted later, 'I told the interrogators at the Royal Patriotic School quite openly that I'd had contact with the Germans. That was how I had been able to get hold of much of the intelligence I had brought over. They didn't seem to understand or accept this principle; they were suspicious of anyone who showed anything but outright hatred for all Germans.'

Though Sneum found the approach of his British hosts absurdly simplistic, even he could see why they were finding his account hard to swallow. He had filmed new technology at Fanoe right under the noses of the Germans. He had rebuilt a plane and flown it out of Nazi-occupied territory. He had stepped onto the wing for a spot of mid-air refuelling. Tommy remembered:

I was aware, as I told them the story of my escape yet again, that it didn't sound very likely. They didn't believe what I was saying, at least some of them didn't, even though they had RAF backgrounds themselves. Perhaps that was the very reason they didn't believe me, because they hadn't heard of such a thing being done before, especially not in a Hornet Moth. They said it was all lies.

But what could I do? I just told them the truth again and again. On the question of the pictures and sketches of the radar, I kept telling Flight Lieutenant Gregory to check for authenticity with the British Legation in Stockholm, and talk to Captain Henry Denham or Squadron Leader Donald Fleet about me. And above all I kept asking Gregory when my films would be back from their laboratory, because I thought that when they saw the quality of those images, it would end the argument. That's when he told me where they had been sent. The post office. Can you imagine?

Before long there was a knock at the door. Gregory, normally a dashing, confident figure, seemed angry and embarrassed when the news was delivered, and with good reason. He had to turn back to Sneum and tell him what had happened. Tommy remembered his own anger at what he heard:

Nearly all my films had been destroyed at the post office in a mix-up. Apparently someone had failed to follow basic instructions, even though I had clearly marked both thirty-metre reels of sixteen-millimetre film with labels written in big letters on their cassettes, in case anything should happen.

I had a roll of reversible 'diafilm', which was positive on one side and negative on the other. I labelled that one 'Reversible'. The other cassette I marked 'Negative'. But the people at the post office probably couldn't read, because they developed the negative film as reversible and the reversible film as negative.

I went mad when I realised what had happened. 'You stupid bastards,' I told them. 'Do you know how many times I risked my life for those films?' They were trying to calm me down but I just kept going. 'Are you intelligence officers? What is intelligent about you? Why did you send them to a fucking post office in the first place?'

I couldn't believe it. They were labelled so that not even an idiot could fail to understand. I demanded to see what was left of them, and that gave Gregory an excuse to leave me to cool down for a while, I suppose. I was thinking, No wonder these stupid bastards are losing the war.

An ugly tension hung in the air for the best part of an hour, until two fresh faces appeared. A gentle-looking giant was first through the door, followed by another man who looked as though he enjoyed a good argument. Reginald Victor Jones, head of Britain's Scientific Intelligence and a personal adviser to Winston Churchill, had just arrived with Charles Frank, his assistant. Gregory, who had made the decision to call in the experts, brought up the rear.

Unbeknown to Sneum, the interrogator had believed far more of the story than he had allowed to show. As a German Jew, he was no stranger to the concept of being doubted for no good reason. But while he had a natural tendency to side with the underdog, he knew that some of Sneum's claims had to be verified by scientific experts.

Jones and Frank were just the men to have alongside him when the remains of Tommy's films were examined. Jones, in particular, had a calm aura about him, which helped diffuse some of the hostility still in the room. Sneum recalled: 'He treated everyone as though they had some good in them, and it was his job to find it.' Soon Jones was studying the precious surviving images as if in a world of his own, with Frank and Sneum looking over his shoulder. Tommy explained: 'They could see what it was but they couldn't really make out the detail because of the damage done, so I tried to explain what was shown. I wasn't an expert but he made me feel like I was. Then we noticed a few clearly definable images. It was an exciting moment, and the scientists eagerly went to work.' They traced the shapes on to clean paper, hoping to form a clearer view of what the devices could be. From frame to frame, a subtle revolving action could be detected. The huge sensors at the centre of each image appeared to be turning towards the sky, which allowed Sneum to write in his wartime report: 'One specialist on this subject, Dr R.V. Jones, got the film which showed this apparatus actually functioning.'

As Jones examined the film further, his face lit up. Even Tommy noticed the sparkle in his clear blue eyes. 'Freya radar,' the scientist announced. 'Hitler's latest defence system. We've seen aerial photographs of these things from France. But we didn't know the Germans were using this type of radar in Denmark.' At last, here was someone who could understand and appreciate the enormity of what Tommy had done for the Allied cause.

It was the latest breakthrough in the intelligence battle against Germany's formidable scientists. From offices on the upper floors of 54 Broadway – the Secret Intelligence Service building in St James's, London – Jones had dedicated all his energies to helping Churchill stay one step ahead of Hitler in the race to develop new technology. The struggle for radar supremacy was crucial to Allied hopes of victory. Only by understanding Nazi advancements in this area could British bombers hope to avoid German night-fighters during raids over the European mainland.

'These are the first pictures I've seen of Freya taken on the ground,' Jones purred. 'Moving pictures, that's a first too. Imagine what he had to go through to get them.' He looked over at Sneum and said: 'Our bomber crews will be very grateful.'

For the benefit of Jones and Frank, Tommy told the dramatic story of his escape yet again. Gregory and his colleagues listened just as intently as the newcomers, checking for inconsistencies with the Dane's previous accounts, and in case they had missed anything which might yet be regarded as suspicious.

'Gentlemen,' said Jones when Tommy had finished. 'I think we have to accept that what we have here is not a double-agent but a man who has demonstrated bravery of the highest order.' He later confirmed Sneum's account of events that day in his book *Most Secret War*:

Why I had been drawn into this episode was that Sneum had brought some undeveloped cine film with him which he said he had taken of the radar station on Fanoe, showing the aerials turning. Unfortunately MI5 had taken the film and had it processed by, I believe, the Post Office, and between them they had ruined nearly all of it; Sneum was justifiably indignant. There were just one or two frames left from which I could see that he very definitely had filmed two Freyas in operation . . . [These frames were] the sole relics of a gallant exploit.

Gregory, Charles and I were all convinced that Sneum was genuine, and we could entirely sympathise with his indignation. Not only had he and his friend risked their lives several times over, but also they had brought with them very valuable information only to have it ruined by the hamhandedness of our Security Authorities; moreover they were treated as spies because their story was so improbable. At the same time, there was an almost inevitable irony about such episodes, because the more gallant and therefore improbable they were, the harder it was to believe that they had really happened.

Gregory agreed that the valour Tommy had shown in order to bring the British this precious intelligence had been truly exceptional. So much so that Sneum later claimed: 'Otto Gregory told me that if I had shown such bravery in a combat situation, I would probably have been recommended for a Victoria Cross. He said he thought I deserved one for what I had done.'

While such an accolade was gratifying to hear, Tommy was already thinking of his colleagues back home, and how he could help them. His stock had suddenly risen so dramatically that he sensed it was the right moment to renew his plea for a Sunderland sea-plane. His wartime report stated the following:

> I informed the British that I had collected together a bunch of Danish aviators, who wished to take part actively in the fight against Germany; and that, because of a promise I had received in Stockholm, I wanted to pick them up as soon as possible, even if it meant me parachuting down into Denmark and collecting them for pick-up at the appointed place, Lake Tissoe.

Perhaps Tommy was a victim of his own success. Although his audience showed a pleasing enthusiasm for the plan, they were far more interested in what he had achieved (and what he might achieve in the future) as a spy than in any friends he had back home. Gregory would doubtless have made all the right noises about seeing what he could do to get the Danish pilots picked up. But he would already have been consumed with other, more pressing questions. Who in Britain should be granted access to Sneum's gold-mine of intelligence? And how could one British covert organisation recruit such a valuable man without the other British covert organisation knowing anything about it?

Being from the Air Ministry, Gregory was attached to the Secret Intelligence Service (or MI6, as it is more commonly known nowadays, the branch of the British Secret Service responsible for overseas security), rather than the newly formed Special Operations Executive, which had been created to cause chaos behind enemy lines in occupied Europe. So he and his masters in SIS set about trying to keep Sneum and Pedersen to themselves, at least until a further plan of action could be devised.

But none of this potentially damaging interdepartmental rivalry would become clear to Tommy and Kjeld until much later. Having made his fresh request for the pick-up of his colleagues back home, Tommy just wanted to get out of the Royal Patriotic School and find his way into the thick of the wartime action.

His hopes were raised when Gregory, brandishing his Air Ministry credentials, cut straight through the red tape and released both newly arrived Danes immediately. Sneum and Pedersen were escorted to a hotel in central London, and waited to see what would happen next. At least they were free.

The following day, however, Gregory turned up at the hotel looking worried. He said they would have to go back to Battersea to 'take care of a few formalities'. When they arrived, it was clear that they were at the centre of a tug of war. Sneum explained: 'The commanding officer at the school was furious because we had been taken away without his permission. We had to go back and sleep one more night there while it was all cleared up. So then it was Gregory's turn to be furious, and I was just as angry. But I controlled myself and just told everyone that I was sure it would be perfectly OK in the end.'

As he lay on a rock-hard bed, Sneum wasn't sure what to make of the British any more. He mused later: 'It seemed to me that for the most part the British were disorganised, deeply incompetent, and hostile to all foreigners, even those foreigners who wanted to help them. With a combination like that, I thought it was no wonder that the Germans looked like winning the war. But the British never know when they have lost, so they never give in.'

Chapter **15**

THE SPYMASTER

EUAN CHARLES RABAGLIATI, head of MI6 Denmark and Holland, was small and slightly built, but instantly recognisable as a character of fearsome intensity. He had grey-red hair, thinning and slicked back, a sharp moustache and a noticeable dent in his head. The depression, large and circular, like a volcanic crater, was visible thanks to his receding hairline. Below it, a silver plate had been inserted to prevent the skull from caving in completely. The plate's owner, as usual, was impeccably dressed in the uniform of a British officer. When he appeared from behind his huge desk inside 54 Broadway, his shiny black shoes gleamed brightly, as if to compensate for the fact that they were almost too tiny to encase adult feet.

Rabagliati spoke in the clipped accent of an English aristocrat, even though his family roots were Scots-Italian. When he met people he didn't know, he preferred to call himself Colonel Ramsden, a name plain enough to be soon forgotten. Although 'Ramsden' had joined the SIS from the Ministry of Information, the forty-nine-year-old's past was far more colourful than that of most civil servants. He had shown tremendous personal courage in the First World War as a fighter pilot in what was then the Royal Flying Corps, becoming the first British ace to shoot down a German plane in the new form of warfare known as 'aerial combat'. He did so by manoeuvring alongside the enemy aircraft and shooting the pilot with a pistol. On another occasion, when he himself was shot down, he survived in no-man's-land for days before crawling to safety.

Rabagliati often flew behind enemy lines and once noticed a substantial build-up of German troops opposite a weak point in the British line. He landed in a field on the British side of the trenches and informed the relevant officers immediately. To his astonishment and fury, they hardly seemed to care, as if they had seen too much carnage already to worry about the fresh threat. The infantrymen were more interested in his plane, still a battlefield rarity in those brutal days of bayonets and trenches. Rabagliati had to use all his tenacity to make sure the war-weary officers reacted swiftly enough to his intelligence to avert a crisis.

It was that kind of initiative and bravery which earned him the Military Cross, the Air Force Cross and six mentions in dispatches. And his courage also won the lasting respect of the enemy, a fact he used to his advantage when the Great War was over. During the 1920s and 1930s, he managed to build up important contacts among the best pilots in Germany. When he went into the insurance business, one of his main clients was Jauch and Hubener in Hamburg.

Hooked on the adrenalin of speed and danger, Rabagliati found his peacetime fix in motor-racing, and drove in the Double Twelve Hours race at Brooklands. There, on 10 May 1930, disaster struck on the notorious banked corner as he pushed his car and body to the limits of their endurance. He clipped another vehicle at 160 kilometres per hour and his co-driver, who had doubled as his mechanic, was killed. Rabagliati himself, having suffered devastating head injuries, was almost left for dead. Then someone noticed he was still breathing, pulled him out of the wreckage and got him into an ambulance. In hospital surgeons patched him up and inserted the plate in his skull, though without much optimism. He spent two weeks in a coma before stunning the nurses by opening his eyes. With his first words after returning to the land of the living he ordered a bottle of champagne.

Though Rabagliati's career in the Ministry of Information was never going to provide a similar buzz to motor-racing, the SIS offered some respite from day-to-day routine as they began to consult him on German matters. Powerful figures at MI6 soon decided they could use a man of Rabagliati's strength and style on a more regular basis, so he was invited to join even before Churchill declared war on Germany. Unsurprisingly, he accepted immediately.

When Britain entered hostilities, Rabagliati sent his third wife Beatrix and her two sons to South Africa for their own safety. Then he moved into a flat in St James's to be near his new office, with only his black Bentley and Hotchkiss sports car for company. Before long, though, he consoled himself with a new infatuation – an SIS secretary called Joan Duff. She was twenty years his junior, over six feet tall and determined to wear high heels. When they walked into London's top restaurants together Joan looked almost twice Euan's height, but he didn't seem to care, displaying a confidence that could never be diminished by his physical limitations.

Back at 54 Broadway he soon became the SIS liaison officer for Holland and Denmark, a strange appointment since he spoke neither Danish nor Dutch. The chief of SIS, Stewart Menzies, and his experienced deputy, Claude Dansey, must have seen other exceptional qualities in Rabagliati, however, for he now ran both departments, which were known collectively as 'A2'.

Without an effective Danish agent, Rabagliati had been waiting for suitable candidates to arrive from the occupied country. So when Flight Lieutenant Gregory called in late June with news of two interesting possibilities, Rabagliati ordered them to be sent directly to his flat at 5 St James's Street, above a hat shop. Next he requested the assistance of a man who passed as Broadway's linguist, a certain Major Thornton, who seemed to have no defined position in the SIS hierarchy, nor even much flare for languages. His job was to assess the linguistic ability of potential new agents and to translate for chiefs of section like Rabagliati. However, since he spoke only very poor German, he was scarcely up to either task.

When Sneum and Pedersen arrived at the address they had been given, both were both struck immediately by the natural charisma of the man who introduced himself as Colonel Ramsden. They followed him up a flight of stairs and met Thornton, who was waiting in a lounge on the first floor. Since Rabagliati spoke no Danish, he instructed Thornton to ask their guests a general question about the situation in Denmark. Tommy recalled: 'Thornton spoke no Danish either, so he phrased the question in broken German. I just put him out of his misery by answering in fluent English.'

From that moment Thornton's role in the meeting was redundant. Before long he excused himself, clearly relieved that his ordeal was over, though somewhat embarrassed that his linguistic limitations had been so quickly exposed.

Rabagliati, who had not lost his air of self-assurance for a moment, quizzed the pair a little more about conditions in Denmark, then came to the point: 'What do you think about going back there for us?' The question was direct and shocking.

'Too dangerous.' Kjeld was adamant. 'We'd be marked men. They'll already know who took the plane.'

Never imagining they would be asked to return to Denmark as spies, they had left plenty of incriminating documentation in the barn in order to deflect any blame away from Poul Andersen. If they did go back, the AS (Special Affairs) Department of the Danish police in Copenhagen would probably be on to them in no time. The Germans would be informed too, and then there was the risk of a full-scale Abwehr manhunt. No, insisted Pedersen, the best way forward was for the British to let them join the RAF.

'Look, I'm sure you're both damn good pilots, you must be to have come this far, and we do appreciate your offer,' acknowledged Rabagliati rather ominously. 'But we're not short of pilots. We've got twenty-five thousand in training already. What we're short of is agents. Your intelligence work so far has been nothing short of brilliant. That's where you can really help us. What do you say?'

Pedersen was shaking his head again.

But Sneum heard himself reply: 'I'd be prepared to think about it. If you really think we can be more use as agents than we can be as pilots, I'll go back to Denmark.'

'I won't be joining you,' said a stunned Pedersen straight away. 'Sorry, Sneum. We can't do more than we've already done over there.' He turned to Rabagliati. 'With your permission, Colonel, I'm going to fly for the RAF, which is why I came here.'

Sneum was disappointed but not angry. He had already put Pedersen in dreadful danger; and he couldn't inflict more on his reluctant friend. Kjeld had earned the right to fight his war in his own way, and his bravery was beyond question. Besides, the RAF was no easy option. In 1941, mortality rates were still high. He had made his choice and Tommy was bound to respect it.

'The Germans would be looking for both of us, so maybe it's better if we split up anyway,' said Sneum supportively. 'But if the British want me to do this alone, I'll go back.'

Although Tommy later recounted this conversation in the full detail shown above, his wartime report on this meeting was rather more protective of Kjeld, whose reluctance to return to Denmark was both sensible and understandable. Sneum wrote:

> On Wednesday, 25 June, we were both called in to see Colonel Rabagliati and Major Thornton, who questioned us about conditions in Denmark. We were asked if we would think about going back to Denmark to work for the British there. This would be of great importance to the British, we were told.
>
> I answered that only one of us could do it, because we were probably being hunted as a pair, wanted men together, and that I would like to be the one to go back because I already had so many useful connections for such a job.

The following day Sneum and Pedersen were both signed out of the Royal Patriotic School for ever. At first they were installed together in Room 65 at Keyes House, Dolphin Square, in the London district of Victoria. But it was clear that they would soon be going down two very different wartime paths. And once they set off on their respective journeys, it was by no means certain that they would ever see each other again. Tommy and Kjeld therefore decided to enjoy a farewell evening in London. But they had no money, and there were no offers of financial help from their hosts. Desperate to have some fun, Tommy looked through their humble belongings and his eye landed on the one item that might fund their big night out. A little later, he pawned the Movikon camera for twenty pounds. And he never returned to the shop to reclaim the piece of equipment which had captured so much vital intelligence for the British.

At the start of the evening, Sneum and Pedersen changed into their Danish naval lieutenants' uniforms. They didn't know when they would get the chance to wear them again, and they were still proud of their homeland, despite Denmark's capitulation to the Germans.

'You know,' said Kjeld as they began a pub crawl, 'I would never have got to England without you forcing me to come with you.'

Sneum smiled because it was probably true.

They tumbled into the Suivie Club, one of the English capital's great night spots, and were shown discreetly to a table in a dimly lit corner. For a while they were happy just to observe the party. It was a good place from which to identify the most beautiful women on the dance floor, and they believed there would be plenty of time to make a move for their favourites later. So they sat contentedly with their beers, although Sneum put ice cubes in his unbearably warm British ale.

Soon they were approached by a British Army captain, who said something that Sneum didn't quite catch. Obligingly, Tommy leaned across the table so that he could hear above the swinging music.

'I said, what are you bloody foreigners doing here?' demanded the captain.

'Oh, I see,' said Sneum, politely. 'Well, I'll show you.'

It took one punch. Tommy later recalled with a chuckle: 'My fist had the force of a mule's kick in those days.'

Within a minute, Sneum had been thrown out of the club, with the captain carried out close behind him. A proud Pedersen slapped his friend on the back to congratulate him on such an efficient performance. It wasn't what they had originally planned for the evening's entertainment, but both Danes had been through a little too much, with the prospect of far worse ahead, to be abused by someone they had risked their lives to help.

Not everyone in England seemed to resent their presence, though. As they cleaned themselves up on the street, Kjeld noticed a prostitute observing them from over the road. He didn't know when, if ever, he would next have the pleasure of a woman's company, so he crossed the road to begin negotiations. Tommy took up the story:

Another girl intercepted Kjeld and she was far more beautiful than the prostitute, I can assure you. This girl said to Kjeld, 'A good-looking boy like you doesn't need to resort to that.' She was smiling to convey her meaning, but Kjeld was probably confused. So she said, 'Come home with me. I won't charge and you'll still get what you want. In fact I'll be very grateful for the company.' Kjeld was a good-looking chap but I still don't think he could quite believe his luck. Anyway, he left me – and the prostitute – in the middle of the street and went off with the other girl. I heard later that they had stayed together for a good few months.

Pedersen had little time to enjoy his new lover in the more immediate future, however. On 27 June, just five days after he had landed exhausted in that field in the north-east of England, he was commissioned as a pilot officer in the RAF and left London for Training School 18, Woking, Surrey. His dream to fly with Britain's finest had come true.

Thomas Sneum, who had shared that same dream, didn't have long to reflect upon the wisdom of the path he had taken, almost on impulse. To all intents and purposes, he was already an agent of the Secret Intelligence Service.

Born to fly, destined to spy: Britain's daring agent Thomas Sneum deep in thought. He used that intensity in his eyes to psyche out enemies – or attract women.

(*Top left*) Days of innocence: Tommy (in the hat) learns to ride.
(*Above left*) The dismantled Hornet Moth.
(*Above right*) Sneum, the dashing hero in Danish navy regalia.

(*Above left*) The very plane that Sneum and Pedersen flew to England.
(*Above right*) Friends for life: Tommy and Kjeld Pedersen get together for the tenth anniversary of their epic flight.

(*Above left*) Else Sneum with Tommy's eldest daughter Marianne. But Sneum chose spying ahead of family life.

(*Above right*) La dolce vita: Tommy in Italy with his second wife Aida. Unfortunately, the marriage didn't last.

Tommy celebrates his third marriage to Katherine, a German doctor. They had two children, Christian and Alexandra.

British families in Copenhagen were rounded up by the invading Nazis on 9 April, 1940, and eventually sent home on a sealed train.

The 'Princes' of Danish Intelligence, a collective thorn in Tommy Sneum's side. (*From left to right*) Colonel Einar Nordentoft, Major Hans Lunding, Captain Volle Gyth.

Chapter 16

SIS, SOE AND A STRAINED MARRIAGE

BACK ON FANOE the following afternoon, there was a knock on the door of the Sneum family home. Christian Sneum found Hauptmann Meinicke, the German commander on the island, standing uncomfortably outside. Tommy later received from his father a detailed account of the conversation, which went as follows:

'May I come in?' asked the German.

The headmaster was too much of a gentleman to refuse, despite his resentment against the occupation, and showed his uninvited guest into the lounge.

'Sir, I'm afraid I have some bad news for you,' began Meinicke solemnly. 'It's your son Thomas. He took a plane and tried to fly out of Denmark with another man called Kjeld Pedersen.'

'Tried?'

Meinicke looked even more uneasy as he explained. 'It seems they were heading for England. But the plane was just a Hornet Moth, a single-engine trainer.'

Tommy's father asked if they had been shot down, and was relieved at least to hear that they had not. 'If this is true, is there any chance they may have got to England?'

'No chance,' the German officer said abruptly. 'The range of the plane was too short.'

Asked to explain further, Meinicke pointed out that the maximum range of a Hornet Moth was less than six hundred kilometres, while England was over seven hundred kilometres from Odense. 'Unfortunately, we can only conclude that your son is now at the bottom of the North Sea. I'm sorry.'

Sneum senior didn't know what to think. He had been told of the short message that Poul Andersen had heard on the BBC a few days earlier which had confirmed the safe arrival in England of two Danish pilots. Since then, he had allowed himself to believe that one of those pilots was Thomas. Now he wasn't so sure.

Meinicke saw what damage his news had caused. 'Mr Sneum,' he said, just before leaving, 'I know this won't come as any consolation, but I'll say it anyway. At his age, I might have done precisely the same thing, had I been in his shoes.'

■ ▓ ■

A week later Else Sneum would hear another version of what had become of her husband; one that was even less accurate than Meinicke's. She had already begun to worry about Tommy's long silence when a letter arrived at her parents' house in Copenhagen. She had been staying there with Marianne while Tommy supposedly established himself in Aalborg. When she recognised the handwriting on the envelope, it is likely that she thought he had finally got round to summoning the two of them to join him. Instead, the letter, posted locally on 5 July, was much more shocking. Sneum didn't keep a copy, but remembered more or less what he had written:

Dear Else,

This is a difficult letter to write because I know the news will break your heart for a while. You will think me a terrible husband and father to our baby. But a man has his pride and there was no work for me here in Denmark. I had to get away so that I can earn us some good money during these lean times, away from the restrictions imposed by the Germans. I sail for America tonight, so don't try to find me because I am already far away. I have been promised a job in New York and I will write again when I have something more positive to report.

Of course, I will understand if you don't want to wait for me. Ours has not been an ideal marriage. The changing events in Denmark have put an awful strain on us. We are both young and I am about to embark on a new adventure. Kiss our little Marianne for me and try to stay strong. Perhaps one day you will understand.

Love, Thomas

Else didn't know what to think. Had her husband gone off to war or simply left her for a new life in America? Either way, the news was dreadful, and left her with a small child to raise without any prospect of help from her husband.

When a stunned Else and her angry parents contacted Christian Sneum, he apologised on behalf of his son and regretted that he could add nothing to the confused picture. Only Thomas could explain his actions when he was ready; until then, the Sneum family would offer all their support in raising their granddaughter.

※ ▩ ※

If Tommy's heroics caused a strain in relations between the Jensens and Sneums, they didn't help relations between Ronald Turnbull and his SOE bosses back in England either. SOE Denmark's quiet beginning under Turnbull was in marked contrast to the shock waves Thomas Sneum was creating in the A2 (Danish) Section of SIS. Turnbull had regarded as premature SOE founder Sir Charles Hambro's demand for a campaign of sabotage against Nazi interests in Denmark. For the moment at least, the tentative Scot wanted to act merely as a channel for information coming from the established Danish Intelligence services. But Tommy's sparkling performance as an intelligence-gatherer was starting to make Ronnie's more measured approach look weak by comparison.

Turnbull worked methodically as he built the foundations of his operation, and explained why he followed such a conservative strategy much later: 'I regarded myself as a young amateur in the intelligence game and these Danish staff officers were experienced professionals.' His main contacts were Colonel Einar Nordentoft, Major Hans Lunding and Captain Volle Gyth. This trio formed the backbone of a group of Danish Intelligence officers who called themselves 'the Princes'. They were exceptionally cautious and made it clear they would be prepared to go into action against the Nazi regime only when the British attempted to liberate Denmark. In the meantime, they promised to prepare a secret army which would rise up in coordination with any planned British attack.

This assurance suited the Princes because it gave them the perfect excuse to do virtually nothing, perhaps for years. However, Turnbull concluded early in his reign as operational head of SOE Denmark that it would be worth far more to the Allies to have these men waiting passively on the inside than to risk aggravating them with a few spectacular but ultimately trivial sabotage missions. And if the Princes said they had established a secret army to help drive out the Nazis when the time was right, Turnbull saw little point in provoking them by setting up a rival network.

In London, though, Turnbull's bosses were rightly wary of relying on assurances from Danish military figures who had done nothing when Hitler had invaded their country and were, in essence, still doing nothing. Ideally, SOE's upper hierarchy wanted action – quick results from their new Danish Section to show Churchill that the fires of resistance in occupied Europe could spread north, too. Failing that, they favoured a hands-on approach to the organisation of the Danish secret army. At the appropriate moment, the British wanted to be able to sound the call to arms themselves, without having to deal with middlemen in Danish Intelligence.

Tommy Sneum was the sort of daredevil character who personified the British vision of what would be required when the tables were finally turned on the Germans in mainland Europe, so perhaps it was inevitable that his brilliance would shine into the rival corridors of London's spy world, reflecting unfavourably on Turnbull's tentative beginnings in Stockholm.

While SIS kept Tommy away from SOE, they were under a moral responsibility to share with their rivals at least some of the information he had delivered. However, Britain's established intelligence service didn't bother to tell the upstarts at SOE that they had recruited Sneum for a covert mission inside Denmark. Even so,

SOE were sufficiently impressed by what they heard to swing into action and exert pressure on their own field chief to take advantage. This was just the sort of dilemma Turnbull didn't want. Sneum had supplied enough information for the Scot to begin creating a secret army under direct SOE control, rather than continuing down his favoured route of channelling everything through the Princes. Nevertheless, he had to find an acceptable response to a communiqué from his superiors in London dated 14 July 1941:

> On 21 June last, two Danish Naval Lieutenants, pilots in the Air Arm, left Denmark in a borrowed Hornet Moth and flew to this country. As all civilian planes were immobilised in Denmark, they had to assemble their machine themselves. From the information they have given us, the following item is of interest as – if the information is correct – it will be of great assistance to us in carrying out our agreed plan.
>
> Holbaek Battery, equipped with 75mm and 15cm guns and 20mm AA guns, is still manned by 600 Danes under Captain Schou. They are said to be pro-Ally to a man and are ready to revolt if a British landing is made. The 600 men have petrol, arms and 11,000 rounds hidden away. Similar Batteries and similar pro-Ally Danish Garrisons are at Roskilde and Naestved. At the latter, there are also German soldiers, housed in some new barracks, built by the Danes.
>
> I feel we should immediately get to work amongst the Danish garrisons.

Turnbull would not have been pleased to receive what in effect was an order to act on Sneum's intelligence and have his own people move in on the Princes' domain. Although Sneum wasn't mentioned by name here, Turnbull's highly placed friends, Nordentoft, Lunding and Gyth, would soon have made it their business to discover the identities of these Danish naval lieutenants who had acted independently, and thereby put them all in such an awkward position.

*   *   *

Such ominous political undertones would eventually catch up with Tommy. But for a young man who had stared death in the face and lived to tell the tale, at the moment it simply felt good to be alive in the capital city of a free country. While Denmark and the task ahead would always be at the back of his mind, here was a chance to sample the good life again.

The Wellington Club in Knightsbridge always offered a fun environment, especially after Tommy began an affair with Rosie, the raven-haired manageress. It hardly seemed to matter that she was married because, of course, so was he. Both seemed to sense the romance had long-term potential, although Sneum wasn't about to be limited to one woman now, not with time so short. No one could have been more exciting or natural than Rosie, but that wasn't the point. For a confident young man, London was a heavenly playground.

The SIS was initially prepared to turn a blind eye to Tommy's nocturnal activities, as long as he showed dedication to their cause by day, and stayed away from certain high-profile haunts. Sneum wrote in his wartime report of this period: 'I got a daily visit from people from the Air Ministry, who wanted reports, sketches and information about various things from Denmark. I was told to keep away from the Danish Club and the Danish Legation. The Danish Club, in particular, was regarded as one of the dirtiest places in London, virtually a centre for German spies.'

But soon his new superiors grew uneasy about the number of women their agent was meeting. In vain, Rabagliati took steps to try to limit Sneum's social life. Tommy was transferred to the Ebury Court Hotel at 24 East Street. There Flight Officer Scrivener, a junior intelligence officer at the Air Ministry, who was also attached to SIS, was a long-term resident. His lifestyle was financed by a possessive mother, who would visit the hotel to check on her boy and then sit in the foyer all day writing letters. Sneum recalled: 'She was a jealous mother who wouldn't allow her son to have a lot of pleasure with other women.' Rabagliati considered the environment ideal, hoping Tommy's passions would be tempered by Mrs Scrivener's austere regime.

Sneum, though, had hopes of his own, and they didn't all revolve around women. He wanted the British to start showing the Danes some proper respect by incorporating them into the existing military structure. In his military report, he wrote:

For a period of 14 days I moved to the Ebury Court Hotel ... where a Flight Officer Scrivener from the Air Ministry lived anyway. Having agreed to go back to Denmark again, I had some conferences with Rabagliati, and worked out some plans with him. At the same time, I had to learn some of the British codes, and in return I told him some things from the Danish perspective. I told him what a boost to morale and how much satisfaction it would give us to have an acknowledged Danish Section in each British fighting service. I also told him about the Danish aviators who were waiting to come over, and how the RAF were very interested to get them over.

But he rejected my statements as no more than a question of prestige, motivated by pride alone, and one had the feeling that the English didn't wish to appreciate the Danish in this way ... even though I proved to them that we had more people in action than De Gaulle's people [the French], in relation to the population and size of forces, and De Gaulle was fully acknowledged. I'm convinced it would have been possible for me to succeed in persuading the British to appreciate the Danish, but I had to stay in the shadows because I wasn't officially there.

For a man who was supposed to be staying in the shadows, however, Tommy was rather busy in the social swirl of England's capital. During his fortnight at the Ebury Court, he did enough drinking and womanising to last most men several summers. In his mind Else and Marianne were now part of another world, far across the North Sea. And when the time came to return to Denmark on his mission, they would have to remain in that other world; for Tommy knew that he wouldn't be able to contact his wife because of the security risks involved. This didn't seem to bother him. In truth, he didn't miss her and he knew for sure now that he didn't love her either. The marriage had been a terrible mistake, a decision taken under extreme pressure. Besides, this was war; he could be dead in a month, like so many other young men. As far as he was concerned, he was single again – and time was short.

Tommy's attitude had a life-changing impact on Flight Officer Scrivener, his previously oppressed fellow guest at the hotel. Since young Scrivener had been designated to keep an eye on Sneum, he had no option but to go out with the Dane on his nights of debauchery. 'His mother thought I would lead him astray . . . and she was right,' recalled Tommy.

Some mornings they would stagger back into the hotel nursing headaches or trying to hide the smiles on their faces. The vigilant Mrs Scrivener was not pleased by this dramatic change in her offspring's behaviour; and it wasn't hard for her to work out who was to blame. Furious, she let her feelings be known in a series of confrontations with Tommy at the hotel. 'Christ Almighty, she was livid with me, this old dragon. But it was time her boy lived a little, and I made sure he did just that,' Tommy chuckled years later.

How much of this was reported to Rabagliati is not known. But it seems unlikely that Scrivener cut his own throat by relaying the full extent of his and Sneum's hedonism. Besides, on many of their nights out they bumped into none other than Flight Lieutenant Otto Gregory, Tommy's erstwhile interrogator in Battersea. Since Gregory was attached to the SIS it may have been no coincidence that their paths kept crossing, but if the dashing flight lieutenant was on a reconnaissance mission to see what Sneum was getting up to, he certainly didn't seem to find it an arduous task. In fact, despite being ten years older, his capacity for fun seemed to surpass even Tommy's. Sneum recalled:

> Gregory had the most beautiful girlfriends you could imagine. He also had a lot of effeminate men hanging around him, and people used to say he was bisexual. If he was, he never tried anything with me, and I liked him for daring to be so different. He was rather wealthy and I've heard he was one of the biggest playboys in London. In that respect we were different. I've never been a playboy. I did what I did in earnest.

Although that was a joke, Tommy did remain deadly serious in all his dealings by day, as he continued to take part in conferences with Rabagliati about the Danish situation and the dangerous task ahead. The older man gradually won Sneum's confidence, even though he didn't always tell his fledgling spy what he wanted to hear. And Tommy seemed to impress his new boss, even though Mrs Scrivener complained vociferously about the wild young Dane. The fun-loving pilot and worldly spymaster did their best to ignore the old woman, which contributed to such an excellent rapport that one day Rabagliati asked a very specific question: 'How highly do you rate Christian Michael Rottboell?'

Tommy remembered later how he answered: 'I liked Rottboell, he was an awfully nice chap. But it was his natural way to be as honest as he could be, he couldn't lie or do anything underhand. That's what I told Rabagliati.'

The colonel looked horrified at Sneum's reply, and screwed up his face. 'Rottboell can't lie? But you have to lie. It's the only way to survive in this game. If you ever bump into him again, don't tell him anything.'

Of course, Rabagliati had not merely been making conversation when he'd posed the question. Rottboell had ignored Sneum's instruction to wait for contact from England. Instead, he had used his political connections to reach Sweden by boat and had headed straight for the British Legation, where he had met Ronald Turnbull. On 28 July, the SOE field chief for Denmark had sent his immediate boss in London, Commander Ralph Hollingworth, the following communication:

1. Young Danish officer named Christian Rottboell visited me this morning with the following story.
2. He and friends Sneum and Pedersen, former a pilot, have made plans to extricate themselves and 20 flying officers from Denmark.
3. Sneum and Pedersen flew off in Moth from Flyn one month ago, in an attempt to reach England. They had agreed with Rottboell to send code message on BBC after arrival indicating day and time when RAF Flying Boat could pick up 20 Danes from Tissoe Lake South East of Kallundberg on Sjaelland, which lies in wooded district free from German troops.
4. Sneum himself visited Air Attaché here some months ago and was handed on to [BLANKED OUT] from CO. This confirmed.
5. Rottboell says he is nephew of Consul General in England, said to be keen vigorous young man.

6. Can you check this story? Think I could use R inside Denmark. He has visa for only two days so please reply immediately if you have any knowledge of the matter.

7. R says they have been listening for message on BBC but nothing comes through.

8. Suggest checking with Consul General if Nephew is tallying with Brown-Blond hair with deep-set strong brown eyes. R says he is mechanic not pilot.

Rabagliati's interest in Rottboell indicated that he thought the young Dane was about to be recruited by the SOE, for what might turn into a rival mission inside Denmark. The spymaster knew that time was short if he was going to get his own, SIS, agent back into Denmark early enough to take control of intelligence operations there for the British. The battle between the rival British departments was gathering pace, with the Danes their unwitting pawns. Tommy Sneum, who didn't even know the difference between SIS and SOE at the time, observed later: 'From what I understand there was a lot of jealousy from SOE people, afraid of their position, scared that they would not be recognised as proper intelligence officers.' But the insecurity ran two ways, with SIS equally concerned that their secret domain had been invaded by a bunch of bright, eager but inexperienced young SOE men, not long out of Oxford and Cambridge.

Linguistically at least, Rabagliati couldn't compete for Denmark against the twenty-eight-year-old Hollingworth, the SOE man who was effectively becoming his rival spymaster in London. 'Holly', as Turnbull called him, spoke such good Danish after working in business there before the war that he could pass as a native. He also had friends in high places, having been posted to SOE at the direct request of the organisation's chief, Sir Charles Hambro. But SIS, and Rabagliati in particular, were determined to show SOE who was boss in the world of covert operations. In the colonel's sphere, that meant winning the race to drop the first agents into Denmark – fully trained or not.

Who would prevail? Hollingworth was young and ambitious. His pointed nose, thin lips and narrow eyes gave the impression that he was more than capable of ruthlessness; and, indeed, he would demonstrate that quality in abundance in due course. Meanwhile, Rabagliati had already shown a killer instinct in battle, and age hadn't diminished the competitive edge he brought to everything he did.

The contest between SIS and SOE was well and truly under way. It would turn deadly before very long.

Chapter **17**

SPY SCHOOL

COLONEL RABAGLIATI SAT DOWN with Tommy in his hotel one day and worked out a plan of action for the pilot's return to Denmark. It would be something to hold on to during his darkest, loneliest moments as a British agent, a rulebook to be followed from the moment he first set foot on home soil. The early days would be the most dangerous. With that in mind, Tommy soon knew precisely whom he should and should not contact, and what his objectives were.

Sabotage or any open defiance of the Germans was out of the question. The Lake Tissoe plan, to pick up the twenty other Danish pilots, was similarly dismissed. The British wanted high-grade, regular intelligence about troop and ship movements, political and technological developments, defences, changes in German officer personnel, or in the civilian attitude towards the Germans; anything, in fact, that might be useful to the Allies. Sneum was given a new series of numbered codes, pertaining to each type of ship, its class and size, to simplify the dangerous job of transmitting back to Britain when the time came. He learned them under the watchful eye of MI6 instructors, whose job it was to ensure that he committed everything to memory.

The training course was held in a mansion called the House of Anna in West Dulwich, London, a white Georgian building with a mock-Greek façade. Tommy remembered:

The training was a scream. The British were trying to teach me the command structure of the German hierarchy. They produced detailed sketches of what they described as the latest uniforms of the Germans in Denmark. But I knew the uniforms had changed some months earlier.

I said, 'It's a good thing I've brought a copy of the *German Soldiers' Handbook* over with me.' Each soldier had this book as part of his basic kit and it was about an inch thick, showing all the exact, up-to-date uniforms and precisely how they should be worn, and weapon requirements in the tiniest detail. What amazed me was that the British didn't even know this book existed. I think I must have brought them their first copy.

This simple act probably saved many lives among the British agents and commandos who were sometimes asked to pose as German soldiers on the European mainland during daring missions to infiltrate and destroy key enemy installations. Duplicates of Tommy's German manual would have been distributed to all SIS sections as a matter of urgency. Thanks to him, German uniforms could now be copied with a precision which made a mockery of the outdated knowledge being imparted by the British intelligence specialists of the day.

Sneum reflected:

They had been too full of their own importance to check their facts properly. I understood the mentality of island people, coming from an island myself. But I have to admit that the arrogance showed by some of the instructors did anger and worry me. Some instructors knew the names of the capital cities of Europe; others didn't, and acted as though it didn't matter too much, because the cities were foreign. At the same time, the British honestly believed they could teach me more about my own country than I knew myself.

When the time came to learn the full range of coding, which was an essential part of any professional spy's work, Sneum felt luckier. Mr Jenkins, his instructor, was a charming, elderly gentleman untroubled by ego.

He was very kind and I appreciated his patience more than anything. He taught me how to create a coded message using a page in a newspaper or book of my choice. You had a personal prefix to your own special code in order to protect communications. You learned your personal five-figure number, then the code. A group of five figures gave the code type. You chose a book to use for coding and decoding the messages you sent. You had a page and a line and you had a prefix for that. Five figures, code, number. You were tested repeatedly, using different novels and newspapers.

The code course went well and Sneum was a model student. But, as usual, once he had worked hard, he liked to play hard. 'As soon as we had finished I took Mr Jenkins to a pub where I knew they had bottles of cold Danish beer. It made a pleasant change from having to put ice in the warm English bitter, because that seemed to shock people. I bought every single bottle of Danish beer they had. The bar staff kept it all in the fridge for me until I was ready to drink each one. Meanwhile, Mr Jenkins told wonderful stories, full of British humour.'

But time was short. Sneum wrote in a military report later: 'I was told that I would soon be going back to Denmark, and therefore there wasn't enough time for me to get sufficiently educated in Morse-Coding to use a transmitter myself. And because of that, they would find a man to go with me.' Perhaps it had always been the intention of Tommy's SIS spymasters to partner him with a radio expert. The added advantage of a two-man team was that if Sneum were killed or captured, the radio operator could take over all intelligence-gathering duties until a replacement agent was sent. Tommy was less than thrilled with the idea of becoming part of a double-act with someone he didn't know, but he decided to say nothing until the radio operator's identity had been revealed to him. That way he could assess for himself the character of the man upon whose competence his life might soon depend.

As July turned into August, the emphasis of the MI6 training turned away from cerebral matters and towards ruthless action. Sneum endured a punishing physical training course, made no easier by the fact that Tommy's fitness had dipped since he had left the Danish Navy. For weeks that summer he had either been sitting in confined spaces or drinking beer. But at least his insatiable appetite for women had kept him in some sort of shape. And a military man of twenty-four finds fitness easy enough to retrieve, given the right routine. Soon Tommy was running up hills and climbing ropes with the best of them, motivated by a sense of what might be waiting for him back home. He knew that his flight to England had probably made him a marked man among the pro-Nazi elements inside the Danish police. It followed that some of the most dangerous officers in the Abwehr would also be aware of his identity. If cornered, Sneum's gift for talking his way out of trouble might take him only so far. So the British wanted to ensure that he was ready for the alternative – a fight to the death.

Tommy had been a hard individual ever since he was first encouraged to stick up for himself at the age of five. He had attended the school in Nordby where his father was headmaster. As if this wasn't tricky enough for Tommy socially, he began his education at least a year earlier than the other local boys in his class. At six or seven, his classmates were much bigger, and ready to pick on him because of his family name. Tommy admitted: 'At first I tried to run, and fortunately I was usually fast enough to get away. But I knew that sooner or later I would have to make a stand.' Since his father was essentially a pacifist, it was Sneum's grandfather, a gnarled old sailor called Thomas Sonnichsen Hansen, who helped him find the courage to fight the bullies. The advice was simple: 'Never give in to anyone,' Sonnichsen Hansen warned little Tommy. 'Ever.'

Tommy, who adored his grandfather, wanted to please him, but the next time he was bullied he lost his nerve and ran away again. He recalled: 'I felt so ashamed that I had let my grandfather down, because I loved him very much. So I found out where this bully played after school, and then I went there, attacked him with a stick and beat him almost to a pulp.'

From those crude beginnings, he had learned other ways to hurt people and defend himself, and built a fearsome reputation for someone of his modest build. He had boxed in the Danish Navy and fought like a tiger when pushed, as Kjeld Pedersen could testify. So Tommy thought he knew enough to get the better of most adversaries already, but the SIS hand-to-hand combat course gave his self-defence a new dimension. He was familiar with some of the throws and moves from his naval training, including the correct hold and procedure for snapping a man's neck. But the MI6 instructors opened up a new world of pressure points and seemingly effortless moves which could incapacitate or kill an opponent.

Once, when Tommy had imbibed perhaps a little too much schnapps, he told the author: 'There is a gap between the cranium and the jawbone, behind each ear lobe. I was taught how to exploit those pressure points with a firm push of the thumbs. I'll show you if you like.' It was the second time he had offered to kill me, and for the second time I politely declined. Anyone who met Thomas Sneum knew immediately that he was not a man to be crossed. He had possessed a ruthless streak since childhood, for instance learning at the age of ten a particularly shocking way to kill ducks: 'You can wring a duck's neck, but it takes quite a lot of energy, and isn't a very efficient way to kill. A quick bite into the duck's skull did the job with the minimum of fuss. With practice, you can crush the skull with your teeth without getting anything in your mouth at all.'

The education Tommy received on the MI6 course seemed to be no more than an extension of the principles of killing he had learned as a boy: namely, attack the weak point with maximum force and a minimum exertion of energy. Armed with his new arsenal of lethal British tips, he knew would be able to dispatch any adversary quickly and silently back in Denmark.

Even so, Sneum's chances of survival as a spy in Nazi-occupied Europe would depend heavily on the calibre of the man chosen to go with him. Given that MI6 had told Tommy there wasn't enough time to get his Morse code fully up to speed, it took them what seemed like an age to come up with the 'expert' who was supposed to send his messages for him. In his military report of his summer in England, Sneum wrote: 'It looked as though it was even harder than they had thought to find a man for me. In the end, they chose Sigfred Christophersen, but he also needed some training. So it all took such a long time that I could have learned [Morse code] for myself.'

When Tommy was introduced to his wireless operator and

partner for the mission, he was sceptical. Sigfred Johannes Christophersen, who had celebrated his twenty-seventh birthday on 11 June, was so tall and lean that he stood out from the crowd. Tommy was concerned that Sigfred's build might make him too easily identifiable for covert operations, but there was something else about him, too. It was as though Christophersen hadn't begun to prepare himself mentally for the enormity of what they were about to do. Also, there was no natural affinity between the two men.

SIS hadn't foreseen any potential problems between the pair. They were both young, enthusiastic and seemingly courageous; and their pasts pointed to similar ambitions. Handsome and hitherto adventurous, Sigfred's story was almost as dramatic as Sneum's, despite unremarkable beginnings. He had joined the Royal Lifeguard Regiment in November 1935 but found army life too mundane. So he applied to the Flying School in Vaerloese, where he enrolled on 1 April 1937. All went well until the following year, when his superiors noticed that he had started to cut corners and no longer flew according to the rulebook. Deemed a liability, he was thrown out of the school on 10 September 1938, his military career in tatters. After six months' unemployment, he went to Germany and found work as a gardener. But he spotted a way to beat the boredom in the middle of January 1940, when he volunteered to become a pilot in the Finno-Russian War. For the next ten weeks he flew for the Finns, although Sneum later insisted that Christophersen had never been involved in any kind of aerial combat during that period. The brief and bloody conflict was over by the end of March 1940, and for Sigfred that signalled another downturn in his fortunes.

He returned to Denmark, only to face a fresh period of unemployment, this time caused by the German invasion. Increasingly desperate, he worked that summer under the occupiers back at Vaerloese airfield. But his conscience was clearly nagging away at him. In mid-October he and two comrades quit their jobs and came up with a brilliant plan to travel to England and serve with the RAF. The trio obtained visas to travel to Turkey on the pretext of buying tobacco there. Five days later, to their own astonishment, they were in Istanbul. Instead of seeking out tobacco merchants, though, they reported directly to the British Air Attaché and volunteered for the RAF. The Air Attaché welcomed the offer and gave the Danes some money for food and lodgings. They were instructed to remain in Istanbul and await further orders. Their patience paid off when, on 10 February 1941, they were told to board a ship. It took them south to the Cape of Good Hope and all the way back north to England, where they arrived on 23 April 1941. Their story was checked at the Royal Patriotic School, just as Sneum's would be two months later.

By the time the British were satisfied, however, Christophersen had heard alarming stories about the mortality rates among pilots in the Battle of Britain. He was therefore more than happy to accept an approach from British Intelligence, who trained him in radio-telegraphy. The course intensified when he was earmarked to accompany Sneum back into Denmark.

One of Christophersen's colleagues on the journey from Turkey had been Jorgen Thalbitzer. He went through with the original plan and signed up for the RAF. Later, he was shot down over France and imprisoned in a German prisoner-of-war camp, from which he subsequently made a spectacular escape.

Sneum met Thalbitzer in the summer of 1941, before the latter's heroics, and the pair got on well. He was less enthusiastic about Christophersen, but he hoped that this opinion would change once they got to know each other better. Perhaps in a bid to achieve some bonding, SIS moved the taller man to the Ebury Court Hotel, but this only exacerbated the tension. By the time the pair were moved into a rented flat at 206 Rodney House, Dolphin Square, it was time for some straight talking. One night after dinner and several beers, Sneum asked his partner why he wanted to leave England so soon after arriving.

'It's too dangerous to stay here and join the RAF,' explained Sigfred. 'Have you heard how many pilots are being killed? It's too risky.'

'What we're going to be doing is a hell of a lot more dangerous than joining the RAF,' Sneum told him. 'Do you know what it'll be like for us if we get caught?'

'I'm not worried about that,' Christophersen said dismissively.

Tommy couldn't believe what he was hearing. 'You're not worried about being tortured or shot?'

'We don't have to let it get to that, do we?' Sneum was speechless, so Sigfred filled the silence. 'I'm in no hurry to die. I'll do my bit, and a lot more. But if we get compromised, I want to survive.'

Tommy was stunned, and as he said later: 'From that moment I considered him to be a danger to the mission, a threat to my safety, and a coward. We all had fears and doubts about how we would react when faced with torture. But you had to suppress those feelings.'

As a two-man team, Tommy and Christophersen were supposed to be ready to protect each other to the death on their return to Nazi-occupied Denmark. Yet here was a man who seemed to be implying that he would rather tell the Germans everything than face an unpleasant ordeal. As far as Sneum was concerned, Sigfred might as well have admitted on the spot that he would sell Tommy's life in exchange for his own. Sneum got up and walked out.

Chapter **18**

A RECIPE FOR DISASTER

THOMAS SNEUM CONFRONTED Colonel Rabagliati at the first opportunity. He couldn't understand how someone like Christophersen had got this far in the selection process. Later Tommy emphasised: 'By now I was completely opposed to using him, and I told the colonel that. I said, "He is afraid, he has warned me that he is only going back to Denmark because he believes it is certain death to stay in England, and he will tell the Germans everything if they get hold of him."'

Rabagliati seemed to think Sneum was exaggerating his concerns, because he replied simply: 'We haven't got anyone else. You'll have to use him.'

Tommy replied: 'I can find you a number of better people you could use.'

But the spymaster wasn't having it. 'They must be trained here,' he insisted.

With a tinge of bitterness, Sneum reflected later: 'They thought if you hadn't been trained in England, you couldn't put your hand on a Morse code key.'

The policy would change later in the war, partly because of what later happened to Tommy. It was a security safeguard which had been put in place to prevent the Abwehr from using their own operators to send false messages, having tortured the relevant codes out of captured agents. SOE in Holland was destroyed through such German tactics, with nearly all the British-run spies eventually shot. So it was no wonder that SIS was keen to keep as much control as it could over radio communications.

'It has to be that way,' said Rabagliati. 'The operators here need to know the personal Morse style of the sender to be sure that he's genuine. They know Christophersen's Morse hand now. It's as simple as that. He'll have to go with you.'

This logic still seemed like nonsense to Tommy. The personnel receiving the messages back in England were subject to such a rapid turnover that, within a few months, Sneum predicted that no one would be left who had even heard of Christophersen, let alone studied his Morse hand during training.

Looking back, Tommy attributed Rabagliati's final decision to go with Christophersen no matter what the risks to the in-fighting between Britain's covert services: 'SOE was also trying to go into Denmark, and there was competition between them and SIS to see who could send the first team in. Personal pride came before the cause.' According to some accounts, SOE were already angling to take over *all* covert operations in Denmark. And with Sir Charles Hambro as a personal supporter, there could be little doubt that Commander Ralph Hollingworth, the rising star of SOE's Danish Section, had a powerful ally where it mattered. For the SIS to be outmanoeuvred in this way by the SOE 'amateurs' would have seemed unthinkable to the long-standing professionals at 54 Broadway. And Colonel Euan Rabagliati especially was not a man who liked to come second.

However, none of these political factors were known to Sneum on that August morning in 1941. In fact, he still didn't even know the name of the organisation that had recruited him. All he knew for sure was that he was being sent into Nazi-occupied territory with a man he didn't like or trust.

*   *   *

About two weeks before radio instruction was due to be completed, Charles Seymour, Rabagliati's number two, arrived at Rodney House unexpectedly. He told Sneum and Sigfred to pack four days' worth of kit. Seymour, who had left a job in the tobacco trade in China to serve his country, was a good-natured twenty-seven-year-old with precious little military experience. He had been brought into SIS by Claude Dansey because his mother spoke fluent Dutch and because he had the right family credentials. At that time he had been known by his real name, Dudley Overton Seymour. He had spent precisely one day in the Tank Corps before his sudden recruitment by MI6 and had mixed feelings about the switch: he had crossed the globe to fight for Britain, and this clandestine organisational work didn't sound like fighting at all. So it was a reluctant Captain Seymour who joined the Broadway team at the start of 1941, as Rabagliati's assistant in the nerve centre of British Intelligence.

Almost immediately he was invited to change his name; not by MI6, but by a secretary who worked inside its headquarters. At twenty-one, Hazel Wonnacott had already been out with a man named Dudley, and she didn't have fond memories of the affair.

'So what do you want to call me?' Seymour wasn't about to let his name spoil a chance of romance.

'Charles. Yes, Charlie, that'll do,' said Hazel.

The name stuck for the rest of his life. By the late summer of 1941, Charles Seymour and Hazel Wonnacott were engaged to be married, with the date set for 6 September. Although the wedding was only days away, Seymour still had to concentrate on his job.

Charlie was more comfortable with the Dutch side of the A2 operation, but his duties naturally extended to Denmark. So here he was, ready to drive Britain's first two Danish agents out of London in the direction of Manchester. They jumped into the sports car Rabagliati had lent Seymour especially for the task, and sped up to their new base for parachute training – Ringway Airport in Wilmslow. Tommy broke into a wry smile years later when he thought about the inconvenient location. 'It all had to be done in the most difficult and expensive way, otherwise it was no good,' he suggested dryly.

First came the preparatory phase of their training, when the agents were protected by a harness. Before their technique had become adequate, however, it was time for the real thing. Over the next four days, they parachuted day and night. Sneum recalled:

'You had to do six jumps to get a certificate, although what use that piece of paper could have been to us where we were going was anyone's guess. Then we had to do a couple of jumps from low altitude. I did at least ten jumps that week.'

Night jumps from low heights were the most treacherous. Tommy would still be adapting his eyes to the darkness when he was jerked upwards by the sudden opening of his parachute; and he would barely have recovered before colliding with the ground below. 'How I didn't break my legs on that first night of jumping, I'll never know,' he said.

In the final twenty-four hours of the course they made three jumps, the last one at night. Due to high winds, the SIS team was advised not to jump, but an uncomfortable Seymour explained that they had to, since there was no more time in which to complete the course. In the murky light, Sneum's parachute opened late and the ground arrived early. He hit at force, which stunned him temporarily, and he didn't react quickly enough to what happened next. Before he knew it, the wind had dragged him across the field. 'I was being scraped and bumped along the ground at speed, face down,' he remembered. 'I couldn't seem to free myself from the harness.' When he finally managed to do so, he sat in a dazed heap, cursing Seymour for ignoring the warnings. Sneum was now going into Denmark with a broken nose and conspicuous cuts and bruises. 'It was a bit stupid of them to send me to Denmark a few days after I'd smashed up my face,' he reflected.

* * *

It was the first week of September when the SIS mission to Denmark received its final green light. MI6 was about to join the war in Denmark. Seymour celebrated by tying the knot with Hazel in Exeter Cathedral, then SIS allowed the newly-weds a five-day honeymoon in the charming Cornish fishing village of Mullion.

Back in London, Sneum and Christophersen were ordered to rip all conspicuous labels off their clothes, and were given a little Swedish and Danish money. The problem was that Danish cash was particularly hard to come by, and when the time came the British had only a single five-hundred-krone note to hand over to their spies. For some reason, it was given to Christophersen, but Tommy decided not to protest. He already had a bad feeling about the mission, so one more piece of stupidity didn't seem to make much difference.

On 9 September 1941, Sneum and Christophersen were put on to a Whitley bomber at a small airfield outside Newmarket, Suffolk, and flown across the North Sea into Danish airspace. Their parachute drop was delayed by thick cloud, and confusion reigned in the cockpit over their precise location. But a difficult flight was about to get worse. Tommy recalled: 'Suddenly we saw tracer fire coming straight up at us, and it looked as if it was going to score a direct hit. The flak was uncomfortably heavy.'

The British crew didn't take long to decide they had to turn back. But no one realised just how close the flak had come to taking their lives until they examined the aircraft, after landing back in Newmarket. Sneum remembered: 'The fuselage was peppered with holes: we counted thirty-seven. We had been lucky and the pilot was surprised at how much damage there was.' The night's trauma had been for nothing, but at least they were still alive.

The weather forecast was so bad the following day that they didn't even try to reach Denmark. Rabagliati could see how wound up Tommy had become, so he took him out for a drive through some of Suffolk's country lanes in his Bentley.

'I want to show you a little trick I learned from my racing days,' he said. 'If you survive the war, you might be able to use it. Good pilots are often good drivers. Do you like fast cars?'

'Yes, sir,' replied Sneum. 'Malcolm Campbell tried for the land speed record on my home island when I was a boy. There were races too, but one of my friends was killed by a flying wheel and that put a stop to it all.'

'Dangerous business,' said Rabagliati sympathetically, and pointed to the huge dent in his skull. 'Don't worry,' he added, 'my brains are still where I need them to be.' Turning his attention to the Bentley, he said: 'See the clutch? When you're racing, you don't necessarily need it. Not if you have a good ear for music.'

Tommy was baffled, so Rabagliati decided to demonstrate. He hit the accelerator on a straight stretch and the Bentley roared forwards, but when he heard the engine strike a certain pitch, he flicked the gear-stick into neutral. On the cue of a new engine note, he changed down into a lower gear. The car had barely lost any speed during this manoeuvre; and at no point had Rabagliati touched the clutch. 'See?' Triumphant, the colonel performed the trick again, then turned to his pupil. 'Now you try.'

They swapped places and Sneum had a go. Soon he had the hang of it.

'You're a natural,' said Rabagliati. 'Don't make a habit of this if you're not racing. Cocks up the car. But it's fun, isn't it?'

Tommy couldn't argue with that. The tension caused by the long wait for that elusive take-off all but dissipated as they sped through the flat Cambridgeshire lanes. Sneum wondered how the colonel might explain a road accident to his superiors, just hours before his protégé was due to set off on an important mission. But Rabagliati knew what he was doing; he had demonstrated his little trick as a precursor to raising more serious matters.

'Look, Sneum, I know we've had a difference of opinion over Christophersen. And I know you dislike him. But he's all you've got, so use him and put up with it. Try to work together as a team.'

'Yes, sir.' Tommy decided it was pointless to argue further.

'And if he really puts you in the shit or becomes a genuine threat to security, there's a simple solution,' added Rabagliati.

'What's that?' Sneum expected more talk of compromise from his British handler.

'Kill him.'

Rabagliati's suggestion was exactly what Tommy had wanted to hear, and perhaps the colonel saw as much in his agent's eyes. 'But you'd need a bloody good reason,' added the older man.

By the time they had returned to the airfield on that September day in 1941, Sneum was buoyant again. He felt as though he had gained a little more control over his destiny because of what had been said on those country roads. And to aid his mood, the weather had improved. It looked as if they would soon be ready to go.

Chapter **19**

INTO ACTION

ON THE NIGHT OF 11 SEPTEMBER 1941, less than three months after his arrival in England, Tommy Sneum climbed back into the Whitley bomber with Sigfred Christophersen, and braced himself for the roller-coaster ride to Denmark. Although Christophersen was still carrying nearly all their money, Sneum put his concerns to one side and drifted off to sleep. This time there was no German anti-aircraft fire to disturb him. Before he knew it, though, the red light came on to indicate that they were flying over the drop-zone at Agerup, near Roskilde, just thirty kilometres west of Copenhagen. Sneum was woken and told to move to the exit door so that he would be ready to jump straight after Christophersen. An English sergeant checked that their static lines were securely hooked on to the rig. Then the two parachutists watched and waited for the green light. It came at 11.40 p.m., and Sigfred was gone in an instant. 'I pushed him,' admitted Tommy later. 'Just in case he hesitated.' Sneum then peered down to make sure that his colleague's canopy had opened. As soon as he glimpsed the white flurry of Christophersen's parachute unfurling in the gloom, Sneum prepared to jump. But there was a problem: 'The sergeant was fooling with the static line, and before he cleared everything we had flown on another kilometre.'

When finally given the signal, Tommy jumped in a hurry. The icy

air battered his face as he hurtled towards the earth and struggled
to fill his lungs with the oxygen his body demanded. Suddenly he
was wrenched up into the night and the parachute's canopy began
to flap noisily above him. Despite the training he had undergone at
Ringway, the shock still stunned him. But he knew there would be
time to regain his composure during the final, quieter phase of the
drop. Or at least he thought there would be: 'The 'chute had just
unfolded when I felt something sharp tear into my legs and
backside.' Before he even had time to bend his legs to absorb some
of the impact, he crashed through a barbed-wire fence backwards
and slammed into the ground with an ugly thud. 'I rolled over on
my shoulder but the sudden jolt of the impact damaged my lower
jaw and some of my teeth. I then felt a terrible pain just above my
buttocks. I thought I must have broken something, perhaps even
my back, and I was worried I wouldn't be able to walk.'

He cursed his luck: 'There are very few hills in Denmark and
somehow we had managed to find one,' he explained with a smile.
'That meant the pilot must have drifted off course.'

Unclipping his parachute, he tried to stand. As soon as he got to
his feet, however, he felt the searing pain from just above his
buttocks again, only this time even more intensely. 'It was
excruciating work just to fold up the parachute,' he recalled. 'I'd
never known anything like it. And I could feel warm blood on my
legs from the cuts.'

At least that meant he hadn't severed his spinal cord. 'I
suspected damage to my coccyx but knew there was nothing I
could do, except to swig cognac from the hip flask I had brought
with me for my cover story – that I had been at a party all night.'
Some party. He had torn one of the legs of his civilian suit,
although at least the everyday shoes in which he had chosen to
jump, against British advice, were still firmly on his feet.

Tommy knew he had to move quickly, whatever the source of
his pain. 'It wasn't nice walking but you can manage an awful lot
in this life if you have to, and I had no choice.' To stay where he
was, on a ridge with no cover, might lead to his capture before
dawn. 'There was moonlight and you could easily see,' he
remembered. 'I looked around to see if Christophersen was
anywhere near by, but there was no sign of him. I didn't know what

had happened to him but I knew that if he got caught they would look for me.'

He spotted a wood below him and headed for that. Once among the trees, he tried to shut out the pain as he dug a hole at the foot of an old, distinctive stump. Then he buried his parachute beneath the roots, replaced the fresh earth and shuffled away as quickly as possible. Only the parachute could prove beyond all doubt that he was a spy. Now he had taken care of it.

There was little point in wasting any more time searching for Christophersen: 'We had an agreement that we should meet the next morning in a certain district of Copenhagen if we got split up on landing.' So Tommy came out of the trees and walked to the nearest road, where he could see a sign in the distance. As he did so, beams from a car's headlights shot across the scene, though the vehicle itself was still some way off. He had time to drop under the cover of some bushes, but the sudden evasive action made him want to scream with pain. He stopped himself from doing so when he realised the type of car that was coming his way. 'It was a Danish police car, going quite slowly. That got me worried. We were in the middle of nowhere, so what was a patrol car doing out there?' As he listened to the growl of the engine pass and fade, he wondered if the parachute canopies had been spotted in the few moments it had taken to land.

Gingerly, he rose to his feet and walked back over to the road-sign. To his horror, he saw that he had landed at Brorfelde, near Holbaek, a full eighty kilometres from Copenhagen. But more worrying than his own isolation was the thought of Christophersen trying to cover that sort of distance to the Danish capital without arousing suspicion. Tommy feared that his untrustworthy comrade would head instead for Holbaek.

'If he got caught they would look for me there too,' Tommy explained. 'So I decided to do what would be least expected of me, and walk fifteen kilometres to the next town after that, Ringsted.'

In fact, Christophersen had decided to lie low until dawn in the field where he had landed, hoping that his descent from the skies had gone unnoticed. This contravened British orders to vacate the drop-zone as quickly as possible. If the area were to be sealed off, he would be trapped, so he was taking a big risk.

Meanwhile, Tommy took another long swig of cognac from the flask, and tipped some of the liquor on to his clothes to support the cover story about his drunken night out. Though the analgesic properties of the cognac increased his mobility, he still found it hard going. Any strange noise or distant flicker of lights made him crawl for cover, increasing his discomfort. Mostly, though, he passed silently through villages and never saw a soul. 'I could sometimes hear people talking behind closed shutters. Or dogs barking – they probably smelled me.'

When he noticed the first streaks of dawn, Tommy knew he would have to face the local population. He looked at his shabby civilian clothes and hoped they would be enough to make him credible. It was not uncommon for young men to fight or get drunk at parties; and despite the old bruises on his face, the fresh damage to his mouth and the blood on his leg, he offered a hearty 'good morning' to passers-by and pretended to be proud of his laddish exploits. 'If asked about my injuries, I was going to say that I had been involved in an argument over a girl. As it turned out, no one asked.'

By the time he reached central Ringsted, it was almost light. He spotted a single taxi parked at a rank, with the driver waiting patiently in the hope of early morning trade. 'You'll have to forgive me,' said Sneum. 'I've had a few drinks and I'm a bit of a mess. Are women worth all the trouble they get us into? Please, take me to Copenhagen so I can forget all about it.'

The driver looked unhappy about his potential fare's state, but he weighed that against the small fortune a trip to the capital would net him. He put a towel out on the passenger seat and told Tommy to get in.

In the meantime, Christophersen had waited until dawn to walk to the nearest railway station at Grandloese, south of Holbaek. Now he was bound for Copenhagen on a morning commuter train, a risky journey if his dishevelled state aroused suspicion among his fellow passengers.

As Tommy's taxi sped through the western suburbs and neared the centre of the Danish capital, the streets were already busy. He felt quietly exhilarated that he had got this far under difficult circumstances. When he asked the driver to stop, however, he realised that he had no Danish money. It was a tense moment as he pulled out some Swedish kronor and tried to explain. He made up a story about having recently returned from a business trip across the Oeresund, only to walk straight into an argument with his two-timing girlfriend. She had gone off with their Danish money, he had fought his love rival and now he was in this rather embarrassing predicament. As one man to another, he hoped the taxi driver would show a little compassion and accept his payment in Swedish money.

Much as he sympathised, the driver wouldn't play ball. He suggested they go to Copenhagen railway station, where Sneum could change his funds into the local currency.

'I thought, Bloody hell, this is going to be dangerous – the railway station in Copenhagen was usually crawling with Germans. But I couldn't think of an alternative.' As he walked into the station, the blood on his torn trousers dark and dry, he avoided eye contact with anyone in uniform. The last thing he wanted was for his forged papers and shaky cover story to be put to the test by the Danish police or their Nazi masters. 'My heart was pounding when I went up to an exchange counter, especially when I saw a doubtful expression on the face of the clerk. Even after I changed the money and began walking back towards the taxi, I thought I might feel a hand on my shoulder and hear the order to stop.' He walked on, and paid off the taxi driver without being challenged. It was hard to know which of the men looked more relieved as they parted company.

Shuffling along quietly, Sneum reached the designated rendezvous point at 10.00 a.m. He had arranged to meet Christophersen outside the home of his sister and brother-in-law, Margit and Niels-Richard Bertelsen, in Njalsgade. But Tommy was horrified to discover they had moved in his absence. As fate would have it, though, he bumped into Christophersen just as the latter turned to leave the same address. Sigfred looked nervous, particularly when he saw the state Tommy was in. 'Relax,' said Sneum as he shook hands with his partner. 'All is well.' They arranged to meet again later, when Tommy had done something about his appearance and injuries.

* * *

Sneum called Professor Ole Chiewitz, a tuberculosis expert and known resistance sympathiser, who had helped him in the past.

'The first time I met Chiewitz,' Tommy recalled later, 'I thought, If God came down again in human form His eyes and smile would look like this. He had the eyes of an angel and the warmest smile I have ever seen.'

But Chiewitz wasn't smiling when he saw the state of Sneum. Quickly he arranged an X-ray in the hospital where he worked. It revealed a vertical crack down the length of Tommy's coccyx.

'Are you in pain?' asked the doctor, his face a picture of bewilderment.

Uncharacteristically, Sneum admitted that he was.

'You shouldn't be able to walk at all,' added Chiewitz's colleague. 'I can't understand it.'

Tommy had marched fifteen kilometres fuelled by adrenalin and cognac when many men would simply have curled up in agony. Now he was told the fracture would mend of its own accord with rest. Chiewitz offered to arrange a bed in the hospital so that Sneum could recover from his ordeal.

'That won't be necessary,' insisted Tommy. 'Please just prescribe some painkillers. I'll come back if I think I'm in trouble.'

Chiewitz persuaded him to wait long enough to see a trusted friend and colleague called Professor Hagedorn, a world-renowned expert on diabetes. When Hagedorn arrived, he collected a urine sample. Although Sneum cooperated, he didn't see the point of this unrelated procedure and said so.

'If ever you need to hide,' Hagedorn explained, 'you can come back into this hospital and we'll be able to prove you have diabetes.'

'One problem,' replied Tommy. 'I don't have diabetes.'

Hagedorn took out some powdered pure grape sugar and dropped it into Sneum's sample before stirring gently. 'You do now,' he said with a smile.

Chapter **20**

A FRAGILE FOOTHOLD

TOMMY WAS MORE WORRIED about having to work with Christophersen than his own physical problems. He had hoped his partner's attitude would harden once their mission had begun. Instead it appeared that the reverse was true. Christophersen had just confided to Sneum: 'Now that we are back in Denmark I feel safe.'

Tommy was astonished at the remark. 'When you're with me, you're not going to be safe,' he warned. 'That's not the way I fight my war.'

He wanted to leave the timid Sigfred somewhere quiet for a few days, allowing him to take the first steps on his mission for the British alone. So he took a tram to the northern suburb of Soeborg, to visit Kaj Oxlund and his wife Tulle. They lived in a leafy boulevard called Noekkerosevej, situated far from the capital's busy centre. Tommy figured that even Christophersen could stay out of trouble there. The Oxlunds had rented a spacious first-floor flat in an elegant four-storey block, the last building on the right-hand side as Tommy walked down the street. He looked forward to the reunion.

When he opened his apartment door, Kaj Oxlund looked shocked to see his old friend standing there. 'Sneum. I thought you were dead.'

Tommy smiled. 'Can I come in, or has Tulle banned your friends?' He saw Oxlund wince at the casual remark, and noticed that the apartment, though tidy, lacked the female touch.

Kaj must have read his mind. 'Actually, Sneum, you might as well know. We've separated.'

Tommy was stunned. 'After nine years? It'll only be temporary, my friend. What happened?'

Oxlund explained that all of his trips to Sweden and throughout Denmark had meant he could never honestly explain his movements to his wife. They had drifted apart, and she seemed to think he was having an affair. Kaj had always said he was going away on business; but since the couple's money worries had worsened, Tulle didn't believe his alibis. She had left just a few weeks earlier, though Kaj had seen it coming for some time. Sadly, he had felt unable to do anything about it.

Tommy had never loved Else quite like Oxlund loved Tulle, but he too knew how much damage the war could do to a relationship. When you were intelligence-gathering, and you couldn't tell your wife a thing about it, the excuses you concocted for your absences didn't do much for mutual understanding.

Nevertheless, before the Nazi invasion, Kaj and Tulle had been as happy and settled as any couple Tommy had ever known. He felt sure those good times still had to count for something. 'She'll be back, Oxlund. You'll see.'

'No, she won't,' the older man replied with a bitter smile. 'I received a letter a few days ago. She's filing for divorce.'

Sneum didn't know what to say by way of comfort, so he told Kaj about his own situation: why he had asked his friend to post that letter to Else during the summer; and that he was no longer with his wife, either. Oxlund offered his friend a beer, as men often do in moments of emotional crisis. Before long they had resolved not to depress each other any further. Seeking to change the mood, Sneum asked if Kaj would like to get involved in something that would be sure to take his mind off his personal situation. 'Could be risky though,' he warned. 'And you'll have some company too, if that's all right.'

The brutal fact was that Tulle's departure was an advantage when it came to the mission. For a start, she wouldn't be able to ask any tricky questions about Christophersen if he came to stay. And Oxlund could put all his energy into resistance work instead of trying to rescue his dying marriage.

In Sneum's absence, Kaj had continued with his intelligence-gathering. All summer he had diligently compiled reports and made sure they reached the British Legation in Stockholm. Disappointingly, the proposed landing of a Sunderland sea-plane on Lake Tissoe had remained nothing more than a distant dream. But there was still plenty of interest to Sneum. And, crucially, Kaj said he was willing to welcome Christophersen, temporarily or otherwise. He could do with the company, he said a little forlornly.

Tommy's next objective on behalf of the British was to make contact with Danish Intelligence. The German occupying forces, obeying an order from Berlin, had left this organisation intact ever since the invasion. Hitler saw no great threat from Denmark, and sought to show the world he was capable of a 'model occupation' in at least one neighbouring country. Meanwhile, to ensure their continued survival, the leading figures within Danish Intelligence, the so-called Princes, were anxious that no one should upset the delicate peace in Denmark. Any contact with the British would be made in great secrecy, if at all, and they certainly had no intention of leading a full-blown Danish resistance movement. Tommy had been trying to find out if these Princes were already sending information to any organisation in Britain. And in spite of their reluctance to rock the boat, he hoped to incorporate them into the new spy ring which Rabagliati had empowered him to create and lead. On hearing of his arrival, however, the Princes warned Sneum, through an intermediary called Bjarke Schou, that they required proof of the incoming agent's story before they were even prepared to meet him. Only if he could produce sizeable pieces of both parachutes – his and Christophersen's – would the meeting take place.

Later Tommy explained: 'The Princes didn't believe I could have flown out of Denmark in the first place, not without the blessing of the Germans.' Furthermore, they doubted the Allies would drop agents in Denmark without consulting them first. Such a policy went against everything that had been agreed with the British through their intermediary in Sweden, a journalist called Ebbe Munck. Not for the last time, the source of this dangerous confusion lay in the interdepartmental rivalry between the Secret Intelligence Service and the Special Operations Executive back in Britain.

Munck, Sneum and the Princes all had no grasp of the difference between SIS and SOE, because the British hadn't told them. The Princes had simply been informed they were supplying information to a very specialised section of British Intelligence, focused on Denmark in particular. In fact, it was Ronnie Turnbull's SOE office, based in neutral Stockholm, which had struck the deal with Danish Intelligence. In return for information, the Princes were told they would be left as the sole agents for intelligence-gathering in their own country. No British spies would be sent into Danish territory unless they were in transit, either on their way to or returning from Germany or destinations further east.

It was because this agreement was in place that Sneum's arrival caused such consternation, and why the Princes demanded such incontrovertible proof of his authenticity. Unbeknown to him, Tommy could hardly have been placed in a more hostile environment if he had landed in Berlin itself. Largely due to the competitiveness among the rival British spymasters, he was already being viewed with extreme suspicion by key compatriots back home. And in this tense climate he could easily be made the scapegoat for anything that went wrong in Denmark.

But all Tommy knew at the time was the importance of recovering the parachutes. The following morning, therefore, he contacted Christophersen and demanded precise details of where the radio man had buried his canopy. Then he came up with a new cover story in case he was challenged: 'I obtained a smock, an easel, some canvases and paints,' he explained. 'Then I went back out to Brorfelde, dressed like an artist in search of a landscape to paint.' He cut a strip off each parachute and hid them between the canvases, knowing all too well that part of the canopy which had saved his life only hours earlier could now get him killed if he was stopped and searched on his way back to civilisation.

When he handed over his proof to Bjarke Schou, the Princes' intermediary, in a graveyard outside Holbaek that night, he felt more anger than relief. The face-to-face meeting with the men behind these demands promised to be lively.

It took place at the Jaegersborg Kaserne in Kongens, barracks that were home to the Royal Lifeguards. Over dinner, Lunding, the hard man of Danish Intelligence, demanded Sneum's British codes. Refusing to take orders from someone he had just met, Tommy in turn demanded to know the codes his hosts used: 'I told them I was serving directly with the British and that made me their superior. They told me I was talking nonsense because their rank was far superior. I wasn't going to accept that, not when they had done so little against the Nazis since the invasion. They had never taken the sort of risks I had taken, yet they had dared to question my loyalty.'

A furious argument erupted, with Lunding and Sneum almost coming to blows: 'Nordentoft intervened by explaining that it had been necessary to test me on the question of the parachutes for security, and that I ought to understand, especially since I had acted independently and not through them. Things calmed down after that.'

The Princes offered Sneum lodgings in a safe-house in St Annaegade, near the Christianshavn Canal, on the Copenhagen island of Amager. In return for the accommodation, and to reaffirm his loyalty to his own country, Tommy would be expected to write Danish Intelligence a full report on his time in England. His codes would remain his own secret as part of the deal. Meanwhile, Christophersen would continue to stay with Oxlund. Sneum chose to play along in order to build some mutual trust, knowing that Rabagliati wanted these people on Britain's side. Besides, to make enemies of the Princes would threaten not just his mission but his very survival in Nazi-occupied territory. His final report, a copy of which he retained into old age, provided some of the source material for the account of his summer stay in England presented above.

* * *

Despite his partial cooperation with Danish Intelligence, Tommy wanted to maintain his independence and set his mission for the British in motion. To do so, he needed money. Making sure he wasn't followed, he headed for the offices of a lawyer called Aage Koehlert Park, who was based in the busy Dronningens Tvaer Gade, near Copenhagen's spacious Town Hall Square. Rabagliati had assured

Sneum that Park would have substantial funds in Danish currency ready for collection. Now was the moment to test that claim.

Tommy gave a false name to a pretty receptionist, who politely escorted him along a carpeted corridor towards a large, plush office. Park was tall, blond and well groomed, so that he looked younger than his fifty-five years. He had the natural authority of a man who had been legal adviser to many of Copenhagen's foreign consulates and legations, but feigned surprise at being visited by a stranger without an appointment.

Sneum uttered the code words he had been given: 'Strange weather when you can't make biscuits.'

He waited for the recognition that would lead to the cash, but Park didn't seem to want to play along. 'I'm sorry, but I can't help you,' the lawyer said.

'I believe it is all arranged,' responded Sneum, trying to maintain an equal air of confidence.

'Oh, you're in the right place,' said Park. 'But this is not a good time. Try again in a few weeks.'

Tommy was taken aback. He had no choice but to leave the building quietly, since to cause a scene might have compromised both men. He couldn't understand how the British could let him down during the most dangerous opening days of the mission. Nevertheless, trying to stay positive, he contented himself with the fact that his first objective had been achieved, as he and Christophersen had at least gained a foothold in Copenhagen.

But amateur sleuths were already at work in the building that housed Oxlund's spacious first-floor flat. The general lack of activity in suburban Noekkerosevej turned out to be part of the problem. It had rendered Christophersen's arrival on the block more conspicuous, because the other occupants of Kaj's building had nothing better to do than gossip about any changes to their humdrum little world. Unfortunately, the only other first-floor apartment was home to the most vigilant neighbour of all – the building's acting caretaker, Hans Soetje. A Danish police report later described how Soetje first laid eyes on the nervous Christophersen:

First a person came after nightfall. He rang the bell, and because Soetje's and Oxlund's bell are so close together and have the same sound, Soetje opened. The person stood outside on the staircase, but pushed himself into Oxlund's doorway so that Soetje couldn't see his face very well.

But soon Soetje got the chance to have a closer look, while at a cigar shop one day, because the same person was also there and tried to buy some tobacco. At this point Soetje realised that this person was actually staying with Oxlund, though he didn't know the newcomer's name. Due to the man's strange appearance, Soetje began referring to him as 'The Russian' when speaking to his wife about him.

'The Russian' was about thirty years old, around 1m 85cm tall, very slender with mousy-blond hair, and a beard that was reddish-blond, as were his moustache and sideburns. He had a pointed nose and sometimes wore horn-rimmed spectacles. He was well dressed in a dark blue felt hat, a blue-grey overcoat and a dark blue suit.

As can be gleaned from this report, the caretaker's eye for detail was ominously impressive.

Chapter **21**

BED MANNERS

FRESHLY INSTALLED IN A top-floor flat at 15 St Annaegade, Tommy aroused considerably less suspicion, and he saw the immediate attraction of the location. Ship movements on the wider waters of Christianshavn, just a few blocks beyond the canal, could be monitored all the way up to the naval base at Holmen. Other factors made the hideout ideal, not least the roof-top escape route it offered, should the Abwehr raid from below.

And Tommy found that his new home contained added attractions. On the ground floor lived an elegant woman named Emmy Valentin, who was, he guessed, ten or fifteen years his elder. He might have been surprised to learn that she had actually turned forty-six on 11 July and was therefore nearly twice his age. However, since his very first lover back home on Fanoe had also been of a different generation, that wasn't necessarily going to put off Tommy. When Emmy smiled, the years didn't seem to matter. Time had in no way diminished her ability to captivate the opposite sex, and she was sophisticated in a way that had attracted Sneum to older women in the past. Tommy remembered: 'Emmy wasn't exactly beautiful, but she was one of those women who attracted men more than the most beautiful women did.' Her figure was shapely, her eyes inviting, so for a sex-hungry young spy in fear of his life, the age difference could be overlooked. What did age matter when he could be dead tomorrow? They began flirting immediately, even though they were not alone.

Emmy lived with her daughter, Birgit, who had mousy-coloured hair like her mother but was taller and more buxom. Tommy recalled: 'Birgit looked good, she was pretty enough, but she was bigger in stature than her mother, and she wasn't so self-assured. Even though she was two inches taller than me, Birgit was the sort of girl all men want to look after. Her mother was the confident one. Emmy was smaller, more fascinating and charming, and she had all the delicacies of a woman.'

But Tommy had the feeling that Birgit liked him every bit as much as Emmy did. This, he reflected, was a situation which called for careful management if he was going to benefit in the way he thought possible without offending either hostess.

* * *

Tommy was still finding his feet and assessing the qualities of his neighbours when a meeting took place in Copenhagen that was later regarded as one of the most dramatic events of the scientific war. In many ways it came too soon for Sneum, although even if he had already been at full intelligence-gathering capacity, it is doubtful that he would have got wind of it.

Professor Niels Bohr, who became known as the father of theoretical nuclear physics and would go on to win a Nobel Prize, had once regarded a young German doctor called Werner Heisenberg as a soulmate. Heisenberg had become Bohr's protégé, and the older man, a Danish Jew, had taught his favourite Aryan student everything he knew. And that was the problem. For what both physicists knew in the autumn of 1941 was enough to threaten the very survival of mankind. Each man realised that science was dangerously close, in theory at least, to constructing a weapon so lethal that its first owner would rule the world. Thanks to uranium and the destructive curiosity of the world's most brilliant minds, the spectre of the atom-bomb already loomed. Bohr, fifty-five and stubbornly anti-Nazi, knew that if Hitler ever laid his hands on such a bomb the free world would become a memory. Heisenberg, at the age of thirty-nine, was a patriotic German troubled by ethics. He was therefore torn between nationalistic duty and his sense of what was right for the world.

Anxious to discuss the moral and scientific complexities of his research, the younger man attended a scientific conference in Copenhagen in the third week of September 1941. Bohr remained conspicuously absent from the series of theoretical lectures and discussions in order to ensure that he remained above any possible accusations of collaboration. But the two men met discreetly one evening, and walked through the brewery district of Copenhagen, choosing a route around the famous Carlsberg House of Honour. As they nervously paced the lanes, looking behind them at regular intervals, both physicists suspected the Abwehr might be tailing them.

There was no time to waste so Heisenberg decided to voice what had been troubling him: 'Do you think it is right to work on the uranium problem at the moment, Niels? There could be grave consequences for the technique of war.'

The older man demurred and Heisenberg thought his professor might be hiding something about the progress made by the Allies in that area. But in fact the terrified Dane was wondering whether his closest friend and protégé had agreed to help Hitler try to win that race. By way of reply, Bohr eventually asked the all-important question: 'Werner, do you really think such a bomb is possible?'

'It would take a terrific technical effort,' answered Heisenberg.

This was hardly the answer to put Bohr's exceptional mind to rest. Heisenberg seemed to be telling him that the bomb was now a very real, if difficult, possibility. For all Bohr knew, the Germans might even be trying to make it already, though he considered success unlikely. A strange psychological stand-off developed between the two men. The meeting had already gone too far for Bohr's liking, so he wished Heisenberg a polite goodnight and quickly decided to act as though their historic exchange had never happened.

As Thomas Sneum had also discovered, the war put terrible

strains upon relationships that once had been positive, productive and even loving. And it was adept at creating distance between those who had previously been very close.

※ 🦟 ※

Oblivious to the extraordinary possibilities being discussed by two of the world's greatest brains in the self-same city, Tommy was already building relationships which would eventually lead him to that same mysterious field of scientific warfare.

On 13 October, Birgit Valentin celebrated her twenty-sixth birthday with a small party, to which Tommy was invited. The new arrival seemed to be the centre of the birthday girl's and her mother's attentions all evening, and Sneum knew that it would be dangerous to favour one over the other. To give too much attention to Birgit, the woman closer to his own age, risked arousing jealousy in her mother, which was the last thing he wanted. After all, Emmy was effectively his landlady. She took care of all the apartments in the building, which belonged to a countess called Elna Trampe. Since the countess was rarely in residence, Emmy treated the house as her own, and handpicked the tenants accordingly. If you upset her in any way, you would be asked to seek accommodation elsewhere. Emmy's trusted friends, on the other hand, knew they were safe. Until recently, the most frequent visitor had been Hans Lunding, and it was he who had arranged Tommy's accommodation, because of his special relationship with Emmy. According to Tommy, they had once been lovers: 'She met him on a train, on a skiing holiday to Norway. They did more fucking than skiing. Her husband was German Consul in Kalundborg, in the north-west of Zealand. I think they had only just got married, but she had already left him to live in Copenhagen.' But to favour Emmy would antagonise Birgit, and Tommy wasn't sure how much the younger woman knew about why he was there. Whatever the truth, it would be advantageous to keep her on side, too. The last thing he needed was the threat of a security leak fuelled by pure petty jealousy.

So there were various complications attached to the sexual adventures Tommy Sneum was contemplating. And that wasn't the only reason why he felt it wise to get out of the building and take plenty of fresh air each day. 'I couldn't just stay in all day because that would arouse suspicion,' he explained. 'I had to behave like any other local, and that meant going out.'

For a spy in Copenhagen, the location of the St Annaegade lair was ideal. Christianshavn was a trendy area, situated quite near the Danish parliament, the Rigsdag. Boersgade and a big old bridge called Knippelsbro were all that separated the two. And yet the island of Amager, of which Christianshavn was a part, had an identity all of its own. It was essentially split in two by the picturesque Christianshavns Canal. The old Snorresbro, an ancient bridge, arched across the canal to link those halves. There was nothing very beautiful about the modern block which included the five floors of 15 St Annaegade. The building's light brown brickwork pointed to the fact that it had been built only in the previous decade. Although neat and smart, it hardly seemed suitable for an aristocrat. Sneum's new base lay between the canal and the tall, green-blue tower of Vor Frelses Kirke, or Our Saviour's Church. Just over the Snorresbro was the old Staerkodder Café, a dark, smoke-filled pub full of simple tables and hard drinkers. Down the road lay the warehouses and offices of the East India Company, handily situated around the harbour itself. The people of Christianshavn were friendly and down-to-earth, and along their narrow stretch of canal they had created a unique disctrict of Copenhagen.

Before he allowed himself to feel too at home, Tommy headed off to re-establish contact with one of his earliest resistance associates, Christian Michael Rottboell. No one had seen Rottboell for some time in Copenhagen, so Sneum decided to cross over to Jutland one day and make the long journey to Boerglum, near its northern tip. He took a train to Aalborg and hitched a ride out onto the Hjoerring road. Just past Broenderslev he turned left onto the quiet country road that led to Boerglum Cloisters and the aristocratic splendour of the Rottboell family residence. It was with some apprehension that he knocked on the huge front door to the main house, remembering that Christian Michael's father had been less than happy about his impact on their lives the previous year. That same overbearing gentleman opened the door and looked at Tommy with a mixture of distaste and confusion.

'Sir, my apologies for turning up without prior warning, but I am looking for Christian Michael,' said Sneum.

'He hasn't been seen since July,' replied Christian Michael's father accusingly. 'Don't you know anything about his movements? After all, you promised me that you would look after him.'

Tommy wanted to explain about the Hornet Moth, the escape to Britain and his recent return. He wanted to tell the older man how he had ordered Christian Michael to stay put, at least until he could send a message from England about how a mass escape from Denmark might be organised. Instead, he just stood there silently.

Rottboell's manners would not allow him simply to slam the door on a visitor, so he invited Sneum in and poured him a drink, then revealed that he was pretty certain Christian Michael had gone to Sweden. Again, Sneum said nothing. It wouldn't have been so hard, the older man continued, because the family had plenty of connections there. Perhaps someone had helped him reach England? Tommy again resisted the temptation to tell his host that Rabagliati had quizzed him about Christian Michael just a few weeks earlier. But surely their paths would have crossed in August if his friend had made it to London? Having finished his drink, Tommy made another promise to Rottboell: that he would try to find out what had happened to his son.

If Christian Michael was not going to be any help, at least there were other old associates Tommy could count on. Kaj Oxlund was already proving to be a tower of strength. And a small but highly motivated band of men, from all sections of Danish society, would help him coordinate a fresh survey of German positions throughout the country. Sneum also learned what he could about the political situation in Copenhagen through more loyal and well-placed contacts. His high-flying uncle, Axel Sneum, and the Conservative leader, John Christmas Moeller, had opened political doors before his flight to England. However, the more he looked at Danish politics, the more it occurred to Tommy that there was no one charismatic or powerful enough to inspire a counter-movement against the depressingly passive toleration of the Nazi occupation.

Frustrated on a number of levels, Tommy returned to St Annaegade and allowed Emmy Valentin to seduce him. Although this was a development which would eventually lead to priceless intelligence, Tommy put his liaison with a middle-aged woman down solely to his own impeccable manners:

It would have been rude to say no to a woman. I couldn't have done that, especially when she was my landlady. Besides, she was very good in bed, so it was a pleasure. Sometimes I would go down to her apartment in the middle of the day and we would have a nice hour, because Birgit had a day job then. Sometimes, at night, Emmy would come up to me. This was a dangerous time anyway, and in war you take your chances when you can get them.

Chapter **22**

THE THREAT

N HIS HEART, Tommy had already left his wife Else for good, even though she was living just a few kilometres across central Copenhagen with their baby Marianne at Else's parents' home in Harald Jensensgade. He knew he had failed in his responsibilities as a father and a husband. But he convinced himself that he had taken on new and more far-reaching responsibilities. And Emmy seemed crucial to the success of his mission, to his very survival. She was reassuring and fascinating, and now she was central to his world, one in which he could be double-crossed, tortured or shot at any time. He decided to live for the moment, and embraced the mutual attraction. Emmy had a 'mature arrangement' with her husband, who was unlikely to cause problems. Her daughter would almost certainly be less understanding, so Tommy and Mrs Valentin were careful to hide how close they had become from Birgit.

Sneum needed all the comfort he could get, because he was about to make his mission a lot more dangerous. Daringly, he decided to return to the Hotel Cosmopolit in order to renew his acquaintance with some of the Abwehr officers based there:

I had to keep up my contact with the Abwehr to get information for Britain. The British knew I was going to do this and wanted me to do it. Personally, I had been more worried about the contact I'd had with the Germans before I had flown to England, in case it was taken the wrong way in London. I didn't have that fear any more.

The Abwehr people were quite relaxed at this time because they were still convinced they were going to win the war. The Cosmopolit was quite an exclusive hotel but you could go into the bar and meet these people. Most of my dealings were with chaps who didn't know who I was; but when a few of them recognised me and asked where I had been for so long, I told them: 'I have been shooting in Jutland and on Fanoe, and I have my family.'

Though his story was plausible, Sneum's tactic represented a massive risk. One phone call to Hauptmann Meinicke on Fanoe to check the facts could have been catastrophic. At first there would have been confusion since, as far as Meinicke was concerned, the plucky young flight lieutenant was dead. But with the help of a detailed description the penny would have dropped soon enough, leaving Sneum's capture inevitable. Indeed, had any suspicious Abwehr officers made the link between the young man standing before them, beer in hand, and the spectacular escape attempt by two Danish pilots back in June, it would all have been over.

Perhaps the horrendous penalty for anyone caught spying served to protect Sneum during these dangerous exchanges. If his sudden reappearance in the Cosmopolit did set off alarm bells inside the heads of any German officers, they must have dismissed such concerns as foolish. After all, no one implicated in the June escape, or secretly loyal to the Allies, would be stupid enough to walk into German Intelligence Headquarters in Copenhagen and casually prop up the bar there. The pilots who had tried to escape to England were supposed to be dead anyway. And even if they had survived somehow, it was highly unlikely that either man would be back in Copenhagen so soon, and certainly not in the Cosmopolit. Simple geography was also on Sneum's side: Odense and Andersen's farm seemed a world away, just like Fanoe. The Abwehr men based in the capital were primarily concerned with events in Copenhagen, and how to keep the occupation there peaceful.

So Tommy was able to exude his usual relaxed confidence, keep his cool and hope that his luck held. He tried not to express any emotion when the conversation in the bar turned to Britain one night. A German intelligence officer, drunk and treating Sneum like a long-lost friend, clearly felt as though he could speak freely, particularly when his boastful revelation merely served to confirm Nazi superiority over the enemy. 'We get running information from England,' he confided with a smile. 'The British think they have caught all our spies, but we still have a good organisation over there.'

If ever Tommy needed further incentive to drink with the loose-talking officers of the Abwehr, this was it, whatever the dangers involved. The problem was that the threat didn't come solely from the occupiers. Occasionally, his arrival or departure from the Cosmopolit was noticed by observers from groups trying to form a resistance to the occupation. To them, Sneum's actions appeared to be those of a man with a death wish. Either that or he was a German agent who couldn't be trusted. Tommy knew he was treading a thin line because pro-Nazi Danish spies often went to the Cosmopolit to give their reports to the Germans. It wouldn't have taken the anti-German elements long to decide that Danish Intelligence should know of Sneum's movements, and the suspicions they had aroused.

Of course, the Princes were already riled by Sneum's mere presence in their sector. They maintained their own indirect contact with London through the smooth-talking Ronald Turnbull, but they had no idea that Turnbull was a field chief in a newly formed 'amateur' organisation rather than an agent of the long-established British Intelligence. It therefore hadn't occurred to Nordentoft, Lunding or Gyth that Tommy Sneum might have been sent to Denmark by a rival British covert service to Turnbull's. The idea that British-run agents could be dropped not only without Ronnie's approval but without his knowledge seemed inconceivable to the Princes. Which explains why they were suspicious of Tommy from the start.

When they heard he was mixing with the Abwehr, the alarm bells began to ring even more loudly. They now considered Sneum to be a security risk, and finally complained to Turnbull about the agent's presence in Copenhagen. Bitterly, they said they felt betrayed by Britain's contravention of the agreement they had struck with SOE. No agents should have been sent to Denmark without the say-so of Danish Intelligence, and yet Tommy continued to insist that he had been recruited in London and sent on a mission to his home country by British Intelligence.

Naturally, Turnbull was confused and then angry to hear about the agents London had sent to Denmark without his knowledge. The last thing he needed was SIS causing complications in his theatre of operations. He felt he already had the territory well covered, and he was confident that it would be only a matter of time before the links he had forged with the Princes bore fruit. They had told him yet again that the best way to handle the occupation was to do nothing until the time was right. Turnbull agreed, and argued their case passionately in communications to London. Sending in British-run agents behind his back, whichever organisation they represented, wasn't the way to ensure the help of Danish Intelligence, he explained.

When urged by his own superiors to be more aggressive in his support for subversive activity in Copenhagen, Turnbull responded with the appropriate reassurances. Privately, though, he shook his head sadly at what he regarded as London's total lack of understanding of the situation in Denmark. He posed the question: what would have a more profound effect on the outcome of the war – to blow up the odd train and suffer inevitable reprisals, or to enjoy the continued support of the men who knew Denmark best, the Princes? Arguing his case with great diplomatic skill, he continued to do nothing. He even protected the identities of the Princes from his bosses, to the exasperation of the SOE hierarchy in London.

It was against this background that Tommy Sneum's high-risk approach to intelligence-gathering had created ripples in Denmark, the previously calm Scandinavian backwater. For Turnbull, this represented an embarrassing situation. Though he could hardly tell the Princes, it was obvious to him that MI6 spymasters had been busy behind the backs of their SOE 'cousins'. SIS had clearly won the race to land the first covert team in Copenhagen, beating their SOE rivals to the punch. And as if that wasn't bad enough, the SIS agent sounded like a loose cannon. Turnbull knew that SOE would now be more anxious than ever to send in their own British-trained agents, to strike back against SIS in the battle for control of

Denmark. The rivalry would escalate until one side prevailed, and only then would all the dangerous misunderstandings come to an end.

Thomas Sneum still knew nothing of this as he prepared for his first transmission in the autumn of 1941. While others viewed his activities with dismay, Tommy himself was satisfied with how he was handling an extremely difficult mission. He had achieved contact with Danish Intelligence and forged a basic understanding with their top officers, despite lingering resentment on both sides. He had found two possible bases for future radio transmissions. And he had gained a foothold in Copenhagen. Furthermore, he had learned plenty about the Nazi occupation from his audacious dealings with the Germans and from Kaj Oxlund's meticulous reports. It was time to tell his spymasters back in London of his successes.

Sneum decided that he and Christophersen would try to transmit from Oxlund's apartment, not least because he didn't want his fellow agent to know the location of his hideaway in Christianshavn. Perhaps he ought to have been more concerned about what Oxlund's neighbours already knew about Christophersen and his increasingly bizarre behaviour.

The caretaker, Hans Soetje, was still calling Christophersen 'The Russian', and the picture he later painted of his new neighbour while helping Danish police write a report would have been funny had it not constituted so much danger for the two agents. The report said:

> Soetje's wife sometimes cleaned Oxlund's apartment, and at certain times when she thought she was alone 'The Russian' suddenly appeared. He never spoke to Soetje's wife except to say 'good day' or 'sorry'. Soetje himself also had to do maintenance jobs in the apartment once in a while, and realised that 'The Russian' was lying down in the bedroom. Soetje never spoke to him, though he realised that 'The Russian' was not on the official list of who was living in the apartment.

Once 'The Russian' appeared with a beard and sideburns, and sometimes a small British moustache. Soetje didn't know if it was a natural beard, but he thought it looked artificial. Once he saw 'The Russian' in bed and didn't think he had the beard, though he wasn't sure if he had seen correctly because otherwise 'The Russian' definitely had a beard at that time.

Amid all this suspicion, Sneum travelled to an evening rendezvous with Christophersen in the first-floor apartment at Noekkerosevej. Sigfred's task would be to send the message after Tommy had encoded it with numbers, using variations from one of three sources chosen back in England. The first of these sources was a thirty-nine-letter word that Sneum had learned as a youngster in order to impress his family and friends. It was a medicine called Monobromisolvalerianylkarbamidtabletter, used by his father for his heart condition. Now it could prove to be a lifesaver for Tommy. The second was a Danish love poem, 'Gaeld', by Erik Bertelsen. It told of a man who was financially poor but romantically rich. The third was *Robinson Crusoe* by Daniel Defoe. It was such a popular book that you could buy the same edition in England and Denmark, without updates or corrections to confuse the code. It was this novel which formed the basis for Sneum's first coded message. The procedure was simple: Tommy gave the British specific page, line, word and letter numbers, and so created new words.

Christophersen and Sneum were not allowed to know each other's code type or source. But both men knew that each message had to be preceded by a personal two-letter, pre-code 'signature'. This was a further safeguard against any attempted impersonation of MI6 agents by the Nazis. Tommy quickly noticed that Christophersen had started to transmit without his pre-code signature so he forced him to begin again, adding to the strain on the radio man's nerves. The evening silence had already done much to unsettle Sigfred. It seemed that every tap he made on the Morse key-pad created an explosion of sound that he feared could be heard halfway down the street. Unfortunately, there was little they could do to drown out the clatter of his work. 'Christophersen's hand began to tremble uncontrollably,' claimed Sneum later, painting a picture of a man who wasn't always as brave as he wanted to be. 'He was already doing what most Danes didn't dare to do, but he got afraid as soon as there was any danger. And I couldn't have that.' Christophersen seemed to fear that the Danish police or even their German masters might locate them as they transmitted.

'For Christ's sake, get a grip on yourself,' hissed Sneum with a glare.

'The equipment's so loud,' whispered Christophersen. 'It's not safe.'

'But you always said you'd be safer in Denmark,' said Tommy, taunting. 'Well, now you've learned something. If you're working with me, you're not safe anywhere. Now finish the message.'

Christophersen must have seen something in his partner's eyes which scared him, because he continued, albeit in a Morse style full of stammers and stutters. It might have sounded confusing to those back in England who were used to his normal Morse hand, but Sneum knew it was better than nothing.

Once Christophersen's shaking fingers had finally completed the communication, both men waited for a response from England. There was none. The poor quality of their British equipment hadn't helped. The transmitter was bulky and heavy, weighing around twenty kilos. Hard to operate, it could be used only with an alternating current; at 7.5 watts. For reliable transmission and reception, a good aerial was also essential; they didn't have one. Tommy recalled: 'We had this ridiculous transmitter, which wasn't powerful enough. It was heavy, it was piss-poor and Christophersen wasn't achieving contact. As far as I was concerned, it was his fault and the transmitter's fault.'

In the hope of receiving some kind of acknowledgement, Sneum ordered Christophersen to send the message again. He complied, but by now his nerves were in tatters. Once he had finished the transmission, tears poured down his cheeks. 'I've had enough, I'm going home to see my parents,' he said at last.

'No, you're not,' Sneum said firmly. 'Not if you want to live.'

Chapter **23**

MEET THE WIFE

STILL FEELING PAIN FROM the cracked bone at the base of his spine, Tommy left Oxlund's apartment a worried man. Later he called Kaj and asked his friend to keep a close eye on Christophersen. 'If he doesn't get a grip, we'll have to kill him,' said Sneum. 'He could jeopardise the whole mission.'

Sneum sought the opinion of another trusted associate, his brother-in-law, the police detective Niels-Richard Bertelsen. Their conversation reminded Tommy just how high the stakes were. He learned that, in his absence, his entire family had been questioned by the authorities about his escape. Fortunately the Germans and the Danish police all thought he had been killed in the Hornet Moth. But if Christophersen were arrested, as seemed possible because his nervousness must already have aroused suspicion, Sneum felt sure that his own cover would also be blown. And then the people he loved could face worse interrogations than they had already endured. Bertelsen reluctantly agreed that they might have to kill the radio operator and find a more reliable accomplice:

Bertelsen and I planned how to kill Christophersen. We would take him down to some marshes in the south of Zealand, shoot him and throw him out of the car so he went under. It would be a long time before his body was found, if ever. I was going to be responsible for the killing, so I decided I wanted some neutral Danes as witnesses. That was because even during the war, to kill a man you were working with was a dangerous business. You had to be seen to have a very good reason. And we did have a good reason. He was scared, he was talking of leaving and going home. He was a security risk.

Before they took such drastic action, however, Bertelsen and Sneum decided that Christophersen should be given one last chance to recover his nerve.

⁂

The more Tommy thought about it, the more determined he became that London should pay for any new transmitter he might be able to acquire. The British had sent agents into Nazi-occupied territory with primitive equipment; now they should make amends.

His next meeting with the lawyer Aage Park, at his offices in Dronningens Tvaer Gade, would show whether the British were serious about backing the young men they had sent into such terrible danger. Tommy was politely shown into Park's office by the same pretty secretary who had caught his eye before. Once again he spoke the code words required of him.

'Oh, yes,' said Park casually. 'I may have better news for you.' He took a little notebook out of a drawer in his desk, studied it briefly, replaced it and excused himself for a moment.

Tommy recalled:

He had left the drawer in his writing desk open. I doubt he had any training for the work he did as a paymaster on behalf of the intelligence services. As soon as he went out, I jumped across the desk and found his notebook. In it were lots of names, people I assumed to be agents. There were mostly Polish and Swedish names. Some of them appeared to be operating in Germany, some further east, others in Sweden. Two names stood out in bold letters, those of a Captain Wahlqvist and Commissaire Runerheim. Their Swedish addresses suggested to me that they were part of the intelligence services over the water, perhaps among the top people.

I memorised as much as I could in the space of a few seconds, and just had time to replace the notebook and return to where I had been standing before Park came back.

Tommy didn't know precisely what it all meant, nor how much the British knew about Swedish operations. Was Park also a paymaster for the Swedish Legation in Copenhagen? If so, he had just gone down a notch in Tommy's estimation, as the young spy was less than impressed by Denmark's Scandinavian neighbours: 'The Swedes were pro-German in my mind at the time,' he said later. 'Although I may have made a mistake about that.'

Oblivious to the fact that his carelessness had just compromised the security of an entire spy ring, Park handed over a small envelope. Tommy quickly counted the cash and looked questioningly at the lawyer, who shook his head and shrugged his shoulders to make it clear that there would be no more for now.

With the meeting over, Sneum returned to his flat to reflect on what had happened. He carefully wrote down the names 'Wahlqvist' and 'Runerheim', and added some of the others still in his mind. This helped him recall several addresses he had seen alongside the names. Once he had memorised all the information, he destroyed the piece of paper. 'I didn't know how these names would come in useful,' he said later. 'I just thought they might.'

Far more important, for now at least, was the money. It wasn't much, given that he needed a better radio, funds for future intelligence-gathering operations, and of course his daily living expenses. But it would have to suffice for now.

* * *

For all the pleasure and comfort she gave him, Emmy Valentin was worth even more to Tommy for the social contacts she had among the upper reaches of the German command in Denmark. 'The Princes had completely wasted Mrs Valentin's contacts among the Germans in my opinion,' he reflected later. 'She had known all kinds of high-ranking officers, even in German Intelligence, because her husband had been German Consul in Kalundborg. Those officers invited Emmy out and they were generous. Hitler paid.'

Sneum was keen to tap into this gold-mine and, as he now had a strong bond with his hostess, he was in a perfect position to take advantage. 'Would you mind living a little more dangerously?' he asked her.

'No, Tommy,' she said with a mischievous smile. 'I don't think I would mind at all.'

Sneum thought he detected a flicker of anger, perhaps even jealousy, in Hans Lunding when the Danish Intelligence officer visited Emmy one day and found the younger man sitting comfortably in her ground-floor apartment. Worse for Lunding, he had to pretend he didn't know Tommy, and he showed such formal courtesy that the spy almost burst out laughing.

His mood was not so buoyant a few days later when he stepped on to a tram and bumped straight into his wife, Else. Tommy recalled: 'We just looked at each other in complete astonishment.' When he had climbed into the Hornet Moth and taken off for England, he had never expected to see Else again. If the flight didn't kill him, he imagined the war probably would. Even when he had survived above the North Sea and accepted his mission back to the Danish capital, he knew that Else belonged to another, forbidden world. British-run agents weren't supposed to contact their families when they went home, and this safeguard would have suited Tommy just fine where his wife was concerned. But an oversight had changed all that, and threatened to ruin everything. 'I realised that she must have been visiting her sister, who lived right by the main canal in Christianshavn,' said Sneum. 'Somehow I had forgotten about her.'

Tommy didn't know what to say, and they shared some awkward moments until the tram reached the next stop. 'Then I told her, "You'd better come with me," and we went to a restaurant.'

Sneum was terrified that his presence in Denmark would now become common knowledge, only a few weeks into his mission. He sat his wife down and looked her in the eye. 'If you talk about this to anyone, you'll be interrogated by the Germans, and that will mean instant death for me,' he said.

Else demanded to know where he was living, but Tommy refused to tell her. Nevertheless, she was determined to see him again, and was clearly prepared to overlook the fact that her husband had lied about sailing to America in search of work.

'We can't see each other,' said Tommy.

A defiant Else reminded him that he had a six-month-old daughter, who was at her sister's house at that very moment. She insisted that he come to see Marianne immediately. Tommy was convinced that Else would cause even more of a scene if he didn't comply, so, within an hour, he was playing with his baby daughter while Else repeatedly swore her sister to secrecy.

When Marianne finally fell asleep, Tommy took Else into another room, and for a while Mr and Mrs Sneum became man and wife again. After so many months of confusion, the passionate Else must have felt that her old life was returning. She was mistaken.

'We can't make a habit of this,' Sneum said as they lay together. 'It's too dangerous.'

His wife suggested that once in a while would be better than never, so they arranged to meet on the first Monday of each month near the parliament building, outside Christiansborg Castle. Tommy was relieved to have averted a crisis. Later he confirmed: 'We met like that a couple of times, and we found the means to go to bed together. After that I didn't go any more.'

* * *

When the police hammered on the door of Carl Jensen's third-floor flat at 2 Harald Jensensgade, it was Else Sneum they wanted to question.

'We are looking for your husband,' they explained. 'Is he back in Copenhagen?'

The quick-thinking Else promptly produced the evidence which might throw the police off her husband's trail, just as it had deceived her for so long. 'This was the last contact I had with him. I received it about three months ago. He is in America.'

The detectives examined the letter. The postmark said 5 July but, intriguingly, the correspondence had been sent from Copenhagen. And, although Sneum had written that he was going to the United States to look for work, there was no hard evidence to suggest he had actually done so.

'Do you think your son-in-law crossed the Atlantic?' The question was directed at Mr Jensen, who said he assumed that was exactly what had happened.

It wasn't clear precisely what had prompted the detectives' visit. Had Else's sister been indiscreet after Tommy's impromptu visit, or was the timing merely a coincidence? Either way, Else must have feared for her husband's safety that day.

Chapter **24**

BROTHERS IN ARMS

ONE EVENING TOWARDS the end of October, Emmy kept a discreet vigil for Tommy's return to St Annaegade and called him straight into her ground-floor flat. She explained that she had been seeking the company of some of her husband's German-officer friends, as Tommy had suggested. Some of them were administrators, others worked in intelligence. When she showed her face in the right hotels, they assumed she was lonely after her separation from her husband, and would invite her out to dinner, sometimes three or four of them together. Emmy would tell them her fears, and confide how much the war was getting her down, because sometimes it looked as though it would never end.

The previous night she had dined with two officers, one of whom she believed was attached to the Abwehr. 'She told me that her husband might have mentioned the Abwehr connection, but I think this German had been one of her lovers in the past,' explained Tommy. But Sneum was more interested in what the German had said than in his level of intimacy with Emmy. For when she had asked how long the war was likely to last, the officer had replied: 'Since you hate this war so much, you may soon have our scientists to thank.'

'It may have been nothing,' Emmy told Tommy as she recounted the conversation. 'Perhaps just some vague boast.'

Emmy had asked her German friend what he meant, but the other officer sitting at their table had looked uncomfortable and quickly changed the subject.

Sneum was anxious to get to the bottom of this casual remark as soon as possible. He decided to have Christophersen send Rabagliati an account of the conversation, so that the British could interpret it as they saw fit. In the meantime, he would send Mrs Valentin back into action.

'Emmy,' he said bluntly, 'you must attach yourself to this man in any way you see fit.'

She looked surprised by the suggestion, but Sneum ignored any hint of indignation that she might have wanted to convey. 'She told herself she did it for the cause, but she liked doing it anyway,' suggested Tommy mischievously in his later years.

* * *

The tension between Sneum and Christophersen was rising by the day. Their radio transmissions were tortuous, and not once had they received a reassuring word from Britain. With no contact from London, there was no proof that Rabagliati was receiving their intelligence.

Christophersen continued to show signs of losing his nerve completely. As far as Sneum was concerned, someone who looked too nervous to blend into the Copenhagen scenery was a liability who would get them both caught if something wasn't done soon. Christophersen was no help with the communication problems either, continuing to blame the equipment while Sneum increasingly blamed the operator. Sneum recalled:

Christophersen was probably still thinking of escaping, so I took charge of the radio at the end of each transmission we attempted. He still had the crystals, which corresponded to the wavelengths we used. You couldn't get the same crystals made in Denmark, so I couldn't transmit without him, but he couldn't transmit without me either. You couldn't get more than one crystal in the transmitter at a time, and I think he must have been going around with four different crystals each day. If he had been caught by the

Germans, they would have known our frequencies. It was ridiculous.

Just as worrying for both men was the suspicion they shared that their transmissions to Britain had not been successful. Something needed to be done, otherwise it was likely that much of Tommy's work would go to waste.

One lunchtime during the second week in November, Christophersen took an irate Sneum to a smoke-filled bar in central Copenhagen and led him towards a young man who was sitting alone in a dimly lit corner. After looking anxiously around the bar and then threateningly into the seated man's eyes, Sneum pulled up a chair. Already livid that he had been led into the company of a complete stranger without any warning, Sneum was speechless when Christophersen said: 'I want you to meet my brother, Thorbjoern.'

For Christophersen, this meeting was like life insurance. Tommy realised that if he tried to liquidate Sigfred, the radio man would quickly be missed. Others within his family might also know of Sneum's threats. 'The introduction of Thorbjoern changed things,' remembered Sneum. 'To kill a man you were working with on security grounds was one thing. But to kill a couple of people was too much. Thorbjoern was innocent; and then there might have been other parties to deal with, too.'

Seeing Sneum's face darken, Christophersen defended his decision to involve his family in the operation. He explained that Thorbjoern could be extremely useful, because he worked for an electrical communications company in Copenhagen that was closely associated with the famous Bang and Olufsen. It was called Gyberg and Jensen. Supporting his brother, Thorbjoern then told Sneum how fiercely anti-German his colleagues were, although no one dared to say as much in public. Even the directors, Werner Gyberg and Robert Jensen, were said to be resistance sympathisers. And from his own dealings with Gyberg, the twenty-two-year-old Thorbjoern felt he could be trusted. It was through his boss that Thorbjoern had heard of a brilliant radio technician, a man knowledgeable enough in the field of communications to have become Bang and Olufsen's chief engineer. His name was Lorens Arne Duus Hansen, and he was said to build his own transmitters for fun. Obviously, this man could be the solution to their communications problems.

'How do you know about the radio?' hissed Tommy.

'I told him everything, Sneum.' Christophersen was unrepentant. 'He needs to know in order to brief Gyberg and Duus Hansen.'

Sneum fixed his eyes on the younger brother. 'If anyone is going to talk to this Duus Hansen, it will be me.' Then, out of anger and because he felt it might help him regain some control over the situation, he issued a new threat, though he knew deep down he couldn't carry it out: 'If you say a word about this meeting to anyone, I'll kill both of you.'

Sigfred, feeling protective of his brother, accused Sneum of overreacting, and claimed his constant threats were putting the mission at risk. The implication that it was Tommy who had begun to show signs of irrational behaviour under pressure, rather than Sigfred, was one provocation too many. To be told that he was losing his grip by someone as nervous as Christophersen seemed so outrageous to Tommy that he became incensed, but he managed to leave before succumbing to the temptation to silence his partner immediately and pemanently.

As he said goodbye to his brother and returned to Kaj Oxlund's apartment alone, Sigfred Christophersen must have sensed the danger he was in. Back in the flat, when the phone rang he forgot protocol and foolishly picked up the receiver. It was Tulle, Oxlund's estranged wife. She didn't recognise the stranger's voice on the other end of the line, and her suspicions cannot have been eased when Christophersen told her she had dialled the wrong number and slammed down the hand-set. Tulle had lived at the apartment for ten years and thought it unlikely that she had made a mistake. When she tried again, there was no answer. She decided that as soon as she had time, she would visit the flat in person to solve the mystery of the stranger's voice, confront Kaj and try to sort out their differences.

Fearing such a visit, or perhaps a more sinister one from the Abwehr, Sigfred Christophersen must have decided that he could take no more. He opened Oxlund's writing desk, took a bundle of cash from the funds Sneum had collected, and left as quickly as his long legs would carry him.

From that moment, Colonel Rabagliati's men were at war – with each other. The only thing they had in common was that they both needed effective radio communication with England. And they both knew where the key to that lay.

Chapter 25

HISTORY-MAKERS

TROUBLED AS TOMMY WAS by Christophersen's disappearance, another development soon took priority. For on Tuesday, 25 November 1941, Denmark signed the Anti-Comintern Pact in Berlin. It was a move that incensed not only Danish communists but most moderate citizens who feared that Germany's next step would be to force Denmark to take action against her Jewish nationals. At 2.00 p.m. the news was broadcast that the agreement had been signed, and almost immediately a large group of students gathered in front of the King's Palace in Copenhagen to demonstrate during the changing of the guard. They sang patriotic Danish songs with great passion and chanted 'Down with Scavenius', a reference to the Foreign Minister who had just signed the pact.

Over the bridge in Christianshavn, Tommy Sneum heard the commotion and went straight to the palace to watch the events unfold. This was, after all, the first substantial public gathering openly to defy the Germans since the occupation had begun. Understandably nervous, Danish policemen began to ready themselves for action under the watchful eye of their German puppet-masters. At this moment Sneum was confronted in the square by Captain Volle Gyth, the lowest-ranking Prince.

'What the hell are you doing?' Gyth hissed. 'If anyone recognises you here, you'll be arrested. Don't you realise, you'll risk all our lives.'

Sneum, who thought the older man was being melodramatic, mocked Gyth's fear. 'We only live once,' he replied. 'And you've got to die some time.'

The police began to move in and demanded that the students leave the vicinity of the palace. The uniformed constables drew their batons to leave the students in no doubt about what would happen if they didn't comply. The demonstrators moved on, but only to where the Rigsdag and the Foreign Office were situated. Tommy followed at a safe distance and saw more sympathisers joining the throng. After a further stand-off, the police drove the demonstrators back, but the mass of angry young Danes began to march down Copenhagen's main shopping street, the Stroeget, towards City Hall. On the way, they passed a fashionable restaurant, where a German officer assumed the passing crowd was on the street to celebrate the signing of the Anti-Comintern Pact. Arrogantly, he marched onto the restaurant's balcony to accept their applause with a Nazi salute. Spontaneously, the demonstrators picked up whatever missiles they could find and began to stone the German. This act of violence provided the police with the excuse they needed: they rushed in, swinging their clubs against their fellow countrymen.

Sneum hid in a doorway and watched with disgust as the beatings increased in ferocity. Still the police failed to restore order, however. As word spread of the brutality that had accompanied the government's signing of the pact, the ordinary citizens of Copenhagen became more irate. Huge crowds expressed anti-German feelings that had festered among many for more than a year and there were serious disturbances in the city centre all night. Outside the Hotel d'Angleterre, where Sneum had dreamed of assassinating a top Nazi, the people sang Allied songs, such as the old British soldiers' favourite 'Tipperary'. Even when arrested and thrown into cells, they refused to fall silent, singing 'God Save the King' and other pro-British anthems until their defiance rang in the ears of their captors.

The following day, students were threatened with expulsion from the universities if they didn't leave the streets and come to order. Although there was more trouble that night, most felt they had made their point and peace was restored after two momentous days.

* * *

Sneum wanted to communicate these events to London, just as Rabagliati would have expected him to, but he didn't have any crystals to use with his radio set. He didn't know what the solution might be, but he did know that it was time to make contact with the chief engineer from Bang and Olufsen.

In the first week of December Tommy called Werner Gyberg and asked him to arrange a meeting with Lorens Arne Duus Hansen. Gyberg told him to go to Kongens Nytorv and sit on the bench furthest from the Hotel d'Angleterre. At 2.00 p.m. Duus Hansen would introduce himself.

There were sixteen benches in Kongens Nytorv, or the New Royal Market, forming a circle around the central monument, a magnificent statue of King Christian V on horseback. Tommy walked to the appointed one and sat down. Even though he had previously socialised in many bars with the German occupying forces, he felt strangely conspicuous now. Stripped of direct contact and beer as a prop, he worried in case his presence seemed suspicious, and he had the sensation that his loitering would be noticed. Even sitting as far away from German Headquarters as possible, he knew he could still be observed from the windows of the hotel. Across the road, the tall masts of sailing ships towered majestically above beer-drinkers in quayside bars, just as they had done for nearly three hundred years. Nyhavn (Newhaven) had once been home to Hans Christian Andersen, and now it almost seemed to be stretching the imagination too far that a city occupied by Nazis could still have a tourist district. Sneum sat and waited for Duus Hansen, rehearsing what he would say. He remembered: 'It was a sunny winter's day and Duus Hansen had been told exactly which bench I was sitting on, because it is a bloody big square. He came down from his office, just a couple of hundred metres away, and when I caught sight of him I got a good feeling.' A smart-looking forty-year-old approached Sneum's bench, and his honest-looking face convinced Tommy to trust him. There was something reassuring about Duus Hansen from the start, an unspoken integrity.

The pair walked and chatted, telling each other a little about what they had done since the Nazis had invaded. Sneum was surprised by his own reaction to a man he hardly knew. 'We got on from the moment we met,' he recalled. 'I had complete confidence in Duus and spoke openly to him, and he spoke openly to me, and already we were friends.'

Then, just when all appeared to be well, Duus Hansen dropped a bombshell: 'Another man, called Christophersen, has been to see me in the last few days. He claims he is the brother of one of the workers at Gyberg and Jensen. He wanted me to help him too; he seemed desperate. He had crystals but no radio.'

Sneum smiled. 'I have the radio. I didn't trust him.'

Later Duus Hansen revealed what he had been told by each spy sent from Britain:

The first with whom I came into contact was Christophersen, who told me that he and a comrade had been dropped into the country to gather information and build an organisation. From England he had brought some quartz crystals together with an incomplete connecting and signal plan. He did not have a transmitter, he explained, because he had thrown it overboard while on a ferry to Fyn, thinking he was being followed. But he had saved the crystals, he claimed, which was the most important thing. So I started to construct a transmitter which suited the given crystals.

Even before the transmitter was ready, however, I was contacted by Werner Gyberg, a business associate, to say that he had been visited by another agent who had been parachuted in, a Lieutenant Sneum. He told both Gyberg and I that we shouldn't deal with Christophersen, whom Sneum said was highly unreliable as an organiser and did not possess the personal courage needed to fulfil the obligations he had been given.

Since the conversation had turned to matters of personal courage, Duus Hansen decided to be disarmingly honest with Tommy, who explained: 'This man would go on to become one of the biggest figures in the resistance, if not the biggest. But the important thing was that even at the start of his involvement, when we met, he knew his value and he knew his limits. He said that he had heard about the torture methods the Germans used, and that he didn't know how he would react, but that he would do his best.'

Tommy felt this admission was a world away from Christophersen's casual confession, after being recruited by the British, that he would cooperate freely with the Germans if he felt in any real danger. Duus Hansen was simply expressing every man's fear – that he might break down under torture. He was aware of his responsibility, as a potential new recruit, to air such concerns at the outset. Making clear that he would try to hold out when subjected to excruciating pain, but didn't know how long his bravery would allow him to do so, showed commendable honesty.

'We all have our limits,' said Sneum supportively. 'We all have those feelings.'

The Germans knew it only too well. Vestre Prison in Copenhagen would become the scene of some horrendous torture later in the war. Even at this stage, in other occupied territories the Nazis were already infamous for putting matches under fingernails before pulling them off completely. They used thumb screws and tongs to distort and crush the fingers themselves. If that didn't crack a prisoner's resolve, they would not hesitate to use the tongs on the testicles of their victims. Some of the most stubborn characters were also softened up with relentless beatings. Although this had not yet happened in Denmark, where the Abwehr and their disciples among the Danish police currently dealt with subversion, Sneum knew that the Gestapo would introduce their sadistic methods sooner or later. Long after the war, Tommy admitted: 'I was afraid more often than people seem to realise. Some resistance people went into interrogations as men and came out as vegetables. Who wouldn't have been afraid? I suppressed my fear, and as a result there were those who thought I was a cold-blooded fellow, someone who even liked the idea of killing people. But I hated it all.'

Back in Copenhagen on that sunny early winter day, Duus Hansen was allowed to see more of the real Tommy Sneum in the space of a few minutes than many others ever came to know. Each

of them had admitted that he was not a superhero. This created
trust and, on that basis, Duus Hansen said he was more than happy
to work with Tommy. However, he wanted to maintain his
anonymity in all his dealings with London, since he didn't know the
spymasters there. Sneum saw the logic of that condition and agreed
to it.

Duus Hansen remembered listening to Sneum's condemnation of
Christophersen and believed his criticism to be justified:

> From his explanation I realised that Sneum was the man to build
> up the intelligence organisation, for he had only brought
> Christophersen along as a telegrapher, and therefore
> Christophersen was in no position to do something on his own
> because Sneum was his superior. Sneum said that the story about
> the transmitter being lost on the way to Jutland was wrong, and
> that he had taken it into his possession, but he was missing the
> crystals. That meant the crystals and transmitter were safe.

The engineer knew he would be able to unite the two, and Tommy
wasn't about to squander the opportunity to bring a true radio
expert on board. This decision would have long-term benefits for
British radio communications behind enemy lines, because Duus
Hansen's innovative genius took the design of transmitters to a new
level.

When he examined Sneum's transmitter, he found the
technology laughable: 'A closer look at the transmitter showed that
it was not fit for purpose, and it was necessary to build a new
transmitter.' Duus Hansen knew he could create a far more
effective radio set which weighed less than a tenth of the
cumbersome and primitive British model. His account suggests that
he met with Christophersen and persuaded the nervous telegrapher
to loan him the vital crystals, however temporarily. For, within
seventy-two hours, Duus Hansen had not only constructed the new
radio, but also teamed up with Sneum for transmission. Duus
Hansen confirmed of that new partnership: 'As soon as I had built
the new transmitter, we tried to contact England.' They worked
enthusiastically, transmitting Tommy's first-hand account of the
Anti-Comintern Pact riots. As usual, there was no reply, but for

the first time Sneum was confident that his message had reached London.

At the end of the war, when Duus Hansen was recommended for the Distinguished Service Order (DSO), his file mentioned the first meeting with Sneum:

> He [Duus Hansen] succeeded in establishing contact with a man sent from Britain by parachute in 1941. There were two Danish parachutists who went to London and came back to Denmark and [Duus Hansen] contacted them. They carried a radio transmitter with them, but could not operate it because they were not very experienced. They were trying to establish contact with London. [Duus Hansen] asked them if he could repair their sets and work and operate them without London knowing about it. This was the start.

In reality, of course, Sigfred and Tommy made contact with Duus Hansen, not vice versa. But it was Tommy alone who gained his trust, so he was perfectly justified in insisting later:

> I recruited Duus Hansen. He would not have become a member of the resistance at that time without me, because he was worried about Sigfred Christophersen. It was because Duus and I got on so well that I was lucky enough to be able to benefit from his help on a regular basis, and that led him to maintain his relationship with the British for the rest of the war.

Others agreed. Although the distinguished Danish historian Joergen Haestrup never accused Christophersen of losing his nerve, he did strongly suggest that the radio operator was responsible for the collapse of the partnership with Sneum:

> Sneum's presence in Denmark was still unknown to the Abwehrstelle. Nevertheless, his mission met serious difficulties, partly because the cooperation between him and Christophersen broke down. There can be no doubt that this was through no fault of Sneum's. Reports from two men, Duus Hansen and the merchant Werner Gyberg, who worked with Sneum and Christophersen, are unanimous on this point.

In short, Sigfred Christophersen acted unprofessionally, while Thomas Sneum commanded more respect and generated more trust.

≡ ❋ ≡

Although he was instantly impressed by the engineer, not even Sneum could have foreseen the impact Duus Hansen would have on the Second World War. Growing in confidence, he went on to become head of radio communications for the Danish resistance and the focal point for most British contact. Fortunately, London soon came to appreciate his worth.

In the summer of 1943, Duus Hansen invented the 'Telephone Book' radio set, so-called because the engineer managed to pack a great deal of superb technology into a very small space. The radio was a spy's dream in Nazi-occupied Europe, more practical and effective than anything British experts had devised. It weighed just one and a half kilograms, making it far more suitable for work in the field.

But he didn't finish there. Acting on a fresh request from London, Duus Hansen invented a high-speed Morse transmission system that helped to protect the lives of countless British agents. By cutting the time during which the feared German detector-vans could trace those transmissions, Duus helped many Allied spies evade capture, and ultimately ensured his own survival as well.

The importance of his continued involvement in the Danish resistance was emphasised in the late summer of 1943, when the British were provided with vital intelligence on Hitler's V-rocket operations on Peenemunde and Bornholm. Had Tommy Sneum not recruited Duus Hansen twenty months earlier, many more Londoners might have been killed towards the end of the war. The engineer had needed someone to convince him that he had the necessary character to prevail in a battle of wits against the Germans. Sneum had provided that inspiration, setting Duus Hansen on the path to his future heroics.

Chapter **26**

INFIGHTING

ELSE SNEUM PRESUMED THAT her husband was still in Copenhagen that December, yet feared he was now out of reach. She hadn't seen Tommy for more than a month, and the rapid approach of Marianne's first Christmas must have sharpened her sense of anguish. While Else's parents had been generous in supporting her and the baby, the traditional breadwinner in her little family remained elusive. Tommy's father had also contributed financially, but Else clearly didn't want to become dependent on either of Marianne's sets of grandparents. Around this time she seems to have decided that she had played the waiting game long enough. She chose to go back to work, leaving Marianne with the Jensens during the day. Taking advantage of extra seasonal demand, Else found a job as a shop assistant in Copenhagen's well-respected Fonnesbech store. If she persevered all through Christmas and the New Year, she could earn two hundred Danish kroner. It wasn't a fortune, but it would give her some control over her own destiny.

＊ ＊ ＊

Sigfred Christophersen also craved independence and normality. As Christmas approached, he decided to attend a seasonal show at the Palace Theatre in Copenhagen. He was about to settle into his seat and enjoy a special evening along with the rest of the festive audience when he was spotted by a young man who recognised him instantly, even though they hadn't seen each other since Sigfred's return to Denmark. How lucky for him that the man in question was one of his younger brothers, Hildur.

Although desperate to speak to Sigfred for the first time in more than a year, Hildur felt that he could not approach his sibling. He had heard through Thorbjoern that Sigfred was back in town, and he knew his two brothers had begun some kind of secret work together. Drawing attention to Sigfred now might endanger him. So Hildur Christophersen kept his distance, and, at the end of the show, he allowed Sigfred to leave the theatre without saying a word. Much later, Hildur confided in a voice betraying the sorrow he had carried inside for many decades: 'I will always remember that evening because it was the last time I ever saw Sigfred alive.'

Shortly before Christmas, Emmy Valentin left St Annaegade to visit relations. It was going to be a busy week for a socialite of Emmy's standing, and there would also be much to do for the Countess Trampe. If she could get some of her family obligations out of the way early, Emmy's own diary would be left a little bit clearer for Christmas itself. She told her daughter Birgit that she should call Tommy on the fifth floor in case of emergency. If any suspicious stranger rang the front doorbell, she should also warn Tommy immediately. A little later, with very different kisses, Emmy bid farewell to her two loved ones on the fifth and ground floors. She said she would be back in four days.

At twenty-six, the buxom Birgit was only a couple of years older than Tommy, and blessed with a vivacity which men found attractive. He had noticed the way she looked at him, but knew the situation would become far too complex if he took advantage of her obvious interest.

The night after Emmy's departure, Tommy heard a knock on his door. He reached instinctively for his pistol and crept up to the little spyhole he had drilled for the early detection of unwelcome visitors. He heard Birgit's whisper and saw her on the landing. She was wearing a flimsy nightdress and asked if she could come in. Deciding it would be less than gentlemanly to tell his girlfriend's daughter to go away, Tommy opened the door. Birgit walked confidently into his room, pulled off her nightdress in the semi-darkness and climbed straight into Tommy's bed. He nearly asked her if she was sure this was a good idea, but there seemed little point. They both knew what was going to happen next and it was a long time before they paused for conversation.

'This is going to make life a little complicated,' suggested Sneum at last.

'Not really,' Birgit explained. 'Perhaps I should have told you. I'm leaving for Germany after Christmas.'

She then revealed that she had met someone who wanted her to work in the Propaganda Department of the Ministry of Information in Berlin, as a secretary behind the scenes for German radio. But that would only be her cover, she explained conspiratorially. In reality she would be sending information back to Denmark, effectively working as a spy. If the Germans grew suspicious, she was supposed to send a postcard to request her withdrawal.

Sneum thought the whole notion ludicrous, since Birgit had no experience or training, would probably be caught and might then be forced to reveal the names of everyone she had met in Copenhagen. He pleaded with her to reconsider.

'I'll think about it,' said Birgit. 'But I've just bought a new fur coat especially for Berlin.'

Tommy couldn't believe how naïve she was being. He had seen her stylish winter outfit already, and now imagined how it would go down in Germany. He remembered later:

She had a big coat and hat, both made of really beautiful furs because she and her mother were rather wealthy. When I told her that she couldn't wear them in Germany, she didn't understand. I had to explain to her that Berlin isn't Copenhagen. All the German women had given their furs to the soldiers on the Eastern Front, because they had summer uniforms in a Russian winter. I told her she would look totally out of place in Berlin and that would arouse suspicion for a start. She wouldn't be popular and she wouldn't be accepted.

Again, he begged her to abandon the entire hare-brained scheme. She promised to give it more thought.

※ ▓ ※

Emmy returned on schedule, and pretty soon Tommy was entertaining both mother and daughter, though never at the same time. With a smirk, he recalled later: 'I have never disclosed before that I fucked Birgit and Emmy. Birgit may have been younger, but Emmy was the better lover.' When the daughter went to work during the day, Tommy would steal downstairs to Emmy. Then, at night, as the mother slept, Tommy would sometimes creep downstairs again, this time to see Birgit.

One morning, however, the young lovers were woken by the sound of Birgit's door being opened. There was no time to move. Emmy Valentin was confronted by the rather confusing sight of her daughter lying in bed with her lover.

'There's nothing going on, I'm just sleeping here,' said Tommy. 'I was just tired. We were talking and I must have nodded off.'

Emmy digested this absurd excuse and said: 'Birgit, I want you out here in one minute.'

When she slammed the door on her way out, Tommy knew he would have to eat a lot of humble pie to extricate himself from this awkward predicament. Later, he reflected with a smile: 'When Emmy found me in bed with Birgit, that was not good.'

Unfortunately for Sneum, much worse was to come.

※ ▓ ※

Hans Lunding banged on the fifth-floor apartment's door with such ferocity that Tommy thought the Gestapo had arrived. Pistol in hand, he peered through the spyhole to see his least favourite Prince red-faced with rage. Sneum opened the door, though he knew that this meeting would be no more pleasant than their first.

Lunding insisted that they go out before he was prepared to tell Tommy what was on his mind, so the two men strolled down to the canal in Christianshavn. There, Lunding erupted: 'What the hell have you been saying to Birgit Valentin? She has just told me she no longer wishes to accept the offer of employment in Berlin. Do you know how long we have been waiting to get someone into Germany?'

'No,' replied Sneum. 'But everyone in the area will know if you keep shouting.'

Lunding lowered his voice to a hiss. 'Finally, we had the opportunity to plant a flower in Berlin. It is so difficult to do this, and at last we had a chance. You have just ruined everything.'

Sneum repeated what he had said to Birgit – that it was a crazy idea which would have resulted in them all being compromised after her swift capture. 'I'm living in the same house as her. I don't want all this nonsense coming back on me. Besides, she was only going to work at a radio station. She wouldn't have been able to gather much intelligence from there.' Then he suggested something which could have signalled the end of his mission in Denmark: 'If you want someone in Germany, send me. I have a cousin, Knud Nielsen. He worked in Berlin three years ago. I resemble him so closely that people in our own families sometimes mistake one of us for the other. He still has contacts in Berlin and he could brief me on what he did there before the war.'

Lunding looked at the young man disdainfully, as though the idea were insane. 'Birgit was above suspicion. That was the beauty of it. Sabotage any more of our projects and I'll kill you.'

Sneum was at breaking point. 'Why don't you try? Because make no mistake, Lunding, if you don't kill me, then one day I will kill you.'

Some of the citizens of Christianshavn had heard the heated exchange and began to look out of their windows. Reluctantly, both men realised they would have to conclude their argument some other time. As they stormed off in opposite directions, each believed the other to be nothing more than a liability to the Allied war effort.

Later, Tommy reflected that there might have been another reason why the argument was so fierce:

Lunding was jealous because he had begun to realise that Emmy was in love with me, a much younger man, and he thought he was a hell of a big man with the women. He was attractive to women, but only because of his military position and standing. He was uneducated, but he could travel to Germany and Sweden to get black-market goods. No one would bother him at customs on the way back in because he was a big officer in Danish Intelligence. But the point is, Lunding wanted to fuck Birgit too. He was about the same size as Birgit, and he wanted to visit her in Germany and fuck her.

Personal issues aside, Sneum remained convinced that he had acted correctly by deterring the daughter of his landlady from embarking upon a career in espionage. Despite his romantic entanglement, he had tried to look at the proposal objectively, and on that basis he was sure that Birgit would eventually have been forced to betray them all. Furthermore, 'Emmy was against Birgit going to Germany too,' he said later.

As the project was aborted, the Princes wondered how they might gain control over Thomas Sneum, the maverick spy who seemed to be disrupting all of their best-laid plans.

※ ※ ※

Back in London, the Danish Section of the Special Operations Executive was extremely pleased with its latest recruitment coup. In Dr Carl Bruhn, they believed they had found the perfect man to lead their proposed new network in Denmark. All summer and autumn, blissfully unaware that MI6 was thinking along precisely the same lines but had worked more quickly, SOE had trained Bruhn and a radio operator called Mogens Hammer for a mission behind enemy lines in Denmark.

The London-based chief of the Danish Section, Commander Ralph Hollingworth, was delighted with the project. Later he would gush:

Bruhn was the best man we ever had in the SOE, full of energy, with a talent for organisation, winning the respect and devotion of all his comrades and exercising great influence upon all who worked with him. His determination may be judged from the fact that he passed his final medical examinations when already training for parachute jumping at Ringway. Indeed his very last exam he passed with distinction only a week before we sent him to Denmark.

By then, however, it was December 1941, and Tommy Sneum had been operating in Denmark for three months. It was highly unlikely that Bruhn would do anything that Tommy hadn't done already, but to the men who mattered in London that wasn't the point. In the corridors of power, the battle for control of Denmark raged on. And, in spite of Ronnie Turnbull's best efforts to convince them otherwise, the SOE hierarchy believed that the best way to win that battle was by putting their own men in the field. They were determined to prove that anything the SIS 'professionals' could do, they could do better. For their part, MI6's spymasters were at pains to resist all interference from men they regarded as upstart amateurs.

Chapter **27**

CHRISTMAS HORRORS

TOMMY DECIDED IT WOULD BE unacceptable to go down to Christmas lunch at 15 St Annaegade without flowers for Emmy and Birgit's table, so on Christmas Eve he left the building in disguise, wearing a pair of spectacles and a false moustache. He found a florist's and was paying for an enormous bunch of red roses when he suddenly became aware of a woman staring at him. To his horror, he noticed out of the corner of his eye the wife of an old Fleet Air Arm colleague. He recalled that her family was pro-German, and therefore probably had contacts among the collaborationist elements of the Danish police. The woman was obviously wondering whether this could really be Thomas Sneum, and seemed ready to engage him in conversation in order to find out. His attempted escape by Hornet Moth that summer had become common knowledge among those who had known him, with many convinced that he had met his end in the North Sea. Now the woman might be thinking not only that he had survived against the odds, but that he had returned on some sort of secret mission for the Allies.

Tommy finished paying and left before she could say anything. However, he realised that he must now assume he had been compromised. Making his way back to Emmy's with the flowers, he took several detours to ensure he wasn't being followed. All the time, he was kicking himself for his carelessness. His life would now be in even more danger than before, and all for the sake of flowers that would fade and die within days.

As they ate their Christmas meal and tried to be cheerful, Sneum's mind was elsewhere, uncharacteristic behaviour when he was in the company of women. But by the end of the meal, a traditional Danish spread of cold meats and fish, there had been more than enough awkward silence, so he tried belatedly to lighten the atmosphere.

'Are you doing anything interesting between now and New Year's Eve, Emmy?' he asked.

'Yes, as a matter of fact: I'm going out with a number of high-ranking German officers. One of them,' she added pointedly, 'I intend to charm rather more than the others.'

Though she didn't seem to want to elaborate in front of Birgit, it was clear to Sneum from Emmy's expression that she was talking about the Abwehr officer who had claimed the war might be cut short by German scientists.

* * *

On the night of 27 December, SOE agents Bruhn and Hammer jumped out of a British plane at Torpeskou, near Haslev, sixty-five kilometres south of Copenhagen. These must have been terrifying moments for the brilliant Dr Bruhn as he hurtled through the darkness and realised that his parachute hadn't opened. He would never see his British wife, Dr Anne Connan, again. Some claimed later that he had forgotten to attach his parachute to the static line. Others blamed a faulty clip mechanism, and suggested that an important life had been wasted for want of a sturdy 'safety pin'.

Whatever the truth, as Bruhn's body smashed into the ground, Hammer knew nothing of the doctor's fate. A tough seaman who had learned his skills on ships' radios, Hammer looked for his partner but failed to find him. After an hour, he had no choice but to leave the drop-zone, having only partially concealed his own parachute. As he trudged away, he might have wondered why Bruhn had been assigned the suitcase that carried the radio transmitter. Already his mission looked in jeopardy. But soon events would take an even worse turn, with consequences not just for Hammer but for the two British agents who had been in Denmark since September.

The following morning a German patrol found Bruhn's crushed body, along with the incriminating transmitter. Searching the area, they uncovered a second parachute and realised that one man was still at large. An order was promptly issued to all troops: 'The first parachute drop of British agents on Danish soil took place during the night of 27/8 December near Koege. One of the agents is dead, but the other succeeded in escaping. As further parachute drops are to be expected, all troops are advised to be especially vigilant.'

Of course, the Germans had never known about the first parachute drop which had delivered Sneum and Christophersen into Denmark, but that was of little consolation to Tommy now, as the manhunt for British agents reached fever pitch. He presumed that the searches were due to the fact that he had been recognised in the florist's shop on Christmas Eve.

So now, of four agents parachuted into Denmark, one was dead, another (Hammer) was bewildered and powerless to transmit as he reached the sanctuary of relatives in Copenhagen, and a third (Christophersen) was on the run and losing his nerve. Meanwhile, Sneum wasn't aware that his predicament had been worsened by the intense competition between the two British intelligence agencies. All he knew was that he was now in deep trouble and would have to use all his cunning to evade capture.

＊ ＊ ＊

On New Year's Day, Emmy Valentin called into Sneum's flat. She pulled out a napkin containing some crude sketches and explained that she had persuaded her Abwehr officer, after several bottles of wine, to draw some U-boat bays and the bomb shelters that housed them. They were all to be found at the docks in Kiel. He had even provided a map. 'The officer was probably in love with Emmy, but even so I don't know how the word "intelligence" could be used to describe him or his department after what he gave away that night,' Sneum said later.

But Emmy hadn't finished. She explained how she had asked her

escort if he was depressed that there appeared to be no end in sight
to the war, now that the German advance to Moscow had stalled in
the Russian snow.

'Don't worry about the war; it'll soon be over,' he repeated.
When asked how he could be so sure, he replied, 'We'll soon have
a little bomb powerful enough to blow the whole of south-eastern
England to atoms.'

Sneum made her repeat the phrase. It still seemed too terrible to
contemplate. Perhaps a drunken officer's bravado had got the
better of him, but Tommy knew the remark had to be taken
seriously. Was such a bomb feasible? He had always been
fascinated by physics, and possessed the intellect and imagination
to grasp ideas that others might dismiss as too fantastic for serious
consideration. His identification of a radar installation on Fanoe
had demonstrated just such a flexible mind, though talk of a super-
bomb was another matter entirely. Sneum knew he would have to
call upon his contacts in the scientific community in order to check
the Abwehr officer's boastful claim.

In his youth, Tommy had been taught physics by Harald Bohr at
a college in Copenhagen. Harald was the brother of Niels Bohr, the
leading authority on nuclear physics, and Sneum realised that Niels
might now be able to provide the key to understanding what the
German had said. The problem was that Harald probably wouldn't
remember Tommy well enough to want to help him; and anyway,
Niels was renowned as a very private individual who liked to spend
his leisure time in the company of a select group of close friends.
Fortunately for the British, though, Niels Bohr and Thomas Sneum
had some mutual friends: two brilliant scientists who also
happened to be resistance sympathisers. Bohr trusted both men
implicitly. These were Professors Chiewitz and Hagedorn, the
doctors who had helped Tommy after his painful landing back in
September. Now Chiewitz was asked to contact Bohr on a matter
of the utmost scientific urgency.

Tommy explained the relationship between the two men:

Chiewitz and Bohr had been friends since school and rode
together. But Chiewitz was like a volcano, he just went all over
the place with his views, telling you what he did and didn't like.

Bohr couldn't have been more different – he was very reserved. But the friendship worked and they always maintained a great respect for each other. I was confident Chiewitz would be able to broach this very sensitive subject with the one man who would have sufficient knowledge and understanding to interpret what we were hearing. So I told Chiewitz what Emmy had been told about a new bomb, and what we wanted him to ask Bohr. Then we just had to wait.

As Tommy was attempting to uncover what were potentially some of the war's biggest secrets, he was being seriously undermined by his own side. The bust-up with Lunding, coupled with the way he had dissuaded Birgit Valentin from accepting her German assignment, had left the haughty Princes with a lasting grudge. They therefore decided to complain again about Sneum and Christophersen to Ronnie Turnbull. For his part, Turnbull believed that the Princes alone could supply intelligence of a sufficiently high grade to have significant bearing on the course of the war. Nordentoft, Gyth and Lunding, then, had effectively brainwashed Britain's man in Stockholm. He still didn't want any British agents – SOE or SIS – in his theatre of operations. And as for any plans for a coordinated Danish uprising – now termed 'The Booklet' – he was quite happy to entrust the timing of all British involvement to the Princes, who could communicate as usual through their dependable Danish messenger, Ebbe Munck.

At this point, Turnbull was eagerly anticipating a personal visit from Lunding. If some sort of formal agreement could be achieved between the two men, it would be a feather in Turnbull's cap, a clear signal to London that he was respected by the most important intelligence officers in Denmark. It didn't matter to Ronnie that nothing would be done to undermine the Nazi occupation of Denmark for the foreseeable future. He was still convinced that Danish Intelligence knew best, and that SOE should therefore do as they said. And he certainly wasn't about to allow an agent of the rival British intelligence agency to get in his way.

With all this in mind, Turnbull sent an urgent message to

London on 10 January 1942. It argued against sending any more
SOE agents as successors to the unfortunate Bruhn and
Hammer:

> ... 4. I fear that if we press on wildly, we may antagonise the
> Princes, who are already upset over continued presence of C's [the
> code name of SIS's chief, Stewart Menzies] two men in 4532's
> [Munck's code number] LAND, and this would endanger whole of
> booklet.
> 5. In addition, it would be tragic if we were to miss visit of one of
> Princes here.

Sneum and Christophersen were being cast as part of the problem,
rather than the solution, because they were upsetting Turnbull's
best contacts by their 'continued presence' in '4532's LAND' –
Denmark. The reputation that Sneum had built for himself during
his dealings with R.V. Jones seemed to count for nothing now. As
far as SOE were concerned, SIS's efforts to gain a foothold in
Denmark had achieved nothing but trouble.

Sneum would need all his nerve in the weeks to come, because
he was up against much more than the German occupiers.
Threatening his survival were the dinosaurs of Danish Intelligence,
an incompetent and frightened spy partner, one Allied intelligence
agency that wanted him out of Denmark, and another that seemed
to have all but deserted him.

Chapter **28**

HUNTED

TOMMY WAS NOW READY TO hunt down Sigfred Christophersen. His brother-in-law, the detective Niels-Richard Bertelsen, was perfectly placed to assist in the search. Within a couple of days he had furnished Tommy with an address for Thorbjoern Christophersen in Kongens Lyngby, north of Copenhagen, and Sneum wasted no time in going there.

Having watched Sigfred and Thorbjoern leave the building, he broke into their apartment. It took only minutes to find what he was looking for. With a mixture of triumph and disgust, Sneum recalled later:

> I got hold of Sigfred's codes, which, contrary to all British regulations, he was keeping inside the lining of one of his jackets. I wrote the whole bloody lot down, so that I could prove to the British I'd got them. I suspected Christophersen would try to convince the British that I was a shit who was afraid of this, that and the other. But he was the one who was afraid. Even so, I believed he would tell the British his own story and substitute my name for his.

Before long the Christophersen brothers strolled back into Thorbjoern's apartment to be confronted by Sneum's menacing presence. Tommy remembered: 'Sigfred froze and began to tremble. He turned white and seemed to realise that the game was up. He probably thought I was going to kill him right there. I wanted to, but I knew I wouldn't get away with it.' So he simply told Sigfred that he knew about his dealings with Duus Hansen and the stories he had made up. He insisted that he would be the one to handle all future contact with Bang and Olufsen's chief engineer. Furthermore, Christophersen would have to hand over all his radio crystals, return the money he had taken, and move back in with Kaj Oxlund. Any future attempts to run away would not be dealt with so gently.

Sigfred knew he was in no position to argue, so he agreed to all Tommy's demands, anxious perhaps to keep Thorbjoern out of the firing line. It must have seemed to Christophersen that Sneum was capable of hunting him down wherever he ran. His best chance of survival now was to do as he was told. Cautiously, Tommy allowed himself to entertain the thought that he had at last gained control over radio communication with Britain. But in Copenhagen that winter, danger was never far away.

Tommy had hidden Duus Hansen's new transmitter in his flat in St Annaegade. He was reluctant to move the equipment, even though he thought he had been recognised at the nearby florist's, fearing that it would only draw more attention to himself. He also felt that St Annaegade still offered enough advantages to make the gamble of staying put worthwhile. If anyone tried to force their way into the building on the ground floor, for example, Emmy or Birgit could act as his early-warning system. He might well be able to escape across the rooftops before anyone reached his hideaway five storeys up.

There were good reasons for keeping cool and trying to behave normally, not least the question of the latest scientific intelligence. Professor Chiewitz hadn't been back in touch yet, and he and his friend Niels Bohr might need clarification on a certain point in the days or weeks to come. If Tommy lost his nerve and went on the run, he would be in no position to offer it. And if he lost contact with Emmy, he wouldn't be able to send her back out to pick the brains of her Abwehr officer, should additional information be necessary.

Despite the risks, therefore, Sneum decided to stay where he was until he had completed his investigations into Emmy's super-bomb lead. Then he received a call from Bertelsen: 'Niels told me that one of his colleagues had asked him, quite out of the blue, whether it was possible that I was back in Denmark. Niels had told him it was impossible.'

This alarming development meant that all local shops immediately became out of bounds for Tommy, in case he was spotted again. The solution was to order essential supplies from the local grocery store. Bags of shopping were duly delivered one morning by a rough-looking boy who looked in need of what little money the errand would earn him. Within sight of the youngster, Tommy took some cash from a pocket in the lining of his coat, which was hanging by the door. He handed the boy what he owed, then turned away to put the provisions on the kitchen table. 'I was away for only a few seconds,' recalled Sneum uncomfortably. 'But it was enough.' In those unguarded moments, the quick-thinking tearaway dipped a greedy hand into Sneum's overcoat in search of more money. He must have been astonished to pull out a pistol instead. Instinctively, the boy hid the weapon under his own scruffy jacket. When Tommy returned to close the door, he was surprised to see the ruffian still standing there. He tossed the boy a coin as a tip, and sent him on his way.

Several hours passed before Tommy checked his overcoat pockets and found that the pistol was missing. 'It still didn't cross my mind at the time that the boy could have taken it, so I searched the whole flat before concluding that my security at St Annaegade had been blown.'

Trying not to panic, he called Emmy on the ground floor and told her that she must, at all costs, prevent any uninvited visitors from entering the building. Then he rang Duus Hansen and Oxlund to tell them how much trouble he was in. They all agreed the situation amounted to an emergency, and that a full and immediate clear-out of the flat was necessary. Bravely, Sneum's two associates volunteered to help, despite the obvious dangers to all concerned. Tommy told them to use a special series of knocks when they arrived at the front door to number fifteen. He also forewarned Emmy and gave her detailed descriptions of both men.

Within half an hour, Oxlund and Duus Hansen were frantically clearing Sneum's flat of any incriminating evidence. Fifteen minutes later, they left in opposite directions with a bag each. The most important task had yet to be performed, however. Since Tommy had slipped up, he insisted that he should be the one to take the biggest risk of all, and move the radio set built by Duus Hansen. He made sure the others had time to vacate the area first, even though he knew time was probably against him.

Unfortunately, the youngster who had stolen the pistol had excitedly tried to impress his friends by letting off a few rounds early that afternoon. Before long, the police had been called to the back streets of Christianshavn in order to disarm the delinquent. The boy knew he was in big trouble unless he told them precisely where he had obtained the firearm.

'The Count,' he said. 'I took it from the Count.'

Knowing that 15 St Annaegade belonged to Countess Trampe, the boy had assumed that Sneum was her aristocratic husband. Armed with the address, the police wasted no time in mounting a raid.

Before Tommy could leave the building with the radio, his telephone rang. It was Emmy, warning that two uninvited visitors were outside the front door. She had pulled a bucket and sponge out into the main hall and was pretending to be cleaning the floor, but she didn't know how long she could stall them. Once she had hung up, the knocks on the door became louder. The two plain-clothes policemen were threatening to break down the door, so Emmy decided to try a charm offensive. As soon as she opened the door, however, they brushed past her.

'We've come to see the Count,' said the leading detective impatiently, looking around for anyone who might be ready to make a break for it.

'Well, you won't find him here,' answered Emmy truthfully.

Before she could delay them, though, they had begun their climb to the fifth floor. They raced all the way up to Sneum's door in no time, and he was trapped. If he tried to scramble out of his window now, they would hear him. He had two choices: try to fight his way past them and risk being shot; or stay where he was and pretend to be out.

He recalled his fear: 'I looked through the little spyhole in his door and recognised one of the men on the other side. It was Detective Esbensen, one of the most pro-German police officers in the whole of Copenhagen. Bertelsen, my brother-in-law, had given me photographs of the most dangerous policemen soon after I landed back in Denmark. Now I was practically face to face with the worst of them.'

It was Esbensen's job to track down anti-Nazi elements and eliminate anyone who might threaten the cosy cooperation that existed between Denmark and the occupying forces. If the first British-run spy in Copenhagen were caught, the consequences certainly wouldn't be pretty for him. Sneum might be sent to Germany for torture at the hands of the Gestapo, packed off to a concentration camp or simply executed. Whatever Sneum's fate, he knew there wouldn't be a happy ending if Esbensen got through that door.

He heard Emmy climbing the stairs in one last attempt to save him.

'Gentlemen, please. Surely there must be some mistake,' she pleaded.

'Who lives here?' demanded Esbensen.

'Just a tenant, a very nice chap,' replied Emmy, looking as casual as she could. 'He passed me on the stairs at lunchtime and seemed in a rush to go out. He hasn't come back yet.'

Esbensen tried the door and discovered that it was locked. 'Do you have a spare key?' he asked. 'Otherwise I'm afraid we'll have to break down the door.'

On the other side of that door, Tommy's heart thumped a little louder as he willed Emmy to think on her feet. She said she thought there might be duplicate a key in her apartment, along with some of the tenant's details. 'You can see the street from there, so you will be in a good position to notice when he comes home. Follow me,' she said breezily.

The last thing Tommy could make out as the trio started to descend the stairs was Emmy declaring herself to be terrible with names. He wondered how long she would be allowed to play dumb as she went through the motions of searching for the key and documents, which of course she would be unable to find. He guessed a minute or two at best. Leaving only a pair of spectacles on a table in his room, he crept downstairs, carrying the precious new radio transmitter in its neat little case. Praying that no creaking floorboard would betray him, he slipped out of the front door and walked away as briskly as he dared. With a smile he remembered: 'Emmy told the policemen they could observe the street from her apartment, and that was true; but you could only see to the left from there. I turned right.' In seconds he was just another a faceless figure on a wintry city street. As he left St Annaegade behind him, he knew that his love triangle with the Valentins had been broken for ever.

He made certain he wasn't being followed before heading to the safety of Kaj Oxlund's apartment in Noekkerosevej. There Tommy uprooted the floorboards, took out the old radio, and installed the new Duus Hansen model in the same hiding place. Within an hour, he had deposited the most cumbersome piece of a British spy's kit in locker number thirteen at Copenhagen's central railway station and been given a written receipt in return. Under the Danish system, the stationmaster retained the key to the locker. So if he ever wanted the primitive radio back, Tommy would need to show the receipt.

When the detectives finally broke into the fifth-floor flat at 15 St Annaegade, they were disappointed to find it almost entirely cleared of possessions. What Esbensen and his colleagues discovered on the table intrigued them, though, especially when they received the results of the tests that were subsequently conducted in a police laboratory. The mystery man, who had so nearly been caught, had apparently made a careless mistake in his rush to escape, one they had reason to believe might lead to his positive identification in time. The glasses he had left behind were most unusual: one of the lenses corrected a short-sighted eye, the other a long-sighted eye. A police doctor confirmed that the condition existed in only a tiny percentage of the population. The authorities therefore started the hunt for a man whose peculiar eye problems would ultimately betray his identity, or at the very least link him to the apartment. 'Carelessly' leaving behind the specially prepared spectacles had worked just as Sneum, who had perfect vision, had intended.

Chapter **29**

BOHR'S BOMBSHELL

TOMMY WAS ON THE RUN and by now he had come to the conclusion that the British were unlikely to help him. He hadn't heard a word from Rabagliati or anyone else in London since landing in Denmark, so he would have to rely on his own contacts, as usual. Though he needed somewhere to hide, even now he didn't want to be too far from the action in Copenhagen. Rather than try to return to Britain, his aim was to weather the storm in the Danish capital and then continue with his mission.

There wasn't much room at Kaj Oxlund's first-floor flat, because Christophersen had returned as ordered. Besides, it seemed more sensible to leave Kaj to keep Sigfred under close observation. After giving the matter some thought, Sneum decided to take up a long-standing offer of accommodation in the basement of a house belonging to Professor Hagedorn, who was attempting to verify the information about Germany's super-bomb with his friend Chiewitz. There was ample space in the basement to hide Duus Hansen's radio apparatus; and the room was self-contained, so Tommy could have his own set of keys and move about freely. Hagedorn would simply deny all knowledge of Tommy's presence if the latter were caught. Though such a claim would certainly be doubted, it would be the professor's best hope of avoiding the same fate as a captured spy.

* * *

As Sneum reorganised his life, so did his estranged wife Else. The spell as a shop assistant in Copenhagen's city centre had provided a distraction from her husband's latest disappearance. Unfortunately, with the Christmas rush over and the demand for staff reduced, she had been laid off by the Fonnesbech store. Once again she was faced with the frustrations of life as a single parent. But once again her family came to the rescue and agreed to finance a career move that might soon hand her back her precious independence.

She enrolled for a course at Miss A. Wiesel, a top secretarial college in Copenhagen. Between 10.00 a.m. and 1.00 p.m. each weekday, she honed her typing, stenography and book-keeping skills. The rest of the time she was happy to spend with Marianne. The college course gave her hope for a brighter professional future, even if her personal life had provided more heartache than she had anticipated.

* * *

Another estranged wife, a former friend of Else, had suffered no less from the impact of the war. Having spent her first Christmas for ten years apart from her husband, Tulle Oxlund had time to reflect upon where it had all gone wrong. Kaj's personality had changed almost as soon as the Nazis had invaded. Then, in the summer of 1941, he seemed to have squandered a handsome inheritance on several failed business ventures. To her intense embarrassment, creditors had started knocking on their door. It was no coincidence that in this awful atmosphere their worst arguments had erupted. Before long, the fights had become violent. That was when she had known it was time to leave, for both their sakes. A formal separation was the next step, but she found it hard to erase the sweeter memories she had from many happy years of marriage.

Her first, pre-Christmas, telephone call to the marital home had thrown up more questions than answers, not least over the mystery man who had picked up the phone. Confused, Tulle called Kaj again in January 1942 to ask what was happening. He was necessarily evasive. Whatever sticky predicament he was in, he didn't want her to know the details; nor, quite clearly, did he want her help. Sadly, she realised she was destined to remain firmly on the outside, looking in.

* * *

Tommy had only just settled into Hagedorn's cellar when he received a visit from his new landlord and Chiewitz. The latter had some very important news. The previous night he had persuaded Niels Bohr to come to dinner. Eventually, he and Hagedorn had steered the conversation towards the possibility of a new super-bomb. As far as they could understand from Bohr, it would be based on the release of nuclear energy. And if he was right, both sides in this war had realised the hugely destructive potential of such a weapon, and would already be assessing how quickly it could become a reality.

Chiewitz continued: 'Bohr says that in Germany two professors in particular, Werner Heisenberg and Otto Hahn, have been working in this field. But that doesn't necessarily mean they have been building a bomb.'

'But it's possible?' Sneum feared the answer.

'Niels says that such a bomb could be built.' There was a stunned silence before Chiewitz added: 'To build it would be one thing. To control it would be quite another. That's what Bohr told me. But he thinks there is one man who might be able to control the huge forces involved: an Italian professor called Enrico Fermi.'

As long as the Allies kept Fermi out of the clutches of the Nazis, Tommy felt there was reason to believe that this devastating new weapon might remain out of Germany's reach, however much pressure Hitler placed on his own scientists. He recalled later: 'Bohr believed that the Germans thought they could develop this bomb. But he didn't think they would be able to do it in practice.'

The fact that they might try, however, was in itself a hugely important piece of intelligence. And what if Bohr was underestimating the ingenuity of the German scientists? Such a mistake had been made before. Tommy knew he had to move quickly to send the British news of what he had just learned. Fortunately, his scheduled transmission to London was imminent.

Now, more than ever, Duus Hansen's expertise would be crucial. Within an hour, Tommy had contacted Copenhagen's most innovative engineer and they had arranged to meet that evening in the coastal village of Skodsborg. Sneum had rented a third-floor apartment at the upper end of the quaint little holiday village in the hope of achieving clearer contact with his spymasters. Sigfred Christophersen, who now considered it too dangerous to be present during transmissions, wouldn't be there to hinder them. Duus Hansen had given up trying to act as peacemaker between the two agents, and Tommy considered Sigfred's absence at key moments a positive advantage. The new partnership had the right crystals and a superb new radio, so why did they need a ham-fisted wireless operator whose nerves were shot to pieces?

Duus Hansen calmly transmitted Sneum's coded message about the potential for an atom bomb in a fraction of the time it would have taken Christophersen to perform the task. The new recruit felt confident that he must have succeeded, even though, yet again, they received no acknowledgement from England. Sneum had already warned him that the British might not see fit to reply.

There was a sense of satisfaction as Sneum and Duus Hansen left the apartment to make their way back to Copenhagen. For the first time, all their problems seemed conquerable; they were alive, they were free and they had done an outstanding job. It was the start of a highly productive phase in Tommy's mission for Britain's Secret Intelligence Service.

With Duus Hansen's increasing help and guidance, Sneum sent the British a treasure trove of information over the coming weeks: ship and troop movements, the names of key German intelligence officers in Copenhagen, lists of their treacherous assistants among the Danish police; all were detailed and dispatched across the radio waves to London with unrivalled speed and skill. In his communications,

Sneum pointed to the strategic importance of certain bridges, the destruction of which would do most damage to German transport links. He also used his political background and contacts to keep Britain informed of any subtle shifts among Denmark's major parties, with particular regard to their relations with the occupiers.

Duus Hansen later recalled this period:

Sneum had told me that people in England would be listening to receive our transmissions at certain times on certain days, calculated from the date of his parachute drop into Denmark. We were not able to get an answer during those early transmissions to Britain, but Sneum told me that he had been instructed to continue sending the messages, even if he didn't get an answer. They would be able to receive those signals even if we in Denmark couldn't receive the English answer. And Sneum told me later that he, through other channels, had learned that the telegrams had been received.

The enmity between Sneum and Christophersen built up so much that further work between the two men was no longer possible. As Sneum saw that the technical questions were now solved, and being independent of Christophersen, he decided that with or without Christophersen's agreement, the latter should be stripped of his duties and sent back to England.

One of the reasons for this decision was also that Christophersen never obeyed orders, rented a room for himself in town, never showed the required care for security, contacted his family, and included his brother in all the details. In this context I can make a remark: it hit me very hard when I realised that Christophersen never dared to be in place personally for the radio transmissions, and yet he asked for all kinds of security measures regarding when a radio should be used. Furthermore I realised that he had very poor training in Morse telegraphy.

Sneum saw Christophersen's brother as being dangerous too, because he also knew all the details, so Sneum considered it to be the right thing to do to get them both out of the country – one way or the other.

Duus Hansen's reference to Christophersen renting a room suggests that he had alternated for a time between his brother Thorbjoern's

apartment and a bolt-hole in Copenhagen city centre. Now he was
back with Oxlund, where Sneum could at least keep an eye on him,
but this soon created more tension than any of them could bear.

Just when the radio problems were solved, another crisis
emerged: Sneum ran out of places to hide. Hagedorn made it clear
that, on reflection, he didn't want a British agent living in his
basement. Understandably, he feared reprisals against his family if
they were caught. Although Skodsborg was safe, Tommy risked
losing touch with important events in Copenhagen if he based
himself so far out of town. Reluctantly, therefore, he moved in with
Oxlund and Christophersen. The beauty of this base had always
been that it was far enough away from the city centre to remain
relatively secure, yet close enough to the mainstream of Danish life
for any agent to keep his finger on the pulse. But home life was
cramped and incredibly fractious, so Tommy decided that the time
had come to do something definitive about Sigfred.

Ultimately, the need to take drastic action for the sake of security
was more urgent than either Tommy or Kaj had imagined. And all
three occupants of the flat would have left in a hurry had they
realised the extent to which they were being observed. For the
caretakers at 1 Noekkerosevej had noticed events in their normally
mundane world take a strange new twist in early 1942; and, as
before, they had an uncanny eye for detail.

Later, Hans Soetje helped the Danish police make out a full
report on the developments in his building, documenting the return
of Christophersen, closely followed by Sneum's arrival. Fortunately
for the spies, he only ever referred to them by the nicknames he had
given them:

> Soetje thinks it must have been the middle of January 1942 when 'The
> Russian' came back to live regularly with Oxlund again. Besides 'The
> Russian' there was also soon a person at Oxlund's whom Soetje called
> 'The Aviator'. Soetje thinks that this man had shown up before, while
> Oxlund was still living with his wife, but he can't remember exactly
> when that was, and 'The Aviator' had been away for a long time.

At this point the nosy caretaker made an erroneous link between
the sudden reappearance in his building of SIS agent Thomas

Sneum and the SOE agents dropped into Denmark just after Christmas. The police report continued:

Soetje had been reading in his newspaper that two aviators had jumped out of an aircraft, and one was killed while the other disappeared. Now 'The Aviator' started to visit Oxlund. Therefore Soetje thought about the possibility that 'The Aviator' could be this person who had dropped from the sky after jumping out of the aircraft and survived.

Luckily for Sneum, Soetje didn't seem to have enough confidence in his theory to act upon it immediately and go to the authorities, preferring instead to exercise his love of other people's business in more trivial ways. The report added: 'It soon became clear that "The Aviator" had taken up residence with Oxlund. He probably slept on the sofa in the living room, while "The Russian" who also lived there slept in the bedroom, on one side of the double bed, while Oxlund slept on the other side of the bed.'

The caretaker's suspicions had been aroused by the routines of the strangers, their appearance and above all by a box they sometimes carried. The police report explained:

Oxlund, 'The Russian' and 'The Aviator' left the building between ten and eleven each morning. Sometimes 'The Russian' left first, sometimes 'The Aviator', and the remaining occupant(s) followed a short time after. They never went out as a trio together in daylight. 'The Aviator' was dressed in Danish officer's uniform with long brown riding boots, but his cap looked too big for him. When evening came all three returned, but either 'The Aviator' or 'The Russian' came first with the remaining pair arriving later.

They purchased large amounts of food and drink and it was clear they cooked for themselves, including big joints of meat. But during blackouts in the city Oxlund came out, either with 'The Russian' or alone, carrying a box with a handle on top, which looked like a big sewing machine. Soetje didn't think anything about it at the time, but looking back he thinks the box must have contained a radio transmitter. He never heard any noise in Oxlund's apartment of the type which might have been caused by a radio transmitter; and if they did transmit, it must have been after the time normal radio transmissions had stopped for the evening.

Soetje did have some radio disturbance on his own radio, and it is possible it could have come from Oxlund's radio, but he never received any complaints from neighbours, as he would have done as caretaker had there been a widespread problem.

It is clear from this report that the fate of Sneum and his colleagues during these tense weeks hung by a thread. Their freedom, perhaps even their lives, depended upon Soetje's and his wife's decision-making. Whether the caretakers resented the occupation, or whether they were simply too scared of the consequences of getting involved, they chose not to act on their suspicions by reporting the mysterious trio to the police at the time. Perhaps they took this decision because a police raid might have damaged the property for which they were responsible, especially if it escalated into a shoot-out. Or it could have been because of something as simple as a party the previous summer. The police report revealed: 'Mrs Oxlund moved out in the first half of July, 1941. On 15 July, Soetje had his 53rd birthday party, and he remembered that Kaj Oxlund was by then living all alone. So he invited Oxlund to the birthday party.'

Had Kaj's natural charm, and the sad end to his marriage, struck a chord with the caretaker? Although he clearly wasn't a great fan of the strange company Oxlund was now keeping, it appeared that Soetje still liked the man he had known for so long. So, for the time being, Kaj Oxlund, Thomas 'The Aviator' Sneum and Sigfred 'The Russian' Christophersen remained at liberty.

Chapter **30**

LONDON BECKONS

WHEN SIGFRED CHRISTOPHERSEN RETURNED to Oxlund's flat wearing a false beard and glasses one day, he was summoned to the kitchen table.

'There's a message for you,' said Tommy. 'It arrived this afternoon. Duus Hansen and I transmitted without you, and for once the British sent a message back.'

Christophersen looked suspicious. 'What did they say?'

'It's coded,' explained Sneum. 'Yours, I assume.'

Sure enough, when Christophersen looked at the piece of paper, he recognised his code name and codes. The message read: 'Columbus ordered to leave Denmark. Go to British Legation in Stockholm then England.' He was stunned.

Sneum, his face blank, waited for an explanation.

'They're pulling me out,' revealed Christophersen. 'I've got to get across to Sweden.'

'What about me?' Tommy's question was impatient.

'Doesn't mention you. Just me.'

Though Sneum offered to help his partner find a way out, Christophersen quickly made it clear that he intended to make his own plans. However, both men were aware that the harsh Scandinavian winter offered one dramatic means of escape – straight across the ice of the frozen sea. In some parts of the

Oeresund, the channel which separated Denmark from Sweden, the ice was up to a metre thick; in others, though, it was considerably thinner. The viability of this option depended largely upon whether Christophersen could summon enough courage to use the elements to his advantage. Sneum was simply grateful that Christophersen was finally preparing to leave, and not before time.

When Christophersen next left the apartment, Kaj sat down with Tommy to discuss the new development. 'So, you're receiving messages from London at last,' he said enthusiastically.

'No, we're not,' replied Sneum.

Oxlund looked confused, then stunned, as though an extraordinary idea had just entered his head.

'I faked the message,' Tommy added by way of confirmation.

By now Kaj wore a mischievous grin. 'Bloody good idea!' he admitted, by way of congratulation. 'But how did you get his codes?'

'Hardly difficult,' Sneum replied. 'This is Christophersen we're talking about.'

* * *

While one British agent and close associate of Sneum began planning a way out of Denmark, another was ready to enter. On the night of 28 February, Christian Michael Rottboell prepared to jump from a British plane as it circled just outside Copenhagen. The previous summer, he had survived his own, less dangerous escape across the Oeresund by boat. He had then reached England not long after Tommy, but they had not met because Christian Michael had been recruited by SOE, rather than SIS.

In choosing Rottboell, SOE made a decision which Sneum had warned against when briefing his own Britsh handlers at SIS. This was typical of the communication breakdown between the two organisations. In discussions with Rabagliati, Tommy had expressed reservations about Rottboell's potential to be a successful field chief, because the young aristocrat was too honest for his own good. In short, Sneum didn't think his friend could lie to save his life.

From the moment he had turned up at Ronald Turnbull's office at the British Legation in Stockholm, however, SOE had earmarked

Rottboell as a young man with the potential to be a future agent and leader. Pretty soon, he was invited to undergo training with the organisation. When Bruhn was killed trying to parachute into Denmark in late December, Rottboell was hurriedly prepared for essentially the same role that Sneum had been performing for SIS since September.

Seemingly oblivious to the potentially disastrous effects of his interdepartmental rivalry with SIS, Ralph Hollingworth, the head of SOE Denmark in London, later recalled proudly: 'I chose Rottboell, though he was very young and had not yet completed his long training in the Special Schools, because he was very intelligent, understood security, and like Bruhn was a man of great integrity, inspired confidence and had all the qualities which make a leader of men.'

As he checked his equipment above the pre-arranged rendezvous point, Rottboell was ready for action and unaware of the problems encountered by the SOE-affiliated reception committee below. Their car had broken down and they were nowhere near the drop-zone. Worse still, there had been no time to let Rottboell's plane know what had happened.

Descending to just a few hundred metres above the appointed place, the aircraft continued to circle as it assessed the situation on the ground. To the pilot, there appeared to be a reception committee as expected, because he could clearly see three cars parked on the road. However, he had still not received any of the signals he needed in order to give Rottboell's jump the green light. Frustratingly, since everything else seemed perfect, the pilot followed procedure and turned back without unloading his human cargo. It was the correct decision. The reception committee must have been bogus, which semed to indicate that the Germans had been tipped off about Britain's latest plans.

※ ※ ※

For his attempt to leave the country that Rottboell was so keen to reach, Sigfred Christophersen had recruited his brother Thorbjoern as a fellow escapee. This tactic suited Tommy down to the ground, because he wanted both of them out of his way for good. The

Christophersens had decided to cross the ice from a point near Kastrup Airport and aim for Malmo in Sweden, as Sneum had suggested.

To Tommy's dismay, however, Sigfred and Thorbjoern returned from the darkness less than an hour after they had set out, claiming the ice was too precarious. Duus Hansen claimed later: 'The first try failed and they came back, saying there was open water in the channel and therefore they couldn't continue, but that they would try again as soon as they had found out where there was continuous ice all the way from Denmark to Sweden.'

The brothers then rejected another short route, from Helsingoer to Helsingborg, because they feared that police patrols would pick them up immediately. After further failed attempts on a short route between Sletten and Rydeback, a crisis meeting was called with the Princes, who had been monitoring the situation with mounting frustration. Nordentoft, Lunding and Gyth met Christophersen and Sneum in the Jaegersborg Kaserne, the military barracks in Copenhagen. Clearly looking for sympathy, Christophersen documented all the difficulties he had experienced.

'I've been giving this some thought,' said Lunding at last. 'I recommend that you try to make your crossing from Stevns to Falsterbo.'

'It's too far,' scoffed Sneum, 'and takes them right across the southern mouth of the Oeresund. We all know how unpredictable the weather and the currents can be down there.'

Christophersen seemed to resent the interruption. He pointed out that it would be his life on the line, not Tommy's, and that Danish Intelligence were the experts in this sort of thing. He and Thorbjoern had vowed to abide by the recommendations of the professionals, and try to trek from Stevns to Falsterbo. Sneum shook his head in dismay. The route lay further south than anything he had been prepared to contemplate. Both points were sparsely populated, which was an advantage, but Falsterbo lay some twenty-three kilometres across the ice from Stevns. They might avoid being spotted; but they might also never see anyone again. The journey would be long and they would be exposed to the worst of the elements. To succeed, the brothers would require extreme powers of physical endurance and mental strength in bitter temperatures.

Sneum doubted the Christophersens had what it took, because they had seemed quite happy to turn back before. And even if they did have the necessary qualities and appetite for what they were about to attempt, they would require luck to find a way through. Tommy didn't want the Christophersens crawling back yet again, so the following day he took Oxlund quietly aside and said: 'Kaj, I want you to go with them. Tell Sigfred you want to join the British forces too.'

Oxlund looked surprised, then expressed scepticism that any of them would make it.

'Maybe you're right,' acknowledged Sneum. 'But I need you to make sure they go through with it this time. If the ice starts to break up and you have to turn back, just make sure you shoot the bastards before you come home. Then put them under the water if you can. It'll buy us some time. If you all get across alive, you can always come back to Copenhagen later, once you've delivered them to the British Legation in Stockholm. Remember, Kaj, you can come home. They must not.'

Oxlund accepted his mission, despite the risk. 'He was very courageous about it,' Tommy recalled. But the time was also right for Kaj to move on. His marriage to Tulle and his business affairs were in tatters. Life in Denmark could never be the same again for him. A fresh start and a direct shot at the Germans from a new base in Britain probably sounded attractive; although the prospect of killing fellow Danes in cold blood must have been far less appealing. Tommy, though, felt such ruthlessness was now essential to eliminate the security threat that the brothers had become. Whether Oxlund was prepared to carry out the gruesome task, if it came to the crunch, was another matter. As he prepared to leave Denmark, doubtless he hoped that he would never have to find out. 'He was soft at heart,' admitted Sneum.

Duus Hansen's recollection of Kaj's mission was chillingly matter-of-fact: 'Sneum's opinion was that the two brothers didn't wish to leave the country. Therefore it was decided that Sneum's landlord, Mr Oxlund, should accompany them over the ice to Sweden and make sure that they would get over, or in any case that they would not come back.'

Chapter **31**

TREK TO THE UNKNOWN

ON THE EVENING OF TUESDAY, 3 March 1942, Kaj Oxlund called his younger sister, Gerda Tapdrup Nielsen, at the home she shared with her husband Svend just outside Copenhagen.

'I'm going to Jutland for a few weeks,' he said. 'Huge amounts of firewood are going cheap. I think I can make some money.'

'A few weeks?' Gerda was already suspicious. 'Why so long?'

'It'll probably take me that long to get into the business,' he explained after an awkward pause.

Oxlund's sister wasn't satisfied. 'By then people won't need firewood,' she pointed out. 'It'll be spring.'

'Then I'll have to work more quickly,' replied Kaj.

'Where can we write to you?' Gerda was worried now.

'You can't,' her brother said. 'I'll be moving around. Look, I'm sorry if it all sounds a bit impulsive. I just wanted to let you know I love you.'

When Gerda told Svend about the conversation, he agreed it had been a strange one. It was almost as if Kaj were saying goodbye for ever. Things hadn't felt right for a while, and this latest exchange added to their concerns. They thought Kaj had made some money in the spring of 1941 from a business connected to the Danish railways, believing he had been paid a handsome commission for one big transaction. They assumed he had been living off that success ever since, because he certainly hadn't been in regular work for a while.

The next day, at around 1.00 p.m., Kaj phoned again, this time from Copenhagen city centre. He told his sister he wanted to give her some clothes, which he would deposit in a locker at Noerreport's train station. He promised to send her the receipt in a letter, together with some cheques and bank documents he wanted Svend to look after, since banking was his brother-in-law's field of expertise.

No doubt the Christophersen brothers were making similar arrangements with their father, a gardener named Johannes Ruder, and their mother, Anne Katrine. Sigfred and Thorbjoern, like Oxlund, were by now focused on the challenge they faced. Kaj must have told the brothers that his only motive for coming with them was to reach England in order to fight alongside the Allied forces. Irrespective of whether Sigfred and Thorbjoern entirely trusted his motives, they had little choice but to comply. They knew he was a close friend of Sneum, and to freeze him out of their plan would only increase the danger they faced.

Late on the afternoon of Thursday 5 March, Tommy prepared a meal for the trio in Kaj's flat. He sent them on their way with one last piece of advice. 'Remember to tie yourselves together with rope just before you step out onto the ice. If one of you goes under, the other two can pull him back out if you're quick enough. Let's hope it doesn't come to that. Keep cool heads and stay together. That way you can still succeed, even on the route you've chosen. Good luck.'

The caretaker, Hans Soetje, saw Oxlund and 'The Russian' leave at six o'clock in the evening, while Sneum remained in the flat, to pack away and remove the possessions they had left behind. Joining up with Thorbjoern, Kaj and Sigfred travelled forty-five minutes by rail from Copenhagen to Koege. There, they changed trains for a half-hour journey to the quaint village station of Klippinge on the Stevns peninsula. The trio stepped onto the snow and trudged enviously past snug cottages with thatched roofs. Soon they hit an open road and began the two-kilometre hike towards a wood between Gjorslev and Raby. Deep inside that wood they had earlier concealed the sledge and supplies that would go with them on the journey to Sweden. Men going to the North Pole could not have prepared more thoroughly. On the sledge were a tent, blankets, sheets for camouflage, an air-pillow and mattresses upon which to rest the following day, some safety rope and an axe. Their provisions consisted of large amounts of food and drink, cigarettes and even warm coffee in Thermos flasks. Each man was to carry his own length of rope and a long staff to help vault across any cracks in the ice. If anyone fell into the water and had to be pulled out, he knew extra woollen socks and dry underwear would be available to aid his recovery. They all put on white overalls so that their darker clothing wouldn't show up against the ice and snow. Now they were almost ready.

Between ten and eleven o'clock, they simply waited, taking shots of brandy for warmth and courage. The smell of the alcohol would also lend credence to the usual cover story – that they were only breaking curfew in some sort of drunken prank. Any close examination of the sledge by Danish police or German soldiers would soon show they were lying, but they reckoned it was better to be well prepared than to give extra credence to an alibi they might never need to use. They checked the equipment and waited for the nearest church bells to sound the hour. By eleven the local population had put up their shutters for the night, and the men were ready to move. All the team's money was given to Thorbjoern, who put it in the inside pocket of his overcoat. Oxlund carried a pistol, though he didn't tell his accomplices.

They crept out into the flat, barren fields, pulling the sledge behind them. They plotted a course for the coast that allowed them to sweep north of the picture-postcard village of Holtug and join a lonely lane to the sea unobserved. Even in summer, this part of the Stevns peninsula is a desolate place. In winter, the cold expanse of land and ice is enough to chill the soul. Encouraging each other, they pressed on through the snow and completed the last three kilometres to the cliffs, where they found the steep path down to the pebble beach. Getting the sledge down the slope must have been tricky, but then they faced a more daunting challenge. It was time to step out into oblivion. The rope they had packed stayed coiled under some extra clothing on the sledge. Perhaps they decided it was sufficiently close in case of emergency.

On a clear day, it is just possible to see Falsterbo's buildings on the horizon. But on a dark night the distant village would have been invisible. Only courage, physical fitness and their compass could bring that world closer. They had just four kilometres of Swedish peninsula to aim for, far across the ice sheets. If they miscalculated by just a few degrees, they faced a hopeless walk on a treacherous course parallel to Sweden's southern coast. In these conditions, they might never sight the land which lay so close.

As they took their first, creaking steps onto the sheet of white, it must have been hard for them to visualise what lay before them. Trusting their lives to a compass lit briefly by a shielded match, they set off on a north-easterly course and hoped for the best. Each man had to conquer the fear of not knowing whether the next step would be his last. But they were all sustained by a powerful survival instinct and a patriotic desire to free Denmark from Hitler's grip. They would need all that mental strength and more.

Disaster struck for the first time after just two hours. The sledge, piled high with their supplies, plunged straight through a weak point in the ice when the trio paused for an ill-advised rest. Thorbjoern, who had been pulling it, was first to be dragged into the freezing water, but soon all three were fighting for their lives, barely able to breathe in the lethal cold. Sigfred and Kaj managed to pull themselves out and find a fragile foothold on a slab of ice. Then they hauled Thorbjoern to safety too. All three men must have known they were now in a battle for their lives, yet a collective decision was taken to press on for Sweden.

Shaking uncontrollably, they marched straight into another weak point in the ice. Perhaps they had been undone by what remained of the shipping lane, through which the steel bows of huge vessels carved a temporary path each morning. The hostile temperatures returned each night to patch the ice-cutters' work, but the newly formed ice didn't always fully repair the gaping scars left by the ships. It was like walking into a minefield, and no one knew which way to turn. All three felt the freezing water assault their senses as they stumbled and scrambled for a firm footing on anything that still resembled a solid surface. A Swedish police report later stated: 'During the hike over the ice towards the Swedish coast they fell into the water several times, losing their sledge in the process. They had suffered a lot from the cold wind, and towards the end they were nearly frozen to the ice.' By now Thorbjoern was all but paralysed by the numbing cold. Nobly, Sigfred gave his younger brother his coat to try to increase his body temperature. Kaj was suffering gravely, too. At the Oeresund's exposed confluence with the Baltic, the temperatures were so severe and the wind so merciless that each man would have felt himself drifting helplessly towards hypothermia. Water froze so quickly on their boots and clothes that it threatened to stick them to the ice like glue. It was a constant battle to keep themselves sufficiently free to place one foot in front of the other.

Still they refused to give up, though. And, as dawn broke, they sighted Falsterbo peninsula. Although salvation was almost within reach, Thorbjoern was fading rapidly. As they clung to life, they discarded their white overalls to make themselves more visible, and cried out for help as loudly as they could. Only the sound of splitting ice answered them. With each crack, the frozen platform beneath them began to disintegrate. Yet dry, dependable land wasn't far away now.

Even closer lay another potential lifeline. A giant sheet of thicker-looking ice appeared before them. Then Sigfred saw a small fishing boat just a few hundred metres away, trying to reach them. It seemed that the boat could come no further because it was blocked by the mighty slab of ice. The fishermen were shouting and beckoning Sigfred to come to them instead, so he pushed on with what little strength he had left, and somehow summoned the energy to reach the more stable ice. Perhaps he thought the others would follow, but Thorbjoern had slumped onto the fracturing ice, unable to keep up. Kaj did manage to stagger onto the thicker ice, closer to the boat, but then he too fell to his knees. If he cried out for help, it appears that Sigfred failed to hear him. At any rate, he didn't turn back, instead pushing on towards the boat.

It took him minutes rather than the anticipated seconds to reach it, and by then the fishermen were adamant there was no way through to Kaj and Thorbjoern. Oxlund attempted to crawl towards them on his hands and knees, but he was becoming stuck to the ice and didn't seem able to get any further. Meanwhile, Thorbjoern was now out of sight, even further away, and still on the thin ice.

The emotions experienced by all three Danes, as the fishermen rowed away with only one on board, can scarcely be imagined. The Swedish police report, later compiled with Sigfred Christophersen's help, told only the bare facts:

Oxlund and Thorbjoern Christophersen were so exhausted as they neared the Swedish coast that they could not carry on to reach a boat which was on its way towards them. Meanwhile Sigfred Christophersen continued and was picked up. As the boat was not able to carry on towards the other two desperate men, they were not taken on board, and the captain of the boat turned around and took Christophersen to the shore. From there he was flown by aircraft to Malmo hospital, and that flight took him back over the ice, where Christophersen could see what had happened to his brother. He lay quietly on the ice, with no signs of life.

The emergency services were alerted as soon as the fishing boat reached the shore. A gyroplane, forerunner to the modern-day helicopter, was immediately dispatched with life-saving supplies. Oxlund would surely have heard the faint drone as the gyroplane neared the scene of the tragedy. But by the time it arrived overhead his military long-coat, already weighing down his weakened body, had become one with the ice.

There was evidence of further horrors as Oxlund refused to give up the struggle for life. He must have fallen forward at some point, probably through sheer exhaustion. In seconds his hands fused with the ice floe. When he pulled them free, the flesh from his palms and the tips of his fingers was torn away. The pieces of skin remained stuck to the freezing surface, gruesome handprints on the ice. Every time he waved towards the aircraft, what remained of his hands spattered the area around him with more blood. He knew he had been spotted, and he must have believed that his rescue was now imminent, but he still couldn't free his knees or the lower fringes of his coat from the clutches of the ice. No matter how he hacked away, he remained trapped, glued in a position of helpless prayer.

From above, the pilot of the gyroplane, Rolf von Bahr, photographed a man who was still conscious, his head swathed in scarves in an attempt to retain the last of his body heat. Although his lower half was stuck to the ice, his arms were outstretched. Von Bahr noticed the blood smeared all over the ice, and watched in horror as the red patches increased with every frantic wave. Sadly, the Swedish pilot realised the ice was too thin to take the weight of his aircraft. But he knew he could still play a part in the stranded man's salvation.

Tommy explained: 'You could take the speed of those gyroplanes down to about thirty miles per hour, so there was a reasonably good chance of dropping a parcel near to Oxlund, so that he could almost touch it.'

Von Bahr did indeed drop emergency supplies with remarkable accuracy. Hot drinks, some rope, food and dry clothes landed in neat bundles agonisingly close to Oxlund. Tommy recalled:

> I've seen the photographs and the nearest parcel seems to be only a couple of metres away, but he just couldn't reach it. He got his arms free but he couldn't reach the parcels because he didn't have the physical force left to do so, even though he knew they were there. What I've never understood is why the bloody hell the pilot didn't send someone down in a parachute, to save Kaj and Thorbjoern.

Kaj fought hard to free his legs and coat from the grip of the ice but he was still frozen fast. He flailed and lunged at the packages, knowing they were potential life-savers, but his increasingly frantic efforts proved futile. All he succeeded in doing was smearing more blood around himself.

By then, two little rowing boats had arrived, and they appeared to be less than a hundred metres away. But their bows were unable to cut through the ice, and already one vessel was in trouble, stuck after trying to carve a path through the massive slab to which Kaj was attached. When the other boat got near enough, someone threw a rope towards the stricken vessel; and once the first boat had been extricated by the second, they both rowed away while they still could.

It was almost the final nail in Kaj Oxlund's coffin. First the Nazi occupation of Denmark, and his decision to resist it, had cost him his marriage. Now it was about to cost him his life. But he was not quite finished yet. Through sheer willpower and a mighty sideways lunge, he used his weight to free one leg. The momentum ripped his coat clear of the ice, and the other leg followed as his body rolled and collapsed in a heap. Almost as soon as he was free, though, he was glued fast again, this time horizontally. If he had been able to look ahead, he would have noticed that he'd moved a little closer to one of the bundles dropped by Rolf von Bahr. But he had no energy left to reach it. He knew the pilot was still watching him from above. He died knowing.

Chapter **32**

CLOSING IN

WHEN TOMMY SNEUM looked back on his friend's death as an old man, he did so with powerful and sometimes conflicting emotions. He didn't feel guilty about sending Kaj Oxlund to his death. 'It was war,' he maintained, 'and Christophersen had to go. Kaj agreed to it all. But I should have killed Christophersen when I first planned it.' And, at his most bitter, he still felt anger towards the sole survivor: 'Two died but that coward Christophersen left them to die. He as good as killed Kaj.' At other times, though, Sneum suggested that all three men bore some responsibility for what happened to them on that awful march:

Oxlund's military coat was so long it almost went down to his heels, and when he fell or even bent down it would have pressed against the ice. It became a solid block of ice, and he didn't have enough power left in his body to pull his coat up. That's easily understood. But they could all have made it if the Christophersen brothers had picked a shorter route across the ice, or they had all taken my advice to tie themselves together with the rope. They had about twenty metres of it.

Feeling more generous one day, Tommy said of Sigfred:

Christophersen was probably so tired and cold that he didn't know what the hell to do in that situation towards the end, because confusion takes over and he wasn't one of the tough guys. He may not have been able to see well or think clearly by then. As I understand it, the Swedish fishermen who got to Christophersen said there was no more room once he was on the boat, and Christophersen may have felt he was in no position to argue. I don't know. I was still furious that he had left Oxlund, though.

And, despite his hatred for Christophersen, Tommy did occasionally acknowledge his fellow agent's achievement in surviving the trek: 'I don't think he was a courageous man in general, but I suppose he had tried to do more than the average Dane, and he did show enough courage to walk over the ice from Denmark to Sweden.'

Historical records related to this extraordinary march over the sea include Christophersen's subsequent police interviews, von Bahr's aerial photographs, and police reports written after Oxlund's body was recovered. Only Sigfred knew the full story, though; including whether he made a conscious decision to leave behind Kaj and Thorbjoern. Since confusion is a common symptom of hypothermia, and Sigfred's survival instinct was all he had to counteract his exhaustion and the intense cold, any condemnation of his conduct seems harsh. Yet it is easy to understand Tommy's anguish: from his point of view, that bid for freedom couldn't have gone worse. He lost a good friend, and the last person he wanted to survive was Sigfred, a man he had plotted to kill on several occasions.

Amazingly, Christophersen sustained no permanent physical damage from his battle with the elements. He had covered twenty-five kilometres on ice, on top of a gruelling five-kilometre snow-trek to reach the Danish coast in the first place, while pulling a heavily laden sledge. But his achievement would not have given him any satisfaction.

The ice floe containing Thorbjoern's body had melted before a recovery team could reach it, and his corpse was swept away by the Oeresund currents. It was discovered further down the coast many weeks later. The Danish authorities arrived in an ice-breaker to retrieve Kaj's body at 8.23 a.m. on 7 March. Even though he had managed to cross the border into Sweden, the Danes argued that his body was their property because he had left their shores illegally. Poor Kaj had marched from Nazi-occupied Europe to the brink of freedom, only to be dragged lifeless back to Denmark by Hitler's puppets. Still nestling snugly in his coat pocket was a pen inscribed 'K. OXLUND'. The fact that he had taken it along was an oversight which now threatened to have devastating consequences for Thomas Sneum.

Tommy's brother-in-law Niels-Richard Bertelsen told him of Oxlund's death. 'I had a drink and thought of him and said, "Bye-bye, old boy,"' Sneum recalled. Sadness and anger flowed through him in equal measure. With another swig of beer, he quietly cursed Sigfred Christophersen, and his stubborn ability to survive. 'I should have killed him,' he told himself, time and time again. Then he wondered what Christophersen might already have told the Swedes about their mission.

Considering the trauma he had suffered, Sigfred Christophersen was actually holding out rather well in Malmo. On 7 March 1942, he was interviewed by Kriminal-Kommissarie Runerheim, one of the names Sneum had memorised from Aage Park's notebook. Runerheim had to begin by confirming what Sigfred already suspected – that his two accomplices were dead. While hiding his grief must have been hard, Sigfred strenuously denied that he was in any way related to Thorbjoern. Instead, he insisted that his name was Erik Moeller, and he gave a false address. A suspicious Runerheim warned that there was no point in lying, since they could check everything with the Danish People's Register. Christophersen stuck to his story. Then he insisted that the third man was Kaj Andersen, a thirty-three-year-old lieutenant in the military. Runerheim immediately suspected the name to be a fabrication. He knew about the incriminating pen found in the dead man's coat pocket, which strongly suggested that a Kaj Oxlund, not Kaj Andersen, had died on the ice. Still, he decided to check out every aspect of the stubborn survivor's story, if only to dismantle it.

* * *

That same day in Denmark, the police endeavoured to trace the relations of a Kaj Oxlund, who was confirmed to have lived in Noekkerosevej. Oxlund's parents, it emerged, were already dead; his wife, Tulle, was recovering from a bowel operation in hospital. The Danish police needed someone to identify the body, but decided that Tulle would be in no condition to perform the gruesome task. That left Kaj's sister, Gerda, as their best hope for a quick, positive identification. Her address was duly found and she was told the grim news by a pair of policemen. In a state of shock, she refused to accompany them to the morgue until her husband had returned from work. After an hour or two, Svend arrived home and together the couple travelled with the policemen to the hospital.

The sight of her brother's frozen body laid out on a slab in such cold and impersonal surroundings was too much for Gerda. She broke down completely, and for some time she was unable to utter a comprehensible word. But to the policemen present, it was obvious that the body did indeed belong to Kaj Egon Emil Oxlund. Nor did it come as any great surprise when it emerged that no Erik Moeller had ever lived at the Copenhagen address specified by the survivor across the Oeresund. The mystery man in the Malmo hospital clearly had some explaining to do. As soon as he was well enough, they would transfer him to a police cell, so that he could be subjected to a more thorough interrogation.

Over the next few days, the Danish police focused on Oxlund's neighbours, in the hope that they might be able to shed some light upon this strange and tragic story. It was during these house-to-house enquiries that Hans Soetje first revealed the strange goings-on at 1 Noekkerosevej.

The Copenhagen force, led by Politikommissaer Odmar, now realised they might be on to something big. If they handled the investigations carefully, they would be able to distinguish themselves before their German masters. Eivind Larsen, head of the Ministry of Justice, would be kept informed of all developments from this point onwards, and Odmar would have known that his superior was in direct contact with Fregatten-Kapitan Albert Howoldt, the head of the Abwehr in Denmark. Most worryingly for Tommy Sneum, Odmar now ordered one of his best detectives, Overbejtent Thomas Noerreheden, to liaise closely with the Germans.

* * *

If the elimination of Sneum was soon to become a priority for the Germans in Denmark, it had long been high on the agenda for the self-styled Princes of Danish Intelligence. They had recently made fresh contact with Ronnie Turnbull, as usual through the Danish journalist Ebbe Munck, who offered to act as middleman for any proposed meeting. Turnbull continued to operate from the safety of Stockholm, where he lived comfortably with his wife and young son. So, if the Princes wanted a face-to-face meeting with him, one of their number would have to make the journey across the Oeresund. However, Hans Lunding didn't need to cross the perilous ice sheets on foot. Even as Kaj Oxlund and Thorbjoern Christophersen perished on the route he had mapped out for them, Lunding was using his lofty position to arrange his passage by ice-cutter from Copenhagen to Malmo. On the afternoon of 6 March, just hours after Kaj and Thorbjoern had lost their fight for life, he carved his way across the Oeresund and reached the British Legation in Stockholm without incident.

For Turnbull, this visit represented the culmination of a year's careful diplomacy. Ever since his arrival in Stockholm, he had been in awe of the Princes. Later he admitted: 'I've always been a bit of a hero-worshipper in all my activities with people who know what they're doing.' Now the Scot knew that his stock would be rising as he provided the link between Danish Intelligence and SOE Headquarters in London. And this was a relationship which had the potential to give SOE the upper hand over SIS, especially now that the latter organisation's agents were in such trouble – with one of them in Swedish custody and the other likely to be uncovered before long by the Danish police. Looking back, Turnbull acknowledged as much: 'I was to one extent lucky in that when I arrived in the middle of that terrible crisis, SIS themselves were in some kind of a mess with their man in Denmark. So that the people [from Danish intelligence] started orientating themselves towards me as being the only person they were willing to talk to.'

But Lunding still knew no more about SOE than Tommy Sneum knew about SIS. As far as each man was concerned, he was simply dealing with 'the British'.

Turnbull's meeting with Lunding took place at the house of the Swedish SOE chief, Sir Peter Tennant. It continued into the early hours of the following day, and Lunding used the occasion to present the so-called P-Plan formally, on the understanding that it would be passed up the chain of command to British Chiefs of Staff as quickly as possible. This plan promised a coordinated uprising against the Germans by a secret Danish army on a given signal from London. The timing would be all important, since it had to correspond precisely with an Allied invasion of Denmark. In order to ensure maximum impact, argued Lunding, in the meantime the Danes would give the impression that they were happy to cooperate with the German occupation.

Turnbull listened enthusiastically to a proposal that effectively provided the Danes with a chance to sit on the fence until the very last stages of the war. He agreed to the P-Plan wholeheartedly, and shared Lunding's opinion that, for now and the foreseeable future, it was best to do nothing to make the German occupation any less stable or comfortable.

Seeing that he had the young Scot in the palm of his hand, Lunding next sought and received a guarantee that no more British agents would be sent into Denmark without the Princes' consent. He argued that too much chaos had already been caused by those dropped the previous year. Since neither man had any knowledge of the scientific intelligence uncovered by Sneum, or indeed the links he had established with Duus Hansen, it's easy to see why Lunding and Turnbull were in complete agreement about future policy. Politically, at least, Sneum's fate was all but sealed by the guidelines they drew up.

Turnbull enthusiastically encoded the P-Plan and added his own personal endorsement. Later that day he sent his communication to Ralph Hollingworth in London:

This morning I completed my conversations with the Prince . . . The Prince made it clear to me that he and his colleagues wanted as much peace and quiet as possible in order to be able to send the balloon up with a bang at the right moment . . . With comparative peace and quiet during the next twelve months they are confident that they can throw in to our help a considerable force at the right moment.

So, a matter of hours after the heroic Kaj Oxlund had met a dreadful end on the ice, Hans Lunding had turned the misfortunes of Denmark's SIS spy circle to his advantage. For his part, Turnbull had made it clear that he wanted London to call off any mission that might cause an unwelcome ripple in Copenhagen. Had there been any substance to the Princes' P-Plan, this might have been a sensible strategy. Had the Princes not already missed the Freya radar stations in their own back yard, the break-out of the *Bismarck*, Copenhagen's importance as an intellectual battlefield in the atom-bomb race, and the importance of Duus Hansen, they might well have been able to claim with justification that they were the right men to handle British affairs in Denmark. In simple terms, the P-Plan made the Princes and Ronnie Turnbull look good. It would also make the ill-fated SIS operation look even uglier than it already was.

As he returned to Denmark, Lunding now felt free to decide how best to deal with Tommy Sneum.

Meanwhile, Gerda Nielsen had the grim task of visiting Tulle Oxlund in hospital and telling her that the man they had both loved was dead.

Chapter **33**

SURROUNDED

BY 12 MARCH 1942, events were taking a turn for the worse in Malmo. Having given Sneum a little time to take evasive action, Sigfred Christophersen was persuaded by Kriminal-Kommissarie Runerheim to start telling the truth. The Swedes knew that he was not Erik Moeller, and Runerheim warned him that to continue to lie would make matters even worse for him. As soon as Christophersen gave his real name and began to tell his story, Runerheim called Politikommissaer Odmar in Copenhagen and invited him over to take part in the interrogation. At the highest level, the Abwehr's chief in Denmark, Albert Howoldt, would also want to know of this vital breakthrough. But first Odmar needed to be sure that he had the whole story, and that any threat of subversion had passed. Otherwise there might be a danger that the Nazis would carry out reprisals against the Danish population for any cooperation they had afforded the spies while they remained free.

Knowing what might be at stake, Odmar was soon conducting Christophersen's interrogations personally. And Sigfred was almost as forthcoming as Tommy Sneum had feared. Perhaps he was still in shock after his ordeal, because once he had decided to admit that he had been sent from Britain, it would have been sensible to claim he was the sole survivor of the December drop that had killed Carl

Bruhn. Christophersen admitted that he had read newspaper reports about that incident, so he knew it was in the minds of his interrogators. Had he used the story, he might have convinced the Danish police that there were no other British agents in the country. Instead, he revealed that he had parachuted into Denmark in September, and even added that he had not come alone. He also confessed that the objective of the mission had been to send intelligence back to Britain on a variety of subjects. Not content with admitting that he was a British spy, though, he revealed the amount of time he had spent in England training for the mission. Worse still, he told Odmar how many times a day he could transmit to Britain during peak periods of activity, and the precise frequency he used. It was only a small consolation that he had at least destroyed his codes before setting foot on the ice.

Together with these astonishing revelations about the mission came a detailed account of virtually his entire life story. Christophersen's fear of Sneum – and the certain knowledge that the latter would kill him one day if his identity were betrayed – was probably all that kept him from giving away his partner's name too.

Even so, the Danish police now had enough information to piece together the rest of the story. They discovered that Sigfred's brother Thorbjoern had worked for Werner Gyberg, the man who set up Tommy Sneum's first meeting with Duus Hansen. They promptly arrested Gyberg, which left Sneum and Duus Hansen one step from disaster, relying solely on the businessman's defiance under interrogation. The only glimmer of hope lay in the fact that the Germans hadn't yet joined in the questioning in a bid to break him.

But even with the Danish police running the show, the future looked grim. Though they knew nothing about Duus Hansen's involvement, they had already put two and two together and realised that Christophersen's fellow agent was Tommy Sneum. There had been the unconfirmed sighting in the florist's near Emmy's house, which had prompted the enquiry about Sneum from one of Bertelsen's police colleagues. Then, in the aftermath of the tragedy on the ice, Oxlund's neighbours, in particular his caretaker, had given the police detailed descriptions of Kaj's associates. One such description bore an uncanny resemblance to

Sneum, and the caretaker had confirmed that this man, 'The Aviator', had also been seen at Oxlund's address prior to the occupation. It didn't take much investigation to establish that Oxlund and Sneum had been longstanding friends. 'The Aviator' had been aptly nicknamed, for the Danish police began to realise that Sneum must have survived his flight in the Hornet Moth and reached England the previous summer. And now there was plenty of evidence to suggest that he had returned as a spy. Tommy had suddenly become the most wanted man in Denmark.

* * *

Fortunately for Sneum, though, he held one advantage over the police – some of their own detectives were on his side. Amazingly, the Copenhagen force had never made the connection between Niels-Richard Bertelsen and his brother-in-law. And so, in the early hours of 14 March, Bertelsen and Sneum were able to enter Odmar's office and read a report detailing precisely what Christophersen had revealed up to that point.

With his worst fears confirmed, Tommy cursed his British spymaster, Rabagliati, for ignoring his warnings before the mission had even begun. But he also cursed himself, for not killing Christophersen when he had the chance. He knew the Danish police would now check all his old contacts and visit his regular haunts. More than ever, it was time to behave in a way the Danish authorities would least expect. 'At the time, I was very much concerned about staying alive, and that's why I moved into the Hotel Astoria,' Sneum explained later. 'I thought it was the one place where the people who were hunting me would never think to look.'

On the face of it, there was nothing wrong with the Astoria: the architecture was a little grim, but that made it no different to many hotels situated next to a city's central railway station. What made it a curious choice as a spy's hideaway was the fact that it was inhabited by half of the middle-ranking German officers in Denmark. It was a place where some of Hitler's luckier soldiers could enjoy a convivial atmosphere, free from the rigours of enforcing an occupation. Ideally placed to welcome colleagues on their arrival in Denmark, the hotel was also a handy venue when giving units a send-off before they were transferred elsewhere.

In a further gamble, Tommy made no attempt to deceive any of the German officers in the Astoria about his naval past. He was quite happy for it to be known that he had been a flight lieutenant in Fleet Air Arm. The way he saw it, he needed the respect and friendship of the Germans in order to make the location work for him. Outrageously, he even used his real name when he introduced himself, confident that he was building a reputation among longer-term residents as an ally and occasional source of information. Meal times meant shared tables, and he tried to keep his cool as he ate with men who could make his worst nightmares come true. 'I just laughed as they tried to test me,' he remembered. 'It seemed to work.'

It wasn't the Germans who grew wary of Agent Sneum during these dangerous March days. Naturally enough, there were members of the Danish resistance among the staff and non-German guests inside the Astoria, locals who discreetly monitored the comings and goings of the occupiers. They would also make a mental note of any Danes seen collaborating with German officers. One morning, two Copenhagen men, tough characters who had also been engaged in the silent fight to gather intelligence on the enemy, entered the Astoria's dining room and spotted Tommy at a table with several Nazis. Sneum spotted the Danish pair, too: 'These men had been present at the reception dinner the Princes held for my arrival back in September. You should have seen the expressions on their faces when they saw me. They were angry, and looked at me as though I were a traitor. I just tried to ignore them because obviously I couldn't explain what I was doing there.' If his own friends on Fanoe had distrusted him earlier in the war, then these acquaintances from the capital would take a far dimmer view of his apparent collaboration. To them, it must have looked as though he had gone over wholeheartedly to the other side, having cracked under the pressure of imminent arrest.

A few days later, an even more dangerous arrival grabbed Tommy's attention. As he finished off a lavish breakfast with his new German 'friends', he saw two Danish detectives, faces he recognised from photographs supplied by Bertelsen. 'It was a very bad moment,' he remembered. 'They were part of the squad whose job it was to hunt down any subversive people who were against the German occupation. I was probably top of their list. I could feel my heart beating and I looked for the best escape route. There wasn't one because they were standing at the door. And I hadn't brought my pistol down to breakfast.' With no exit available, Tommy just sat there, trying to avoid eye contact with the policemen, and continued his conversation with the enemy officers. He felt the Danish detectives studying the guests methodically, as if they were looking for someone in particular, until their gaze settled on his table. 'To behave normally at that moment was the hardest thing of all,' he said. 'I was scared stiff they would recognise me.' Then, however, the policemen simply walked away. The sea of German uniforms in Sneum's corner of the room must have thrown the detectives off the scent. Either that or they had come to the hotel with a completely different agenda. As he watched them leave, Tommy hid his relief in the same way he had suppressed his fear, by sipping his coffee as though nothing had happened. However, the incident told him he had to get out of the Astoria as soon as he could. His stay had been interesting and eventful, but it had run its course.

While he was packing his bags after breakfast, there was a knock on the door and Sneum heard someone whistling 'The Marseillaise' outside. Taking his pistol, he opened the door cautiously and saw a man he recognised as a messenger for the Princes. He was summoned to meet Lunding and Gyth at the Jaegersborg Kaserne barracks at seven o'clock that evening. No further explanation was given, but Tommy was left in no doubt that he had to comply.

Later, as he checked out, a German officer tapped him on the shoulder. He froze, then turned round with a manufactured smile on his face. The German, an acquaintance during his stay, was smiling too. He just wanted to say goodbye.

Having ensured he was not followed, Tommy arrived at the barracks at the given time. Lunding and Gyth were already there, along with Major Per Winkel. Lunding seemed to be relishing the prospect of this latest encounter with his least favourite spy. 'Sneum, every day you stay here, you become more of a liability.

You've recently been seen in the company of German officers again. What the hell do you think you're playing at?'

Tommy was in no mood for a dressing down. 'Gentlemen, in order to evade capture, it is often necessary to hide in places where you are least likely to be hunted. I'm sorry if that surprises you.' Later, Tommy revealed: 'They were scared of me. They thought I was going on too hard and not being careful enough, that the Germans would find out. But I had always told them that if you want results you must take risks. They were scared for their own safety, I think.'

Lunding ordered Sneum to leave Denmark for Sweden immediately, or face the consequences. Gyth tried to soften the threat by suggesting that once the heat had died down, he might be able to return.

Tommy was suspicious, especially when Lunding advised him to reveal his true identity at once if the Swedish authorities apprehended him. He didn't see why he should cooperate with the Swedes, even when Lunding insisted that it would be in his best interests to do so. The Swedish police would pass the information back to the Danish authorities, the Prince explained, and the Germans would be satisfied that Sneum was safely under lock and key. Then, after a couple of weeks, when the storm had blown over, the Swedes would let Tommy out, so that he could make his way to the British Legation in Stockholm. From there, he could make his way back to England.

It all sounded too good to be true, and Tommy continued to voice his concerns.

Gyth, the most refined of the Princes, saw that the agent remained deeply sceptical. Using his natural charm, he tried to assuage any doubts. 'Sneum, you have my word of honour as a gentleman. The deal with the Swedes has been done. You just have to put together another plan to escape from Denmark.'

'And don't be long, Sneum,' warned Lunding, with much less warmth.

Chapter **34**

DEFIANCE AND LOYALTY

AS HE TRIED TO STAY one step ahead of the Danish police, who might yet deliver him to a German torture chamber, Thomas Sneum was contacted in mid-March by his cousin, Knud Nielsen, the port-master in Copenhagen. Nielsen revealed that an entire brigade of German soldiers, accompanied by heavy armoury, was preparing to leave for Oslo in the next forty-eight hours.

The firepower about to sail to Norway was considerable. Squadrons of Hotchkiss tanks, snatched from the French during the lightning advance on Paris in 1940, were at the forefront of the shipment. Knud, Tommy's doppelgänger, detailed the precise number of tanks involved, as well as the individual names and types of the ships that would transport the armoury and men. Sneum's vigilant cousin even knew the calibre of the guns and the number of troops for whom bedding on the vessels had been prepared. Despite Lunding's bleak warning, escape from Denmark was no longer Tommy's immediate priority.

He contacted Duus Hansen and asked the trusted radio engineer if it was possible to transmit to England that same evening from Skodsborg. However, the weather forecast suggested to Duus Hansen that their best chance of success would be from the island of Fyn, the following day. They travelled separately, with each man showing sufficient nerve to play his part in cordial exchanges with

German officers along the way. When they reached their destination, they transmitted as planned in double-quick time. Duus Hansen was helped by the fact that Sneum knew the appropriate coded letters and numbers for every type of German vessel, from battleships to U-boats. His previous summer's homework in England had paid off handsomely. The British received the intelligence, and Sneum learned later that they bombed and partially destroyed the German convoy before it reached Oslo.

Tommy's last safe-house in Denmark was the apartment of a long-time resistance sympathiser called Arne Helvard, who had also been a colleague in Fleet Air Arm. 'We'd known each other even before that,' revealed Tommy later. 'We had been at a technical college together.' It was while at polytechnic in Copenhagen in 1934–5 that Arne and Tommy had first discovered the thrill of flying. They trained on gliders, as many would-be aviators did in those days. Tommy recalled: 'We flew a glider called a Stamer Lippisch, a big German monster, but with the help of a motor-winch we could gain a height of thirty to forty metres. On a good day, we got down safely without incident.' The rush of the wind as it whistled past the cockpit was a wonderful substitute for the growl of a powerful engine, and flying soon became an addiction for both men.

Arne was more than two years older than Tommy, who was still a few weeks short of his twenty-fifth birthday when they shared the safe-house. Helvard had a receding hairline and acne, proving that some afflictions arrive before their time while others linger longer than they should. But Arne's cheeky demeanour won him plenty of friends, and he had one other precious attribute. Tommy explained:

> He was one of those annoying bastards who can drink ten pints a night and hardly put on any weight at all. He was a character. When everyone else was enjoying a party, for example, Arne would suddenly come up with a deep piece of philosophy to wrong-foot us. But on serious occasions he could be flippant – he loved going against the flow.

One day, for example, the commanding officer at Avnoe air base, Erik Rasmussen, noticed that Helvard was looking unhealthy, so he must have been drinking even more than ten pints a night at that point. Rasmussen told him he needed some physical training to tone him up. Helvard said, 'My right arm's getting plenty, sir. It spends all night lifting heavy glasses of beer. And my left arm does plenty of bending and stretching when I smoke my cigarettes.'

Fortunately for Arne, his superiors liked him, despite his cheek, partly because they knew what a plucky individual he was when it came to the crunch. In 1939, as a coastguard and a flight lieutenant in the Reserve, he won a medal for bravery. Somewhat awkwardly, given what happened soon after, that medal was awarded by the Germans. Arne had come to the rescue of German sailors whose ship had struck a mine. A life was a life, and it was Arne's duty to save stricken mariners, whatever their nationality. As Tommy explained, he had more than enough skill to fulfil the role. 'Arne was a bloody good pilot and he came down in a sea-plane to save them. He didn't want to take off again because several of the German crew were hanging on to his floats, so he just eased the sea-plane into shore.'

After being demobilised on 30 April 1940, three weeks after the German invasion, Helvard was unemployed for a time before finding temporary work at Aalborg Airport. In October 1940, however, he landed a dream job with the Danish Airport Authority, the DPPA, at Kastrup Airport. He soon found he could monitor all the comings and goings of German aircraft and dignitaries, and pass the intelligence on to Sneum's spy ring without arousing suspicion.

Tommy trusted Helvard enough to want to include him in his plans once he accepted that the treacherous ice on the Oeresund would have to be tested again. If Sigfred Christophersen could survive a crossing, then so could he, Tommy reasoned. He asked Arne to join him on the escape attempt, which he believed would be made at some point in the following fortnight. They would walk across the sea to Sweden and then try to reach Britain from there, giving Helvard the chance to fly against the Germans with the RAF. Arne took it as a compliment to be invited, and said he would think about it.

But if he went, Helvard would be leaving plenty behind. Above all, there was his fiancée, Vita Nielsen, to consider. He loved her very much and they had big plans for the future. For the moment, she still lived with her parents in a fifth-floor flat on Leifsgade. But she hoped to start a new life with Arne in a house of their own, which could happen as soon as they tied the knot. Somehow, where others had failed, this romance between Arne and Vita had remained strong enough to withstand the pressures of the occupation – until now. What troubled Helvard most was the idea that, if he went, he wouldn't even be able to tell Vita why he was leaving her. Furthermore, Arne's mother, Angla Eugenia, who lived alone in Hobro, would also have to be kept in the dark.

※ ※ ※

Tulle Oxlund was trying to piece together the events leading up to her husband's death. Stories from her former neighbours in Noekkerosevej all pointed to Tommy Sneum's presence in her marital home during the preceding months. What had they been up to? The identity of Kaj's other flatmate – the strange, tall man with sharp features and a penchant for disguises – was also a mystery. Whatever they had all been doing, it had obviously gone horribly wrong. Now Kaj was dead, and Tommy seemed to be on the run.

Tulle moved back to her parents' home in the town of Ringsted, to the south-east of Copenhagen, so that she could grieve quietly. When an old friend rang her soon after her arrival, Tulle naturally expressed surprise, since few could have learned so quickly of her return. It had barely been a fortnight since her estranged husband had died. The friend was called Peter and he had also known Kaj in the past. He explained that he too had suffered a bereavement recently, and suggested they meet at a restaurant called Wiwex for dinner the following night. Tulle heard herself accepting without really knowing why she had.

The evening went pleasantly enough as they picked at their food and drowned their sorrows, until the conversation began to take a strange turn. Tulle was just starting to open up about Kaj when her escort asked about his friends in his final months, and in particular

Boffins at work for Britain

(*Above*) R.V. Jones of British Scientific Intelligence: Sneum's ally, and a trusted advisor to wartime leader Winston Churchill.

(*Above left*)The Nazis' secret weapon, Freya radar. This example is similar to the device filmed by Sneum on Fanoe.

(*Above right*) Vital images of Freya radar in action, meticulously traced from Tommy's damaged film by R.V. Jones.

(*Above left*) Practical and highly effective, one of Duus Hansen's radios.

(*Above right*) Lorens Arne Duus Hansen: Sneum's brilliant recruit liaised with the British and helped to reduce the threat to London from Adolf Hitler's V-Rockets.

Deadly duplicity: Britain's covert wartime services, the Secret Intelligence Service (SIS) and the Special Operations Executive (SOE), set up rival chains of command to spy in Denmark.

(*From left to right*) Colonel Euan Rabagliati of SIS sent Thomas Sneum and Sigfred Christophersen back into Denmark after they received clearance as friendly 'aliens'.

(*From left to right*) SOE's Head of Danish Section, Commander Ralph Hollingworth RN, ran Stockholm-based field chief Ronald Turnbull and Copenhagen-based agent Christian Michael Rottboell, who was killed in a shoot-out during his mission.

Stuck to the ice: a desperate Kaj Oxlund pleads for help as an aircraft flies overhead. But vital supplies and a rope land just out of reach, and poor Oxlund dies on his mission for Sneum before he can be rescued.

(*Above left*) Enjoying life: Kaj Oxlund and his wife 'Tulle' before the war destroyed their marriage.

(*Above middle*) Thorbjoern Christophersen: Sigfred's younger brother died out on the ice near Oxlund.

(*Above right*) Arne Helvard: he crossed the ice to Sweden with Tommy Sneum, and they eventually reached Britain.

Still looking smart and lethal: Tommy Sneum in 2001, reenacting the moment he threatened to shoot the author in Switzerland. *(Photo by Dave Pinnegar)*

Firm friends: Tommy Sneum and the author in 2006, the year before Britain's former spy passed away.

Thomas Sneum. Tulle was startled and asked why he wanted to know.

Peter came to the point. 'Your husband was involved in certain activities. He may have done things that weren't good for the fragile peace that exists in our country. We believe Thomas Sneum was also involved in those activities. Do you know anything about it?'

Tulle had a question of her own. 'Who are you talking about when you say "we"?'

'I'm a member of the Danish Nazi Party,' replied Peter quite openly.

Tulle felt the anger welling up inside her. She stood up and sent the table and its contents crashing into the man. Having been humiliated in Ringsted's plushest restaurant, the Nazi leapt up, drilled Tulle with a menacing stare and insulted her loudly. With that, he marched out, past waiters who were already trying to put the table back on its legs.

Tulle tried her best to apologise to the manager. 'The problem is,' she said tearfully, 'I'm afraid I can't pay. I didn't bring any money.'

'That's quite all right, madam,' replied the manager, who had witnessed the whole spectacle and was clearly on the same side as the late Kaj Oxlund had been. 'It's on the house.'

※ ※ ※

Detective-Sergeant Roland Olsen was a resistance sympathiser. But on 24 March 1942 he was put in a difficult position. Olsen was aware that the Danish police department was now liaising directly with the Germans, and that a middle-ranking Abwehr officer, Oberleutnant von Grene, was their point of contact on the delicate matter of the recently uncovered spy ring. He therefore fully understood that his superiors were under strong pressure to deliver firm results for their German masters. Given his own anti-Nazi leanings, however, Olsen didn't want to deliver anything to von Grene, especially not one of the spies in question. So he was less than thrilled to receive a call at the police station that day from a Copenhagen restaurant, Café Bunis, informing him that a man they believed to be the hunted resistance figure Thomas Sneum had just reserved a table and was due to arrive in a few hours' time.

Later Olsen wrote down his own account of these tricky moments. 'I sat in my office and thought about it. The Germans would think of Sneum as an enemy spy. And now we, the Danish police, were supposed to arrest him because the Germans would want him delivered to them. But for spies in wartime there is only one sentence in court – death. Then it is back-against-the-wall time, and one salvo of gunfire ends it.' While these thoughts were going through Olsen's head, he came clean about the phone call from the restaurant in a frank conversation with his boss, Politikommissaer Odmar. Olsen explained later: 'I told Odmar what I knew, that I would go to the restaurant but that I would not bring Sneum back under arrest. We could invent some story or other for the *Herrenvolk* [Germans] instead. We talked about it a little, and Odmar said he understood my point of view.' But Odmar, who wasn't an outright Nazi, still wanted Olsen to find a quick solution to the Sneum affair before the Germans had time to react. Everyone feared the backlash if the agent continued to operate in Copenhagen for a second longer.

However, a message soon came through from the restaurant to say that the reservation made by the suspect had been cancelled. Olsen suddenly had a few more hours in which to come up with an answer. He felt that Werner Gyberg might help him find a way through this minefield, but Gyberg was behind bars and being questioned after the death of his employee, Thorbjoern Christophersen. With no other options, though, Olsen released an astonished Gyberg on 25 March and left him in Copenhagen's Town Hall Square. Under the terms of the deal, Gyberg had to return within twenty minutes, having used his temporary freedom to arrange a meeting with Sneum for that very night. Worryingly for Olsen, however, there was still no sign of the businessman after half an hour. The detective recalled:

To think about something else, I bought some pigeon feed. This was the police department's biggest case, about spies and parachutists, and there I was, acting like I didn't care. German soldiers passed by, the sun shone on the Town Hall, but still no

Gyberg. Finally he arrived and took me to his house. Duus Hansen turned up, took my pistol, and disappeared again. Eventually Sneum arrived through the back door of the cellar, and we greeted each other.

Tommy recalled later: 'We arranged a meeting for that night with Duus Hansen, at his office just off the Town Hall Square. Olsen was going to be present with Gyberg and I agreed to attend with my brother-in-law, Bertelsen.'

Having set up the meeting, Gyberg was taken back into custody until the evening. 'I knew you'd come back,' said Olsen.

'I wasn't so sure,' replied Gyberg.

That night the meeting went ahead as planned, and Olsen had the chance to sit down and talk with Duus Hansen for the first time. They would form an understanding which lasted for the rest of the war, and helped to keep Duus Hansen one step ahead of the Abwehr. By risking his life to attend the meeting, Tommy had therefore laid the foundations for the future police protection of Duus Hansen against the constant threat of discovery by the Germans. That, in turn, gave Duus Hansen the platform to assume a leading position in the Danish resistance. And his increasing importance led ultimately to his pivotal role in the delivery of precious V-rocket intelligence to the British later in the war.

Sneum's position in late March 1942 contrasted sharply with Duus Hansen's. It was obvious that Tommy's time had run out in Copenhagen, and he would have to leave at the first opportunity. Men he didn't trust had told him as much already. Now men he did trust were telling him exactly the same, and he knew his mission for the British was over. Later he recalled: 'We had the typed reports of Christophersen's latest revelations to the Swedes, and my friends told me that the Germans were increasing their efforts, and one day they would be sure to find me in a small country like Denmark. If I left, it would be better for Gyberg too. Those were some of the reasons why I agreed to go.'

Before planning his escape, Tommy suggested that Duus Hansen should renew attempts to contact the British-run spy who had survived the parachute drop that had killed Carl Bruhn just after Christmas. They all assumed that Bruhn's partner must still be free somewhere in Denmark, and Sneum was convinced that the man would welcome such an approach if it were made discreetly. He was working for the British after all, just as they were.

Although he didn't know it at the time, by arguing strongly for this new link Tommy opened the way for Duus Hansen to work for SOE as well as SIS in the years to come. It was a piece of simple common sense unheard of at the time. The fierce interdepartmental rivalry between Britain's two covert services, and the wasteful duplication it ensured, had almost killed Sneum and could still prove to be his downfall. Yet here he was, an SIS agent unwittingly doing SOE a favour, because he knew that the only important war was the one being waged against Hitler.

Duus Hansen's account of his extraordinary meeting with Gyberg, Olsen and Sneum emphasises Tommy's importance right up to the end of his mission:

> Police investigations led to the fact that Sneum had to leave the country, as his continuing work was impossible, due to the Danish police's and the Germans' knowledge of it. But the whole investigation led to the establishment of some very useful connections inside the police [Roland Olsen]. Already, before Sneum had left the country, two other parachutists were dropped near Haslev. One [Bruhn] was killed while the other, [Mogens] Hammer, started organisational work within the country. We had tried to get in contact with Hammer without success, and it was a deal between Sneum and me that I should do everything to get in contact and achieve a successful working relationship with this man, which I managed to do.

Chapter **35**

LIVING ON THE EDGE

THE MORNING AFTER that historic meeting, something happened which might yet have trapped Sneum. Politikommissaer Odmar ordered Detective Sergeant Olsen to surround 2 Harald Jensensgade, the building where Else Sneum's father, Carl Jensen, had a third-floor apartment. There was no time for Olsen to forewarn Tommy or the occupants of the targeted apartment, because he was sent to the location with two other detectives, Kaj Andersen and Oestergaard Nielsen. Olsen must have been praying that Sneum hadn't decided to say goodbye to his wife and baby before trying to escape to Sweden.

The policemen set up surveillance of the building, and Olsen's colleagues prepared to pounce. Odmar had issued strict instructions that anyone leaving the apartment was to be apprehended. If Sneum had been stupid enough to have had any contact with his family in those final hours, he certainly would have paid the price.

Tommy, though, had been more preoccupied with the risks involved in placing his future in the hands of the Swedish authorities. He had sought a final assurance from the Princes that he wouldn't be left to rot in a Swedish jail. Later he remembered: 'I received that guarantee and told Arne Helvard it was time to get across if he was coming. He said he was.' But Sneum was still sufficiently worried about the fate which awaited them on the other side of the border to request a final conference that morning with Niels-Richard Bertelsen, who took a chance by visiting Tommy's last Copenhagen lair in an unmarked police car.

'There's going to be a problem with the Swedes, Niels-Richard,' Tommy said. 'I just know it. I've never trusted them.'

His brother-in-law didn't see how he could help, and reminded Sneum that the best way to steer clear of trouble was to avoid capture. But Tommy suggested that Bertelsen could influence events as a last resort. He told the policeman how, before Christmas, he had stumbled across the names of some Swedish agents operating in Poland and Berlin. 'I'm going to give them to you,' he said. 'If I do get caught over there, and they lock me up for longer than Lunding says they will, you can threaten to give the names of their agents to the Germans. If you don't get a postcard from Stockholm by the start of June, with a code word to confirm my freedom, and you know I didn't freeze to death on the ice, then you'll also know they've locked me up and thrown away the key. So you send an anonymous letter to the Swedish Legation in Copenhagen, warning that their spy ring is about to be blown because of what they've done to me. You tell them another letter has been put away for safe keeping with all the relevant information on their spies in the east, and that letter will be handed over to the Germans if I'm not released immediately. That'll make them think twice. I'll be out in no time.'

'I don't think I could do that,' said Bertelsen, looking horrified. 'It's madness.'

'Take these names anyway,' Sneum told the policeman, handing him a piece of paper. 'Keep them and hide them, and only use them if you think it is absolutely necessary. There are twelve names on the list. For every genuine name of an agent, two on the list are false.'

Later Sneum explained his ruthless logic:

I gave my brother-in-law a number of names of personnel who didn't exist, so the Germans would never be sure who was real and who wasn't. They would have a hell of a lot of work to do to clear up the mess, if it came to that. But I felt pretty sure that the Swedes would back down.

Spying is a dirty game and at that point I thought that if the Swedes played dirty, then I was prepared to fight dirty. I didn't have a high opinion of the Swedes and I believed that the work I was doing was more important. I didn't think anyone in Germany could get any decent information out anyway, because a transmitter wouldn't have lasted five minutes there before it was discovered.

From my point of view, I just wanted to have something in reserve if it all went wrong for me in Sweden. I wanted to know in my own mind that I hadn't used all my ammunition already; that there was something still in reserve. And if these agents were so important, then the Swedes wouldn't risk compromising them by detaining me.

Bertelsen listened to Tommy's explanation on that tense day in March 1942 and shook his head. 'I think you've forgotten who your true enemy is,' he observed sadly.

'Right now,' Tommy replied bitterly, 'it feels like almost everybody.'

It wasn't true, of course, because, even under the most mind-bending pressure, Sneum had already shown that he could think of resistance men such as Duus Hansen, Olsen and the unknown parachutist before he concentrated on trying to save his own life. He still knew that the Nazis were the only real enemy.

But many years later, Sneum had a better insight into the sort of man that more than six months of spying in Nazi-occupied territory threatened to turn him into. The constant fear, the lack of support from Britain, the death of Oxlund, the feeling of being hunted and the suspicion that Danish Intelligence didn't have his best interests at heart – all those factors led him to look after number one at all costs once his mission in Denmark was over. He reflected: 'In the spy game you have to tell so many lies that in the end you can hardly distinguish between truth and lies, and you don't even trust your nearest friends.'

In all the chaos, Tommy might have felt a temptation to visit his wife and baby one last time, and rediscover a sense of the person he had been before the invasion, a man with control over his destiny. Others had been banking on him succumbing to that temptation. It was mid-morning when Odmar ordered Olsen and his two colleagues to raid Carl Jensen's apartment, where Else and Marianne were staying. The operation took place under the watchful eye of Thomas Noerreheden, who had liaised with the Germans and wanted to make sure everything ran smoothly. Noerreheden knew they would have to move quickly to be effective, and urged his officers to hurry to the third floor before any evasive action could be taken inside the apartment. Carl Jensen opened the door before it was broken down.

'We're looking for Thomas Sneum,' said Noerreheden as his colleagues dashed past the owner and searched one room each.

'I haven't seen him since last June,' replied Else's father honestly.

Within minutes it became obvious that Sneum was not in the apartment. Noerreheden hoped for a new lead and asked Jensen if his son-in-law had access to a summer house somewhere along the coast. Else's father replied that, to the best of his knowledge, he did not.

The officers then turned their attention to Jensen's wife Gerda and their daughter Else, who were in the living room with Marianne. They were both asked when they had last seen Thomas Sneum. They both answered: 'June last year.' Else was promptly put in a police car and taken to Copenhagen's central station.

Politikommissaer Odmar was following events closely. He had already instructed four detectives from the Criminal Investigations Branch – by now closely affiliated to the Abwehr – to observe proceedings at the station. As the interrogation began in earnest, Criminal Detective Normander and his colleagues Harry Jensen, Rasmus Christensen and Emil Petersen watched for signs of weakness in Else's story. Olsen later said of this interview: 'In the department they believed Sneum had had some contact with his wife, which in fact turned out to be the case. It was decided that she should be shadowed and her telephone tapped. Then she was brought in for an interrogation by my department.'

Under intense pressure, Else tried to stick to what she could say truthfully without endangering her husband: that Tommy had left home on 18 June 1941, and that she had received a farewell letter from him dated 5 July. She insisted she had no idea where Tommy was now, and maintained a friendly demeanour even under intense pressure. This composure gave Olsen the nerve to try something which might have rebounded on him in spectacular fashion had his audacious move been discovered by his pro-Nazi colleagues. He recalled:

> She denied having any contact with her husband, and during the questioning some of our young officers were given a good look at her, because they were going to be shadowing her when she left the police station. Mrs Sneum handled the questioning without any problems, and as she left she said goodbye to all the personnel in the office, offering her hand to each and every one of us. This was exactly what I had been waiting for.
>
> On a piece of paper, I had written some instructions for her on how to behave over the next few days. The piece of paper was neatly folded, and when it was my turn to shake hands, it changed from my hand to hers.
>
> It was a shot in the dark, as I had never seen her before, but we were lucky beyond all expectations. She got the piece of paper and behaved as though nothing had happened. She left as though everything was totally normal from her point of view, and no one realised anything about what had just happened.

When Else left the station that afternoon, she was followed by Detectives Normander and Jensen, who had orders to shadow her indefinitely, in case she should lead them to her husband.

Olsen revealed: 'She understood the content of my note and followed the instructions. And as she had a sense of humour, in the following days she had quite a lot of fun leading her police shadows a merry dance.' Else Sneum hadn't been given the opportunity to enjoy herself so much in ages, and she wasn't going to pass up the chance to make her own amusing contribution to the Allied war effort by wasting police time.

Meanwhile, other Danish police officers checked all mail to and from the Jensen family home for the slightest clue as to Sneum's whereabouts. They grew similarly frustrated. The correspondence revealed nothing, though it seemed increasingly likely that the elusive Tommy would turn up soon enough, dead or alive. Even Britain's best spy couldn't remain at large for ever in the midst of such a manhunt.

Chapter **36**

WALKING WITH GHOSTS

TOMMY AVOIDED HIS ESTRANGED WIFE and daughter throughout this dangerous time, focusing instead on escape. Emotional complications could be fatal for a spy in occupied territory. He and Arne Helvard would head for Sweden and then Britain. Nothing else mattered.

Sneum and Helvard met late on the afternoon of 26 March at Copenhagen's central railway station, where they both deposited some of their personal effects in lockers. They avoided locker number thirteen, where the original British radio, now not only cumbersome but entirely useless without its crystals, still lay neatly packed away in its case. However, Tommy fully intended to take the receipt for that locker to Sweden, where he thought it could be used to his advantage.

He joined Arne on a northbound train to Skodsborg. Originally, Tommy had seen Skodsborg only as an ideal location from which to improve radio communications with Sweden and Britain. Now, though, he believed the northern end of the village would provide the perfect stepping-off point for their escape across the ice. Though this part of the coast was patrolled by the Danish police, who had observation boxes at strategic points along the sea front, the local lookouts were known to be less than dedicated to their tedious task. Tommy and Arne would also wear white for camouflage against the snow and ice, so that if searchlights were shone in their direction, they might still blend into their surroundings unnoticed. On the Swedish side the following morning, they could pose as fishermen, mingle with those already on the ice, and slip away unnoticed.

Their ultimate target was the Swedish town of Landskrona, seventeen kilometres across the frozen sea. But Tommy believed they might not even have to reach the mainland to achieve their objective of escaping Denmark's Nazi occupation. In the middle of the channel, the island of Hven lay just inside Swedish waters, and only eleven kilometres from Skodsborg. The small number of Swedish police who were based there might feel obliged to take any unauthorised visitors across to their own mainland for processing. However, they might equally call in their Danish counterparts to repatriate two of their citizens. So Landskrona remained the favoured destination, because it appeared to guarantee Tommy and Arne's long-term freedom.

They were joined at the Skodsborg flat by Sneum's cousin Knud Nielsen, who would help with the first phase of the escape attempt. In the meantime, they cooked themselves a meal and enjoyed a few beers, teasing each other to shake off the fear that this might be their last supper. Little more than a fortnight earlier, two out of three men had died on the ice. Since then, the daytime temperatures had risen slightly, a potentially deadly development which meant the ice was probably breaking up during the day. Although the bitter nights still repaired most of the cracks, Tommy feared that the spring sun might have done lasting damage to their hopes.

Anticipating a scenario where they might need to jump across the fracture lines, Tommy insisted they take a pole each, between two and three metres long. Such props would do no harm to their alibi, since many fishermen took the same precautions when stepping out onto the ice to carve their fishing holes. If they were forced to vault across cracks to stay above the water, the poles might become lifesavers. They could also be used to rescue a freezing man who had fallen through the ice and needed help to claw his way back out of the water.

Tommy had walked over frozen seas before, from Fanoe to the Danish mainland at Esbjerg. He felt sure his experience would help

Arne survive too, especially if the pair were tied together with rope. He was determined to do all he could to avoid the tragedy that had befallen the other men a few weeks earlier, though he knew there were no guarantees. 'Of course I was scared,' he admitted later. 'I would have been stupid not to be. But I always forced myself never to show other people that I was scared. If you show fear as a leader, you are not a leader any more.'

Knud Nielsen knew the importance of running checks and cross-checks before stepping onto the ice. At 11.00 p.m., he went over Arne and Tommy's kit and made sure their clothing was adequate. Over several thermal layers, the two men were wearing bulky white, hooded anoraks and white trousers. Even their boots had been painted white to help avoid detection in the first vital minutes. In order to reach their stepping-off point without arousing suspicion, however, they had realised it would be necessary to wear normal clothing over their whites. If confronted, it would be better to look like locals breaking the curfew for a spot of illegal fishing than to be seen for what they were – highly organised resistance men dressed for an evasive expedition across the ice. Therefore, they put on their naval overcoats before they began the short walk towards northern Skodsborg's beach.

Knud accompanied Tommy and Arne on this crucial phase of their journey. When the time was right, he would take charge of the discarded overcoats and hurry back to the apartment for the night. Together they carved a path through the deep snow. Each man marched in the footsteps of his predecessor, in order to minimise the evidence they left behind. They also kept in step, to try to sound like just one person. Nights were particularly silent during the occupation, and the crunching sound of three men trudging through the snow at midnight could have raised the alarm even before they stepped onto the beach.

There were dangers lurking on the sea front now. Only forty metres to the left of the point at which they were due to descend to the ice, a police lookout post could be made out in the darkness. Two hundred metres further along the promenade, there was another. Tommy had hoped that neither police box would be manned, but a flicker of light in the first cabin disappointed him. Looking closer, he saw the silhouetted shoulders and head of the policeman; for a moment, it seemed certain the officer would spot them. As he lit a cigarette, however, the lone watchman turned away to survey the promenade in the other direction. All three men managed to hurry to the beach unchallenged, praying their footprints would not be spotted in the gloom. Wasting no time, Sneum and Helvard took off their overcoats and threw them to Nielsen. In that instant, they became virtually invisible. Using their staffs, they then negotiated the six steps down to the beach, tied themselves firmly together with rope, and trudged across the five or ten metres of smooth, snow-covered sand. Without hesitation, they stepped onto the creaking ice and, in seconds, they were gone. Even from a few metres above sea level, Knud now couldn't make them out. It was as though they had stepped off the edge of the world. He wondered for a moment if they had fallen through the ice already, but he knew he would have heard something if they were in trouble. So he turned and headed back for the warmth of the apartment, leaving Helvard and Sneum to their fate.

In the reassuring light of day, you could often see the cliffs of Hven, just a few kilometres away from the Danish mainland. In the best visibility you could even see the skyline of Landskrona. But in the darkness, there was precious little to guide them. Tommy and Arne were met merely by silence and black cold. Only the impact of the freezing air reminded them they were still alive; and neither man knew exactly what lay under his next footstep. Surrounded by the void, Helvard hesitated. Feeling the rope pull him back, Sneum pressed on, urging his partner to follow him more closely. Tommy wanted to a find a rhythm and rely on the simple action of walking for reassurance. He explained later: 'You have to keep moving on ice because if you stand still you could go through.' The first creaking of the ice did nothing to dispel the thought that the spirits of recently departed men lurked somewhere in the night. But once they were about a hundred metres away from the shore, they began to exchange banter, and create a distraction from their fear.

'Breathe through your nose,' whispered Tommy, having noticed that Arne was using his mouth.

'Why? It's harder.'

'You'll conserve your body heat better, and cough less. Try not to ask questions and just do as I say. You might live that way.'

They wore berets under their white hoods to slow the loss of heat through their heads; Sneum was aware that every tactic they could employ in order to preserve that precious heat for a little longer might eventually prove crucial. Very soon they had begun to achieve a rhythm, marching side by side. Two former glider pilots, firm friends, with distant dreams of flying again. As the last remnants of light from the shoreline faded to black, that unity became their comfort.

'Looks nice, should be a pleasant trip,' said Tommy cheerily to boost morale. In reality the words of his grandfather, Thomas Sonnichsen Hansen, were echoing in his head: 'If you fall beneath ice, never give in to panic and never be fooled by appearances. The lighter-coloured ice looks inviting from below, because it appears to offer escape from the darkness. But it's a nasty trick of nature, because that white ice is the thickest ice, and will lock you in below it. The dark ice is thinnest – that's where you can break through. Strike at the dark, not the light.' If they did fall through at night, however, it would probably be impossible to distinguish between the darker, weaker ice and the lighter, thicker surface which would trap them. Meanwhile, the fate of Thorbjoern and Kaj continued to hang in the air like the mist, haunting them every step of the way. Tommy hoped that the cold had taken Thorbjoern beyond fear when he had finally gone under. Sneum knew what it was like suddenly to find yourself thrashing around below the surface. 'I went under once as a boy,' he explained. 'If you fall through, the ice closes. It is an awful feeling and you do panic a bit. You have to get your elbows and upper body back up on the ice straight away, before the hole closes completely.'

The darkness enveloped them, and smothered them so completely that Sneum had to fight his fears to maintain his composure. 'I told myself to be pleased about the darkness, because it meant there were no enemies around us,' he said. Stubbornly, he tried to focus on Sweden, and Britain beyond. But it wasn't easy. Even though they were heading for the medium-sized town of Landskrona, there were no lights twinkling in the distance, and they had nothing but a compass to confirm the accuracy of their route.

He and Arne were engulfed in a ghostly haze, which conjured strange shapes in the night against a black, forbidding backdrop, and played cruel games with the imagination. Meanwhile, the bleak monotony of the frozen wasteland beneath their feet became almost as hard to bear as the constant fear of falling through it. There was nothing to use as a landmark or reference point. It wasn't as though waves had frozen as they rose or died; the ice was almost perfectly flat and featureless. There were no frozen boulders, no ships, no stranded small boats. Just a vast sheet, an awful uniformity hiding its weak points.

The two pilots trudged on, hour after hour, wandering ever further away from Denmark. Their fitness and determination were sorely tested against the biting cold. Then an awful groaning beneath their feet alerted them to fresh danger. They had stepped onto unstable ice. A sharper, splitting sound warned that their weight might take them down at any moment. Using their poles, they launched themselves towards what they hoped would be a more secure surface. The fear that they might land in freezing water instead lasted for as long as they were in the air, seconds seeming like an eternity. Instead their momentum took them onto what felt like firm ice. Scarcely daring to trust their feet, they scurried away before the fresh sheet could also betray them.

Tommy believed they must now be near the middle of the Oeresund, close to the daytime shipping lanes. He thought he could just make out the little island of Hven to their left, though he knew it could well be a trick of the eye. So, ignoring the possible mirage, they straightened their course and pressed on for the preferable target of Landskrona. Later Tommy reflected: 'We didn't have any trouble until we were south-east of Hven. But in the morning, just before dawn, we could feel that the ice was starting to move under us, and it cracked sometimes.'

As the first weak colours of dawn streaked the horizon, there was an almighty roar, as if the gods of winter and spring had begun to do battle. Sneum admitted:

It was like rolling thunder and then we got scared, because two massive slabs of ice, the size of football pitches, just broke apart. If the fragmentation continued we knew the ice wouldn't be able to carry us. If the ice keeps breaking, finally you find yourself on such a small flake that you just go down with it, because it can't carry your weight. I knew how dangerous these conditions were from my childhood, walking on ice around Fanoe. When I had fallen in as a boy I had been lucky to survive.

If that happened so far out in the Oeresund, they faced the same fate as Thorbjoern. From the southern end of the channel, where the younger Christophersen brother had died, a storm was now blowing with terrible ferocity. A swirling wind whipped up the cold air and flurries of sleet and snow flew in all directions. 'We didn't realise that such a heavy storm was moving north so quickly,' Tommy explained. 'We didn't have a weather forecast.'

But the natural forces unleashed above the ice were nothing compared to the dangers lurking below. The stretch of sea shaken by the storm had begun to exert untold pressure on the thick slabs of ice above it. The original, thunderous sound heard by the men was a fracture that threatened to open all the way down the Oeresund's main shipping lane. Vast areas, carved up by ice-breakers the previous morning, had healed overnight in a brittle callus. Now the storm had sliced open the old wound, leaving Tommy and Arne perilously close to a channel of water filled with freezing debris.

In the distance, beyond the widening gap in the ice, Sneum could see dark figures, like matchstick men, near the Swedish shoreline. The thin light had brought out the morning fishermen near Landskrona; and now the distant crowd seemed to be warning away the two intruders. Frantic shouts carried kilometres across the ice floes which were steadily breaking into pieces.

'Oh God, Sneum, look.' Helvard pointed south and Sneum followed his gaze to the source of his concern.

The latest fracture line was heading straight for them. The previous morning's ice-breaker had clearly chopped its way along this line, riding up on the slabs with its rounded bow and crushing them as it sank back into the water. Now the underwater turbulence had reopened all that a frozen night had begun to heal.

Sneum recalled: 'The storm from the south-east had brought all the water in from the Baltic, which had lifted the ice and made it break up again. That was the greatest danger to our survival. The ice all around that line was breaking into flakes, and we didn't know when we were going to have to step onto a flake that wasn't big enough to carry our weight.'

Their wooden poles came into play again as they reacted instinctively to avoid the bubbling veins of water now appearing at their feet. 'As soon as a crack opened up, we jumped in unison,' said Tommy. But for a few perilous moments they lacked firm direction. Sneum was the one who finally came to a decision. 'Come on!' he yelled, pulling on the rope which tied them together. 'Back to Hven. It's our only chance.'

The main fracture was almost upon them. If they didn't outrun it, they would surely fall through. But Helvard hesitated for a crucial moment, apparently frozen in fear. Tommy explained Arne's confusion: 'Helvard hadn't been to sea until he joined the navy. He didn't understand the ice like I did, because he'd been brought up in the country. He had never been in a situation like this before and I think he must have been more scared than me. I knew we had to turn back to Hven, but Arne didn't turn as quickly as I did.'

Since they were still attached by the rope, it looked certain that they would both be killed, but the fracture deviated slightly as it tore past them. Even so, the consequences appeared to be no less devastating than a direct hit under their feet:

When the biggest crack in the ice opened up, it blocked our path back to Hven. It was as wide as a bed is long, and I screamed at Arne to run at it and use his pole when I did. If you didn't have a run-up, you didn't have the momentum to get yourself lifted into the air, or the forward movement to land where you wanted to. It was a bit like pole-vaulting, but there was no real bend in the pole because it was made of wood. All the more reason why we really had to run at it.

Helvard snapped into action and they both charged at the ice as it ripped apart in front of them. Ramming their staffs into the softening surface and leaping for their lives, both men hung in the air long enough to land in a heap on the other side. Sneum, struggling for breath, was first to drag himself to his feet. He pulled Arne up quickly and said: 'Come on, keep moving, let's get out of here!'

They stumbled back towards Hven, their only chance of survival. Adrenalin kept their exhausted limbs pumping as they skipped across the crumbling surface, praying all the time that they wouldn't fall under. The sleet and snow whipped into their eyes as the worst of the storm caught up with them. Tommy began to notice more matchstick men, moving towards them from the island. At first they seemed far away, unreachable; but Sneum and Helvard fought on like men possessed until the matchsticks became real people. All of a sudden their rescuers, Swedish policemen, grabbed each man by the arm and dragged him away roughly. 'We thought they were our saviours but they treated us like criminals,' Tommy observed wryly. 'Still, at least they were dragging us onto solid ground, and that was good to know.'

For five or six hours, Sneum and Helvard had been tormented by the creaks and groans of the ice beneath their feet, and had felt the vast slabs shifting menacingly as they moved to the rhythm of the silent currents below. Now they were being scraped across a beach by their captors, towards a grim-looking building on the cliffs above.

It might not have been the mainland, but it was at least Sweden. And perhaps the first firm stepping stone back to London.

Chapter **37**

SPILLING THE BEANS

TOMMY SNEUM AND ARNE HELVARD were trapped in Malmo Prison. The governor, Einar Karstengren, was rumoured to be a Nazi. Since their escape to a supposedly neutral country, life had been full of strange twists and turns. On the island of Hven they were locked in a shed as punishment for refusing to give their names. They tried to keep moving in order to prevent the onset of hypothermia, until at last they were put on motor-sledges and driven across the ice to the Swedish mainland. A comfortable night at a police station in Helsingborg saw the town's chief constable, Olaf Palm, lay on the most extraordinary hospitality, including a lavish dinner in their cell served professionally by the head waiter of a local hotel. But then, before their transfer to the bigger Swedish city, Palm warned his guests to prepare for the worst. Tommy remembered how awkward his host had looked as he broke the news. 'I feel obliged to tell you,' Palm began, 'that they are going to send you to Germany, or at the very least back to the Germans in Denmark.'

'I got scared when I heard that,' admitted Sneum. 'I knew that if the Germans got their hands on me, they would shoot me or torture me, or more likely both. I had heard about so many people being tortured, and the Germans scared everyone with their methods. I was almost sure I would have broken down. I needed to avoid it.'

As their fate hung in the balance in Malmo, they had their mugshots and fingerprints taken. Then all they could do was wait for the arrival from Copenhagen of Politikommissaer Odmar, who would help to decide what was to happen to them.

* * *

If Tommy thought that Colonel Rabagliati might be able to exert some influence over his and Arne's precarious predicament from back in Britain, he was wrong. By then, the political wind had turned against the Secret Intelligence Service.

On 30 March 1942, Colonel Harry Sporborg of the Special Operations Executive's Scandinavian Section revealed how he intended to outmanoeuvre his rival Rabagliati to gain control of British dealings with Denmark:

> It seems to me that we have a chance to create a really good Secret Army in Denmark and although this might never be used it might be extremely useful at a later stage in the war . . . If the Chiefs-of-Staff approve and authorise us to go ahead along the lines I suggest, we must then approach the Foreign Office and get them to modify their policy towards Denmark to fit in with the plan . . . We must consider carefully who is allowed to see the documents and how they are to be presented. I agree that A.C.S.S. [Claude Dansey, the assistant chief of SIS] should see them and I think he should show them to Colonel Rabagliati also. I would really like it if the copy sent could then be returned to us, as for many reasons I think it would be wise not to have it in the files at Broadway [SIS Headquarters].

Under this plan, SOE's field chief for Denmark, Ronnie Turnbull, would have authority from the very top to receive on behalf of Britain whatever information the Princes chose to provide. In return, the British would essentially leave Denmark alone for the foreseeable future, and SIS's involvement would end.

Tommy Sneum, working for the wrong covert organisation, therefore became expendable in the eyes of the power brokers in London. If the Princes wanted him locked up and kept out of the way, that is how it would be. Rabagliati's hands were well and truly tied.

※ ▓ ▒

Oblivious to the political games being played in London, Tommy was concerned about striking the right note during his vital interrogation in Odmar's presence. He wanted to appear as cooperative as possible, so that he and Helvard could avoid being delivered into the hands of the Germans. He had by now given his real name to the Swedes, and freely admitted that he was Sigfred Christophersen's spy partner. He did this because he knew that the Copenhagen police had worked out as much already. At the time, he thought he was beyond the clutches of the Nazis in Denmark. But then Palm told him that Sweden's neutrality might not count for anything. So Tommy knew he was going to have to give his captors a little bit more.

When the interview with Odmar began, Sneum was clear in his own mind where he would draw the line. Surviving police records show just how far he went.

'Thomas Christian Sneum declines to give any information about what happened to him in England after he had volunteered for the Royal Air Force. And he declines to talk about what happened to Kjeld Pedersen,' began Odmar's report.

Tommy did admit that the British had dropped him, along with Christophersen, near Brorfelde in September 1941. He was also happy to reiterate that his relationship with Christophersen had broken down due to the latter's incompetence and lack of nerve. Since Kaj Oxlund was dead, Tommy then implicated his late friend in most of his activities. He admitted that he had known about Oxlund's attempted escape across the ice with the Christophersen brothers before it had happened. As the police seemed to have independent verification from Helvard's neighbours that Tommy had stayed with Arne during their final days in Denmark, there seemed no point in denying that, either. However, Sneum continued to insist that Helvard had no knowledge of his spying activities on behalf of Britain, claiming that his friend had wanted to escape to England for his own reasons.

Unbeknown to Tommy, though, Arne had already confessed that

he was a spy. The police report stated: 'Under questioning, Helvard admitted that he had spied against the Germans after being employed at Kastrup Airport. He was collating all sorts of information about the airport with regard to manpower, hangars, airplanes, numbers and types, anti-aircraft artillery, and so on. All this information he says he gave to Oxlund, and didn't know what he did with it.'

The logic of both men exaggerating poor Kaj's role was flawless. But why Helvard admitted to being a spy is a mystery. One can only assume that he thought he would take some of the heat off Sneum. Perhaps he was assured that their chances of avoiding the Gestapo would improve if their confessions could be extracted in a more civilised manner in Sweden. Whatever his reasoning might have been, the Danish police didn't need much brainpower to realise that Kaj, Arne and Tommy were all part of the same spy ring, even if the latter two never confirmed their own relationship within the set-up.

Their partial cooperation gave them a fighting chance of survival, but in itself it wasn't enough. Odmar demanded to know the whereabouts of the radio that the British-run spies had brought with them. He explained that he had to be able to give the Germans something tangible, or else he would be obliged to escort the culprits back to Denmark for some brutal interrogation. Fortunately, of course, Tommy had prepared for just such an eventuality. He told Odmar that if he looked among his personal effects he would find a receipt for locker number thirteen at Copenhagan railway station.

Effectively, he had just handed the Nazis a British radio. On the face of it, this seems a terrible betrayal. As far as Tommy could see, however, the discovery would only lull the Germans into a false sense of security. If they thought British spies had to rely on such cumbersome and old-fashioned equipment, the enemy would probably feel confident that they were well ahead in all aspects of radio communication. Whereas in reality, partly thanks to Duus Hansen, the Allies now held the advantage.

'When your life is in danger, you do what you can to save yourself,' admitted Tommy later. 'But there were still things I wouldn't have done.'

For example, Odmar's report noted: 'Sneum declines to give any information about whether the radio transmitter which they brought with them has been used. And he declines to give any

SPILLING THE BEANS 265

information about codes, signals or transmission times. He doesn't say if he was able to transmit himself, but says it was necessary for Christophersen to leave Denmark because he had lost his nerve.'

Sneum wasn't going to betray his friends. He admitted that he had met Werner Gyberg, but claimed he had posed as an innocent radio ham, using a false name – 'Lieutenant Wolff'. That, he hoped, would clear the still-imprisoned Gyberg of all charges that he had been involved in any attempt to get hold of a radio receiver. And it worked: Gyberg was subsequently released. Even more significantly, Tommy did not name the man who represented the future of resistance radio technology – Duus Hansen. It would take more than a persuasive Danish policeman to extract the names of the key people Tommy had left behind, or indeed any confirmation that he had seen his wife during his mission. Odmar's report added: 'Sneum insists that no one – especially not his wife, his parents-in-law, his parents or other members of his family – had any idea that he had been back in Copenhagen, since he knew the police would look for him at family addresses.'

Only time would tell whether trading the old radio would help to win Tommy his freedom. Meanwhile, his wife Else was coming under almost as much pressure to talk at her parents' house in Harald Jensensgade, Copenhagen. Thomas Noerreheden led the questioning again and, supplied with an up-to-date file by Odmar, he showed Else mugshots of Tommy, taken by the Swedish police since his capture and transfer to Malmo. 'Is this your husband?' the detective asked.

Else confirmed that it was. There was no point in denying the obvious.

Noerreheden closed in for the kill. 'Else, enough is enough. The truth now. When was the last time you saw him?'

Else must have been very angry at the way she and Marianne had been abandoned, but the safety of her parents would also have come into the equation as she weighed up what her response should be. Finally, she delivered her answer: 'June last year,' she said defiantly.

* * *

On 31 March, Odmar and Noerreheden opened locker number thirteen at Copenhagen railway station. They were not disappointed by what they found. As Sneum had promised, inside a case were a primitive-looking radio transmitter and receiver along with some English-made headphones. On closer inspection, it became apparent that the radio crystals were absent, rendering the equipment useless. So the British frequencies would remain a mystery. But here was solid proof that the spy ring had existed. It was the sort of evidence which would make these two detectives look competent in German eyes. Odmar decided to search the surrounding lockers. In one he found a travel case containing various items of khaki uniform, which appeared to belong to a lieutenant in the Army Reserve. In another were a cap and riding boots belonging to the same man – Kaj Oxlund.

The following day Odmar authorised Noerreheden to hand over the most interesting items from the haul to the Abwehr, and Oberleutnant von Grene duly welcomed the Danish detective at the Hotel Cosmopolit. The English-made radio transmitter and receiver were said to be of particular interest. A delighted von Grene then informed his superior, Fregatten-Kapitan Howoldt, of the find. In time perhaps they could persuade the Swedes to hand back the original owners of this equipment, Thomas Sneum and Sigfred Christophersen. If that happened, Roland Olsen's vision of Sneum being machine-gunned up against a wall would become reality.

Chapter **38**

THE GAMBLE

THE SWEDISH AUTHORITIES were worried about sending British agents back to Denmark, when there was every chance that such a move could result in their torture or execution in Germany. The Danes were equally concerned about German reprisals if Sneum and his colleagues were allowed to reach Britain. So Tommy, Arne and Sigfred, each in his own cell, continued to suffer in Malmo Prison.

Meanwhile, Christian Michael Rottboell, the friend who had wanted to join Tommy and Kjeld Pedersen in the Hornet Moth, parachuted back into Denmark on behalf of SOE. Rottboell therefore effectively became Tommy's replacement as Britain's representative in Copenhagen. The Princes of Danish Intelligence were no happier about his arrival than they had been about the presence of his predecessors, Sneum and Christophersen. Hans Lunding thought he had persuaded Ronnie Turnbull to put an end to the night-time parachute jumps, but Turnbull really had no influence over such critical policies. It was his Danish Section boss in London, Commander Ralph Hollingworth, who insisted they should continue.

Once on the ground, Rottboell achieved one notable success: he managed to persuade John Christmas Moeller, the chairman of the Conservative Party, to escape to Sweden. The politician, who had known Tommy Sneum and his family since before the war, didn't leave Denmark alone. He packed his family into a secret compartment on the escape boat, and the voyage to freedom went like clockwork. They later flew from Stockholm to Scotland and arrived in London in mid-May 1942. Christmas Moeller was soon elected chairman of the Free Danish Council, which became the closest thing to a Danish government-in-exile during the war.

Rottboell remained in Copenhagen, working with Duus Hansen. Their activities would soon become more hazardous than ever.

By late May, Sneum's imprisonment in Sweden had reached a critical phase. It was clear to Tommy that, for whatever reason, the Princes had been unable to keep their promise to have him freed. He explained: 'I had planned to go back to England, give them my reports and then parachute back into Denmark, all inside three months. But it wasn't turning out that way.' He wondered whether the cautious old professionals of Danish Intelligence had exerted enough pressure to secure his release. In reality, the Princes had used all their influence in the other direction – to ensure that he was kept under lock and key in Sweden, so that he could never threaten their cosy existence again.

Tommy and Arne had spent a total of eight weeks in jail by now. Tommy felt his spirits sink by the day, as the monotony and solitude began to get the better of him: 'I was let out of my cell to empty my piss-pot in the morning but I wasn't allowed to speak to anyone. Twice a day all the other prisoners went out for exercise surrounded by guards with machine-guns, rifles and pistols. I was just taken to a back yard to walk on my own with a policeman watching me. There was no way out.'

Unless Tommy gambled soon, he feared he could be left to rot behind bars until the end of the war. He had realised that the spy world was a murky one long before he had left Denmark. Either you played dirty or you lost – and he didn't intend to lose. He insisted upon a new meeting with Einar Karstengren. 'Because of the time I have now spent here,' Tommy warned the prison governor, 'a very serious situation has developed outside, which could present a grave threat to Swedish lives. You need to contact Captain Wahlqvist of Swedish Naval Intelligence, here in Malmo; and Kriminal-Kommissarie Runerheim of the Malmo police. I suggest you do it straight away. Tell them to hurry to the prison without delay.' Karstengren knew that Wahlqvist and Runerheim were key spymasters in Swedish Intelligence, and it was with some satisfaction that Tommy noted the concern etched on the governor's face as he left the cell. He had set the wheels in motion for a bitter game to begin. Sure enough, Runerheim arrived at the prison later that day.

Tommy recalled: 'He was a tall fellow, good-looking, well dressed, probably in his mid-forties. He looked strong, confident and formidable. I knew this wasn't going to be easy. He was accompanied to my cell by the Nazi, Karstengren. Then the prison governor left the cell to Runerheim and myself.'

'Why have you brought me out here?' demanded the police chief, clearly irritated. 'I'm extremely busy.'

Undaunted, Sneum drilled him with a stare. 'You know why. You made an agreement with some Danish officers we both know. The agreement was that I would be released within two weeks. Now there is talk that I could be handed over to the Germans. If that happens, I promise you I won't be the only one.'

'What are you saying?'

'I'm talking about your precious agents in Poland and Germany,' said Sneum menacingly. 'I know you have networks there. And I gave one of my people in Denmark some instructions. If he doesn't get my coded postcard from Stockholm by the end of the first week in June, he's going to send a letter to the Germans. He'll tell them all about your spies in Poland and Germany. Your name is on the list, too. It could be messy.'

Runerheim tried to smile. 'You're bluffing. We haven't any such spies.'

'Haven't you?' Tommy asked knowingly.

The Swedish policeman looked at the prisoner disdainfully. 'Give me some names, if you're so clever.'

Sneum laughed. 'So that you can warn them and work out how I got the information? Don't be so bloody stupid.'

'I knew it,' said Runerheim dismissively. 'You don't have any names.'

'I knew your name, Runerheim, and I know a lot more. I have a lot of information that you really wouldn't like to come out. You'd better be careful, or I'll reveal the whole lot.'

Runerheim just stood there, seething. It was as though he were about to ask Sneum what he wanted, but had too much pride.

So Tommy made it simple for him: 'You'd better find an excuse to release me and my friend – and quick.' Then he turned his back and began to make his bed.

Runerheim stormed out of the cell, and Sneum listened as the furious clatter of the Swede's footsteps on the stone corridor grew faint. Sitting on the bed, Tommy suppressed any sense of guilt by remembering the significance of the scientific and military intelligence he had sent to the British, and reminding himself that he needed to be free to do such work again. Furthermore, it was not only the Swedish spy ring that was in danger of being blown if he were ever delivered for torture by the Germans. People he knew and cared for, professionally and personally, would be at risk if he cracked.

Back in Copenhagen, Niels-Richard Bertelsen was well aware that his brother-in-law's postcard from Stockholm hadn't arrived, and it didn't take the policeman long to find out why. Late night checks in Politikommissaer Odmar's office revealed that the Danish police chief had approved Tommy's long-term incarceration in Malmo. Bertelsen knew that Tommy would want him to start issuing threats to all the relevant people in Copenhagen, warning that agents in Nazi-occupied Europe risked discovery if the Swedish didn't let Sneum go. However, Bertelsen knew he could never go through with it. So he hoped Tommy would prove convincing enough in Malmo to win his ugly game of brinkmanship without further assistance.

Since Tommy believed he could be handed back to the Germans at any time, he hadn't lacked motivation as he played his part. He felt abandoned, and a cornered animal's survival instinct had kicked in. Later, he insisted:

I needed to get to Britain because I had a lot of important information. More important, I thought, than anyone else would have. Remember, we had never had any reply from the British about the German super-bomb intelligence. On another level, where the genuine names on the list I had given to Bertelsen were concerned, it was my life or theirs. To me, they were just names. If you were going to be put up against a wall and shot, what would you do? I gambled that the Swedes would see sense so that no one was put in any danger.

Chapter **39**

THE CONSEQUENCES

BEFORE MAY HAD COME to an end, prison guards marched into Sneum's Malmo cell with Arne Helvard. 'Get your things together,' said Helvard with a smile. 'Looks like they're finally releasing us. Christophersen has already gone.'

Starved of company for so long, they talked without sleeping as the night train made its way from Malmo to Stockholm. If there were sensitive matters to discuss, they moved into the corridor outside their compartment. No guards watched over them, but Tommy occasionally imagined that some of their fellow passengers might be members of Sweden's secret service. As long as these observers said nothing and did nothing, Tommy didn't care. As for Karstengren, Runerheim and the rest, they could all go to hell.

When the two Danes arrived in the Swedish capital the following morning, Sneum sent the vital postcard with its coded message to Bertelsen. As he did so, he told Arne how he had secured their release. Helvard looked shocked, scared and grateful all at once. Tommy, for his part, was relieved that his brother-in-law would no longer be dragged into his cut-throat world. Now that the dirty tricks were no longer necessary, they could focus on reaching Britain so that they could return to war.

As a first step, they made their way to the British Legation at

Strandvagen. There, Tommy was relieved to find the familiar face of Henry Denham, the Naval Attaché, still serving Britain from his Scandinavian outpost. It seemed an eternity since Denham had sent Sneum back into Denmark to photograph the Fanoe radar installations. In reality, it had been little more than a year, though much had changed.

If Denham had been forewarned of the circumstances surrounding Sneum's release from Malmo, he certainly didn't show it. Instead, he promised to arrange visas for Tommy and Arne, so that they could fly on the new British air service from Bromme airfield in Stockholm to Leuchars in Scotland. It might take a week or two, he warned, but he would make sure there was space on one of the planes. In the meantime, they would have to survive in Stockholm as best they could, because there was no money available to keep them comfortable.

Tommy's solution to his latest predicament was typical: 'I found a girl over there,' he revealed later. 'And I think Arne had friends in Stockholm.'

It was mid-June when the two men called the Legation and were finally told to head to Bromme airfield. There, they were directed towards a fifteen-seater Lockheed Hudson that was waiting on the tarmac. Christophersen was already sitting on the plane. However, the seating arrangements seemed to have been planned with this awkward scenario in mind: Helvard joined Christophersen at the front of the plane while Sneum was ushered to the back, and directed to a seat next to a man he thought he recognised. Swiftly, he traced the soft, handsome face to his visits to the British Legation in Copenhagen and the fast-moving days of April 1940; it was Ronald Turnbull. As they exchanged pleasantries, Sneum recalled that Turnbull had been a press attaché two years earlier in the Danish capital, and that they had sometimes attended the same parties. Turnbull was full of charm and fun, so Tommy couldn't know that his status as an SIS agent meant he had been regarded by SOE's field officer as the opposition over the previous nine months. He didn't sense any relief in Turnbull that a dangerous rival had finally been removed from the Scandinavian stage.

Ronnie was leaving his beloved Thereza and their son Michael behind temporarily, while he took part in a series of meetings in London, many of them relating to the situation in Denmark. Sneum's exit from the Danish stage had made Turnbull's life simpler in many ways. The loose cannon, the thorn in Ronnie's side, the SIS man who had tried to upset the Danish status quo with his risk-taking, had become a casualty of SOE's recent rise to prominence.

The three-hour flight passed amicably enough. Tommy couldn't deny that Turnbull was a witty, intelligent man whose company was easy to enjoy. He remembered: 'I was having a nice conversation with Turnbull; he was very charming. We talked about the war, and, since we were both destined for London, we talked about England. He asked if I had been there before and I said that I had, the previous summer. He asked if I liked London, and I said I had enjoyed myself there.'

As Turnbull went his own way at Leuchars airfield, Tommy, Arne and Sigfred were met by military policemen. Tommy recalled: 'We were arrested, driven to the nearest railway station and put on a night train bound for London, accompanied by a heavy police escort. I thought it was normal procedure, because the British wouldn't want immigration officials to know that I was an agent. I didn't think about trying to escape.'

The silent tension between Sneum and Christophersen was uglier than ever, and even their guards must have felt awkward.

Once in the capital, the Danish trio were transferred to a police car for what Tommy assumed would be a short journey across the West End. He felt sure their destination would be St James's Street, where he had met 'Colonel Ramsden' for the first time. Sneum hoped to have a long, serious talk with the man who had put him through so much pain. The colonel had become a father figure during the tense days before the mission, for instance when he had shown Sneum some of the basic tricks of motor-racing in his powerful Bentley. He was charismatic and good fun. However, in Tommy's view, he had made two fundamental errors of judgement at the planning stage: he had selected Christophersen for the mission and he had seen fit to equip his two-man team with a primitive radio.

As he prepared what he wanted to say, Sneum was curious

to see Londoners going about their daily business, surrounded by the ruins of buildings destroyed in the Blitz. Nothing seemed to dampen the spirits of these people, who had been bombed but never occupied. Yet Tommy himself became alarmed when he noticed that the police car seemed to have bypassed St James's and was heading towards one of the bridges over the Thames.

* * *

There was a very good reason why Rabagliati's office would not be the first port of call. For the head of SIS's A2 (Danish and Dutch) Section was now too busy trying to save his own skin to devote much time to Sneum. Rabagliati was already falling foul of political games among the Free Dutch, because he had declared allegiance to one of that community's more controversial figures. Until that summer, the SIS hierarchy had been fairly loosely defined below 'C' (the chief, Stewart Menzies), 'ACSS' (the assistant chief, Claude Dansey), and the chief of staff, Commander Rex Howard, who ran day-to-day business at Secret Service Headquarters at 54 Broadway. Heads of section were generally considered of equal importance to one another, and with no clear order of seniority these men sometimes competed for resources and respect. Rabagliati, though, with his fine military record and aristocratic breeding, considered himself to be superior to an equally haughty Jewish colleague – Commander Kenneth Cohen. However, the latter was a key player, since he had taken charge of the all-important French Section.

A personality clash erupted when the undeniably snobbish Rabagliati refused to recognise the seniority of Cohen, who had just been promoted to statutory head of A Section. Effectively, the commander had been handed executive responsibility for France, Holland, Denmark and indeed the rest of occupied Western Europe. Rabagliati went over his rival's head to complain about the promotion, and even threatened to resign in protest. To his astonishment, he was promptly asked to make his offer of resignation formal. His bluff had backfired disastrously. It seems incredible that a fit of pique, based certainly on snobbery and perhaps on anti-Semitism, could effectively have removed Sneum's spymaster from the arena just when Tommy needed him most.

§ § §

As the police car carrying the three Danes crossed the Thames and moved purposefully through Clapham, Tommy began to wonder if something had gone wrong. Then he remembered that the Royal Patriotic School, where he had been vetted following the Hornet Moth flight, was near by. Perhaps he would face another interrogation there. Disturbingly, however, the car took them even further south, far beyond the school's location. It soon reached Brixton, where the driver turned off the main road and down a side street. Sneum saw vast walls rising above the houses and the daunting arch of an iron gate. Before he knew it, Brixton Prison had swallowed the police vehicle, and Tommy found himself incarcerated yet again.

Chapter **40**

THE ORDEAL

TOMMY SNEUM DEMANDED to see Brixton Prison's governor. His request was refused. Instead he was again separated from Helvard and Christophersen and thrown into a small cell in the bowels of the jail. He tried to ignore the familiar stale smell. It was best to be positive and patient while he waited for Rabagliati to arrive. Though his cell was no more than four metres long and two metres wide, even more cramped than his home of the last couple of months in Malmo, he tried to see the funny side. This wasn't the best of British welcomes, but what did it matter? He wouldn't be staying inside for long.

When the door was unlocked and Tommy was escorted along the corridor to a dimly lit interrogation room, he still wasn't unduly worried. He expected the confusion to be resolved quickly, so that he could be back in the outside world before nightfall.

A British Army officer, no more than twenty-four and rather too proud of his pencil-thin moustache, was waiting to conduct the interrogation. He was an MI5 interrogator and he had clearly been expecting the new prisoner. The initial exchanges seemed friendly enough, if clinical and routine. Tommy willingly gave his name and rank, before being invited to tell the complicated story of his mission, from the moment he had landed in the Danish countryside. Hour after hour, he explained the difficulties he had encountered, from the misjudged parachute drop to the break-up of the Oeresund ice during his last escape. He was careful to include in his account the successes that had made his mission to Nazi-occupied Denmark worthwhile. The only questions he refused to answer concerned his contacts in the field, because he wanted to protect their identities. Rabagliati had told him before his departure that he was entitled to withhold names during any initial interrogation on his return. They would sit down together for a more detailed debrief in due course, he imagined.

Sneum's evasive tactics didn't seem to impress MI5. As he stubbornly resisted the pressure, the atmosphere began to change. The young officer began to focus on Tommy's imprisonment in Sweden, and the information he had divulged there. Sneum insisted that Christophersen had told the Swedes most of those details already, but the interrogator disagreed. Sneum, it was pointed out, gave away not only his real name but the whereabouts in Copenhagen of their radio. Tommy explained the logic behind this, and emphasised that his Danish friends had designed far better radios since, therefore leaving the Germans with a misleading idea of the technology now available to the Allies. He also pointed out that he had been encouraged to cooperate to an extent, in order to secure his release.

It didn't take very long for the young interrogator to come to the most damaging chapter of Sneum's detention in Malmo – his threat to expose Swedish agents in Poland and Germany. 'You were going to betray us,' the officer suggested.

Tommy began to realise that the Swedish and Polish names he had committed to memory weren't working solely for Sweden, but also for the Allies. Naturally, that left him with some explaining to do. 'That was a bluff,' he insisted. 'I only brought that threat into play when they had kept me in jail too long.'

The interrogator shook his head. 'From what I can see, you would quite happily have blown an entire organisation. They didn't think you were bluffing.'

Tommy smiled at this. 'My dear fellow, that is the idea of a bluff.'

The interrogator wasn't convinced by this defence. He also had information on Sneum's whereabouts during the penultimate week of March, when he had stayed at the Astoria in Copenhagen. The British knew that this was a hotel frequented by German officers and Nazi sympathisers, and they didn't buy Tommy's claim that he had decided to hide in the last place anyone would expect him to be. Nor was Sneum very tactful when he freely admitted that he had enjoyed the company of many of these Germans, just as he had enjoyed mixing with Abwehr officers in the Hotel Cosmopolit the previous year.

Sneum explained later: 'The Brixton interrogators said I had been trying to deliver all Britain's secrets to the Germans. I told them they were talking nonsense, because the Danes I had contacted to set up the resistance were still working. If I had really squealed, they would have been stopped. But the English couldn't cope with the fact that I liked some Germans.'

The young interrogator was staggered by this confession, but Tommy was determined not to sound ashamed of what he had done, and insisted that fraternising with the enemy had paid off handsomely. He recalled: 'I told the British this: "If you want proper information about the enemy, you should be grateful that a man had the courage to go in and make friends with them and get that information."' He was able to give the names of some German officers, albeit admitting that he didn't think those names were genuine, since it was common practice for everyone in that community to use aliases.

The interrogator seemed far from satisfied and the exchanges became more heated. Tommy accused the young officer of being naïve, and he attacked the British for their xenophobia. 'I think the majority of regular German Army people are decent and well disciplined. Most are also against Hitler,' he dared to suggest.

'If you regard the Germans so highly, why didn't you stay over there with them?' came the reply.

'What do you actually know about Germany?' Tommy fired back accusingly. 'Did you get good information or not?'

To the interrogator's ears, Tommy was sounding ever more like a collaborator or, worse still, a double-agent. So the British officer voiced a theory that the Princes had shared for some time: that Sneum couldn't have escaped from Denmark in the Hornet Moth the previous summer without German help. Tommy pointed out that, were he really a double-agent, he would hardly have warned the British about the claims of a drunken Abwehr officer, who had boasted that the Germans still had an effective spy ring in Britain, and received 'running information' from it.

But since Sneum wasn't more specific, this did little to strengthen his case, because the British had more substantial allegations against him, from his very own spy partner. Christophersen had already accused Tommy of inventing the radio message ordering him over to Sweden, the one that had effectively sent Thorbjoern Christophersen and Kaj Oxlund to their deaths. Astonishingly, Sneum freely admitted that he had done just that.

'I told the British what I had done when they interrogated me,' he confirmed later. 'I said that Christophersen was my radio operator, and I had the right to get rid of him if he wasn't doing his job. It had been the only way I could get him out without killing him. I had tried to solve the problem quietly.' On this point, at least, the British seemed to accept Tommy's reasoning, as he revealed: 'After that the British never bothered me about it.'

One problem for Sneum was his refusal to come up with the names of people who could support his story about Christophersen's loss of nerve, or indeed Tommy's own loyalty to the British cause. He had decided to protect the identity of Duus Hansen, for example, who had gently sided with Sneum in his dispute with Christophersen. Indeed, until he could talk to someone he knew he could trust, he was determined that the identities of all of those who had given him assistance in Denmark would remain secret.

He demanded to see either Colonel Ramsden or Otto Gregory, and asked for a message to be sent to R.V. Jones, the scientific expert. When he received no satisfactory response, he played what he thought was his strongest card: namely, that he had important information about a German bomb that might soon be powerful enough to blow up the whole of south-east England. 'I told them I didn't want the Germans to win the war because of this bomb. I suggested that the British make one themselves or steal one from the Germans.'

This seemingly outlandish claim about a super-bomb was met with derision, probably because the young interrogator was far too junior to have heard about the potential for such a development. But the warning was doubtless passed up the intelligence line for further analysis, where it would have been treated much more seriously. Indeed, when Tommy tried to raise the subject again during a subsequent interrogation, he was told urgently: 'Forget about it! Shut up!'

Tommy observed later:

> Hardly anyone knew that the potential for such a bomb existed, and the importance of Enrico Fermi – maybe twenty people in the whole of Britain. And there was little old me, just a flight lieutenant, saying it. Just mentioning Fermi's name or talking about the bomb was probably enough to get you locked up. It was top, top secret. I realised I knew too much, and they obviously realised it too. That was dangerous for me.

Ironically, however, Tommy's information about German efforts to make an atom bomb were already out of date. In autumn 1941 the Allies and Germany had both come to a crossroads in their respective nuclear-fission programmes. But during the first half of 1942 the Allies had forged ahead in the race, while the Nazis, and in particular the new Minister for Armaments and Munitions, Albert Speer, had recently been advised by Professor Heisenberg that such a weapon could not be built in time to make a difference to the war.

If the British knew that the Germans had scaled down their efforts, it might even have sounded to them as though Tommy had been 'turned' and that he was trying to strengthen the Nazis' bargaining position should they ever need to sue for peace. To those in Britain who knew nothing about the potential for an atom bomb, however, Sneum's claims would have sounded staggering in their gravity, especially his first radio communication to that effect, sent in partnership with Duus Hansen from Denmark in January 1942. As an old man, Tommy alleged: 'Otto Gregory told me that when he talked to his superiors at the Air Ministry about my atom-bomb intelligence, they said it was the biggest and most important news they ever got.'

Whatever the truth about the way in which the British

intelligence community greeted and assessed Sneum's claims, the sensitivity of the issue meant it was safer to keep him under lock and key. Tommy was a one-off, very hard to read, and the pressure from his interrogators as they tried to break him down was sustained and unpleasant. The faces sometimes changed, but the questions remained the same. Sneum was interviewed for at least ten hours on that first day, with several intelligence officers working in shifts. On the second day, the process started all over again, and lasted from morning until evening. The third day brought the same exhausting routine as he was subjected to more verbal abuse from eager young British officers.

'I was interrogated by God-knows-how-many different British intelligence people,' he said. 'The questioning was relentless.'

They had clearly been well briefed on the situation in Denmark, but seemed to have no idea about the harsh realities of an agent's struggle to survive. Time and again the interrogators returned to what they knew for sure – that Sneum had threatened to expose Swedish spies in Nazi-occupied Europe. They rejected his insistence that he was fundamentally loyal to the Allied cause and had been forced to fight dirty, simply regarding his tactics as outright treachery.

Tommy wondered when the British people who knew him best – Rabagliati, Gregory and Jones – might walk through the door to call off the dogs, as had happened the previous June. This summer, however, there was no respite and the questions kept coming as the days rolled by. With each interrogation, MI5 seemed to demand ever more detail, as though Tommy should be able to remember absolutely everything he had done, on each individual day, for seven months. It seemed as though the British were trying to catch him out at every turn. If he gave a solid account of an event to one interrogator, it was seized upon and used against him by the next. At the height of summer, with little food or water, this relentless pressure was exhausting. Sneum felt as though he were edging along a high wire, with the British determined to make him trip and fall. He was numb with fatigue and confusion.

After a week, the interrogators, sensing that he might be at his most vulnerable, finally took Tommy to a larger cell, where he was reunited with Arne Helvard. As soon as they were left alone with coffee and cigarettes, both men began to look for a microphone. 'I found one up in a grille in the corner and smashed it,' Tommy admitted. It was time to let off some steam about their incarceration, and they insulted the British in every way they knew. Tommy revealed later: 'We talked about what big shits the British were, how we had risked our lives for them and how they had treated us like criminals in return. I said that the Germans might never have gone into France if the British had adopted a stronger stance towards them in the first place.'

What neither man knew was that the British had refined their interrogation techniques, and the microphone had been placed in such an obvious position because the prisoners had been meant to find it. A popular MI5 technique was to lull prisoners into a false sense of security so that a second, more ingeniously hidden microphone could pick up their conversation, once they had dropped their guard.

The atmosphere became even more hostile when Tommy and Arne were separated again and the interrogations started afresh. 'They didn't rough us up, but it was difficult just the same,' Tommy admitted. 'It was constant pressure, talk, talk, they never gave me time to think.'

Ten more agonising days passed before the questioning came to an abrupt end. By then Sneum had concluded: 'The British didn't like me because I was too independent, I argued with them, and I knew too much about the scientific war.'

When Tommy was told to prepare for a change of scenery, he asked if he was to be released. His optimism brought scornful laughter from the guards. He was simply to be taken to a new cell, in a block that had been set aside especially for foreigners. He recalled: 'Christophersen was in a ground-floor cell just two away from mine. I saw him sometimes but I didn't have anything to say to him, and it was too late to do anything. I would have been hanged as a murderer.'

Most of Sneum's new neighbours, it turned out, were Hungarians, but the route to 'Little Budapest' took him down corridors which ran through the central artery of the close-knit prison community. Here the majority of inmates were British, and Tommy encountered a problem. 'The rumours had already spread among the other prisoners that I was a very dangerous spy,' he remembered. As he was escorted through the prison, cells on all floors suddenly came alive with banging and chanting. 'They shouted at me, "You fucking spy," and all that nonsense.' The prison warders just smiled, and did nothing to silence the inmates. Perhaps the screws had even orchestrated it all for their own amusement. Realising there would be no punishment for their unruly behaviour, the prisoners intensified their campaign. Sneum had to face this abuse on a daily basis, whenever he was taken out of his cell, and there was no one to share the burden of being a hate figure. Judging by the more neutral reaction of their fellow inmates, Helvard and Christophersen appeared to be under less suspicion.

The half-hour Tommy was given in the exercise yard each morning or afternoon should have been the highlight of his prison day. Instead, it provided the platform for some of the most intense verbal abuse. The occupants of the cells overlooking the tiny yard were quick to spread news of the foreign spy's arrival. 'Nazi traitor,' they yelled incessantly. Eventually their insults began to hit home, and Tommy withdrew into himself. Apart from the Hungarians, with whom he could at least share the dubious status of distrusted foreigner, he was surrounded by black-market spivs and violent criminals. These men were seeing out the war in the relative safety of a London prison, while they called for the head of a man who had risked his life for the Allied cause. Every day the abuse from the British inmates echoed louder inside Tommy's head.

'German spy!'

'Scum!'

'Hang the bastard!'

'What are you waiting for?'

'Traitor, you're going to die!'

The prison governor, Mr Benke, who had taken up his post only the previous year, was appalled when news of the victimisation reached him. He ordered the guards to put a stop to it, and for a few merciful days, the cells fell silent when Tommy walked past. He felt relief and hoped for acceptance. Then, inexplicably, the chanting started again with fresh venom.

As the days turned into weeks, life no longer felt worth living. All Tommy's senses were under assault. The stench of prison life in high summer, with hundreds of sweaty men crammed into tiny spaces, was stomach-churning. One day the prisoners were ordered to tidy and prepare their cells for inspection. Seeking to restore order in his own mind, Sneum complied until his tiny living space was sparkling perfection. Before long a large, red-haired prison officer by the name of Griffith entered Tommy's cell on his tour of inspection. He seemed to have taken even more of a dislike to Sneum than the other inmates and glared contemptuously around the cell as he searched for fault. When he could find none, he became visibly agitated.

'Your bed, Sneum. Look at it! What a bloody shambles.'

'I've just made it,' said Tommy defiantly.

'It's a mess.'

'I don't think so, sir.'

Griffith marched over, pushed Sneum against the wall and pulled apart the bed. 'Well, it's a mess now, isn't it? Make it again, you slob.'

Sneum's icy blue eyes drilled Griffith with such intense aggression that, for all his own sadistic tendencies, the officer was taken aback. Then he called Sneum's bluff. 'Go on, son, I know what you're thinking. Why don't you have a go? Throw a punch and see what happens to you.'

Tommy was confident he could floor the overweight warder without a problem. He also knew how deeply satisfying that punch would be. But for how long? He would be playing into Griffith's hands – enjoying a short-term victory but a lasting defeat. If he knocked out a warder, they would have an excuse to lock him up for ever. Griffith would have all the time in the world to plan and exact his revenge.

Smiling, Griffith seemed to read his mind again. 'Don't worry about the consequences, Sneum. You couldn't get into more shit than you're in already, even if you killed me. It's all over for you, boy.' Tommy said nothing but wondered why Griffith suddenly seemed so sure of himself. 'That's right, Sneum. The rope's waiting for you. Haven't you been told? You're due to swing in five weeks.'

Although he tried hard to hide his fear, Tommy was unnerved by this. A malevolent grin spread across Griffith's face as he saw the news hit home, and he left the cell whistling cheerfully. Sneum slumped onto the mattress, which had been left in a heap on his cell floor, and wept as quietly as he could.

The next day, as he walked towards the exercise yard, Tommy experienced no abuse at all. There was mostly silence, although one or two prisoners shouted words of sympathy or encouragement from their cells. Sneum was convinced these were the same men who had been victimising him previously. The kindness was chilling.

They began to treat me with more respect because they had heard I was going to hang. They told me straight: 'You've been condemned to death. We'll think of you.' A lot of them said that: 'We'll be thinking of you when it happens.' One said: 'You can ask for a Bible.' I was scared, but I was pleased when I found out my fellow prisoners liked me. I began to realise that some of the finest gentlemen in Britain were in Brixton.

Chapter **41**

A DIPLOMATIC INCIDENT

SIS HAD BEEN BUSY REORGANISING its A2 Section. Rabagliati's successor overseeing operations in Holland and Denmark was the newly promoted Major Charles Seymour, his former number two, the man who had driven Sneum up to Ringway Airport for parachute training. With his resignation so surprisingly accepted, Rabagliati had asked Seymour to walk out too, as a gesture of solidarity. Seymour had refused, determined that there should be some continuity within the department, for the sake of any agents still in the field. He also failed to see why he should sacrifice his own career and prospects of promotion just because of Rabagliati's personality clash with a colleague. As if to prove the point, he even took over the colonel's old office, a particularly painful twist for Rabagliati as he stepped aside for a man half his age.

Since he had handled Tommy in the past, Seymour must have known about the Danish agent's imprisonment in Brixton. However, he had only just got his feet under the table in Rabagliati's office. To rock the boat so soon and campaign for Sneum's release, especially as Tommy had threatened the lives of fellow agents, would have been a very risky career move. And Seymour was amiable, rather than a born risk-taker in the Rabagliati mould.

Office politics had therefore worked devastatingly against

Tommy. Only the previous summer, Rabagliati and Seymour had shown so much faith in his ability that they had asked him to risk his life for them. Now, for very different reasons, neither man was anywhere to be seen when Tommy needed their help in return.

To make matters worse, Sigfred Christophersen was released by the authorities. For Sneum, living in the shadow of the noose, his former partner's freedom was hard to swallow. It was even rumoured that Christophersen was to be offered a place in the RAF in recognition of his services. The chance to fly. It was all Tommy had ever wanted for himself.

One day Griffith entered Sneum's cell wearing a sadistic smile and told him he would be executed in a few days' time. In the meantime he would be moved to a cell nearer to the gallows. 'They're just making sure the mechanism is working smoothly,' he said, taunting his prisoner. 'You'll be dropping through the trapdoor soon enough.'

Tommy later claimed: 'They had this holding cell before execution in Brixton, and I was put in there. I thought: Fuck. Now they're really going to kill me, the bastards. I was in this empty cell, which looked much like all the others, except that nobody contacted you.'

That changed when Sneum heard a strange squeaking as something heavy was pulled along the corridor outside. The contraption sounded as though it was running on wheels. As it came closer, however, he saw it was nothing more lethal than a trolley laden with reading material. 'Books? Want anything?' An elderly man was asking the question to everyone he passed. The prison librarian had reached Sneum's cell on his weekly round.

'Do you have any Somerset Maugham?' Tommy asked, bringing mild astonishment to the librarian's face. 'I like most English writers – except Shakespeare.'

The librarian looked horrified. 'What don't you like about Shakespeare?'

'I just think he's overrated,' Sneum replied. 'But any Somerset Maugham would be fine.'

'I'll see what I can do for my next round,' the librarian promised.

'Let's hope I'm still here when you do your next round,' said Tommy in a brave attempt at black humour.

Soon he was told he was on the move again, and he began to brace himself for the noose. Instead, he was taken into the exercise yard. There he was greeted with a spontaneous round of applause. Then he heard a shout: 'Back from the dead, you lucky bastard!'

Tommy looked up to see he was sharing the yard with a young man of about his own age. A wide, warm grin had spread all over the other man's face. Sneum had seen him before, and remembered feeling a little jealous of his popularity, not to mention the privileges it appeared to have earned him. The regime in Brixton clearly didn't consider this character a threat; it was as though he had been there a long time, behaved well, and now was just finishing his half-hour of exercise without an escort. Tommy, though, was confused by the man's little quip, delivered in a thick cockney accent. The Londoner smiled at the warder who had brought out the Dane. With a nod of his head, the guard allowed Sneum to approach his fellow prisoner.

'Bill's the name,' said the man. 'Griffith said they were going to hang you. Either he was playing a cruel trick on you or someone high up must have changed their mind. Anyhow, even Griffith says it's not going to happen now.'

Relief swept over Tommy, and it was all he could do to fight back the tears. Deep inside he also felt a burning anger. Bill smiled sympathetically as he watched his fellow inmate struggle with his emotions. Sneum managed to introduce himself, and Bill revealed that his buoyant mood was not down to Tommy's reprieve, but because he had been given his own imminent release date.

'I robbed a post office,' he said, clearly feeling free to confess to his crime now that he was leaving.

'Did you get anything better than stamps?' asked Tommy with a smile.

'Yes, a lot of money,' claimed Bill. 'Trouble was, they caught me.'

As they took a stroll and engaged in small-talk, Sneum's mind was racing. 'Could I give you a telephone number?' The question was sudden and desperate considering they barely knew each other.

'You can if she's pretty,' laughed Bill.

'I mean for someone who might help get me out of here too.'

Sneum explained that the next time they saw each other, he

would have the number of a man named Otto Gregory ready for Bill, scribbled on a small piece of paper. Somehow the number, for the RAC Club in London, had stuck in his mind since the previous summer.

Bill looked worried, so Tommy gave him an alternative – to pass the number to another Dane who was still in the prison but likely to get out soon – Arne Helvard.

Their conversation was suddenly cut short by the warder: 'Right, that's enough, you two! Sneum, back to your cell.'

But at least Tommy now had new hope.

For a few anxious days, Bill was nowhere to be seen. Then one morning Sneum spotted him leaving the exercise yard, and managed to slip him a tiny scrap of paper with the information he would need. Tommy felt strangely elated. No one could keep him down for long, he told himself. The Germans hadn't managed it when they invaded his country, and the British who had stabbed him in the back wouldn't manage it either. But he never saw Bill again.

Arne Helvard was freed in mid-July, at about the same time that the Free Danish leader, John Christmas Moeller, learned of Thomas Sneum's imprisonment in Brixton. Even before Helvard reached him with the news, Christmas Moeller might have been tipped off by Frank Stagg, a pro-Danish member of the Special Operations Executive. Stagg, a naval commander, had joined SOE in the autumn of 1940 as principal assistant to Harry Sporborg, then head of the Scandinavian Section. By the summer of 1942 he had climbed sufficiently high in the SOE hierarchy to be privy to information regarding Sneum's incarceration, and he was not afraid to speak his mind. Just as Helvard was being released, Stagg hosted a dinner for Christmas Moeller and other friends of the Danish cause at the Thatched House Club in west London. At that event it seems likely that the SOE man expressed similar views to those he would later put in writing: 'The treatment of Sneum on his return to London in 1942 was a disgraceful chapter in the English handling of one who had given us what radar specialists described as "the most valuable piece of radar intelligence yet received" – and the damnable handling also went over to his companion in flight, Helvard.'

Stagg and Christmas Moeller decided to campaign on Sneum's behalf, even if it made them unpopular. Perhaps it was no coincidence that Stagg left SOE later that month, at the height of the controversy over Sneum. His records are said by the Foreign Office to give no official reason for his departure, although Ralph Hollingworth, the London-based head of SOE Denmark, described Stagg at around this time as 'irresponsible and erratic'. Maybe Hollingworth meant that Stagg had decided to speak out about Britain's treatment of Sneum, against SOE wishes.

As Free Danish leader, Christmas Moeller was appalled that he had been kept in the dark about Sneum's imprisonment. Neither, he soon discovered, had he been informed of other key SOE developments, which he knew would have a vital bearing on the situation back home. For instance, no one had told him of a proposed meeting in Stockholm between Captain Volle Gyth of Danish Intelligence and Ronnie Turnbull, or the preparations for the dropping of a fresh wave of SOE agents into Denmark. Incensed, Christmas Moeller decided to hit back. He demanded that Mogens Hammer, codenamed 'Arthur', must be contacted in the field and told that Moeller had severed his SOE links. Moeller's letter was dated 19 July 1942:

Dear Commander Hollingworth,

I am writing this letter to you after long and careful consideration. It is absolutely impossible for me to work under the conditions which have been offered me during the last two months, and I therefore feel we should cease taking up any more of each other's time. The question as to how I shall arrange to carry on my work must be my own affair.

You know that I left Denmark by request and because a Danish politician was very greatly desired as adviser . . .

I have since been kept in complete ignorance of everything that has happened. In between I get scraps of information, that SNEUM is in prison, that there is now money in Denmark, that the Prince [Gyth] is going to Stockholm in a few days, that three new men are going to Denmark etc. – but it is quite outside your thoughts that these three should have a talk with me, without mentioning that it is obvious that my advice is not asked as to whether they should be sent . . .

I must therefore demand that the following message be sent to Arthur:

'Christmas Moeller has demanded that we should inform Arthur and . . . the Princes . . . that he has had no part in or knowledge of the messages we have sent and are sending since his departure from Denmark, and it should not be assumed that Christmas Moeller has anything to do with our work. Christmas Moeller will try by another means to secure for himself communications to Denmark . . .'

Yours, J. Christmas Moeller

Sneum was now at the centre of a full-blown diplomatic incident between Britain and the Free Danes.

Helvard, meanwhile, was accepted by the RAF and sent to North Africa to fly Handley Page Hampdens. He probably felt he had done as much as he could for Tommy for the time being. By leaving his fiancée Vita, Arne had paid a heavy price to fly again, and he wasn't about to pass up his chance.

Chapter **42**

SMEAR CAMPAIGN

FIGHTING FOR HIS CREDIBILITY, Commander Ralph Hollingworth wrote to George Wiskemann, head of SOE Scandinavia, to defend himself over the Sneum affair and the complaints of the Free Danish leader: 'Since SNEUM belongs to SIS and has never been one of our bodies I was not at liberty to tell Christmas Moeller that he was in the hands of MI5 interrogators until I had obtained permission from SIS.'

Fearing his job was on the line, Hollingworth then came out with all guns blazing. He decided that he would indeed have his SOE team get in touch with Hammer. And if he was going to tell Hammer that Christmas Moller had washed his hands of SOE, he was determined to land his own blow first. With regard to Christmas Moeller's grievance over Sneum's imprisonment, he mounted an argument designed to make a ·mockery of the politician's objections. In the message, which he sent to Hammer on 22 July 1942, Hollingworth alleged that Sneum and Christophersen had 'given a great deal of information to the Germans about our activities in Denmark'. In particular he emphasised that 'Sneum had spilt the beans'.

The timing of SOE's 'warning' to Hammer about Sneum's alleged treachery seems strange, unless the main motivation behind it was to strengthen Hollingworth's defence in the face of Christmas Moeller's onslaught. After all, SOE must have known for several months what Sneum told the Swedes during his time in Malmo Prison. The Princes of Danish Intelligence would have kept

Ronnie Turnbull fully informed of the agent's desperate tactics under interrogation. Therefore, if Hollingworth had really seen Sneum as a security risk to Hammer in Denmark, he could have warned his agent to that effect between April and June.

On the very day that the message was sent to Hammer, SOE's latest crop of agents held a farewell luncheon at the Three Vikings restaurant in Glasshouse Street, London, before preparing for a parachute drop into Denmark. This meal would spark a full-scale hunt by MI5 for a possible traitor. During the investigation, Hollingworth tried to implicate Sneum, even though the Dane was still in prison at the time of the party.

No one could foresee such repercussions on the day of the luncheon itself, which began at midday and lasted four boozy hours. Hans F. Hansen, Knud Erik Petersen and Anders Peter Nielsen wanted to relax and enjoy themselves one last time, knowing that a dangerous mission lay ahead. What they didn't know was that the Germans would be warned not only of their imminent arrival in Denmark but of plans to send a further three Danish agents back to their homeland soon afterwards.

Convinced, as ever, of Sneum's loyalty, Christmas Moeller continued to vent his fury about his fellow countryman's imprisonment in meetings with the British later that week. On 27 July, M.L. Clarke, secretary of the Danish Committee and an official in the Northern Division of the Foreign Office, made a list of Moeller's grievances, as they had been told a few days earlier to his confidant, Christopher Warner, the committee's chairman and another key figure in the Northern Division. The grievances included the controversial treatment of Sneum:

> Mr Christmas Moeller said that this man, who had flown backwards and forwards between Denmark and this country more than once (as far as I could understand it) was now in prison here. Could he not be released? I said that I thought this was also a matter for Sir Charles Hambro. I have since made enquiries and understand this may not be the case, and that the matter should be looked into.

By this last remark, Warner meant that he had originally believed that Sneum's fate lay in the SOE chief's hands, since he thought

Sneum had been an SOE agent. When he made further enquiries, however, he learned that Sneum had in fact been an SIS agent, which explained the necessity for further investigation.

But Christmas Moeller wasn't prepared to wait around while the matter was 'looked into' by the appropriate British department, and demanded the right to visit Sneum in Brixton Prison. He had known the young man for years through Tommy's uncle, Axel, who was also a politician. Fully aware of Sneum's efforts on behalf of the British since the German occupation, Christmas Moeller trusted him completely. When he was granted permission for the visit, he was accompanied by his wife Gertrud, who brought jam as a gift for her compatriot. The couple both expressed their surprise at Sneum's haggard appearance. Tommy looked so much older than the young man they had known during happier times in Denmark.

Christmas Moeller outlined his efforts to secure Tommy's release, and claimed that neither SOE nor SIS seemed willing to take any responsibility for his imprisonment.

Sneum was baffled. 'Sorry, sir, but I don't know what you mean by all these initials.'

'Don't you know who you were working for?' asked the Free Danish leader, clearly shocked.

'I just assumed it was British Intelligence,' replied Tommy.

So Christmas Moeller had to explain the difference between the Special Operations Executive, which had facilitated his own escape from Denmark a couple of months earlier, and the Secret Intelligence Service, which had dropped Tommy into Denmark. He also had to break the news that the man who had recruited Sneum no longer had any influence, and that SOE was now the only service running active agents in Denmark. As far as Christmas Moeller could see, Sneum had been the victim of a political game, but he assured the young man that he wasn't going to stop bothering the British until they let him out.

Even the tenacious Christmas Moeller probably didn't understand the size of his task. To release Tommy would require the British to defy the Princes, who were still arguing that Tommy was a traitor. And as SOE relied on the Princes for the vast majority of their information from Nazi-occupied Copenhagen they didn't want to offend them.

Decades later, the celebrated Danish resistance hero Stig Jensen wrote to Tommy to confirm that Danish Intelligence had made Sneum pay for his threat to expose Swedish spies in Germany and Poland:

> Afterwards they say such a bad joke has to be punished. They warn England and get you put out of business. Was that any way to behave? Do they not understand the mentality of a desperate prisoner? They should have forgiven you and said: 'here is a healthy man who did something stupid (which was actually intelligent); here is a man who has qualities we can build on.'
>
> [Volle] Gyth admitted that it was out of revenge (you cannot call it a precautionary measure) that they tried to have you blacklisted in England.

The smear campaign against Sneum used whatever tools it found handy. At the end of summer 1942, Mogens Hammer sent the British the disturbing news that a German-run spy was operating in London. Of course, one of the last things Tommy had done in Denmark had been to instruct Duus Hansen to link up with Hammer, the SOE radio operator, in order to strengthen the resistance network in Copenhagen. So it was thanks to Sneum that Hammer was now up and running. Yet his important communication, relayed via Sweden, could have been the final nail in Tommy's coffin.

On 1 September 1942, Commander John Senter, director of SOE's Security Section, wrote to Dick White of MI5:

> The following is an extract from a telegram received yesterday from Stockholm:
>
> 'German Intelligence received message some time ago about impending arrival of paratroops in Denmark ... German Intelligence also knew these men had held goodbye feast on 22nd July in London. There is evidently a traitor in London.'

The hunt for that traitor was on, and it wouldn't be long before Sneum's name found a prominent place on the list of suspects. The shadow of the noose loomed large again. Tommy needed a friend like never before.

Chapter **43**

—————

POWERLESS

WHEN BRITAIN'S FIRST AGENT into Denmark was frog-marched into the governor's office at Brixton Prison, he feared yet another interrogation. Instead, he was astonished to see Squadron Leader Otto Gregory of the Air Ministry and SIS sitting in the governor's chair. Mr Benke had apparently been told to make himself scarce.

'What the bloody hell are you doing here, Sneum?' The dashing squadron leader looked genuinely baffled.

'I've been here for months. Where the hell have you been?'

'My dear boy, I had no idea you were here. I've been away.'

It was true: Gregory had been on SIS business in Russia, and there had been plenty of changes in his absence. On his return he had discovered that a message had been left for him at the RAC Club. He had heard about Tommy's imprisonment and here he was, though he had to admit that he was powerless to do very much. From what he could gather, the 'security people' still weren't satisfied with some of Tommy's answers, and it would suit the political climate to keep him exactly where he was. Gregory suggested that it might even be safer for Sneum to stay inside.

Tommy recalled: 'Gregory told me: "Watch your back if you get out. There are people who want to liquidate you." He had risked his career to come and see me, but if someone threatened his friends he would do anything to stop them. He wasn't a big man

but he was a man of courage. He was probably the best friend I
ever had in England.'

⁕ ⁕ ⁕

Back in Copenhagen, it was Christian Michael Rottboell's radio
operators who needed to watch their backs as the Germans closed in
for the kill. On the night of 4 September 1942, the Abwehr sealed off
the entire area around 8 Vinkelager, where Paul Johannesen, one
such radio operator, was transmitting to Britain. As the house was
stormed, Danish police were ordered into the front line, but the
Abwehr's Alsatian dogs alerted Johannesen to his imminent capture.
He had time to pick up a pistol and open fire as the door flew open.
A Danish policeman named Ostergaard Nielsen was killed and
several others were wounded. Tragically, Nielsen was himself a
member of the Danish resistance, but he had found no way to avoid
carrying out German orders on that particular night.

Seeing himself hopelessly outnumbered, Johannesen shouted, 'You
won't get me alive.' Then he ran into another room and swallowed
his 'L' pill, supplied by SOE in London. As the cyanide went to work
on his body, Johannesen screamed, 'Forgive me,' and died in agony.
It is not known whether he was talking to God or trying to apologise
to his colleagues for the incriminating evidence he had left in the flat.
On a blank page of a notebook, the Germans found the
distinguishable imprint of an address. It threatened to lead the Nazis
to SOE's leader in Denmark, Christian Michael Rottboell.

At the time, though, it appeared that Mogens Hammer was in
most immediate danger of capture by the Germans, so he was ordered
out of the country. When he initially refused to go, his spymaster in
London, Ralph Hollingworth, expressed the hope that he would soon
see sense. Then he added ruthlessly: 'but if a man becomes a real
danger . . . he should be liquidated'. Fortunately for Hammer, he saw
the light just in time, and escaped to Sweden by kayak.

⁕ ⁕ ⁕

Whether Hollingworth's ruthlessness would prove terminal for his
least favourite agent, Thomas Sneum of the rival SIS, remained

uncertain. That seemed to depend on how effectively Hollingworth could persuade others to share his view that Tommy was a traitor. While he attempted to do so, he seems to have kept everyone else in SOE's Danish Section, even his second-in-command Reginald Spink, in the dark over Sneum's imprisonment. Spink gave his version of events years later: 'For some strange reason, which never became evident to us in SOE, Sneum was put straight into jail on his return to England. We were told about Sneum's arrest by Christmas Moeller, who had come to England on SOE's request, and to whom Sneum had demanded to talk.'

It was early September when Spink reported Christmas Moeller's revelations to Hollingworth, who appears to have feigned ignorance before telling his sidekick to contact Commander Senter if he was concerned. So it was that a bout of sanity at last broke out in the interdepartmental war between SIS and SOE. Spink simply wanted to ensure that justice had been done, even if the endangered agent had belonged to the rival SIS, so he did indeed go and see John Senter, the head of SOE's Security Section. Senter had been a barrister during peacetime, and soon agreed that a qualified lawyer should visit Sneum to assess his case. Since this might turn into a trial of sorts, he put forward a man who was well equipped for the task.

Flight Lieutenant Hugh Park had also been a peacetime barrister, and a good one at that. Much later in the century, he would become a judge, and then a knight of the realm. In the early 1980s, following the occupation of the Iranian Embassy in London, which was famously broken by an SAS raid captured live on television, Park sat in judgement upon the few terrorist survivors. Back in 1942, however, he was only thirty-two, and a new recruit to the General Section of SOE, which came under the umbrella of Senter's Security Section. Park, like Senter, used his natural talent for cross-examination to help Special Section, which dealt with counter-espionage. Their job was to detect any 'turned' SOE agents as they arrived back in Britain. Now Senter ordered Park to concern himself with the complex case of Thomas Sneum, and dispatched him to Brixton along with Spink, so that they could make a joint assessment of the spy. Park and Spink made a good double act. The former was a highly qualified interrogator; the latter an expert on Denmark. Together they would form a small but formidable jury.

It was Spink's first and last experience of prison. He felt nervous as he was driven through the huge gate and found himself inside Brixton's high and threatening walls. Instead of being taken to Sneum's cell, Reggie and Park were invited to wait in a reception room near Governor Benke's office. The prisoner was brought into these more spacious surroundings and, after brief and formal introductions, the process began. Tommy was disappointed that his visitors were neither friends nor the SIS spymasters who might have been able to order his release that very day. Nevertheless, he sensed that the meeting must be important, and initial signs were encouraging. These men didn't display the arrogance, ignorance and mental cruelty of his former interrogators. They were patient and interested in what he had to say.

Sneum was sure he had heard Christmas Moeller speak favourably of Spink, and the Free Danish leader seemed to have assessed this particular Englishman's personality correctly. Here, at last, was someone who listened. Although Sneum had told his story countless times already, he soon noticed a difference in his own delivery. With such a receptive audience, he was able to convey the pressures he had been under and the practical problems he had encountered far more calmly.

Spink knew Denmark intimately, having been an adviser to the British Legation in Copenhagen until the occupation: he spoke the language, knew the current conditions and understood the people. He wasn't even shocked to hear that Sneum had socialised with Germans, knowing only too well that nothing could be achieved without some sort of contact with the enemy. Park also displayed a keen interest in Denmark, a country he would visit at the end of the war in a successful bid to recover missing SOE money. But his enquiries were more pointed than Spink's, and he posed some tough questions on the controversial topic of Sneum's behaviour in Sweden. Tommy invited his latest jury to step into his shoes: at best he had felt neglected by the British and at worst double-crossed. In those desperate circumstances, he had chosen to protect himself from the threat of being returned to the Germans. Yes, he had played a dirty game in Malmo and had probably gone too far.

Ultimately, however, he insisted he had betrayed no one. Moreover, his achievements had been considerable, given all the infighting which had marred his mission. He had left behind the foundations of an effective resistance network, one which didn't rely upon the Princes of Danish Intelligence. He had also made the first inroads into areas of scientific intelligence which others seemed unable to grasp. As for the accusation that he was pro-German, Sneum explained that he simply saw Germans as human beings too. If this was a crime, he was guilty. Yes, he had been ruthless and headstrong in Copenhagen at times, but he had recruited good men to the Allied cause. Indeed, the men who remained operational in Copenhagen would provide the biggest testament to his loyalty at the end of the war.

Spink and Park listened carefully for three hours. They had been given reports from other men who featured in Sneum's story, disgruntled characters who told a very different, damning tale. Presumably they would also have known all about the claim that there was a traitor operating within Danish circles in London. Could that traitor be Sneum? Or could Sneum be feeding this German spy information for use against those SOE agents who had stolen his thunder on the Danish stage? They put their questions to Sneum calmly. Sneum insisted he knew nothing about such a traitor.

But where did the truth lie? Spink and Park left Brixton to consider all they had been told in more comfortable surroundings. With minimum disagreement, they compiled a joint report for the attention of their respective SOE superiors. Unusually, their findings remained entirely free of political or departmental bias. On the basis of their objective understanding of what had happened to Thomas Sneum over the previous year, they offered a series of no-nonsense recommendations. If their SOE bosses were prepared to follow their suggestions, there would soon be liaison with SIS too, in order to determine Sneum's fate.

* ※ *

Since their falling-out in June 1941 over the lack of space in the Hornet Moth, the war had taken Thomas Sneum and Christian Michael Rottboell on very different paths. However, their stories had also displayed a certain continuity. Sneum had been an agent for SIS in Denmark and had then found himself imprisoned in Sweden for his efforts. While he was adapting to life in a Malmo cell, Rottboell, the SOE agent, had landed in Denmark and taken over British interests there. Christian Michael had then organised the escape to England of Christmas Moeller, whose subsequent support for Sneum had undoubtedly helped him survive.

The hangman's noose remained a threat to Sneum for as long as he was left in Brixton, but Rottboell's situation suddenly became even more critical on the night of 25 September 1942 in Copenhagen. Unbeknown to Christian Michael, seven Danish policemen, acting on German orders, had surrounded his headquarters at 29 Oeresundgade. As they stormed the hideout, it might have crossed Rottboell's mind to surrender quietly. After all, the Princes had recently brokered an agreement with the Danish police to guarantee that any captured resistance men would be imprisoned in Denmark and not sent to the Gestapo in Germany. Several key Danish policemen had even claimed they were willing to stand up to the Germans in order to ensure that the agreement was honoured.

Unfortunately, in the panic at Oeresundgade, Rottboell didn't stop to weigh up his chances of remaining free from the clutches of German torturers. Instinctively, he grabbed a pistol as the Danish police stormed through his door. Seemingly caught in two minds as his hands were quickly thrust behind his back, Rottboell neither opened fire nor released his grip on the weapon. Somehow, the gun went off accidentally in the struggle and then fell to the floor. As with the Johannesen raid earlier that month, a Danish policeman was hit in the commotion. This time the officer, Inspector A. F. Ost, miraculously escaped injury, because the bullet bounced off his belt buckle. Christian Michael wasn't so lucky. Seeing a shell hit their colleague's midriff, other policemen opened fire with machine-pistols, some before they had time to realise that Rottboell had now been disarmed. For one accidental bullet, Rottboell's own body was riddled with twelve. He died instantly.

Duus Hansen knew that Rottboell had been working around the clock since Johannesen's death just to keep the resistance alive. He wrote later: 'The whole organisation had to be changed because we thought that old contacts might now have been known to the Germans. This work took so much out of Rottboell, who saw it as his duty to ensure the safety of others, that he didn't have time to address the question of his own protection and security.'

Thomas Sneum had been unable to keep the promise he had made to Rottboell's father at Boerglum Cloisters two years earlier, to 'look after' his boy. It was something he regretted later in life, showing more remorse over this particular piece of misfortune than any other: 'I made that promise but I wasn't there to honour it, and I'll always feel bad about that,' he said.

Chapter **44**

———

A NEW BETRAYAL

OVER IN BRIXTON, the caged agent already sensed that events were moving quickly behind the scenes. For some time, rumours had been sweeping the prison that Governer Benke was in deep trouble over some infringement of security. Then Tommy was called to the interrogation room.

Waiting in the room, situated next to Benke's office, was an intelligent-looking man of about thirty, whose thin frame scarcely filled out the army officer's uniform he was wearing. The man leaned forward as Sneum entered, as though compensating for short-sightedness. But beneath his rather intellectual exterior, Major Leslie Mitchell of SIS possessed great courage, a sharp knack for practical diplomacy and a sense of humour which had served him well since the start of the war. Already, however, Sneum's case had tested his diplomacy and humour to the limit – and the pair hadn't even been introduced yet.

Like Sneum, Mitchell had distinguished himself with a daring contribution to the secret war in Scandinavia. He had set up a ferry system between Nazi-occupied Norway and a remote cove in the Shetland Islands. Special agents, radio transmitters, ammunitions and explosives were ferried into the fjords for the waiting Norwegian resistance. The transport route was so dependable that it soon became known as the Shetland Bus.

Then, in the late summer of 1942, Mitchell was promoted and brought south to London, in order to oversee SIS dealings with Scandinavia. Charles Seymour, new head of the joint Danish/Dutch A2 Section, had his hands full with Holland. Still adjusting to his wide-ranging responsibilities, he hadn't been able to address the confusion caused by SOE's takeover in Denmark. So Mitchell was told to keep a close eye on what was left of SIS Denmark in case the organisation was one day invited to assume British intelligence-gathering there again. In the meantime, Denmark could still be used as a transit point for SIS traffic between Germany, Sweden and Poland.

Mitchell's first major headache at home was how to deal with the lingering problem of Thomas Sneum. Squadron Leader Gregory had submitted a critical report about Sneum's treatment and detention inside Brixton Prison. Mitchell did not know how Gregory had learned of Sneum's whereabouts, but he soon discovered that the squadron leader had visited Brixton personally, something he had not been granted authority to do. Mitchell called Governor Benke to demand an explanation. When he received no conclusive reply, he decided to meet the source of the controversy in person.

'You've been rather clever, haven't you?' said the major after introducing himself. 'Somehow you got a message out of this prison to one of my colleagues, Squadron Leader Gregory. Since you had no obvious contact with the outside world at the time, I'd like you to tell me how you achieved that.'

Sneum refused to do so. He enjoyed protecting Bill. It had taken two Brixton prisoners who hardly knew each other to show SIS and SOE what true trust and cooperation were all about.

'This is a great shame,' said Mitchell when he had to admit defeat for the day. 'Because I have just received an SOE report from a barrister called Park and a fellow called Reginald Spink, from their Danish Section. The report recommends that we allow you to be released from here. You are not helping me to follow those recommendations.'

Tommy looked him in the eye. 'I'm sorry you feel that way, Major Mitchell. But my position remains unchanged,' he said. It might have been Sneum's imagination, but he thought he saw something akin to respect in Mitchell's eyes.

Some time between 25 September and 3 October 1942, Leslie Mitchell returned to the jail with the appropriate papers, bundled Sneum into a car and drove him away. The major said they were bound for Bedfordshire, where a new life awaited Tommy. He wouldn't be entirely free, but it would be better than prison. Sneum was to stay on a farm with the father of a junior SIS man called Gordon Andrews.

Tommy wanted to trust Mitchell, but he also remembered Gregory's warning about it being safer inside Brixton. He remembered his childhood and going on duck shoots, when trained birds would lead the wilder ones to their deaths. He wondered whether he too was being led to his execution somewhere in the English countryside. Sneum watched and waited. If the car stopped in the middle of nowhere he would try to make a break for it. It didn't, and soon they had reached their destination.

Milton Ernest was picturesque. The River Ouse flowed to the west of the village, though anyone passing through might never have known it was there. On a gentle slope beyond the village green stood All Saints Church, first built almost a thousand years earlier, after the Norman invasion. In nearby Radwell Road, two pubs stood almost side by side; from the outside, the Queen's Head looked classier than the Swan. All over the village, grand signs pointed the way to large farms and manor houses. The biggest of these properties was Milton Ernest Hall, from which the Americans were coordinating bombing raids on the continent.

Sneum soon saw that his new home was to be another mansion. A tower, crowned with a weathercock, sprouted incongruously from the more modest contours of the main building's roof. The sign at the start of a long driveway read 'Milton Ernest House'. The establishment thought itself so grand that visitors were even expected to sign in at a lodge by the outer gate. Willow trees adorned lawns in front of the main building. Tucked away to the right were some modest farm buildings, where the bulk of the daily agricultural business was done. At the back of the house nine rolling fields made up the remainder of the three-hundred-acre property. Beyond those fields lay Twinwoods airfield, where American Mustangs took off to do battle in the skies of Europe.

For Sneum, whose love of flying surpassed all other passions, this new existence would be torture. All around him were airfields and American pilots, fighting the kind of war that he had always wanted to fight. Instead he was grounded, sentenced to what amounted to continued imprisonment. His only hope of action, it appeared, would be as a farm labourer, and even that small outlet for his frustration would become a reality only if his behaviour in his new surroundings proved exemplary. The British were clearly still at pains to ensure that, one way or another, Tommy Sneum's war was over. But he wasn't beaten yet.

Turning on the charm, he received a warm reception from his host, Leslie Andrews, and the farmer's much younger wife, Irene. 'He was in his sixties; she was only about thirty,' Sneum recalled. 'She was slim, dark-haired and attractive.'

He maintained his charm offensive and soon won concessions. 'First I was allowed into the village only if I was accompanied by a security man. Then I was allowed in without an escort. "Where's his manservant today?" I heard one woman say. They thought the security people were my staff and I was some kind of lord.'

Tommy was happy to be put to work on the farm after months of inactivity in prison. Irene seemed to take an interest in his lithe young body as he worked. She began to show the newcomer increasing affection and asked him to call her Reeny. Typically, Tommy took every opportunity to get close to her. 'She was in love with me from the beginning and we began an affair,' he confirmed. 'It was always going to happen. She called me Tommy and I began to call her "sweetheart".' They took advantage of her husband's many trips away and long hours in the fields. Before long, they were so intimate that she was helping Sneum to make secret visits to London, without his absence ever being noticed by those who should have been keeping a close eye on his movements. 'The security was very slack by then and I was even left to play golf on the farm if I felt like it. Reeny didn't join me – she was only sporting in bed.'

Gordon Andrews of SIS realised that Tommy was having an affair with his stepmother, but he chose not to tell his father. 'Gordon said he was sorry for his dad but he knew Mr Andrews was unable to have sexual relations,' claimed Tommy. 'The clock had stopped at half past six, so to speak. Gordon told me he could understand why Reeny wanted a younger fellow. I don't think he really liked his father very much.'

*   ▦   *

The police in Copenhagen were preparing for the return of Thomas Sneum, and would have been amazed to know that he had been packed off to live anonymously in the English countryside. First, they had prison mugshots of Sneum and Helvard sent over from Sweden; then they dug out records of police interviews conducted with Kaj Oxlund's neighbours. Paying special attention to any descriptions of the clothing worn by suspicious visitors to Noekkerosevej, two of whom had since been identified as Tommy and Arne, they were able to build up accurate pictures of both men. Using the latest technology, they compiled wanted posters of both Sneum and Helvard, which were promptly distributed around the city. Both the Abwehr and the Danish authorities were convinced that, sooner or later, the British would send their most experienced spy back into the field, perhaps with his sidekick.

Tommy explained:

In late 1942 the head of the Abwehr in Copenhagen, Fregatten-Kapitan Albert Howoldt, told the Danish Army's liaison officer, Colonel Vagn Bennicke: 'We have put a stop to the Danish resistance movement. The only man we haven't been able to catch is Sneum, but we'll do that one day because he will have to come back. The British don't have anyone else of his calibre.' The reason I know he said this is because Bennicke told Bertelsen, my brother-in-law.

Sneum's account was later confirmed by Stig Jensen, the resistance hero who became one of Tommy's employers after the war. He wrote Sneum a reference which included the following:

Mr Thomas C. Sneum, who during the German occupation of Denmark was able to escape to England and later was parachuted into occupied Denmark again in order to take an active part in the

Danish resistance movement, was known by everyone who cooperated with him under those circumstances to be an exceptionally composed, resourceful and steady man – even in the most difficult situations. He even gained the respect of the German occupation forces for those qualities, and the Germans expressed their recognition of Captain Sneum as an efficient and dignified adversary to the principal Danish liaison officer.

Chapter **45**

ALL'S FAIR IN LOVE AND WAR

I T IS FAIR TO SAY that the Danish seamen sent back to Copenhagen as SOE agents were not of the calibre of Thomas C. Sneum. Even Ronnie Turnbull later said: 'My boss, Commander Hollingworth, seemed more interested in quantity than quality.' Some of the new agents were no more mindful of security than Sigfred Christophersen had been, others even less so. The worst culprit in Denmark itself was Hans Henrik Larsen, who parachuted back into his native country in February 1942. Soon after his arrival, he began to drink heavily and started to boast to strangers about his activities. By spring, he had been identified in resistance circles as a dangerous liability. The final straw came when Larsen, codenamed 'Trick', was ordered to escort a Swedish girl who was wanted by the Danish police to safety. He simply refused to comply. London approved his liquidation.

In a communication from Stockholm, Ronnie Turnbull reported what he described as the 'rather gruesome story', which he later likened to the murder of Rasputin. It involved 'L' tablets – the poisonous capsules that agents in the field were expected to swallow in order to avoid capture and interrogation. Larsen, explained Turnbull, was invited to a party and

came in as usual in an inebriated condition and was very easily persuaded to accept a vermouth and water in which one L tablet had been dissolved. 'Trick' gulped it down and was given two more tablets in similar drinks. After the third glass, he merely complained of sleepiness, and went home. The next day he was still very much alive, although he admitted to a slight headache. His would-be assassins were totally bemused, and decided they would have to find a less subtle way to kill him. Eventually, Larsen was driven to remote countryside, ostensibly to identify a future dropping point for parachutists and supplies. There, in the wilderness, he was shot dead.

Hollingworth was furious that the original execution had been bungled. These were ruthless times, and any threat to security had to be eradicated efficiently and quickly. SOE even launched an inquiry into why 'Trick' hadn't been dispatched more promptly. The investigators were stunned to discover that their agents had failed to distinguish between the lethal 'L' and mere knockout pills. But Hollingworth was even angrier that agents had sought to use their 'L' tablets to do the job in the first place. They had been prepared to sacrifice their own means of suicide, leaving themselves vulnerable to interrogation if caught.

On 22 March 1943, MI5 gave Major Geoffrey Wethered the task of investigating penetrations into both SOE and SIS. He therefore took over responsibility for finding the traitor among the Danish in England from his predecessor, a Major Blunt. On 9 April, Wethered gave an account of events that would put a new question mark against Sneum's loyalty, particularly in relation to Mogens Hammer and the wave of SOE agents sent into Denmark the previous year, known as 'Table Top':

Major Blunt took me round this morning to meet Spink and Hollingworth (SOE). We discussed the TABLE TOP leakage, and the following points of interest emerged:

. . . Hollingworth referred to an SIS agent named SNEUM, who had escaped to this country in late [*sic*] 1941 and had been sent back to Denmark by SIS without much training, taking with him a wireless operator. It appears that both these men were blown in Denmark and escaped to Sweden. During their adventures, however, they appear to have given a great deal of information to the Germans about our activities in Denmark, to such an extent that SOE sent a message to ARTHUR [Hammer] on July 22, 1942, informing him that SNEUM had spilt the beans. None of this was told to us until today.

Wethered also describes Hollingworth's suspicions with regard to the Princes, also known as the HAMILCAR organisation:

They are opposed to acts of sabotage arranged in their country, in case these might spoil their plans of seizing power from the Germans ultimately, and SOE have noticed that information which should reach them through HAMILCAR about sabotage seems sometimes to have been suppressed . . .

An additional point about the HAMILCAR organisation it that although it does a good deal of ship watching on the Danish coast for its own purposes, information about this is not passed to SOE, but is suppressed – presumably for the same reason as sabotage information is suppressed.

By now, almost two years had passed since the Princes had 'missed' the breakout by the *Bismarck*, but clearly they were still up to their old tricks, judging by these remarks. It seems that by the spring of 1943, both MI5 and SOE felt that no Dane could be fully trusted. One man was more guilty than the rest, however – the mystery spy who had fed German Intelligence and then disappeared.

Wethered could not rest until he had that traitor in his sights. At some point over the next month, he or a member of his investigation team visited Sneum in Milton Ernest to interrogate him. They suspected he was the traitor and said so. Sneum pointed to the facts. He had been in prison in Brixton throughout the summer of 1942, and effectively under local arrest in Milton Ernest ever since. How could he have known anything? And even if he had been given any information about Danish operations, how could he have passed that intelligence on to the Germans?

Given the earlier warning he had received from Otto Gregory – that there were people in London who wanted him liquidated – the latest accusations spelled grave danger for Tommy. He was living in an isolated place, so he decided it would make sense from that point on to make sure civilians were never far away from him. He claimed: 'Even in Bedfordshire it began to feel like I was always under threat of death. I had those bastards coming out to the farm but they couldn't kill me openly.'

Where Wethered's team of investigators were concerned, however, Tommy needn't have worried. On 26 April 1943, Wethered submitted a short report on the likelihood or otherwise of Sneum being the traitor. It was entitled: 'B1b. note re. case of SNEUM and TABLE TOP organisation 74X'. MI5 withheld it from a file labelled KV6/40, which was otherwise made available at the National Archive in Kew, west London, some sixty years later. On 11 July 2006, however, the Security Service revealed this much: 'the gist of 74X in KV6/40 is that SNEUM was not in any position to leak to the Germans information regarding TABLE TOP'.

Although this confirmed that Thomas Sneum was still suspected of treachery as late as spring 1943, it also revealed that Wethered was convinced that Sneum simply couldn't have been the traitor, due to the physical constraints he was under at the time of the leaks. Effectively, that meant Sneum was off the hook. But Tommy's former spymasters wouldn't have been pleased when unforeseen circumstances allowed him to return into wider social circulation.

In May 1943 Sneum left the village of Milton Ernest under a cloud after his relationship with Reeny was discovered by her husband. 'He came back early one day and found us in my bedroom,' recalled Sneum. 'I was still pulling my trousers up so it was obvious what had been happening. It wasn't a funny situation at the time, because there were guns all over the farmhouse, and he looked angry and upset enough to use one.'

Leslie Andrews controlled himself long enough to call his son Gordon, then ordered Sneum's instant removal from his property. Suddenly SIS and London's Free Danish leader had a crisis on their hands.

Chapter **46**

WHEN LIFE IS TOO SHORT

SINCE JOHN CHRISTMAS MOELLER had exerted so much pressure to have Sneum released from Brixton Prison, he now bore much of the responsibility for his fellow countryman's future. Therefore, Sneum was quickly moved to London and housed in Christmas Moeller's basement flat. He was even given a job in the politician's office, which mainly consisted of translating documents. His opinion was sometimes sought on the quality of various snippets of intelligence which found their way through from Denmark. But Sneum still felt like a spectator, cheated of his place at the centre of the action.

By night, however, he was anything but a passive observer as he made up for lost time by trying to bed as many women as possible. 'In those days, it felt like I only had to take a woman by the hand and she would go straight to bed with me,' he admitted with a chuckle. 'I even had two women at the same time, but I didn't like it when they started giving each other attention when they should have been giving it all to me.' He brought many of his conquests back to his new home, and it seemed as though his appetite was insatiable. 'I found I could stay up for three nights and four days without sleeping,' he claimed.

His hosts soon found it hard to turn a blind eye to his playboy lifestyle, and Christmas Moeller's wife, Gertrud, finally lost patience and insisted that Sneum be confronted about his behaviour. The politician called his guest into the main house and came straight to the point: 'You run around with too many girls, Sneum. Sooner or later it's going to get you into serious trouble.'

'I'm in trouble already,' joked Tommy. 'Some of them can be terribly jealous and suspicious.'

Gertrud insisted that it was no laughing matter. 'We felt sorry for you when you were in prison,' she explained. 'We can understand that you want to enjoy yourself after being locked up all that time. But you have a wife in Denmark and you're leading a life of debauchery here, Tommy. There's no other way of putting it. You should love your wife.'

'What's the point of loving a woman in Denmark when I'm in England?' asked Tommy with unanswerable logic.

But Christmas Moeller backed his wife: 'It's not acceptable, Sneum. Remember, this is our household and we make the rules, even for the cellar flat. No more women – agreed?'

Sneum was too stubborn to have the terms of his private life dictated to him. 'How can I agree to something like that?' he asked in desperation.

Gertrud was prepared for just such a response. 'Then my husband and I have no alternative but to tell you that you are no longer welcome to stay here.'

John Christmas Moeller clearly regretted that it had come to this. 'From now on you'll have to live with my secretary, Peter Knauer. And I should warn you that Peter's wife had a strict upbringing in Australia, and she won't put up with any of your nonsense. Besides, you won't have your own flat any more, just a room. Since you have abused your newfound freedom, you will now have less of it.'

Sneum recalled: 'I carried on having affairs but Christmas was right – Mrs Knauer didn't like it.' For a week or two, he would fall deeply in love with a woman, before he reminded himself that he was essentially in love with all women. He remembered: 'I fell in love with a doctor from Kensington Hospital. Her mother was English, her father from Senegal. Her name was Audrey and she was lovely. In fact she was the most beautiful girl you could ever imagine. She wasn't very sexual at the start but I soon made her feel sexy.'

At the time, Sneum was socialising with another member of the Danish resistance who had managed to escape, Ole Killerich. Although he was older than Tommy, they had much in common. 'He had gone to live with Emmy Valentin after I had left for England, and he had shagged her before coming to London,' revealed Sneum. Now their romantic paths almost crossed again. 'Killerich was in love with Audrey's friend, another doctor from Kensington Hospital. The two women were colleagues and close to each other, so we all got on very well together.'

Despite his romantic distractions, Sneum noticed that he was still followed occasionally. It was as if someone had decided that a grave mistake had been made in granting him freedom. And he knew that it wasn't just elements within SIS who harboured lingering doubts about him. Fortunately for Tommy, though, he still had many female admirers in the close-knit Danish community. One was a former secretary to Commander Frank Stagg, the SOE officer who felt that Sneum's imprisonment was 'disgraceful'. Although Stagg had since left SOE, disillusioned that his efforts to persuade the British to work more closely with the Danes had fallen on deaf ears, his secretary had remained in the Danish Section.

'I had a relationship with this girl from SOE for a while,' Sneum said. 'And she warned me that they were still suspicious of me and following me.'

These hostile undercurrents didn't lead Sneum to modify his playboy lifestyle, however. During the war, the general feeling was that time was short, and life should be enjoyed while it still could be. It was a philosophy also embraced by Sneum's former spy partner, although his idea of personal fulfilment was rather more traditional.

Sigfred Christophersen was no longer working for SIS, but he had become involved with someone extremely well connected to that murky world. Perhaps it was more than coincidence that he had chosen to court a private secretary in the Foreign Office. If he had wanted to cultivate further ill-feeling towards Sneum in the corridors of power, he could hardly have chosen a better channel for his bitterness. Mary Anita Blackford Wood was five years younger than Christophersen, who had now turned twenty-eight. As romance blossomed, the couple soon realised they had much in common, since their families shared a background in market gardening. Sigfred's father was a nurseryman, and had introduced his son to the trade before the war. Anita's father was a horticultural contractor, and she too retained a keen interest in plants and flowers.

Thanks to her administrative role in the Foreign Office, Anita already knew something of Sigfred's story. But it appears that he soon gave her full details of how Sneum had repeatedly threatened to kill him during their mission. She must also have learned of Christophersen's escape to Sweden, and how his brother Thorbjoern and Kaj Oxlund had died so horribly on the ice. It seems that Sigfred soon convinced Anita that there was only one villain of the piece – Tommy Sneum. He also warned her that if, for any reason, he should die unexpectedly or mysteriously, Sneum would probably be behind it.

Anita foresaw a happier future, especially when Sigfred proposed. Although he had known her only a matter of months, this was wartime and strong bonds were often forged quickly. Anita accepted and their wedding day was fixed for 2 June 1943. The ceremony was held at the Register Office in Anita's home town of St Albans.

By then, Sigfred was Pilot Officer 151948 of the RAF and stationed far to the north, in Harrogate, Yorkshire. However, he was given a special weekend pass to tie the knot, and the couple spent their wedding night in a St Albans hotel. Unfortunately, with the war never far away, there was no time for a proper honeymoon. That following Monday, Anita Christophersen returned to her duties at the Foreign Office. Her husband was already back in the cockpit in Yorkshire, preparing for the day when his skills might be needed against the fighters of Hitler's Luftwaffe.

※ ※ ※

Thomas Sneum would have given anything to be able to fly again and test himself in real action. His work translating and summarising intelligence reports in John Christmas Moeller's office was occasionally interesting, but Tommy hated working indoors. He knew that a daring spy wasn't meant to sit behind a desk.

Leslie Mitchell, the man who had finally authorised his release from Brixton, seemed to understand. He began to come to the office and asked Sneum for his opinion on various matters connected with Denmark. This, though, didn't do much to lift Tommy's spirits. He could never forget how some of his former resistance colleagues had found their way into the RAF. Many, such as Kjeld Pedersen and Arne Helvard, saw action every week, while he was left behind to push a pen in London. During his isolation in Milton Ernest, Tommy had tried to hide his jealousy from Arne, who visited him after returning from North Africa. Helvard was now stationed in nearby Cambridgeshire, where he was being trained to fly bombers. Tommy recalled: 'Helvard came to see me and we talked about flying. He thought it was a bit stupid that he had more flying hours than the instructors on his course. I was just envious of his situation because I couldn't fly.'

At midnight on 21 June 1943, precisely two years after Thomas Sneum had taken off with Kjeld Pedersen in the Hornet Moth, the midsummer skies came alive over south-east England. Bomber Command sent 705 planes into the air for a massive assault on the German city of Krefeld. The target lay just to the south-west of the industrial sprawl that merges Duisberg and Essen with Dortmund. It was to be a night Krefeld would never forget.

At 00.14 hours on 22 June, Flying Officer Arne Helvard climbed into a Stirling III, registration BK712 HA-D, at Downham Market airfield. The man who had accompanied Tommy Sneum across the icy channel separating Denmark from Sweden was ready to risk his life again over enemy territory, this time to be part of the massive raid. Helvard, who had been attached to 218 Squadron, was joined in the Stirling by seven new colleagues. Pilot Officer W.G. Shillinglaw of the Royal Australian Air Force was his only superior in the cockpit. Five of the crew were British sergeants: R.P. Goward (flight engineer), P.D. McArdle (navigator), T.R. Lunn (bomb aimer), A.E. Gurney and E.D. Hart (air gunners). The last crew member was a New Zealander, Flight Sergeant D.J. Ashby-Peckham (wireless operator).

Pilot Officer Shillinglaw and Flying Officer Helvard were taking their Stirling over Belgium en route to Germany just before 1.30 a.m. when they were spotted by Lieutenant Heinz-Wolfgang

Schaufer in a Messerschmitt fighter. When he saw Schaufer closing in for the kill, Helvard must have known that his chances of survival were slim. The Stirling had none of the manoeuvrability of the German plane; and the clear, moonlit skies of a midsummer's night that virtually guaranteed an accurate bombing mission also left many brave crews at the mercy of the enemy.

It is not known if Shillinglaw and Helvard had time to attempt any form of evasive action before Schaufer unleashed his machine-guns on their cockpit and fuselage. Even if he survived the spray of bullets and resulting flames, Arne could do little to prevent the Stirling from hurtling towards the Belgian fields below. Although he had a parachute, he was unable to escape from the crumbling cockpit. As one of the pilots, he would probably have felt a responsibility to wrestle with the controls until all hope was lost. By then, it would have been too late to eject.

The final impact of the crash was timed at 1.33 a.m. The villagers of Langdorp, Brabant, around sixty kilometres north-east of Brussels, knew long before they reached the smouldering wreckage that no one could be saved, and after the war the Air Ministry concluded that the eight crew members had died instantly. Their broken bodies were buried that same day in Langdorp churchyard. By then, the occupying German forces had arrived to supervise, and to their credit they gave the Allied crew a respectful send-off, with full military honours. Three or four German officers were present, along with six ordinary soldiers. Three rounds were fired over the grave, which was draped in a Union flag. Although no civilians were allowed to participate, a floral tribute was also placed at the graveside.

Helvard had prepared for death or capture. At the time of the ceremony, only three of the crew were identified – Hart, Lunn and an airman known as 1438341 Sergeant Turton. Arne had assumed the name Turton in order to protect his family and fiancée from any reprisals back home. He had been selfless to the last. It was typical of a man who had successfully spied against the Germans at Kastrup Airport, survived the treacherous ice floes between Denmark and Sweden, and stayed loyal to Tommy Sneum when the British thought their agent had been 'turned'.

His colleagues in the hundreds of remaining bombers made sure that Germany paid dearly for the Luftwaffe's marksmanship. The devastation caused to Krefeld that night was unmatched up to that point in the war. Forty-seven per cent of the city centre was obliterated as a bomb-induced fire raged out of control. A total of 5,517 houses were destroyed and 72,000 people lost their homes, as the Allies sought to break both the back of German manufacturing and the collective will of the country's people. For 1,056 citizens of Krefeld, their lives ended as city buildings collapsed and burned in the firestorm. A further 4,550 German citizens were injured in the carnage.

If the price for Hitler's madness was disturbingly high on the ground, the price in the sky was also considerable. During the night, forty-four Allied aircraft were lost, including nine Stirlings. These were some of the highest Bomber Command casualty figures of the entire war. In the bright moonlight, once spotted and singled out for attack, poor Helvard and many others never stood a chance.

Chapter **47**

THE ACCIDENT

IN LONDON, CHRISTMAS MOELLER asked Sneum into his private office and began to shuffle uncomfortably in his seat. It was obvious something was seriously wrong. Tommy waited for the older man to speak. The politician came straight to the point: 'I don't know whether you've heard, but your friend Helvard has been shot down. I'm sorry.'

Tommy recalled feeling numb. 'I didn't know how to feel, apart from sad, because we didn't know if he had survived or not. Many people were shot down, survived somehow, and turned up at the end of the war.'

In Arne's case, though, hope slowly faded. At least he had rediscovered the supreme freedom of flight that he and Tommy had first tasted as teenagers before he met his end. Not that his fiancée Vita, waiting back in Copenhagen, would have seen it that way when she heard that all her dreams had been shattered.

Sneum felt helpless, living out his life in a tiny, claustrophobic office, desperate to make any kind of impression on the war that was passing him by. But the monotony was broken temporarily in early July 1943, when SIS suddenly awarded him £2750. They didn't call it compensation; instead, the sum was described as 'agent's back-pay'. It appeared to be a sweetener, a belated attempt to buy back Sneum's loyalty after a year's freedom had been denied him. Perhaps they felt he would be less dangerous if they managed to make him feel that he was still on their side.

The sum was a fortune for any young man to have in his pocket. Was it some sort of trap, Sneum wondered, to induce him to behave so erratically that he had to be silenced for ever? He didn't really care if it was. Temporarily rich in an exciting city, he was determined to spend his new-found riches in style.

On the first Friday night after he received the money, Sneum took an old girlfriend called Rosy, the manageress from the Wellington Club, to another watering hole which had become a favourite Danish haunt in the West End of London. Rosy was one of Tommy's favourites, and there were good reasons why. He recalled: 'She was dark-haired, not the most beautiful, but she had nice tits. She was an inch or two taller than me, but then most of them were. What made Rosy special was that she could fuck all day long, and she was the sexiest girl I had in England.'

Tommy was looking forward to a good drink and another night of passion when something suddenly distracted him in that West End pub. For there, to his amazement, he spotted Kjeld Pedersen, propping up the bar alone.

'You learned to fly properly yet?' yelled Sneum across the crowded room.

'My God, they've let you out!' shouted back Pedersen. 'They must be mad!'

The Danish pilots met in a bear-hug, their first since falling exhausted into each other's arms in a field near Newcastle back in the summer of 1941. So much had happened since they landed the Hornet Moth and chose separate paths in service of the British. Kjeld explained that he had only recently heard about Sneum's difficulties, because he had just come back from North Africa for a spot of leave. He had been there since 6 December 1942, with 33 and 94 Squadrons, flying Hawker Hurricanes. He was due to face another six months running the gauntlet above the German guns in the desert, and had already built up quite a thirst.

'Well, you're lucky, because we have money to spend,' said Sneum with a smile.

'I've got some, don't worry,' Kjeld assured him.

Tommy was still grinning. 'I think I may have a little more.'

'What is this, a competition?' Pedersen was reaching for his wallet.

'Not unless you have about three grand in there,' said Sneum, grabbing his friend's arm. 'Now, we're going to split it between you, me and Rosy here, and see who can spend the most in a weekend.'

Pedersen's mouth dropped open. 'How much?'

The trio took the best shops, restaurants and clubs by storm. For forty-eight hours the champagne flowed, the party raged and cash changed hands in extraordinary amounts. 'We ate goose-liver paté and drank the best champagne, Dom Perignon,' Tommy explained. Even then, they found it impossible to get rid of more than a thousand pounds between them.

At the end of their orgy of spending, the trio exchanged wonderful presents. Watches, jewellery and the finest clothes were opened by each laughing participant in turn, to the astonishment of fellow customers in the most elegant restaurants and hotel lobbies. Everything was paid for in cash with perfect nonchalance, to the bemusement of stunned staff in each top establishment. Perhaps it was inevitable that they attracted unwanted attention. They began to notice that they were being followed by young men who looked to Sneum like SIS agents. He didn't care. MI6 had financed the party, so he thought it fitting that their representatives should be allowed a taste of the anarchy. In full view of the agents of his former employers, Sneum continued to spend like there was no tomorrow. They drank to Helvard. They drank to flying. They drank to living for the moment.

Mrs Knauer, Tommy's landlady, didn't understand living for the moment, and she was running out of patience. He explained: 'Reeny, from the farm, came to London and stayed with me sometimes at the house. Mrs Knauer didn't like that. But then I was also going out with Rosy and Audrey simultaneously, so the Knauers and Christmas Moellers were angry with me for that, too. I had all this money, I had to spend it, and a lot of it went on whoring and fucking. I've always loved women.'

However, he would have swapped it all for the chance to get back into the Danish resistance. Nevertheless, the man he had recruited, Duus Hansen, was doing a fine job in Tommy's absence. And he was about to make London, Tommy's playground, a safer place for the duration of the war.

※ ▦ ※

On 16 July Duus Hansen received a radio message from an SIS department known to him as 'Hannibal'. It read: 'Can you report on activity at Peenemunde near Greifswald where enemy are producing and experimenting with long-range rockets. Believe new radio apparatus on Bornholm connected with these experiments. We would like description of rocket and emplacement and scale of rocket and projector production at Peenemunde.'

Even to Duus Hansen, whose network now included the Princes of Danish Intelligence, this must have sounded like an impossible mission. But it was clear that the British were extremely anxious about Hitler's new rocket technology, because he received a similar request from Ralph Hollingworth of SOE. Once again, rival British departments were vying for centre stage in Denmark.

Duus Hansen made discreet contact with resistance sympathisers in the relevant locations, to see what they might unearth. The Danish naval officer in charge on the island of Bornholm, Lieutenant Commander Hasager Christiansen, was one such man. Fate was about to hand him a vital role in helping the British to understand Hitler's V-rockets.

Back in London, Tommy Sneum knew something big was happening, and all of a sudden he was glad that he had taken the opportunity to enjoy himself while he still could:

> Mitchell took me to one side and said: 'Would you be prepared to go back to Denmark if necessary, in spite of everything we've done to you? I may have a mission for you.' I said that I would be prepared to go, but I didn't ask what the mission was because I knew I would be told when it was deemed to be the right time. I knew the game.
>
> Bornholm had been mentioned at around that time. They were asking so many questions about sea conditions between Denmark and Bornholm, near Peenemunde on the German coast. I'm sure I

knew about Peenemunde too. I don't think I knew anything about rockets at that time, but I did know from my time in the Danish Navy that the Germans had a special base there. I thought the British were eventually going to send me to Germany itself to find out about Peenemunde. They seemed to want someone who knew the local sea and could speak German. Part of me wanted to bite their hands off to get myself back into action. Another part of me thought: I hope they're not going to send me in there, because it will be a bloody dangerous job.

Even for Christiansen, who was on Bornholm in an official capacity, the environment would almost cost him his life. But to go into this highly sensitive area with no connections on the inside would surely prove fatal. So Tommy waited to see if he would be handed a suicide mission.

* * *

Just before midnight on 9 August 1943, Pilot Officer Sigfred Johannes Christophersen underwent another pre-flight briefing at the large air base of 12 Pilot Advanced Flying Unit in Grantham, Lincolnshire.

With 137 hours of flying time already under his belt since joining the RAF more than a year earlier, a weary Christophersen was about to take to the skies again in a Mark I Blenheim, serial number K7050. This time he would face the added challenge of night-flying. Sigfred knew his long hours in the versatile Blenheim had prepared him for a future in the cockpit of either a night-fighter or a bomber. His advanced course was nearly at an end, and soon it would be time for real action.

Christophersen probably harboured mixed feelings about the prospect of aerial combat. Even before teaming up with Sneum in 1941, he had seemed to dread the idea of running the gauntlet of German flak and night-fighters with an Allied squadron over occupied Europe. Indeed, he had told Sneum before their mission that he considered it safer to return to Denmark as an agent than to fly for the RAF, the path chosen by most pro-Allied Danish pilots. Now, though, the spying option no longer existed.

Though Sigfred had hardly covered himself in glory while on active service for SIS, and had even been accused of cowardice by Sneum, he had still shown more bravery during the war than many men. With the help of his late brother Thorbjoern, he had also led Sneum to the genius of Duus Hansen. Now he was on the point of proving to the British and to himself that he still had the stomach to fight the Nazis. He was in the final stages of training for a new chapter in his war, and he had conquered the worst of his fears.

By 1.30 a.m. on 10 August, a confused Christophersen was flying over the fields of Lincolnshire, trying to follow a flare-path which would guide him back to the airfield. Due to elaborate defence measures, this wasn't as easy as it might have been. Decoy airfields (called 'Q sites') had been built all over Lincolnshire to fool the enemy into dropping bombs on worthless targets. Although they looked inviting, the runways were lethally short, if they existed at all. And they certainly weren't built to accommodate a Blenheim, especially if the pilot wrongly thought he had plenty of time to taxi to a halt.

It is not known whether Christophersen suffered added complications, such as engine trouble. Since little was left of plane or pilot by 1.36 a.m., a thorough examination was ruled out. His Blenheim had crashed into fields near Bottersford, by the Great North Road, a kilometre to the east of Allington. On impact, the plane had exploded into flames. Although an ambulance was called at 1.47 a.m., Flying Officer Small and Flight Sergeant Cox must have known when they saw the fire that their dash to the crash site was futile. Their examination of Sigfred's charred body concluded that death had been instantaneous due to multiple injuries and burns. His remains were taken to the station mortuary at Grantham.

The following day, Squadron Leader Frigurson-Sibson commenced his investigation into the accident. He believed that Christophersen's fatal error had been to lose sight of the flare-path. Sigfred had attempted his landing close enough to the genuine airfield to suggest that he had mistaken one of the Q sites for the real thing. What had been designed to fool the Germans had apparently been responsible for the death of one of the RAF's own advanced trainees.

Perhaps, back in 1941, Sigfred Christophersen had foreseen his own fate. In death, he had proved that his dread of joining the RAF had been well founded.

There is no evidence to suggest that the accident was suspicious. When Anita Christophersen was informed of the tragedy, however, it wasn't long before Sigfred's heartbroken widow suggested that Tommy Sneum might be behind it. She had no evidence to back up her claims, though. So, despite her protestations, Christophersen's death was accepted as a terrible but all-too-common accident in the rush to prepare pilots for aerial combat. Sigfred was buried at Grantham cemetery, Lincolnshire.

Predictably, Sneum was less than devastated when John Christmas Moeller told him that his old spy partner was dead. And he wasn't about to pretend he was unhappy. He was more sorry for some of the other Danes who wouldn't see the end of the war. Of the five men who had taken part in epic walks across the Oeresund from Denmark to Sweden in 1942, Sneum was now the only one left alive.

Chapter **48**

REWARDS AND MEMORIES

ON 22 AUGUST a rocket bearing the serial number 'V83' crashed into a turnip field on the Danish island of Bornholm, having been fired from Peenemunde on the German coast. Lieutenant Commander Hasager Christiansen was quickly alerted and managed to take several photographs before the Germans arrived on the scene. He had one reel developed at a photographic shop on Bornholm itself, and sent prints to a new member of the Princes group, Lieutenant Commander Poul Moerch of Danish Naval Intelligence. Another, undeveloped reel of film was smuggled out of Bornholm at the same time.

Soon Duus Hansen was sending a message to Ronnie Turnbull in Stockholm, asking the Scot to let 'Hannibal' (in other words, SIS) know about the precious images, and to get back to him as soon as possible with details of where he should deliver them. Turnbull seized his chance to take control and ensure that SOE, rather than SIS, gained the credit for an extraordinary intelligence coup. 'It wasn't a question of "stealing SIS's thunder", as one historian claimed,' insisted Ronnie. Even so, he replied to Duus Hansen like this:

You enclose a message to Hannibal in which you mention different telegrams about collaboration and coordination of plans. As a matter of fact these messages did not come from

Hannibal, which is our intelligence organisation [SIS], but from the operational people [SOE]. I wonder how it was you thought they came from Hannibal, since new intelligence questionnaires from Hannibal have always been prefixed Hannibal and other communications about our operations from my headquarters are still referred to as London. My headquarters are prepared to guarantee absolute full secrecy of your special messages to my headquarters undeveloped. I entirely agree that such matters are so all-embracing and secret that it is necessary to take strictest precautions to the end.

Duus Hansen duly sent the films to Turnbull, who was able to say later:

In the end it was me, it was my office, that was able to send over the V1 intelligence, of course obtained by the people with whom I had insisted we must have good relations, which was Danish Intelligence. I sent the films on to Britain undeveloped. That was of supreme importance to the war effort and in London it was quickly distributed to the correct people.

Just how grateful those people – including R.V. Jones of British Scientific Intelligence – were could be gathered from the congratulatory message Duus Hansen received from SOE on 27 August: 'Please tell Bannock [Hasager Christiansen and his colleagues on Bornholm] that Hannibal is delighted with the vast amount of intelligence material that they have been able to send. It is greatly appreciated by all departments concerned.'

In his book *Most Secret War*, R.V. Jones correctly hailed Hasager Christiansen as the true hero of the hour, particularly since he was arrested by the Germans and tortured for months before being rescued and awarded the Distinguished Service Cross. Indeed, it will be recalled that Christiansen's name followed immediately after Tommy Sneum's in the dedication Jones penned to the great spies of the Second World War. Jones revealed that he received 'three independent sets of copies' of Christiansen's photos, 'and it seemed that someone was determined that the information should reach us'.

One of those determined men was Duus Hansen, and his importance as intermediary and coordinator in securing and delivering the V-rocket intelligence which saved many lives in London cannot be overestimated. At the same time, it should be remembered who recruited Duus Hansen for the British in the first place – Tommy Sneum.

What happened next is more widely known, and well put by the historian E. H. Cookridge in his book *Inside SOE*:

> On this occasion rivalry in London was forgotten and the vital information from Denmark was shared by all the secret departments and submitted to Churchill and the Allied Chiefs of Staff. German V-1 rocket operations began in June 1944, but Hitler's plan to 'plaster London with 5,000 V-rockets every day' was never fulfilled. RAF and American aircraft carried out the famous raids on Peenemunde; on August 18 the heaviest Anglo-American raid ever concentrated on a single target almost completely destroyed the research station. Many thousand V-1 and V-2 rockets had been manufactured and were launched, but the elimination of Peenemunde, together with the heavy bombing of Bornholm and the French and Dutch rocket ramps, broke the back of Hitler's vengeful offensive.

In a sense, though, the most crucial element in the defence of Britain against the V-rockets had been accomplished a year before that raid, at the end of August 1943. Perhaps by coincidence, perhaps not, Tommy was stood down in early September: 'One day Mitchell came to me and told me that I wasn't going back to Denmark after all. He said there was no need since the Germans had taken a more heavy-handed control of everything in the country on 29 August, because suddenly there was open hostility. Every Dane was prepared to be a spy and the political climate had changed completely.'

Had the German crackdown been the real reason, or had Sneum been on stand-by in case Duus Hansen, Danish Intelligence and Hasager Christiansen had failed to deliver the required intelligence? If the latter is true, it is possible that Tommy's recruitment of Duus Hansen had ultimately saved his own life. The success of the

Danish spy ring in satisfying British requests for V-rocket secrets simply made it unnecessary to send in a second agent.

All Tommy knew was that he was going nowhere. It was the final straw:

Knauer and Christmas Moeller told me that I had been doing nothing but boozing and shagging, but at least I could say that I had been doing a useful job in the office. But what I really wanted to do was get out fighting, and I couldn't do that while I remained with Christmas Moeller. So I left London in late 1943. Christmas Moeller had found me a place at Plymouth, where the British were forming a Danish Section of their Royal Navy. I was given the honour of being the very first to join. My serial number was D-DANE-X-1.

I thought that if I got into the navy then one day I would be flying again, even though the British told me that it wouldn't happen. They were worried that if I got shot down and survived someone might recognise me and then I would be tortured by the Germans and end up telling them everything I knew, which was plenty. So I became a commando instructor in Plymouth, but that turned out to be a load of rubbish. They weren't even using live ammunition on key training exercises, and I got very angry about that. How could they ever learn properly if they weren't exposed to realistic conditions?

I enjoyed my leave more, because I got to drive a lorry and there were pretty girls all over the place, out on the road just like I was. You'd drive all day alongside them, listen to something nice on the radio, check into the same hotel and eat together. After that I'd say: 'What about going up?' and they'd say, 'Well, OK.' Look, I was good in bed and I knew women liked me. That was just a fact. But it didn't make me entirely happy because what I really wanted to do was fly.

One day Tommy took a break from his amorous routine and returned to London to help a Danish naval colleague who felt he was owed some money by the British. On the way out of the Danish Legation, he came face to face with one of the men he blamed most for having him imprisoned and grounded – Captain

Volle Gyth. Sneum refused to shake the hand of the Prince, who himself had escaped to Sweden after the German crackdown. When asked to explain his rudeness, Tommy stated bluntly: 'You people are traitors and you had me locked up. I think you had better come to lunch right now and tell me why.' Trying to maintain his composure, Gyth politely declined that ominous invitation, and one for dinner. Then Tommy asked a question which must have sounded menacing in its simplicity: 'Are you home later?'

'You don't know where I'm staying,' laughed an increasingly nervous Gyth, who had been given an SOE safe-house while he tried to persuade the sceptical British to support Danish Intelligence in exile. 'And I can't give you my address because it's confidential, since my mission here is of a somewhat secretive nature.'

'I'll see you this evening at seven,' Sneum promised confidently. Tommy explained later:

I knew a place SOE had rented for the use of visitors from Denmark. It was in Romney Court, Shepherd's Bush, and I decided that SOE were such stingy bastards that they probably hadn't bothered to spend money on a new safe-house. So I went to the address with a few bottles of beer and explained to the doorman that I was a friend of Captain Gyth, who had asked if I could be let in to make myself comfortable until he got back.

When Gyth came home that evening he got a nasty shock. I had a pistol, and I told him: 'It's all over for you tonight, Gyth.' I was happy to see the fear on his face after everything I had been through because of the intrigues created by Danish Intelligence. He had a good idea that I was going to shoot him unless he told me exactly what had happened to get me locked up in Sweden.

He admitted that Danish Intelligence had told the Swedes to make sure I wasn't in a position to spy in Denmark again for the remainder of the war. That meant stopping me from getting to England too, in case they sent me back. So the Swedes locked me up on the instructions of the Princes; and therefore it was Danish Intelligence who effectively forced me to make that threat to blow the Swedish agents. Which caused me to be locked up again in England.

Gyth told me that everyone thought I was a loose cannon who

took too many risks. By then both the Danes and the English thought I was a bit of a crazy bastard, when in fact I was just more courageous than they were. The only way they could get a knife in my back was to spread stupid stories about me. For example, Gyth admitted that the Princes had expressed their doubts to the English that I could have flown out of Denmark in the Hornet Moth without the help of the Germans.

Perhaps the biggest problem I had was that I was very young in those days, and that made it difficult to get the respect from these people that I deserved. And a lot of it was my own fault because I have never been very diplomatic. If you tell people what you suppose is the truth, you will always be unpopular.

Now, at last, Tommy felt he had heard the truth; not that it made him feel any more diplomatic than usual. And the way that Gyth was sweating suggested that he still believed he was going to die.

He thought I was going to do it, because I pointed the pistol at him and went round to the back of his chair. He must have thought he was going to get a bullet in the back of the head. But I just said this: 'I'm not even going to touch a dirty dog like you.' Then I left.

There was a terrible stink about it the next day, after I got back to Plymouth. Security people soon arrived, and I had to explain myself. I told them: 'None of this would have happened if you had shown the slightest common sense over where you housed Gyth. How can you call yourselves "Security" when your precautions aren't secure? Or do you call yourselves "Intelligence"? Because you're not intelligent either.

They were bloody angry, but they knew at the end of our little chat that I wasn't going to kill Gyth, because I would already have done it. Eventually things died down, and I think some of my old friends in London might have helped me to avoid being locked up yet again.

In May 1944 Tommy decided to use his leave to go to London again, though he was seeking fun rather than revenge over the Princes or SOE. He strolled through the West End on the lookout for pretty girls, but instead bumped into a distinguished-looking

Norwegian gentleman whose face he recognised instantly. It was Hjalmar Riiser-Larsen, who in his younger days had been a polar explorer. Now aged fifty-four, he was Commander-in-Chief of the Royal Norwegian Air Force. A fine pilot, Riiser-Larsen was also a controversial leader who loved to do things his way, even if his methods antagonised those around him. No wonder he had already taken a shine to young Tommy Sneum, who must have seemed like a chip off the same Scandinavian block.

Tommy recalled:

I had met Riiser-Larsen a few months earlier, while I had been living and working with Christmas Moeller. We had chatted a couple of times at social occasions and got on well because we could talk about flying – he had been a naval pilot too. I had always been in civilian clothes on these occasions, but he soon knew a bit about me. The big difference this time, when we bumped into each other, was that I was dressed in my British naval uniform.

Riiser-Larsen stared at Sneum in mock-disbelief, and said: 'What the hell are you doing in that uniform?'

'They wouldn't allow me to fly,' Tommy explained, 'so I joined the navy.'

The Norwegian invited Tommy to a French restaurant he knew, so that he could hear all about it. 'I told him: "I've had some trouble with SOE and SIS. They're keeping me out."'

When Sneum had finished his story, Riiser-Larsen sat for a moment in silence. Then he uttered seven matter-of-fact words: 'You had better come over to us.' Before the tears in his eyes could embarrass him any further, Sneum was given the confirmation he craved. 'It'll be no bother. I'm going to see to it that you fly again.'

Some busy and egotistical men might make a casual promise over a merry lunch and then forget all about it. Tommy knew that he would soon find out if Riiser-Larsen was such a person, or if his own, long-cherished dream was about to come true at last.

'Eight days later I joined the Royal Norwegian Air Force,' said Sneum decades later, his delight clearly eternal.

He did so by presenting himself at Kingston House in west

London, which acted as the Free Norwegian Headquarters during the Second World War. Saying he was applying for transfer from the Royal Navy, he simply mentioned the name of the top man, as instructed. As if by magic, 'Riiser-Larsen' opened all the necessary doors.

Tommy was back. His high-powered Norwegian acquaintance had been as good as his word. But the path from Kingston House to the cockpit of a plane wouldn't be quite so straightforward.

Chapter **49**

COMING HOME

'**D**ID YOU GET ANY twin-engine experience in Denmark before the war, Sneum?' The Royal Norwegian Air Force officer was trying to be helpful, but he wasn't about to arrange for a Dane to be trained from scratch. Not when he would have to handle the speed of a Mosquito at the end of his refresher course.

'I have three hundred hours of twin-engine flying time,' Tommy said boldly.

He chuckled as he remembered his outrageous boast. 'I had never even sat in one,' he admitted.

But the bluff won him a place at an operational training unit (OTU) for twin-engine pilots in Oxfordshire. The problem was that Sneum knew he would have to come clean to somebody sooner or later, otherwise he would risk killing himself behind the controls.

'Once we were at the OTU, I identified a colleague who looked trustworthy and took him aside. "I've never been in a Mosquito or any other twin-engine plane, so you'd better show me," I said.'

The other pilot could have reported him there and then. Tommy might have been back in the British Navy before he could blink. Instead, he was introduced to one of the Second World War's finest aircraft.

To understand the quality of the Mosquito you only had to go back to January 1943, and listen to an old acquaintance of Tommy –

the Luftwaffe chief, Reichsmarschall Hermann Goering. An ex-pilot himself, Goering knew that the Mosquito, made of wood and built like an aerodynamic work of art, had no equal. She flew faster than a Spitfire, due to her beautifully tapered wings and 1250-horsepower Rolls-Royce Merlin engines, and was ahead of her time in terms of raw power. Goering had said: 'It makes me furious when I see the Mosquito – I turn green and yellow with envy. The British, who can afford aluminium better than we can, knock together a beautiful wooden aircraft that every piano factory there is building, and they give it a speed which they have now increased yet again.'

Tommy knew what it was like to feel envy. He had been jealous of the RAF pilots who had flown against the odds to do battle with the Luftwaffe, while he was grounded by his own superiors. And he had been envious of the German pilots who had patrolled his own Danish skies during the occupation. True, Tommy had stolen six hours of death-defying glory in a Hornet Moth, but that wasn't much for a pilot-warrior to live on during four years of conflict in the skies above him.

Now he wanted some of that speed Goering had coveted, and he was prepared to risk his life again to get it. In his own mind, the thrill that awaited him justified everything. Even the early versions of the Mosquito were the fastest operational planes of their day, darting through the air at 611 k.p.h. That made the 'Wooden Wonder' 30 k.p.h. quicker than a Battle of Britain Spitfire and 80 k.p.h. faster than the Hawker Hurricane. Later Mosquitoes flew at 668 k.p.h. with an 1800-kilo bomb-load. Tommy's Hornet Moth had become paralysed by the cold in midsummer at an altitude of 1500 metres, and its range was less than 600 kilometres. The Mosquito had a ceiling of 13,500 metres, and a range of 2900 kilometres. Even Sneum wondered whether his rusty skills would be enough to handle this modern miracle of aviation.

He knew full well why he had been asked about his previous twin-engine experience: 'They were very, very particular about who they let into the Mosquito force. The Mosquito, I knew, was a difficult plane to fly because of the high speed through the air and the high landing speed, too.'

The colleague Tommy had chosen as his confessor must have known he was taking a chance by aiding the Dane's deception. But they climbed into the two-seater cockpit of a Mosquito together, and the more experienced man set about trying to show the novice how he might fool the instructor into believing he knew what he was doing. Nevertheless, when the time came to take off for real with his instructor, Sneum was sure the expert would realise the truth.

'You're a bit rusty, aren't you?' said the older man quickly. 'But you're doing OK.'

Tommy remained receptive to the demands of both plane and instructor, and his skills came rushing back to him. Adrenalin coursed through his veins, just as it had the very first time he had flown as a teenager. He was soon at one with the machine. The pilot within had clearly never left him.

'I found that flying was fundamentally the same, no matter how many engines you have,' he remembered with a smile.

All too soon, though, he faced the ultimate challenge of his first high-speed landing. His entire being was focused on getting it right. The tarmac rushed past as he met it, and the kiss was smooth. 'I got lucky,' he admitted later. 'I was due to do two or three landings, but the first one went so well that when we came to a halt the instructor wrote on his pad: "Above average to excellent." Then he told me: "OK, all yours, just take a navigator with you."'

To all intents and purposes, Tommy had just been given the green light to fly solo. 'I enjoyed that feeling so much when I went up again,' he recalled. 'And the navigator had no idea that I had never been in Mosquitoes before. He seemed to think I was an experienced twin-engine pilot.'

Four years of frustration were blown away in the wind as the Mossie scythed through the sky under Sneum's instinctive guidance. The power of the plane and majesty of life among the summer clouds inspired him.

'I can't put into words what it felt like,' he said apologetically, 'except to say that it was like coming home.'

Tommy Sneum won a place in a Norwegian squadron within the wider structure of Coastal Command, essentially defending Britain from German attack. This reflected a compromise Riiser-Larsen had reached with the British, who were keen to avoid the risk of Tommy being shot down over enemy airspace, in case he gave away all their secrets. Ironically, he was often stationed at Leuchars in Scotland, where he had been apprehended as a perceived threat to national security only two years earlier.

'We'd sometimes fly over the sea towards Norway in our Mosquitoes, and find the odd U-boat to attack. But skirmishes were very limited because by the time we got so far it was almost time to turn around and come back.'

On one occasion, however, while stationed in Wales, Tommy was sent on what he described as a 'training reconnaissance flight', though his Mosquito was armed with live ammunition.

I'd been ordered not to get involved in anything. But I saw a German ship running out in Irish waters. There was no mistaking it, because I knew every ship the Germans had from my spying days and I could identify them. This particular ship fired on me, so I got mad and attacked. I just went in once and gave them a heavy burst of fire, then I got away. They had a lot of guns and I didn't want to get shot down, but I think I did some damage.

When I got back to base I knew they would check the ammunition, so I had to tell them what had happened. It was an English-run airport in Wales, so first I got a bollocking from the English and then I got another one from the Norwegians. As a matter of fact, I think they were pleased, but they had to give you a dressing down.

Tommy Sneum had always tried to do things his way, and that continued right up to May 1945:

I was out with Lars, my navigator, flying eighty kilometres due south of Cape Clear in southern Ireland. I was keeping a sharp lookout for submarines when we received a call-up on the radio: 'Back to base immediately.'

We had only been flying an hour and a quarter, and it was meant to be a six-hour patrol, so I replied: 'Everything under control, I'm continuing.' But they came back again, even more emphatically: 'Come back immediately.' That was it, the war was over.

Tommy celebrated VE Day, 8 May, in London with Lars and his old girlfriend Rosy:

> They had grounded us in case we got drunk and crashed the planes. We took a tube to Green Park and spivs were selling flags for pounds. They must have made a fortune. We weren't allowed to pay for any drinks because of our uniforms and it was amazing I was still standing by the end of the night. I went back to Rosy's for a while – to change my shirt, you understand – and then we came out again because the party was still going.

Having tried and failed to arrange for Sneum to lead his squadron of Mosquitoes to Copenhagen as the first Allied planes into Kastrup Airport, later that summer R.V. Jones gave him a familiar job – taking photos of German radar installations. It wasn't quite the climax to his war that Tommy had foreseen: 'I had volunteered for a squadron going to the Far East but the bloody Japs gave up,' he pointed out. 'At the time, people thought it was a bloody good idea to drop atom bombs on Hiroshima and Nagasaki, but later many people thought differently.'

The atomic potential that so few had dared to imagine back in 1941, when Emmy Valentin and Sneum had debated the meaning of a German officer's careless boast, had finally been realised in August 1945. Not even Niels Bohr, the father of theoretical nuclear physics, had believed that the atom bomb would actually be made and used in anger.

With Tommy's active service over, there was a sense of coming full circle when he was given a letter of authorisation from R.V. Jones in September 1945. It read: 'Sneum has been loaned to us to assist in the task of photographing a number of radar sites. The photographs are required for the official history of the battle against the German night-fighter force. Sneum is particularly qualified for this work as he distinguished himself doing similar work for us during the German occupation.'

Inevitably, Fanoe was one of those sites. The British had never totally destroyed the Freya installation, though simply knowing it was there and how it worked had saved the lives of countless Allied pilots. The island's biggest hero arrived unannounced, and took the opportunity to surprise his parents. 'I crept into the house while they were sleeping and woke them up. They hadn't seen me for years and there were tears of joy all round,' Tommy remembered.

The reunion with Else and Marianne was less happy: 'Marianne didn't know I was her daddy because Else didn't want that. Else was playing the piano in a bar in Copenhagen. She had a new boyfriend and a new life. She was scared Marianne would get attached to me. I didn't feel I knew either of them any more. Although, unfortunately for Marianne, I could see she looked a bit like me.'

* * *

Kjeld Pedersen, Tommy's co-pilot in the Hornet Moth, also survived the war. After his wild weekend on the town with Tommy and Rosy, he returned to North Africa and continued to risk his life there until 28 January 1944. By March, he was back in England with 234 Squadron, then based at RAF Cottishall, Norfolk. In April, he was posted to 1 Squadron and began to fly Spitfires. He advanced across Europe with the squadron in the last year of the war, emerging unscathed. 'Oh yes, and he shagged Else after the war,' revealed Sneum casually. 'He also became a very good pilot in the end.'

The relationship with Else seemed more surprising. 'Yes,' repeated Tommy. 'Kjeld and Else got together for a while. My best friend and my ex-wife! Can you imagine? She certainly had her revenge for the way I treated her. But you know, it's funny, I didn't mind about Else and Kjeld. I probably deserved it. And besides, he asked my permission first!'

Furthermore, Else had been true to Sneum when it mattered, when his survival had depended on her ability to resist the pressure of the Danish police. And in truth, after their epic Hornet Moth flight together, Kjeld meant much more to Tommy than his wife did.

'Kjeld and I remained friends for life,' Tommy said proudly. 'He became quite a big noise in the Danish RAF, a lieutenant colonel, but we stayed as close as ever because we had the same interests. As we grew older we used to swap books, because we were both very well read. He had a wonderful sense of humour, Kjeld. He died in 1982, and that hit me harder than anything.'

The white towel and broomstick that Kjeld had thrust through the plexiglas roof of the Hornet Moth on that midsummer's night in Odense in 1941 remained on a wall at RAF Acklington for as long as the air base existed. The British flyers liked to stare at the filthy towel – two metres long when Tommy and Kjeld took off from Elseminde, but only ten centimetres by the time they landed at Bullock Hall Farm over six hours later. The RAF boys stationed in the north-east of England often thought of what those Danish pilots must have been through while that towel was being ripped to shreds. Any newcomer who spotted it would ask for an explanation. So the Acklington pilots had the perfect excuse to tell their favourite tale time and again.

THE HORNET'S STING

THE BRITISH SECRET SERVICE, for whom Tommy had risked his life, were not overly appreciative in the aftermath of the war. It was 1948 before anyone in British officialdom decided that he was worthy of some small recognition for his efforts. On 19 April of that year, R. Dunbar of the Foreign Office wrote to Alec Randall, the British Ambassador in Copenhagen, with the following news:

Sir,

With reference to your dispatch No. 30 (G.35/17/48) of the 27 January 1948, I have to inform Your Excellency that The King has been pleased to approve the award of the King's Medal for Courage in the Cause of Freedom to Flight Lieutenant Christian Thomas Sneum, Danish Naval Reserve Forces, in recognition of valuable services of a special nature to the Allied Cause during the war.

Owing to difficulties of supply and manufacture, the actual medal has not yet been struck. In the meantime, however, I enclose a piece of the appropriate ribbon and, in accordance with His Majesty's Commands, I request that you take such steps as you may consider proper to ensure its delivery, with due formality, to Flight Lieutenant Sneum. The medal will be forwarded to Your Excellency as soon as circumstances permit.

Tommy's view of the British hardly improved when he realised that they couldn't even present him with the medal he had been awarded. It was the following January before the Treaty Department of the Foreign Office saw fit to send Sneum's medal to Copenhagen, along with fifty-two others. There was another familiar name on the list of Danish recipients of the KMC that year: Birgit Valentin. Partly thanks to Tommy, she had survived the war without being compromised by the Nazis. It was a credit to her that she had been judged by the British to have been as courageous as Sneum himself, for her contribution to the Allied effort in Nazi-occupied territory.

However, the romance between the two was not rekindled at the medal ceremony, even though Tommy was officially single again by then, and still only thirty-one. Deep down, Sneum felt that his original exploits, in gathering Freya radar intelligence, had alone warranted a far higher recognition of his bravery. Much as he liked Birgit, he didn't see her as his equal when it came to spying. Yet now she was deemed by the British to possess the same warrior spirit as he did. Right or wrong, that assessment seemed faintly absurd in his eyes.

Sneum knew that the British had never been fully convinced of his loyalty, even though they readily acknowledged the contributions of many of the resistance figures with whom he had worked. Emmy Valentin received an MBE, as did Lorens Arne Duus Hansen. Much more controversially for Sneum, so did Hans Lunding, his chief detractor among the Princes of Danish Intelligence. Lunding was arrested by the Germans in August 1943, as they tried to quell widespread unrest in Denmark. He later claimed to have been close to execution when saved by the Allies' advance across Europe. Sneum's brother-in-law, Niels-Richard Bertelsen, was arrested in the same clampdown in Denmark. He endured the horrors of a German concentration camp before finding his way home at the end of the war, his face yellow with hepatitis.

There was no such ordeal for Ronald Turnbull, who continued to operate from the safety of Sweden while others put their lives on the line across the Oeresund in Denmark. Although that relative comfort was sometimes disturbed by the necessity of taking dangerous flights to Britain and back, those risks were hardly in the same league as Tommy's. Even so, Ronnie received an OBE.

Sneum never received the medal he deserved, and recalled: 'R.V. Jones told me that I must have had some enemies high up. Otherwise I would have been more highly decorated.'

In another snub, he had hoped to be promoted by Denmark's Fleet Air Arm when he returned home for good after the war. Instead, he was told that if he wanted to rejoin, he would have to start at the lowly rank he had been given before 1940. Since others had failed to fight and been promoted in his absence, Tommy was understandably disgusted and walked away.

R.V. Jones wrote later:

It might be thought that after all this Sneum would have become the national hero that he deserved to be. But he found himself cold-shouldered by those in control of Denmark at the end of the war, perhaps for this very reason. Some of them had been equivocal so long as Germany was in the ascendant, and their patriotic record would bear no comparison with that of Sneum, who had committed himself to resistance as soon as the Germans invaded Denmark. It would have endangered their positions if Sneum came back, and they were able to make play of his imprisonment in Brixton; he ultimately left Denmark to live in Switzerland. If they survive, the men who go first are rarely popular with those who wait for the wind to blow.

It was actually some time before Tommy moved to Switzerland. He remained in the Royal Norwegian Air Force until 1947 after being slighted by the Danish equivalent. Then he returned to England, where he dabbled in sales, public relations and advertising, while getting his adrenalin fix by taking courses in fire-fighting and rescue. His love for flying would never die, and later he delivered planes to their base airports for British and Scandinavian aircraft manufacturers. Soon he was a different kind of agent – for the British aircraft industry and various Danish firms – but the adrenalin rush was missing. So he became managing director of an air-charter and air-ambulance company in Denmark, often demonstrating his own death-defying piloting skills to help save the lives of others.

There were more thrills when he spent ten months in Turkey during 1951 as a construction supervisor and then test pilot for a Turkish state aircraft factory in Ankara, before returning to Denmark. There, he hit the headlines for the wrong reasons when, in 1955, Else had him thrown into jail in a dispute over maintenance payments for Marianne. Tommy, who had divorced his wife years earlier, took his punishment on the chin and came out smiling for the cameras on the day of his release.

'Everybody put me in prison,' he joked. 'The Swedes, the British, even the Danes. But each time I came out, I grew more important.'

He celebrated his freedom by moving to the city he called 'the most beautiful in the world', Rome, and dividing his time between the capital and another Italian paradise, Lake Como. 'I had met my second wife, Aida, who was simply lovely. We spent two very happy years of marriage moving between Rome and Como, where her father had a big business.' There is a marvellous photograph of the couple in an Italian restaurant (see picture section, p. 3), looking as happy as any lovers ever have, living la dolce vita. Behind the scenes, Sneum was working on the idea of an international air-ambulance service in cooperation with the Red Cross and the Sovereign Military Order of Malta. Sadly for Tommy and Aida, the magic of their romance didn't last, although Sneum was soon immersed in his next professional challenge.

Stig Jensen, the Danish resistance hero, had offered Tommy a position in his press, publishing and advertising firm. 'But I didn't like working in an office,' Tommy confirmed, unsurprisingly. He was also tiring of the mixed reception he still received in his own country. In 1961 all this persuaded him to pack his bags and leave for Switzerland. He would be based there for the next forty-five years.

Tommy's next job title might have sounded boring, but it allowed him to travel and meet more women. He became administrative director of the European Association of Advertising Agencies. 'I was always on the move and that suited me down to the ground,' he said. 'You can have a girlfriend in every town.'

But even confirmed womanisers are vulnerable; and in Munich, Germany, he fell in love with his third wife, a stunningly beautiful neurologist called Katherine. 'She was twenty years younger than me and she stayed good-looking as she got older,' observed Sneum. However, although Katherine gave him two more children, Christian and Alexandra, yet again the marriage didn't last. Most women found Tommy's forceful personality difficult to handle in the long run, and Katherine may have been too young at the time to cope with him. He raised the children in Switzerland, and though they probably didn't see their mother as often as they would have liked, he did a good job.

By the time I met Tommy, Chris and Sandra had grown into fine adults and flown the nest, though they still helped their father to face the frustrating onset of old age whenever they could. I also met a middle-aged Marianne, his war baby with Else, when she came to visit one day. The relationship between father and daughter was clearly strained, perhaps still a casualty of that war. Sneum was such an uncompromising character that in some ways he had become more isolated than he would have liked. But at least that meant he had time to sit down and tell his extraordinary story.

Time had changed Tommy's appearance but not his views. He had made it his business both during and after the war to find out precisely who had been responsible for his imprisonment. In later life he was still bitter about Britain's Special Operations Executive, and specifically blamed its Danish Section for what had happened to him: 'The SOE were shits and sent people to their deaths without bothering about it,' he alleged. 'They always talked about fighting for England, but they were really fighting for their own positions. Hollingworth and Turnbull had never been in the field but they had me put in prison.'

In 1953, Hollingworth still sounded proud that SOE had won the spying game against SIS in Denmark when he answered a letter from the Danish historian Jorgen Hastrup:

When you touched upon the short-lived rivalry between Sneum, working for SIS, and SOE, do not forget that normally it was not SOE's job to collect intelligence, except in so far as it was essential to its own work. In a larger country SIS would feed SOE with intelligence. After the Sneum affair, however, the position was reversed as far as Denmark was concerned, and we became the channel to SIS.

What Hollingworth, with a touch of flippant triumphalism, described as 'short-lived rivalry' almost cost Sneum his life.

In the fullness of time, Ronnie Turnbull developed a healthier perspective. Although it was true that he never spied behind enemy lines, I learned that sending men to their deaths *did* bother him, particularly the Rasputin-like liquidation of Hans Henrik Larsen by his own side in Denmark, a killing which had been authorised by SOE in London. I heard this from Ronnie himself, having tracked him down to São Paulo, Brazil. He was perfectly happy to discuss the war years on the phone, and we developed a good relationship which we maintained in his final years. Tragically, his Brazilian wife Thereza, with whom he was so happy during the war, was killed in a car crash in Copenhagen way back in 1945. But his love affair with Brazil lived on, and eventually he remarried and moved there.

By the twenty-first century, after decades of speaking Portuguese, Turnbull's Scottish lilt had taken on a strange, nasal quality, but the eighty-five-year-old often sounded half a century younger than he was. During one conversation I asked him about Sneum, and how SOE had effectively cast the SIS agent into the shadows in 1942.

'At that stage, SOE wouldn't have wanted to be involved in any dirty business against any individual agents,' he maintained. 'It may be there were wheels within wheels. A security problem rather than a political problem.'

It crossed my mind that there wouldn't have been a 'security problem' had Tommy not been forced into a corner as a result of the 'political problem' of interdepartmental rivalry, but I didn't want to interrupt Ronnie when it was all coming back to him.

'Sneum,' he continued. 'Yes, he came in at a time when the Princes had a better idea and were very much in control. They worked from a broader platform and they were able to deliver. I didn't know to what extent Sneum had been trained and we decided to go with the Princes. They were the professionals.'

The whole story might have been very different if Tommy had

bumped into Ronnie at the British Legation in Stockholm in February 1941, instead of meeting Donald Fleet and Henry Denham. If Turnbull had seen Sneum's Freya radar intelligence, something the Princes had failed to supply or even understand, the Scotsman might not have been so dismissive of the spy who ended up working for SIS instead of SOE.

'I didn't give Sneum too much thought,' admitted Ronnie.

'Except when the Princes complained about him,' I pointed out.

'Yes, then I took notice,' agreed Turnbull. 'It was my duty to pass on that kind of information. I think Sneum was arrested in the end. Maybe it was his bad-tempered behaviour. I think they picked him up in England.'

'Weren't you on the plane that took him to Scotland from Sweden?' I enquired.

'I don't think so ... I might have been. I don't remember,' Ronnie replied.

By the time he was locked up, Tommy understood the feasibility of the atom bomb, thanks to information supplied by Niels Bohr. Ironically, the man who eventually put Bohr on a plane from Stockholm to Britain on 30 September 1943 was none other than Ronnie Turnbull. But what had the Princes been able to tell Turnbull about the race to develop the atom bomb, given that they were supposedly the 'professionals' and 'very much in control'?

'I didn't even know about it,' admitted Turnbull.

I wondered whether Ronnie considered it a shame that Bohr had not been spirited out of Denmark earlier, to add his colossal intellect to the development of an Allied atom bomb. 'I should have said so, yes,' he replied, with refreshing honesty. Though he added, quite truthfully, 'Bohr himself determined the timing.'

But how hard had the British tried to persuade Bohr to leave Copenhagen earlier? Even in 1943 neither the Princes nor Turnbull, by his own admission, understood the extraordinary scientific breakthrough that Bohr and Heisenberg had dared to debate in Copenhagen two years earlier. They were no more alert to atomic science than they had been to Freya radar. Sneum, on the other hand, knew the significance of both technologies, and had even given the British the name of Enrico Fermi, the Italian professor whom Bohr believed held the key to controlling such a bomb.

Sure enough, on 2 December 1942, Fermi demonstrated just how such awesome forces could be controlled. At the University of Chicago, he pulled out ZIP, a weighted safety rod, just far enough to send a nuclear pile critical, then tamed the monster he had created by pushing ZIP back into its original position. His success meant that it would be only a matter of time before the bomb was built.

If Sneum could gather so much crucial intelligence, what else could he have achieved had he not been caught in the crossfire between SOE and SIS? It was a thought-provoking question, and one I dearly wished Sneum and Turnbull to debate together. I asked Ronnie if he would be prepared to meet the spy Britain had left out in the cold, or talk to him over the phone.

'Yes, I would,' said Turnbull enthusiastically, to my great surprise. 'There is a lot of interest in all this, even now. And I'd love to visit Denmark one last time before I kick the bucket.'

I put the same proposal to Tommy. 'No,' he said. 'There was a time when I wanted to kill Turnbull. I don't want to do that any more, but I don't want to meet him, either. And why waste the price of a phone call to Brazil? I know what he did and so does he. At the very least, Turnbull chose the wrong heroes to worship. I don't think he had very much knowledge of people's character and ideas.'

'You might be surprised,' I suggested. 'Did you know, for example, that he has admitted that his boss, Hollingworth, was more interested in quantity than quality when it came to the SOE agents they sent into Denmark?'

'He said that?' It was unusual to see Tommy astonished. 'Then, for once, I agree with him. But I still don't want to talk to him.'

At the risk of infuriating Tommy, who was by now a firm friend, I suggested that it was getting rather late in the day to be so bitter. I even dared to tell him that I liked Ronnie, as a result of the many telephone conversations we had enjoyed. There was a silence, and I feared that Tommy's volcanic temper might erupt.

'Unfortunately, it is true: I have felt bitter for far too long about what happened back then, and it has actually more or less destroyed my happiness in life,' he admitted poignantly.

I never did manage to organise their reunion, and Ronnie

Turnbull died shortly after his return to his native Scotland in 2005. Tommy lived on, and was no less fascinating or provocative as he neared the end of his life. Sometimes, apparently for fun, he used to make boasts about having 'penetrated' the British Secret Service, and waited for my reaction. Once I asked him if the British really had caught all the German spies in wartime England, as was often claimed. Tommy sat there with a fiendish smile on his face, saying nothing. The silence set my heart and mind racing, and I no longer knew if he was being playful or serious. I even revisited the evidence, and wondered whether my friend Sneum had fooled everybody, including me.

Dick White and Geoffrey Wethered of MI5 had been certain there was a traitor in London's Danish circle, but they had never been able to find him. Tommy was investigated and cleared. I wrote to MI5 for clarification of a document they had withheld from a file relating to their investigation of Sneum in 1943. They wrote back and revealed: 'Sneum was not in any position to leak to the Germans information regarding TABLE TOP [the SOE organisation in Denmark].' They meant that at the time of the leaks he was either in prison or under local arrest in Bedfordshire. But we know he smuggled at least one message out of prison, and his sexual prowess earned him plenty of rides to London during his so-called local arrest. So could MI5 have got it wrong?

For that to be true, R.V. Jones must also have been mistaken when dedicating Tommy's paperback edition of *Most Secret War* to 'one of the heroes of this book and the war'. Could the brilliant professor's assessment have been based on the Sneum he had known before the spy became embittered by his treatment at the hands of the British authorities? Did Tommy ultimately turn on his captors? Ralph Hollingworth seemed to think he might even have gone over to the Germans long before. Could he have been right all along?

It was all starting to play on my mind, so, making sure he wasn't armed, I plucked up the courage to ask him straight. 'It's too late for anyone to do anything about this, Tommy, so perhaps you could tell me the truth, if you've been hiding anything up to now. Were you a double-agent?'

'No,' he replied, without taking any apparent offence. 'I never told the Germans anything they didn't know already.'

He understood why I had to ask the question. Maybe he had been suspected in some quarters all his life because he positively encouraged suspicion, perhaps to remain the centre of attention. He also loved a battle of wits, especially when he knew that he alone held all the answers. Uncertainty in others seemed to amuse him.

'You are still a mystery,' I told him.

'Well, I think a mystery is rather a good thing to be,' he replied with a smile.

The British Secret Service's refusal to release Tommy's file only perpetuated that mystery, and we all knew time was running short. When I asked him how he wanted to be remembered, he had obviously already thought about it.

'As a fighter,' he said simply.

It was an apt self-portrait. Sneum fought against everyone who tried to control and tame him. That was the essence of the man. Now his fighting days were nearly over. The last time I saw him was in November 2006.

'I feel bloody old,' he said with a familiar throaty chuckle.

'You're not even ninety,' I told him. 'What are you moaning about? Eighty-nine is nothing these days.'

'Shut up and pass me the whisky,' he ordered, still smiling.

When he issued an order, it was unwise to cross him.

Tommy Sneum died on 3 February 2007, still a few months short of his ninetieth birthday. Like all the best spies, he took some of his secrets with him. His passing wasn't sad, because time had worn out his body. For such an active man that meant the moment had come to move on.

Tommy's son Christian organised a fitting funeral service in Denmark, and his death notice in the Danish papers included an English line: 'If they survive, the men who go first are rarely popular with those who wait for the wind to blow.' That poignant observation from R.V. Jones provided one last swipe at those who had treated him shabbily in his own country. Tommy's ashes were taken to the Sneum family's resting place on the island of Fanoe, where his story had begun.

Over in England, the Sneum family gave me the honour and

responsibility of marking Tommy's passing in an appropriate manner. I immediately contacted St Clement Danes, the church in the Strand, London, where Arne Helvard's name, among those of many other fallen heroes, was already commemorated. A plaque on one of the outer walls confirmed that this was also the right place to remember Thomas Christian Sneum. It read:

St Clement Danes

Built by the Danish community in the ninth century and rebuilt by William the Conqueror.

Built again by Sir Christopher Wren in 1681, the steeple added by James Gibbs in 1719.

Gutted by German incendiary bombs leaving only the damaged walls and steeple 10 May 1941.

Adopted in 1956 by the Royal Air Force, restored by Antony Lloyd and reconsecrated in the presence of Her Majesty Queen Elizabeth II, 19 October 1958 as the central church of the Royal Air Force.

By sheer coincidence, in two days' time the church was due to hold its Battle of Britain Commemoration Service, and RAF men of all generations would be there in strength. The Reverend Richard Lee of the RAF was most courteous, and agreed to remember Tommy in his prayers. I attended, hoping simply to hear his name read out. What followed was entirely unexpected, and some of us will be eternally grateful to the reverend for his extraordinary warmth and generosity of spirit.

In a church packed with serving RAF officers and veterans, Reverend Lee climbed into the pulpit and began his sermon. Luckily, the event was filmed, so what he said was recorded. The first part went like this:

Welcome to St Clement Danes – central church of the Royal Air Force. It is no stranger to conflict, since it has been torn down and built up many times. The church was built first of all to reconcile the community of Denmark with the community of England, which is particularly fitting today as we remember in our prayers a man called Thomas Christian Sneum. You may never have heard of him. But he was an exceptional man. He was a pilot, he was a Dane. And when his country was invaded he escaped in an aircraft called a Hornet – which I'm told is a rather souped-up Tiger Moth, if such a thing could exist – carrying secrets about radar. He flew across the North Atlantic – the North Sea, sorry, just testing the navigators among you – he flew across the sea and halfway across of course he had to refuel. So he stepped out onto the wing with the fuel to put in the wing, and he refuelled the aircraft on his own.

At this point some of the pilots in the congregation began to look at each other quizzically. I had forgotten to mention Kjeld Pedersen when I recounted the story of the Hornet Moth flight to Reverend Lee, and of course the RAF men were now wondering how on earth Tommy could have kept the plane steady with no one at the controls, and poured fuel into the tank with no protection from the high winds. I hope this moment would have amused Tommy, though I felt a fool for not having been more thorough in my briefing. Nevertheless, Reverend Lee continued:

He flew to this country and he was hired – to put it bluntly – by MI6 and asked to go back to his country and be a spy. So he went to spy, and when he was discovered, he and another colleague walked across the frozen sea from his Danish island to Sweden.

He died on Friday and the funeral service took place yesterday. Because they knew that this service was taking place, the Danish people asked us to pray for him. A man you never knew, who did marvellous things for peace and freedom. You will never meet him, but in this church he is remembered today.

What a send-off. What a tribute. Tommy would have loved the idea of being remembered by airmen, and along with so many other pilots, at such a distinguished RAF gathering. I hoped he was listening somewhere in the clouds, as he had finally been given centre stage by the British, for whom he had risked his life so many times.

It was interesting to hear Tommy Sneum described as a man 'who did marvellous things for peace and freedom'. I had never regarded him as a man of peace, though he was certainly a freedom-fighter. In a way he was the very embodiment of freedom. He loved life, even though his personal happiness was sometimes spoilt by bouts of bitterness over his treatment during the war, a state of mind he readily acknowledged. Tommy lived life to the full regardless, and hit extraordinary heights as he pursued and embraced that freedom. He refused to be grounded by the Danes, the Germans, the Swedes or the British. His spirit was a force of nature nothing could contain, and it allowed him to soar above and beyond the horizons of the average human being, to tease and outwit those who sought to bring him down.

* * *

Just before Christmas 2007, Christian Sneum, a commercial pilot, flew his plane and passengers to London City Airport, bringing with him some papers he had found as he went through his father's personal effects. I was not expecting to see anything new, because Tommy had always assured me that he had shown me everything of relevance to his story.

But when I laid eyes on one particular document it rendered me speechless, and not just because it had been written on the very day I was born. Marked 'Confidential', it was from Major General R.E. Lloyd, CB, CBE, DSO, Director of Military Intelligence, The War Office, Whitehall, London SW1. Dated 5 January 1962, it read:

TO WHOM IT MAY CONCERN
This is to certify that:
Captain Thomas Christian SNEUM
a Danish National, presently resident in Switzerland at Arosastrasse 127, Zurich 8, rendered valuable and loyal assistance to the Allied Cause during the late war.

In the early months of the war Captain SNEUM, who was at that time serving in the Royal Danish Air Force, escaped from Denmark to England, bringing with him information of the greatest value to the Air Ministry.

Captain SNEUM then volunteered to return clandestinely to Denmark in order to obtain further information. After a course of training, he parachuted back to Denmark.

Captain SNEUM fulfilled his mission with considerable energy and when he could no longer continue to operate, he made a most gallant escape from Denmark across the ice to Sweden, arriving there early in 1942. Soon afterwards he was evacuated to England.

Unfortunately, certain remarks attributed to Captain SNEUM had preceded his arrival and as these appeared to cast some doubt on his loyalty, he was interned in Brixton Prison whilst investigations were being made.

The result of these investigations was to clear Captain SNEUM completely of any imputation against his loyalty to the Allied Cause and he was accordingly released.

Thereafter Captain SNEUM served in the Danish Section of the Royal Navy and was later transferred to the Royal Norwegian Air Force, in which he served as a pilot.

It is desired to emphasise that Captain SNEUM's detention in Brixton Prison in 1942 does not in any way reflect adversely on his conduct. On the contrary, Captain SNEUM's courage, energy and loyalty to the Allied Cause throughout the war are now beyond question.

So there it was, proof at last that Britain had unequivocally hailed Tommy a hero, and long before that moving service in St Clement Danes in 2007. It had taken seventeen years to paint his wartime conduct and achievements in such glowing terms. And the fact that Tommy had seen fit to secure such a reference as late as 1962 was an indication of just how long the post-war smear campaign against him had continued. The King's Medal for Courage, awarded to him in 1948, had been tantamount to damning him with faint praise, given his remarkable exploits, and certainly hadn't been sufficient to silence some of his critics.

Major General Richard Eyre Lloyd's tribute seemed to reflect the wartime opinion of Otto Gregory of Air Ministry Intelligence, who had argued that Sneum deserved something closer to the Victoria Cross for his achievements. However, since the vast majority of Tommy's heroics had not come in open combat, and since his record had subsequently been clouded by suspicion, he would never receive the ribbons or the recognition due to him.

The letter in itself constituted something special, though. And I had to smile, because Tommy had been in possession of it on the first day I met him, and yet had allowed the debate about his loyalty to continue for years. Why?

Once he had told me: 'Always keep something in reserve, close to your chest, never use all your ammunition unless you have to.'

He had followed his own rule to the end. Now it was as though Tommy had enjoyed a last little joke with me, from beyond the grave, mocking me for having doubted him. For it seemed inconceivable that he had simply forgotten about that letter, which he knew could provide the perfect answer to any suggestions of treachery. More likely he had cultivated my suspicions for his own amusement, and ensured that I would remain intrigued. That way he knew I would return for a fresh round of verbal chess, sometimes armed with a bottle of schnapps or whisky, on other occasions bringing a new document or discovery from the English war files.

None of this stopped me from feeling guilty about some of the questions I had asked of a man I had befriended. Then I remembered one of the last things he ever said to me: 'You have always treated me very fairly.' Tommy had faced plenty of questions in his lifetime, so a few more hadn't made any difference. He knew deep down that he would always have the last laugh. The extraordinary letter of support from the Director of Military Intelligence guaranteed that.

Thomas Christian Sneum, the man who had flown to freedom in a Hornet, had saved his most potent sting for the very end.

Index

Aalborg 116, 157
Aalborg airstrip 50, 100, 241
Abwehr (German Intelligence) 14–
  16, 46, 102, 111, 129, 134–5,
  160–2, 169, 173–4, 176, 182,
  184, 194–6, 200, 208, 229,
  233, 243, 245, 250, 266, 279,
  280, 296, 298, 308, 312
  see also German Intelligence
Ackermann, Eric 4
Admiralty 34, 100
Agerup 140
Air Ministry 120–1, 281, 297, 319,
  355
Air Ministry Intelligence 100–7,
  356
Allied convoys 53
Allies 4, 10, 14–15, 22, 40, 53, 59,
  104, 118, 126, 148, 155, 161,
  179, 190, 193, 207, 219, 231,
  251, 264, 278, 281, 282, 284,
  301, 319, 320, 325, 343, 344,
  349, 356
  see also Anglo-American air raids
Amager 150, 157
Amble 89, 90
'Amniarix' 4
Andersen, Hans Christian 180
Andersen, Poul 47–50, 57, 62–5,
  95–6, 111, 116, 161
Anderson, Kaj 247
Andrews, Gordon 306, 307–8, 313
Andrews, Irene 307–8, 313, 323
Andrews, Leslie 307–8, 313
Anglo-American air raids 330

Ankara 346
Anti-Comintern Pact 178, 179, 183
anti-German protests (Danish) 178–
  80, 183–4
Ashby-Peckham, Flight Sergeant
  318
Assens 74
Atlantic 53
atom bomb 154–5, 196–7, 200–1,
  205, 207–8, 232, 271, 280–2,
  340, 349–50
Avnoe airstrip 10, 22, 69, 100, 241

Bang and Olufsen 175, 180, 200
Baston, David 89
BBC see British Broadcasting
  Corporation
Belgium 318, 319
Benke, Mr 284, 297, 300, 304, 305
Bennicke, Colonel Vagn 308
Berlin 190, 248
Bertelsen, Erik 165
Bertelsen, Margit 144
Bertelsen, Niels-Richard 28, 29,
  144, 167–8, 199, 201, 203,
  228, 234, 236, 245, 248–9,
  270–1, 272, 308, 344
Bill (Brixton inmate) 289–90, 305
Bismarck (battleship) 53, 232, 312
Blenheim aircraft, Mark I 325, 326
Blitz 275
Blunt, Major 311
Boerglum 157, 303
Bogart, Humphrey 21
Bogoe 75

Bohr, Harald 196
Bohr, Niels 154–6, 196–7, 200,
    207–8, 340, 349
Bond, James 3
'Booklet, The' (Danish uprising
    plan) 197
Bornholm, Denmark 33, 185, 324–
    5, 328, 329
Brazil 348, 350
Britain 2, 3, 10, 24, 31–2, 34–5, 48,
    49, 52, 69–70, 101, 103, 106,
    110, 114, 118, 126, 135–6,
    148–50, 158, 160–3, 174–5,
    181, 183–4, 197, 200, 205,
    208–9, 215, 217, 233–4, 241,
    246, 249, 251–2, 256, 262,
    267, 270, 272–3, 279–80, 286,
    291–2, 297–9, 329–30, 338–9,
    345, 347, 349–50, 356
Britain, battle of 132, 353
British, and the German Fanoe
    installations 10, 11, 12, 17, 22,
    23, 43–4
British Army 113, 277
    Royal Lifeguard Regiment 131
    Tank Corps 136
British Broadcasting Corporation
    (BBC) 96, 116, 123, 124
    anti-German propaganda 32
British Intelligence 101, 127, 132,
    136, 149, 163, 195, 197, 282,
    295
    see also MI5; MI6; Secret
        Intelligence Service; Special
        Operations Executive
British Legation, Copenhagen 32,
    34, 273, 300
British Legation, Stockholm 23, 31,
    34, 35, 40, 102, 123, 148, 213,
    214–15, 217, 230, 238, 272–3,
    349
British Scientific Intelligence 4, 7,
    103, 329
Brixton Prison 276, 277–86, 287–
    92, 294–6, 297–8, 299–302,
    304–6, 312, 314, 318, 345,
    356
    'Little Budapest' 283–4
Bromme airfield 273–4
Brorfelde 142, 149, 263

Bruhn, Carl 191–2, 194–5, 198,
    215, 233–4, 245–6
Bruneval Raid 4
Bullock Hall Farm 94, 342

Café Bunis, Copenhagen 243–4
Campbell, Malcolm 138
Chamberlain, Neville 32
Chemielewski, Jerzy 4
Chiewitz, Professor Ole 144–5,
    196–7, 200, 205, 207
Christensen, Rasmus 250
Christian, King 23, 69
Christiansen, Lieutenant
    Commander Hasager 4, 324–5,
    328–30
Christianshavn 153, 157, 164, 170,
    178, 190
Christophersen (née Wood), Mary
    Anita Blackford 316–17, 327
Christopherson, Anne Katrine 219
Christopherson, Hildur 187
Christopherson, Johannes 219
Christopherson, Sigfred Johannes
    263, 266, 310
    courts and marries Mary Wood
        316–17
    death 326–7
    early life 131–2
    in Malmo prison 233–5, 245, 267
    release 272, 273
    spills the beans on Danish
        operations 4–5, 233–5,
        245, 293
    returned to Britain his following
        Malmo incursion 274, 276,
        277, 278, 283, 284
    in the Royal Air Force 288, 325–
        7
    in the SIS
        on the ground in Denmark 4–
            5, 146, 148–9, 151–2,
            164–6, 167–8, 174–7,
            178, 181–5, 186–7, 195,
            197–8, 199–200, 205,
            208, 209–12
        ordered out of Denmark by
            Sneum 213–14, 215–17,
            219–23, 226–8, 241, 265,
            280

Christopherson, Sigfred Johannes –
  continued
  in the SIS – continued
    sent to Denmark 137–9, 140,
      141–4
    training 131, 132–3, 134, 135–
      6
Christopherson, Thorbjoern 175–6,
  181, 187, 199–200, 209–10,
  215–17, 219–24, 226–8, 230,
  234, 244, 256, 258, 263, 280,
  317, 326
Churchill, Winston 4, 31, 51, 70,
  97, 103, 104, 110, 118, 330
Clarke, M.L. 294
Closquet, Jean 4
Coastal Command (British) 338
codes 128, 130, 134–5, 165–6, 185,
  199, 209, 213, 214, 240, 265
  Morse 128, 130, 134–5, 165–6,
    185, 209
  pre-code signatures 165
Cohen, Commander Kenneth 275–6
Connan, Anne 194
Conservative Party (Swedish) 267
Cookridge, E.H. 330
Copenhagen 1–2, 9, 14–15, 18, 20,
  25–9, 45–7, 51, 53, 57, 59, 61,
  69, 95, 111, 116, 140, 142–4,
  150–1, 153–9, 160–4, 171–2,
  174–6, 178–85, 186–90, 193–
  5, 199–204, 205–6, 208, 210–
  12, 214, 216–17, 219, 232,
  233, 239–40, 244–5, 248, 250,
  264–6, 267–8, 270, 278, 295–
  6, 298, 301–2, 308, 310, 321,
  344, 348–9
Coquet Island 89
Cox, Flight Sergeant 326
Criminal Investigations Branch
  (Danish) 250

Dahl, Jens 28
Danish Airport Authority (DPPA)
  241
Danish Army 308
Danish Army Intelligence 22
Danish Army Reserve 47
Danish Club 120
Danish Committee 294

Danish Fleet Air Arm 8–9, 11, 23,
  28, 51, 55, 56, 69, 84, 94, 193,
  236, 240, 345
Danish Intelligence 52, 53, 117–18,
  148–50, 164, 249, 329, 330
  'the Princes' (HAMILCAR) 118–
    19, 148–50, 162–3, 169,
    178–9, 189–91, 197–8, 216,
    230–2, 236–8, 247, 262–3,
    267, 268, 291–2, 293–6,
    301, 312, 324, 328, 332–3,
    344, 348–9
Danish Legation, London 120, 331
Danish Naval Intelligence 328
Danish Navy 9, 14, 128, 129, 325
  see also Danish Fleet Air Arm
Danish Nazi Party 243
Danish police 129, 151–2, 166,
  167, 171–2, 178, 179, 182,
  193, 202–3, 208, 210–12, 229,
  230, 234–5, 239, 243–6, 250–
  1, 252, 254–5, 263, 264–5,
  298, 302, 308, 310, 341
  AS (Special Affairs) Department
    111
Danish resistance 185, 236, 243,
  245, 295–6, 298, 301, 302–3,
  308–9, 310, 316, 318, 323,
  346
Danish Royal Air Force 341
Danish secret army 118, 119, 231,
  262
Danish troops 70
Dansey, Claude 108, 110, 136, 262,
  275
De Gaulle, Charles 121
De Havilland 46
De Havilland Hornet Moths 47,
  49–51, 53–60, 62–7, 68–73,
  74–80, 81–7, 88–92, 94–6,
  102, 115–16, 119, 123, 158,
  167, 170, 193, 235, 267, 276,
  279, 301, 318, 322, 333, 337,
  341, 342, 354, 357
De Havilland Mosquitoes 35, 336–
  9
Defoe, Daniel 165
Denham, Captain Henry 34–7, 40,
  42, 45, 53, 102, 273, 349
Denmark 1–2, 5, 8–17, 18, 20, 22–

3, 25–9, 32–4, 36, 45–51, 52–
    60, 61–7, 68–73, 74–80, 81,
    93, 95–6, 100–1, 104, 106,
    111–13, 115–21, 123–4, 126–
    8, 130–3, 134, 136–8, 140–5,
    146–52, 153–9, 160–6, 167–
    72, 173–7, 178–85, 186–90,
    193–8, 199–204, 205–12, 213–
    17, 218–21, 227–32, 233–8,
    239–46, 247–51, 252–7, 261,
    262–6, 267–8, 270, 274, 278,
    281, 282, 291–2, 294–6, 300,
    302–3, 305, 308–9, 310–12,
    314–15, 318–19, 324–5, 327,
    328–30, 340–1, 344–6, 348–
    50, 352, 354
Double Twelve Hours race 109
DPPA see Danish Airport Authority
Duff, Joan 110
Dunbar, R. 343
Duus Hansen, Lorens Arne 175–6,
    180–5, 200–2, 204, 205, 208–
    9, 213, 216–17, 231–2, 234,
    239–40, 245–6, 249, 264–5,
    268, 280–1, 296, 302–3, 324,
    326, 328–30, 344

Ebury Court Hotel, London 120–2,
    132
Elseminde farm 47, 48, 49–50, 53–
    60, 62–7, 68–73, 92, 342
Esbensen, Detective 203, 204
Esbjerg, Denmark 9, 12, 13–14, 16,
    38, 77, 79, 100, 253

Falsterbo 216, 221, 222
Fanoe 7–14, 16–17, 18–19, 21–3,
    27–8, 33, 35–7, 38–44, 62, 70,
    75–6, 78, 80, 99, 102–5, 129,
    153, 161, 196, 236, 253, 258,
    273, 340–1, 352
Felkin, Squadron Leader Denys 100
Fermi, Enrico 207, 281, 349–50
Finno-Russian War 131
First World War 10, 108–9
Fleet, Squadron Leader Donald 34,
    35–6, 40, 42, 102, 349
Fleming, Ian 3
Follett, Ken 3
Foreign Office 4, 33, 262, 291,

    316–17, 343
Northern Division 294
Treaty Department 344
Forest, Flight Officer 96
France 104, 283
Frank, Charles 103–4, 105
Free Danish 290, 291–2, 293, 295,
    300, 313
Free Danish Council 268
Free Dutch 275
Free Norwegian Headquarters 335
French 121
Freya radar 104–5, 232, 340, 344,
    349
Frigurson-Sibson, Squadron Leader
    326
Fyn 47, 74, 239–40

German Army 279
German Intelligence see Abwehr
    (German Intelligence)
German spies 101, 120, 162, 351
Germans 248, 269, 270, 313
    and atomic weapons 207–8
    in Belgium 319
    in Denmark 7–17, 18, 20, 22–3,
        25–9, 32–4, 36, 47, 50, 56,
        57, 60, 62–6, 74–80, 95–6,
        100, 102, 104, 111, 112,
        113, 116, 118, 126–7, 131,
        133, 134, 144, 148, 158,
        160–2, 164, 166, 167, 169–
        70, 173–6, 178–82, 195,
        208–9, 215, 229–30, 231,
        234, 235–8, 239–41, 243–6,
        250, 261, 263, 264, 266,
        267, 279, 294, 298, 300–1,
        302, 303, 308–9, 312, 328,
        329, 330, 332, 344, 345
    and the Fanoe radar installations
        7–8, 10, 11–13, 17, 21, 23,
        33, 35, 36–7, 38–44, 70, 75–
        6, 102
    and the First World War 109
    and the invasion of France 283
    and the invasion of Russia 76–7,
        97, 196
    in North Africa 322
    potential victory of 9–10, 107
    radar technology 104–5

Germans – *continued*
  Sneum's associations with 4–5,
    13–15, 16
  uniforms 127
  use of torture 182, 329, 331
Germany 168, 261, 269, 302, 305,
  318, 320, 346
  Allied bombing of 318–20
  and the Anti-Comintern Pact 178
  and atomic weapons 281
  potential victory of 9–10
  and V-rockets 325
Gestapo 182, 203, 264, 302
Gibbs, James 353
Gloucester Hill Farm 89
Goering, Hermann 10–11, 26, 337
Goftenhafen (later Gdynia) 53
Goward, R.P. 318
Grandloese 143
Grantham 325, 326, 327
Gregory, Lieutenant (later Squadron
  Leader) Otto 100–3, 105–7,
  110, 122–3, 280, 282, 290,
  297–8, 305, 306, 312, 356
Griffith (prison officer) 285, 288,
  289
Gurney, A.E. 318
Gyberg, Werner 175, 176, 180,
  181, 184, 234, 244–5, 246,
  265
Gyberg and Jensen 175, 181
Gyth, Captain Volle ('Prince' of
  Danish Intelligence) 118, 119,
  162, 178–9, 197, 216, 237,
  238, 291, 296, 331–3

Hadersley 75
Haestrup, Joergen 184
Hagedorn, Professor 145, 196,
  205–6, 207, 210
Hahn, Otto 207
Hambro, Sir Charles 52, 117, 124,
  135, 294–5
HAMILCAR see Danish
  Intelligence, 'the Princes'
  (HAMILCAR)
Hammer, Mogens (ARTHUR) 5,
  191, 194–5, 198, 246, 291–2,
  293, 294, 296, 299, 312
Hansen, Hans F. 294

Hansen, Thomas Sonnichsen 256
Harald Jensensgade 160, 171, 247,
  265
Hart, E.D. 318, 319
Hastrup, Jorgen 347–8
Haw-Haw, Lord (William Joyce) 33
Hawker Hurricanes 89, 90, 322,
  337
Hawker Nimrod biplanes 9, 69
Heisenberg, Werner 154–6, 207,
  281, 349
Helsingborg 261
Helvard, Angla Eugenia 242
Helvard, Arne 28, 240–2, 247,
  252–60, 261–4, 267–8, 272–4,
  276, 277, 282–4, 290, 292,
  308, 318–19, 321, 323, 353
Himmler, Heinrich 26, 29, 30, 31
Hiroshima 340
Hitler, Adolf 5, 7, 9, 10, 13, 26, 29,
  31–2, 33, 43, 75, 94, 104, 118,
  148, 155, 169, 185, 207, 221,
  228, 235, 246, 279, 317, 320,
  324, 330
Hobro 242
Holbaek 142, 143, 149
Holbaek Battery 59, 119
Holland 135, 305
Hollingworth, Commander Ralph
  4–5, 35, 123–5, 135, 191–2,
  215, 231–2, 267, 291–2, 293–
  4, 298–9, 310, 311–12, 324,
  347–8, 350, 351
Holmen naval base 153
Holtug 220
Home Guard 93–4
Hotchkiss tanks 239
Hotel Astoria, Copenhagen 235–6,
  279
Hotel Cosmopolit, Copenhagen 14–
  15, 160–2, 266, 279
House of Anna, London 126–31
Howoldt, Fregatten-Kapitan Albert
  229, 233, 266, 308
Howard, Commander Rex 275
Hven 253, 255, 257, 259, 260,
  261

Iranian Embassy, London 299
Isle of Man, internment camps 98

Jaegersborg Kaserne, Copenhagen 216, 237
Jaegersborg Kaserne, Kongens 150
Japanese 340
Jauch and Hubener 109
Jenkins, Mr (SIS instructor) 127–8
Jensen, Carl 19–20, 61, 117, 171–2, 186, 247, 250
Jensen, Gerda 117, 186, 250
Jensen, Harry 250, 251
Jensen, Robert 175
Jensen, Stig 295–6, 308–9, 346
Jensen, Sylvest 47
Jews 29, 178
Johannesen, Paul 298, 302
Jones, Reginald Victor 4, 103–4, 105, 198, 280, 282, 329, 340, 345, 351, 352
Jordan, Harold 4
Junker aircraft 22, 41, 43
Jutland 59, 64, 75, 77, 157, 161, 183, 218

Karstengren, Einar 261, 268–9, 272
Karup airstrip 100
Kastrup 28, 29, 33, 50, 100, 216, 241, 264, 319, 340
Keyes House, London 112
Kiel 195
Killerich, Ole 316
Kingston House, London 334–5
Klemm aircraft 66–7
Klippinge 219
Knauer, Mrs 315, 323
Knauer, Peter 315, 331
Knivholt airstrip 100
Koege 219
Kongens Lyngby 199
Krefeld, Germany 318, 320

'L' tablets (suicide pills) 298, 310–11
Lake Como 346
Landskrona, Sweden 253, 255, 256, 257, 258
Langdorp, Brabant 319
Lars (navigator) 339–40
Larsen, Eivind 229
Larsen, Hans Henrik 310–11, 348
Lee, Richard 353–4

Leuchars airfield, Scotland 273, 274, 339
Lille Belt Channel 74
Lindballe (mechanic) 56–7
Lloyd, Antony 353
Lloyd, Major General R.E. 355–6
London 97–8, 99–107, 110–14, 120–3, 126–33, 134–6, 191, 192, 197, 198, 205, 215, 263, 268, 274–5, 299, 307, 310, 312, 314–18, 321–5, 330, 331–4, 340
Luftwaffe 8, 10–11, 16, 26, 35, 45, 76, 80, 97, 317, 320, 337
Lunding, Major Hans ('Prince' of Danish Intelligence) 118, 119, 150, 156, 162, 170, 189–91, 197, 216, 230–2, 237–8, 239, 248, 267, 344
Lunn, T.R. 318, 319

Malmo 216, 228, 233
Malmo prison 261–6, 267–71, 272, 277, 278, 293–4, 300, 302
Mandoe 77
McArdle, P.D. 318
Meinicke, Hauptmann 9–10, 13–14, 16, 76–7, 79–80, 115–16, 161
Menzies, Stewart 110, 198, 275
Messerschmitts 41
109 fighters 76–7, 79–80
MI5
  hunting and interrogation of double-agents 3, 4, 101, 196, 277–84, 293, 294, 311–13, 351
  on pilots as spies 101
  and Sneum's Fanoe radar film 105
  and Sneum's file 3
MI6 1, 106, 108, 110, 126, 128, 130, 136, 137, 163, 165, 191–2, 323, 354
  see also Secret Intelligence Service
Michels, A.A. 4
military police (British) 274
Milton Ernest 306–7, 312–13, 318
Milton Ernest Hall 306–8
mine-laying 100

Ministry of Information, Berlin 188
Ministry of Information (British)
108, 109–10
Mitchell, Major Leslie 304–6, 318,
324, 330
Moeller, Gertrud 295, 314–15
Moeller, John Christmas 158, 267–
8, 290–2, 293–5, 299, 300,
302, 314–15, 317, 321, 323,
327, 331, 334
Moerch, Lieutenant Commander
328
Morpeth 96, 97
Morse code 128, 130, 134–5, 165–
6, 185, 209
Munck, Ebbe 148, 149, 197, 198,
230
Munich 346

Naestved Garrison 59, 119
Nagasaki 340
Napoleon Bonaparte 10
National Archive, Kew 313
Naval Intelligence (British) 34
Nazis 4, 10, 29–30, 249, 281, 326,
344
and atomic weapons 207
Danish 243
in Denmark 1–2, 12, 18, 22, 23,
25, 26, 32, 33, 34, 46, 48,
59, 69, 75, 78, 96, 117, 118,
130, 133, 144, 150, 158,
162, 164, 179, 180–1, 182,
197, 206, 233, 236, 243,
263, 264, 278, 279, 295,
298
and the Fanoe installations 7, 42
and Malmo prison 261
in Norway 304
radar advances 104–5
use of torture 39
Newcastle 97, 322
Newmarket 138
Nielsen, Anders Peter 294
Nielsen, Gerda Tapdrup 218–19,
232
Nielsen, Jens 16
Nielsen, Knud 190, 239, 253, 254–
5
Nielsen, Oestergaard 247, 298

Nielsen, Svend 218–19
Nielsen, Vita 242, 292, 321
Njalsgade 144
Noerreheden, Thomas 230, 250,
265–6
Nordby, Fanoe 16, 17, 18–19, 78,
129
Nordentoft, Colonel Einar ('Prince'
of Danish Intelligence) 118,
119, 150, 162, 197, 216
Normander, Criminal Detective
250, 251
North Africa 292, 318, 322, 341
North Sea 7, 10, 22, 51, 55, 57, 66,
72, 73, 77, 80, 81–7, 88–9, 94,
116, 121, 138, 170, 193, 354
Norway 29, 239, 304, 339
Nurnberg (ship) 100

Odense 48–9, 51, 53, 56, 57–8, 60,
62, 63, 64–6, 95, 116, 161,
342
Odmar, Politikommissaer 229–30,
233–4, 244, 247, 249–50, 262,
263, 264–6, 270
Oeresund 1–2, 3, 23, 144, 214,
216, 217, 221–5, 226–8, 230,
241, 253–60, 278, 327, 344
Olsen, Detective-Sergeant Roland
243–6, 247, 249–51, 266
Operation Barbarossa 76–7, 97
Oslo 239, 240
Oslo Report 4
Ost, A.F. 302
Oxlund, Kaj 22–3, 35, 40, 45, 62,
234–5, 264, 266, 308, 317
accompanies the Christopherson
brothers from Denmark to
Sweden 218–25, 226–8, 230,
232
business problems 218–19
death 225, 226–8, 230, 232,
242–3, 249, 256, 263, 280
helps Tommy on the ground in
Denmark 146–8, 150–2,
158, 164, 167, 176, 200–2,
204, 205–7, 210–12, 213–
14, 217
Oxlund, Tulle 23, 146–8, 176, 206–
7, 212, 217, 232, 242–3

Palm, Olaf 261, 263
Park, Aage Koehlert 150–1, 168–9, 228
Park, Flight Lieutenant Hugh 299–301, 305
Pasborg, Oda 25, 26–7, 28–9, 30
Pedersen, Kjeld 23–4, 33, 45, 51, 53–60, 61–7, 68–73, 74–80, 81–7, 88–98, 99, 106–7, 110–14, 115, 123, 129, 263, 318, 322–3, 341–2, 354
Peenemunde, Germany 185, 324–5, 328, 330
Petersen, Emil 250
Petersen, Holger 46–7
Petersen, Knud Erik 294
Petersen, Ove 15–16, 41
Plymouth 331, 333
Poland 248, 269, 305
Poulsen, Olaf 99–100
'Princes, the' see Danish Intelligence, 'the Princes' (HAMILCAR)
Pringley, Wing-Commander 96

'Q sites' (decoy airfields) 326

Rabagliati, Beatrix 110
Rabagliati, Euan Charles 108–12, 120–5, 126, 134–5, 136, 138–9, 148, 150–1, 158, 174, 177, 180, 205, 214, 235, 262, 263, 274–6, 277–8, 280, 282, 287–8
RAC Club, London 290, 297
radar
    on Fanoe 7–8, 10, 11–13, 17, 21–3, 35, 36–7, 38–44, 45, 62, 70, 75, 76, 80, 99, 102–5, 196, 273, 340, 349
    Freya 104–5, 232, 340, 344, 349
radio operations 128, 130–1, 134–5, 165–6, 174–7, 180–5, 200, 202–4, 205, 208–9, 211–12, 213, 239, 264–6, 278
'Telephone Book' radio set 185
RAF Acklington 89, 94–5, 96, 342
RAF Cottishall 341
Randall, Alec 343
Rasmussen, Erik 241

Rasputin 310, 348
Red Cross 346
Riiser-Larsen, Hjalmar 334, 335, 338–9
Ringsted, Denmark 142, 143, 192, 242, 243
Ringway Airport, Wilmslow 136–7, 141, 287
Rocard, Yves 4
Rodney House, London 132, 135–6
Rome 346
Romoe 77
Roskilde Garrison 59, 119
Roth, Henry 4
Rottboell, Christian Michael 23, 24, 33, 45, 58–9, 123–4, 157–8
    death 302–3
    recruited by the SOE and sent to Denmark 214–15, 267, 268, 298, 301–3
Rottboell, Mr 24, 157–8
Royal Air Force (RAF) 8, 24, 35, 45, 48, 51, 97, 99, 102, 111–12, 114, 121, 131, 132, 241, 263, 288, 292, 317, 318, 325–7, 330, 337, 342, 353–4
    12 Pilot Advanced Flying Unit 325, 326
    Bomber Command 318, 320
    Squadrons
        I Squadron 341
        33 Squadron 322
        94 Squadron 322
        218 Squadron 318
        234 Squadron 341
    Training School 18 114
    see also RAF Acklington; RAF Cottishall
Royal Australian Air Force 318
Royal Flying Corps 108–9
Royal Lifeguards 150
Royal Navy 100
    Danish Section 331, 333, 335, 356
    see also Naval Intelligence
Royal Norwegian Air Force 334–5, 336–40, 345, 356
Royal Observer Corps 89

Royal Patriotic School for Orphan
    Daughters, Battersea 97–8, 99–
    107, 112, 132, 276
Runerheim, Commissaire 168, 169,
    228, 233, 269–70, 272
Russia 297
German invasion of 76–7, 97, 196

St Annaegade 150, 153–4, 157,
    173, 187, 193, 200, 201–4
St Clement Danes Church 353–4,
    356
Sanky, Flying Officer 100, 101
SAS (Special Air Service) 299
Scandinavia 304–5
Scavenius, Foreign Minister 178
Schaufer, Lieutenant Heinz-
    Wolfgang 318–19
Schleswig-Holstein (ship) 100
Schou, Bjarke 148, 149
Schou, Captain 119
Scotland 268, 273, 274, 339, 351
Scrivener, Flight Officer 120–2
Scrivener, Mrs 120, 122, 123
Secret Intelligence Service (SIS) 3, 5,
    34–5, 106, 109–10, 122, 124,
    127, 131, 135, 300, 316, 334
    54 Broadway building 104, 110,
        135, 136, 262, 275
    British Scientific Intelligence 4, 7,
        103, 329
    Denmark and Holland (Section
        A2) 108, 110, 117, 275,
        287, 305
    French Section 275
    'Hannibal' department 324, 328–
        9
    interdepartmental rivalry with the
        SOE 106, 124–5, 135, 149,
        163–4, 192, 195, 214, 215,
        230, 246, 262, 273, 274,
        299–300, 305, 324, 328–9,
        347–8, 350
    and Major Leslie Mitchell 304–6
    MI5 conduct anti-spy
        investigations into 311–13,
        351
    and the V-rockets 324, 328–9
    see also MI6; Sneum, Thomas, in
        the SIS

Security Service 313
Senter, Commander John 296,
    299
Seymour, Major Charles 135–7,
    287–8, 305
Shakespeare, William 288
'Shetland Bus' 304
Shetland Islands 304
Shillinglaw, Pilot Officer W.G. 318–
    19
Siddons, Lieutenant 100, 101
Skodsborg 208, 210, 239, 252, 253,
    254
Small, Flying Officer 326
Sneum, Aida (Thomas's second
    wife) 346
Sneum, Alexandra (Thomas's
    daughter) 347
Sneum, Axel (Thomas's uncle) 158,
    295
Sneum, Christian (Thomas's father)
    19, 20–1, 30, 78–9, 115–16,
    117, 250, 341
Sneum, Christian (Thomas's son)
    29, 347, 352, 355
Sneum, Else (Thomas's first wife)
    18–23, 26, 27, 42, 147, 186,
    347
    birth of her first child, Marianne
        47
    bumps into Tommy in Denmark
        during his SIS stint 170–2
    first pregnancy 18–19, 20
    left by Tommy 61–2, 116–17,
        121, 160
    post-war life 341, 346
    questioned by the authorities on
        Tommy's location 250–1
    returns to work following
        childbirth 186
    takes secretarial course 206
    and Tommy's capture by the
        Swedish police 265
Sneum, Harald (Thomas's brother)
    65, 77, 78
Sneum, Karen (Thomas's mother)
    19, 30, 79, 341
Sneum, Katherine (Thomas's third
    wife) 346–7
Sneum, Margit (Thomas's sister) 30

Sneum, Marianne (Thomas's
        daughter) 47, 61–2, 116, 117,
        121, 160, 171, 186, 206, 250,
        265, 341, 346, 347
Sneum, Thomas
    children
        daughter Alexandra 347
        daughter Marianne 47, 61–2,
            341, 347
        son Christian 347
    in the Danish Fleet Air Arm 8–9,
        11, 21, 193, 236, 240, 345
    death 352–5
        funeral 352
        memorial service at St Clement
            Danes Church 353–5, 356
    and the end of the war 339–41
        return to Fanoe 340–1
    in England
        in Brixton Prison following
            Malmo incursion 276,
            287–90, 291–2, 294–6,
            297, 299–302, 304–6,
            312, 345, 356
        due to hang 285–6, 288
        interrogation 277–86, 293
        release 305–6, 314, 318
        reprieval 289
        visited by Otto Gregory
            297–8
        first wartime stay 89–96
        interrogation 96–8, 99–107
        recruited into the SIS by
            Rabagliati 110–14
        released from interrogation
            107
        in the SIS 110–14, 118–21,
            126–31, 132–3, 134–9,
            140
        joins the Royal Navy Danish
            Section 331, 333, 356
        joins the Royal Norwegian Air
            Force 334–5, 336–40,
            345, 356
        in London after his Milton
            Ernest stay 314–18, 321–5
        awarded back-pay by the SIS
            321–3
        meets Kjeld Pedersen 322–3
        told about Helvard's death
            321
        told of Sigfred
            Christopherson's death
            327
        in London on leave from the
            Navy 331–4
        confronts Volle Gyth about
            his wartime
            incarceration 331–3
        in Milton Ernest following
            release from Brixton
            Prison 306–8, 312–13,
            318
        returns to Britain following
            Malmo release 273–6
    independent espionage work
        and the Abwehr 14–16, 46,
            102
        dreams up assassination plots
            in Copenhagen 25–30
        escapes Nazi-occupied
            Denmark in a stolen
            Hornet Moth 46–51, 53–
            60, 61–7, 68–73, 74–80,
            81–7, 88–92, 342
        escapes Nazi-occupied
            Denmark to Sweden 33–7
        Fanoe radar surveillance 7–8,
            10, 11–13, 17, 21–3, 35,
            36–7, 38–44, 45, 62, 70,
            75, 76, 80, 99, 102–5,
            196, 273, 340, 349
    interview with the author 1, 2
    invited to join the Luftwaffe 10–
        11
    IQ 12
    in Malmo prison following
        capture by Swedish police
            261–6, 267–71, 272, 277,
            278, 293–4, 300, 302
        release 272–6
        threatens to expose Swedish
            agents 268–71, 272, 278,
            296
    post-war life 2, 341–7, 350–1
        awarded the King's Medal for
            Courage 343–4, 345, 356
        legacy 352
        life in Rome and Lake Como
            346

Sneum, Thomas – *continued*
  post-war life – *continued*
    lifelong friendship with Kjeld
      Pedersen 341–2
    moves to Switzerland 2, 345,
      346–7
    on Rottboell's death 303
    on the SIS-SOE rivalry 347–8
    in Turkey as construction
      supervisor and test pilot
      346
    work as administrative director
      of the European
      Association of Advertising
      Agencies 346
    work as managing director of
      air-charter/air-ambulance
      company 345
  recognition
    awarded the King's Medal for
      Courage 343–4, 345, 356
    post-mortem, by British
      Military Intelligence 355–
      7
  in the SIS 118–21
    atom-bomb information 196–
      7, 200–1, 207–8, 271,
      280–2, 349–50
    becomes expendable 262–3
    believed to be a double-agent
      3–4, 5, 279–80, 299–301,
      351–2
    combat skills 129–30
    file 352
    internal investigations into
      311–13, 351
    parachute training 136–7
    recruitment 110–14
    return to Denmark 4–5, 146–
      51, 153–9, 160–72, 173–
      7, 178–85, 186–91, 193–
      8, 199–204, 205–12, 213–
      17, 219
      atom-bomb information
        196–7, 200–1, 207–8,
        271
      attempts to extract
        information from the
        Abwehr 160–2, 173–4,
        194, 195–6, 200, 229

      bumps into his wife Else
        170–2
      and the Christopherson's and
        Oxlund's departure
        213–14, 215–17, 219,
        224, 226, 228
      financial support 168–9
      hunts down Sigfred
        Christopherson 199–
        200
      journey 140–5
      meets the Princes of Danish
        Intelligence 148–50,
        189–91
      moves into his last Danish
        safe-house 240–1
      moves into the Hotel Astoria
        235–7
      parachute drop 140–1, 145,
        167
      plots to kill agent
        Christopherson 167–8
      preparation for 126–31,
        132–3, 134–9
      quits Denmark 241, 245–6,
        247–9, 252–60
      radio operations 165–6,
        174–7, 180–5, 200,
        202–4, 205, 208–9,
        211–12, 213, 239, 264–
        6, 278
      and the recruitment of Duus
        Hansen 175–6, 180–5,
        330
      spinal fracture 145, 167
      tide turns against 193–4,
        195, 198, 201–4, 205–
        12, 228, 230–2, 233–8,
        239–41, 242–6, 247–51,
        252–4
  Stig Jensen's account of 308–9
  training 118–21, 126–31, 132–
    3, 134–9, 140
  Turnbull on 348–50
  and the V-rockets 324–5, 330–
    1
  and women 2, 3, 20–1, 47–8,
    59–60, 113–14, 121–3,
    273, 314–16, 322–3, 331,
    340